Tear out this answer mask
to use when answering
questions in the programmed
completion exercises (see
the section entitled To
the Student for further
directions).

Tear out this answer mask
to use when answering
questions in the programmed
completion exercises (see
the section entitled To
the Student for further
directions).

Study Guide

MARKETING

Study Guide

MARKETING

Concepts and Strategies

EIGHTH EDITION

William M. Pride
Texas A & M University

O. C. Ferrell
Memphis State University

HOUGHTON MIFFLIN COMPANY   BOSTON   TORONTO
DALLAS   GENEVA, ILLINOIS   PALO ALTO   PRINCETON, NEW JERSEY

To Jack and Grace Burkett — W. M. P.

To Norlan and Phyllis Nafziger — O. C. F.

Sponsoring Editor: Diane L. McOscar
Development Editor: Susan M. Kahn
Project Editor: Mary Ann Carberry
Production Coordinator: Frances Sharperson
Senior Manufacturing Coordinator: Priscilla Bailey

Cover photography by Geoffrey Gove.

Printed in the U.S.A.

Library of Congress Catalog Card Number: 92-72396

ISBN: 0-395-63889-5

123456789-WC-96 95 94 93 92

CONTENTS

TO THE STUDENT

This study guide has been designed to be used with *Marketing: Concepts and Strategies,*
Eighth Edition, by William M. Pride and O. C. Ferrell. We have developed this study
guide (1) to assist you in learning the definitions, concepts, and relationships presented
in our textbook, and (2) to help you evaluate your knowledge and understanding of these
materials.

For each chapter in *Marketing: Concepts and Strategies*, this guide contains eight parts:

1. Chapter outline
2. Chapter summary
3. Matching exercises
4. True or false statements
5. Multiple-choice questions
6. Minicase
7. Programmed completion exercises
8. Answers to objective questions

The chapter outline sets forth the basic structure of the chapter. You should find the
outline helpful if you read it before reading the text chapter.

The chapter summary provides an overall perspective on the content of the text
chapter. We suggest you read this summary before reading the chapter in the textbook
because the summary can act as a preview and make you aware of the major topics and
relationships presented in the text chapter. This awareness will help you grasp the
chapter material more easily. Before you attempt to complete the questions and exercises
for a specific chapter, we suggest you reread the study guide summary to refresh your
memory about the contents of the text chapter.

The matching exercises should help you focus on the important terms in a chapter.
We suggest you do these exercises shortly after reading the text chapter to allow you to
master important definitions quickly.

The true or false statements and the multiple-choice questions should help you test
your understanding of marketing terminology, concepts, and relationships. Some of
these exercises deal with definitions and details; others focus on the broader aspects of
marketing decisions and activities.

The minicase presents marketing situations aimed at helping you apply some of the
concepts and relationships discussed in the text chapter. The minicase is followed by
several multiple-choice questions.

The programmed completion exercises offer a method for both learning and testing your knowledge. Like the other exercises, the programmed completion exercises pertain to your understanding of both specific details and more general relationships. When working with these exercises, you should use the perforated cardboard mask that can be torn out from inside the front cover of this book. This mask is used to cover the correct response word(s) that completes each question. To begin, cover the answers in the left-hand column. After you answer a question, move the mask down so that the answer is exposed. In this way, you can evaluate your answers immediately. Do not be overly concerned if your answers are not exactly the same as those suggested. The purpose of these exercises is to improve and evaluate your understanding of marketing topics and relationships, not to encourage you to memorize.

The last part of each chapter supplies the answers to the matching exercises, true or false statements, multiple-choice questions, and minicase questions. These answers are provided to help you evaluate your understanding of the material in the text chapter. To this end, you should refer to these answers only after you have completed the questions.

This study guide is a self-help tool. It can help you learn and evaluate your knowledge only to the extent that you use it correctly and regularly.

The authors both acknowledge and appreciate the assistance of Pam Swartz, Gwyneth M. Vaughn, Jennifer Maloney, José Mireles, Marissa Salinas, Zed Eric Stephens, and Debbie Thorne in reviewing and editing the materials for this study guide.

William M. Pride
O. C. Ferrell

Study Guide

MARKETING

1 AN OVERVIEW OF STRATEGIC MARKETING

CHAPTER OUTLINE

Marketing defined
Marketing consists of activities
Marketing is performed by individuals and organizations
Marketing facilitates satisfying exchange relationships
Marketing occurs in a dynamic environment
Marketing involves products, distribution, promotion, and pricing
Marketing focuses on goods, services, and ideas
Why study marketing?
Marketing activities are used in many organizations
Marketing activities are important to businesses and the economy
Marketing knowledge enhances consumer awareness
Marketing costs consume a sizable portion of buyers' dollars
The marketing concept
Evolution of the marketing concept
Implementing the marketing concept
Marketing strategy
Marketing opportunity analysis
Marketing strategy: target market selection
Marketing strategy: marketing mix development
Marketing management

CHAPTER SUMMARY

Marketing is broadly defined as a set of individual and organizational activities aimed at facilitating and expediting satisfying exchanges in a dynamic environment through the creation, distribution, promotion, and pricing of goods, services, and ideas. Producers, intermediaries, and purchasers must perform a multitude of activities to market products effectively. Both individuals and organizations are marketers. An individual who owns a store or who wants to sell a car must perform marketing activities to facilitate the exchange. All organizations—business and nonbusiness alike—carry out marketing activities as a way to facilitate exchanges.

Four conditions must exist for an exchange to take place. First, exchange requires participation by two or more individuals, groups, or organizations. Second, each party

1

must have "something of value" that the other party wants. Third, each party must be willing to give up its something of value to receive the something of value the other individual, group, or organization holds. Fourth, the parties to the exchange must be able to communicate with one another to make their something of value available. The something of value that the two exchange parties hold is usually a product or a financial resource (cash, credit).

Satisfaction is important to both the buyer and the seller in the exchange process. For the buyer, satisfaction can stem from the product that meets expectations or from the exchange itself. For the seller, satisfaction can stem from doing business with a particular customer, from making a profit, or from meeting some other organizational goal. Most important, a buyer who is happy with a transaction probably will buy again from the seller. That customer is the cornerstone of repeat business.

Marketing occurs in a dynamic environment, where laws, regulations, politics, societal values, economic and competitive conditions, and technology are constantly changing. It involves the development, distribution, promotion, and pricing of goods, services, and ideas. A good is a physical entity that can be touched; a service is the application of human or mechanical effort to people or objects. Ideas include concepts, philosophies, images, and issues.

The study of marketing is relevant for many reasons. First, about a third of all civilian workers in this country work at some type of marketing activity. Second, marketing activities are important to business organizations and to the economy. These activities help businesses create and sell products and generate profits. Third, marketing is all around us, and as consumers we have a responsibility to understand its effects—its costs, its benefits, and its flaws. This responsibility becomes even more important when we consider the final reason why the study of marketing is relevant: marketing costs consume about half of every dollar we spend.

The marketing concept is the management philosophy that a business organization should try to satisfy its customers' needs through a coordinated set of activities that allows the organization to achieve its goals. Providing customer satisfaction is the major thrust of the marketing concept. This means not only creating and distributing satisfying products but altering, adapting, and developing product offerings to keep pace with changes in consumers' needs and preferences. Although the emphasis here is on customer satisfaction, the organization's goals—increased profit, market share, or sales—are also important. The marketing concept stresses that a business organization can best meet its goals by providing customer satisfaction. An organization whose overall activities are consistent with the marketing concept is said to be market-oriented.

Businesses have not always accepted the marketing concept. During the late nineteenth century, management maintained a production orientation. In the 1920s, businesses began looking at sales as the major means of producing profits. Not until the 1950s did managers move into the marketing era, adopting a customer orientation.

To implement the marketing concept, top managers must adopt it wholeheartedly, using it as the basis of every goal they set and every decision they make. This commitment necessitates an information system and possibly the restructuring of the organization so that customers' needs are understood and satisfying new products can be created. But even with these changes, a firm's new marketing approach may not function perfectly. First, the firm's ability to satisfy customers' needs is limited. Second, the firm may be unable to learn what these needs are. Third, by satisfying one segment of society, the firm may be contributing to the dissatisfaction of another. And fourth, employee morale during a restructuring can be a problem.

Marketing management is a process of planning, organizing, implementing, and controlling marketing activities to facilitate and expedite exchanges effectively and efficiently. The overall goal of marketing management is to facilitate highly desirable exchanges and to minimize the costs of doing so. To achieve this goal, the organization must develop and manage a marketing strategy, a plan for the best use of its resources. To develop and manage a marketing strategy, management must focus on four generic marketing tasks: market opportunity analysis, target market selection, marketing mix development, and management of marketing activities.

To keep up with varying customer preferences, organizations must use market opportunity analysis, which can be accomplished by various alternatives, such as the modification of existing products, the introduction of new ones, and the elimination of undesirable ones. To pursue any of these alternatives successfully, an organization must rely on internal organizational factors, including organizational objectives, financial resources, managerial skills, organizational strengths and weaknesses, and cost structures. Forces in the marketing environment also play a vital role in how an organization plans for the future. Political, legal, regulatory, societal, economic and competitive, and technological forces all affect the marketer's ability to facilitate and expedite exchanges. They do so in three ways: First, the environment has a specific influence on the kinds of products customers need or want. Second, these forces influence how a marketing manager performs certain activities. Third, environmental forces can affect a marketing manager's decisions and actions by influencing buyers' reactions to the firm's marketing mix or mixes. At times these environmental forces create opportunities; at other times they create problems. The marketing manager must be able to adjust to major changes when they occur in the marketing environment, to capitalize on the opportunities the changes provide.

A target market is a group of persons for whom a firm creates and maintains a marketing mix that specifically fits the needs and preferences of that group. Marketing managers may define a target market to include a relatively small number of people or a vast group of people. Although a business can focus its efforts on one target market through a single marketing mix, it often focuses on several target markets by developing and employing multiple marketing mixes. The identification and analysis of target markets form the foundations on which a marketing mix is developed.

The marketing mix consists of four major components: product, distribution, promotion, and price. The marketing mix is built around buyers. To provide consumer satisfaction, a marketing manager must create and maintain a marketing mix that fits consumers' needs for that general type of product. To do so, the marketing manager must use up-to-date in-depth information and must understand the marketing variables.

The marketing mix variables are associated with many different decisions and activities. The product variable involves developing, altering, and modifying the product—all activities that help create a want-satisfying product. The distribution variable involves keeping products available in necessary quantities and accessible locations and holding total inventory, transportation, and storage costs as low as possible. The promotion variable facilitates exchanges by informing one or more groups of people about an organization and its products. The price variable involves setting pricing policies and determining product prices—one of the most critical components of the marketing mix.

Within limits, a marketing manager can alter marketing mix variables as consumers' preferences and needs change.

Managing marketing activities involves planning, organizing, implementation, and control. Marketing planning is a systematic process that focuses on the assessment of opportunities and resources, the determination of marketing objectives, the development of a marketing strategy, and the development of plans for implementation and control. Organizing marketing activities involves developing the internal structure of the marketing unit. The implementation of marketing plans depends on the coordination of marketing activities, the motivation of marketing personnel, and effective communication within the unit. Finally, the marketing control process consists of establishing performance standards, evaluating actual performance by comparing it with established standards, and reducing the difference between wanted and actual performance.

MATCHING EXERCISES

Use the following set of terms to identify the sentences and phrases below. On the blank line next to each sentence or phrase, place the letter of the term that the sentence or phrase describes. Do not use a term more than once.

a. Price variable
b. Marketing management
c. Marketing mix
d. Promotion variable
e. Marketing concept
f. Production orientation
g. Sales orientation
h. Customer orientation
i. Marketing opportunity analysis
j. Target market

k. Distribution variable
l. Product variable
m. Exchange
n. Service
o. Marketing strategy
p. Goods
q. Marketing environment
r. Strategy
s. Marketing
t. Product

Product variable 1. The aspect of the marketing mix that deals with researching consumers' wants and developing a product that meets those wants.

target market 2. A group of persons for whom a firm creates and maintains a marketing mix.

Exchange 3. Participation by two or more individuals, groups, or organizations, with each party having "something of value" that the other party wants. Each party must be willing to give up its something of value to get something of value the other party holds, and all parties must be willing to communicate with one another.

Distribution variable 4. The marketing mix variable in which marketing management attempts to make products available in the quantities needed to as many customers as possible and to hold total inventory, transportation, and storage costs as low as possible.

Production
Orientation 5. An era characterized by new technology and new ways of using labor; an orientation encouraged by the scientific management movement, which, to increase worker productivity, championed rigidly structured jobs and pay based on output.

Marketing 6. Individual and organizational activities aimed at facilitating and expediting satisfying exchanges in a dynamic environment through the creation, distribution, promotion, and pricing of goods, services, and ideas.

Marketing
mix 7. Consists of four major variables: product, price, distribution, and promotion.

Product 8. Everything (both variable and unfavorable) that one receives in an exchange; it is a complexity of tangible and intangible elements, including functional, social, and psychological utilities or benefits; it includes goods, services, or ideas.

Sales
Orientation 9. During this era, businesspeople believed the most important marketing activities were personal selling and advertising.

Marketing
Strategy 10. A plan for selecting and analyzing a target market and creating and maintaining a marketing mix.

Promotion
Variable 11. A major marketing mix component used to facilitate exchanges by informing an individual or one or more groups of people about an organization and its products.

Goods 12. Physical, concrete things you can touch; tangible items.

Price Variable 13. A critical marketing mix variable in which marketing management is concerned with establishing pricing policies and determining product prices.

Marketing
Environment 14. The element that surrounds both the buyer and marketing mix and consists of political, legal, regulatory, societal, consumer movement, economic, and technological forces—variables that affect a marketer's ability to facilitate and expedite exchanges.

Service 15. An intangible that is the result of applying human and mechanical efforts to people or objects.

Marketing
Concept 16. The managerial philosophy that an organization should try to satisfy customers' needs through a coordinated set of activities that at the same time allows the organization to achieve its goals.

Customer
Orientation 17. In this era, businesses found that they must first determine what customers want and then produce it, rather than make products and try to change customers' needs to fit what they produce.

Marketing
Opportunity
Analysts 18. The process of pursuing new ways to market products using a variety of analytical means.

Marketing
Management 19. The process of planning, organizing, implementing, and controlling marketing activities to facilitate and expedite exchanges effectively and efficiently.

TRUE OR FALSE STATEMENTS

T   F   1.   Many people who work for nonbusiness organizations are involved in marketing activities.

T   F   2.   An organization's marketing activities are aimed directly or indirectly at helping to sell the organization's products.

T   *F*   3.   According to the authors, marketing is defined as selling and advertising.

T   F   4.   Marketing begins after goods and services have been produced.

T   F   5.   All kinds of organizations, such as churches, schools, and hospitals, perform marketing activities.

T   F   6.   The consummation of a specific exchange between two parties does not in itself determine whether marketing activities have occurred.

T   F   7.   Products can be goods, services, or ideas.

T   F   8.   A good is a tangible object possessing physical features.

T   **F**   9.   The customer orientation of the marketing concept means that business activities start within a firm and end with consumers.

T   F   10.   The marketing concept calls for the coordination of a firm's activities.

T   F   11.   Because the marketing concept is a management philosophy that affects all types of business activities, it must be implemented by top management in the organization.

T   **F**   12.   Marketers are under very little pressure to provide high living standards and ideal lifestyles through socially responsible decisions and activities.

T   **F**   13.   When implementing the marketing concept, the business organization should strive to build products to fit the needs of each consumer.

T   F   14.   The production orientation that began during the Industrial Revolution was the result of new technology and new ways of using labor.

T   F   15.   Consumer product companies should consider spending time and money to research consumers' needs.

T   F   16.   Marketing mix variables are totally controllable.

T   **F**   17.   Marketing activities are associated with two general kinds of marketing variables: marketing mix variables and consumer variables.

T   F   18.   One primary goal of a marketing manager is to create and maintain a marketing mix that satisfies consumers' needs for a general product type.

T   F   19.   Through the marketing mix variables a marketing manager can develop and change marketing decisions and activities.

T **F** 20. A sales orientation developed after 1920, when businesses realized that products would have to be "sold" to consumers.

T **F** 21. Marketing mix variables are often viewed as "controllable" variables because the marketing manager can change them.

T **F** 22. Forces in the marketing environment do not directly affect the marketing manager's ability to perform certain marketing activities.

T **F** 23. Forces in the environment are sometimes called "uncontrollable" variables because marketing managers cannot directly control them, although they can influence them.

T **F** 24. Firms should not be concerned about how they are viewed by political officials.

T **F** 25. By the early 1950s, businesses found that they must first produce a product and then try to change customers' needs.

T **F** 26. A marketing strategy involves selecting and analyzing a target market and creating and maintaining a marketing mix that will satisfy that target market.

T **F** 27. The management of marketing activities involves planning, organizing, and directing.

T **F** 28. Financial resources and managerial skills are two of the primary internal organization factors.

MULTIPLE-CHOICE QUESTIONS

_____ 1. Approximately what percentage of a buyer's dollar is used for paying the costs of marketing activities?
   a. 50 percent
   b. 60 percent
   c. 45 percent
   d. 40 percent
   e. 25 percent

_____ 2. Approximately what percentage of U.S. civilian workers employed by business organizations perform marketing activities?
   a. 30 to 35 percent
   b. 50 to 55 percent
   c. 25 to 33 percent
   d. 33 to 38 percent
   e. 50 percent

_____ 3. An organization's marketing activities are
   a. an essential part of all organizational activities.
   b. aimed directly or indirectly at helping to sell the organization's products.
   c. developed for the sole purpose of producing profits through exchanges.
   d. the lifeblood of the organization.
   e. utilized by the firm only in the event of a profitable exchange.

_____ 4. To survive in a capitalist economy, a firm must
   a. grow.
   b. generate immediate profits.
   c. generate long-run profits.
   d. attract more capital.
   e. produce more products.

_____ 5. Which of the following is *not* a marketing activity?
   a. Promotion
   b. Storage
   c. Product development
   d. Wholesaling
   e. Production

_____ 6. Which of the following statements most completely defines the term *marketing*?
   a. Marketing is the transportation of goods from manufacturer to retailers so that goods are available when and where consumers want them.
   b. Marketing occurs when consumers go shopping and make purchases.
   c. Marketing consists of individual and organizational activities that facilitate and expedite exchanges within a dynamic environment.
   d. Marketing is the efficient organization of the firm's activities into a single customer-oriented entity.
   e. Marketing includes all those activities involved in the production, transportation, and ultimate sale of products.

_____ 7. Even universities are involved in marketing activities. Which of the following is *least* likely to be considered a marketing activity?
   a. Addition of a new course of study requested by many students
   b. Application to the state government for building funds
   c. Expansion of the school cafeteria to include fast-order foods
   d. A fine arts series sponsored on campus
   e. Extension of free-time hours in athletic facilities to meet demand overflow

_____ 8. The intangible "something of value" that is provided by applying human and mechanical efforts to people or objects is called a(n)
   a. service.
   b. product.
   c. good.
   d. market variable.
   e. exchange variable.

9. Concerning marketing activities, which of the following statements is *most* correct?
   a. Most of the approaches, concepts, and activities are used by business organizations.
   b. Many marketing activities are performed to support exchanges even though some situations do not result in exchanges.
   c. The consummation of a specific exchange must occur for marketing activities to occur.
   d. Marketing activities must be performed by individuals, not by organizations.
   e. Marketing activities can be justified only if an exchange occurs and if profit results from the exchange process.

10. The customer orientation of the marketing concept stresses the importance of the customer. The main thrust of this statement is that organizations should
    a. create new products whenever possible.
    b. provide products that will satisfy short-term needs.
    c. avoid duplication of products already on the market.
    d. get the products into the hands of consumers.
    e. provide customer satisfaction.

11. To provide customer satisfaction, marketing activities must begin with
    a. the creation of high-quality products.
    b. a focus on customers to determine what will satisfy them.
    c. putting the product in the hands of consumers.
    d. attempts to alter product offerings to keep prices as low as possible.
    e. attempts to satisfy existing customers' needs.

12. Marketing activities start and end with the
    a. firm.
    b. consumer or client.
    c. long-run objectives of the firm.
    d. exchange situation.
    e. marketing intermediaries.

13. A marketing manager must decide what combination of variables is needed to satisfy consumers' needs for a general type of product. What are the essential variables that the marketing manager combines?
    a. Product variables, price variables, consumer variables, and promotion variables
    b. Marketing environment variables
    c. Product variables and promotion variables
    d. Product variables, price variables, and consumer variables
    e. Product variables, price variables, promotion variables, and distribution variables

14. Some of the variables in the market environment are
    a. political forces, legal forces, societal forces, and economic forces.
    b. social forces, technological forces, political forces, economic forces, production, and consumers.
    c. promotion, product, price, and distribution.
    d. consumers, producers, and wholesalers.
    e. consumers, product, economic forces, and social forces.

15. Concerning marketing mix variables, which of the following statements is *most* accurate?
    a. Marketing mix variables often are viewed as uncontrollable because marketing managers cannot change them.
    b. Marketing mix variables cannot be altered by marketing managers.
    c. Marketing mix variables can be altered but cannot be controlled by marketing managers.
    d. Marketing managers can control marketing mix variables to a limited degree.
    e. Marketing mix variables can be altered and controlled by marketing managers.

16. The marketing mix ingredient that is the easiest to control is
    a. product.
    b. consumers.
    c. promotion.
    d. price.
    e. not the same for all situations.

17. Which of the following statements about marketing environment variables is *most* correct?
    a. Marketing managers have more control over these variables than over most marketing variables.
    b. The strength of the variables in the marketing environment is relatively stable as compared with that of other variables in the market.
    c. Marketing environment variables affect consumers but do not affect the marketing mix.
    d. The forces in the marketing environment influence marketing managers but do not directly affect their ability to perform certain activities.
    e. These forces influence consumers' reactions toward a firm's marketing mix.

18. A group of persons for whom a firm attempts to create and maintain a marketing mix that fits the needs and preferences of that group is known as a
    a. customer group.
    b. target market.
    c. consumer target.
    d. marketplace.
    e. primary market.

____ 19. When a target market is being chosen, which of the following need *not* occur?
a. Managers should try to evaluate possible markets to determine how entry into them would affect the firm's sales, costs, and profits.
b. Marketers should consider whether the firm has the resources to produce a marketing mix that meets the needs of the target market.
c. Marketers must analyze the size and number of competitors who are already selling in the target market.
d. The firm must decide whether to focus its marketing efforts on one or several target markets.
e. Managers should ensure that choosing a particular target market will not adversely affect employee morale.

____ 20. In strategic marketing management, marketing managers focus on generic marketing management tasks. Which of the following is *not* one of these tasks?
a. Market opportunity analysis
b. Target market selection
c. Management of marketing activities
d. Economic opportunity analysis
e. Marketing mix development

____ 21. Chimney Sweeps employs people to clean fireplaces and chimneys in homes and apartments. The firm is primarily the marketer of a(n)
a. service.
b. good.
c. idea.
d. image.
e. physical entity.

____ 22. If ConAir, a blow dryer manufacturer, is focusing on customer satisfaction, it will find that what consumers really want is
a. more watts.
b. more speeds.
c. higher heat settings.
d. attractive hair.
e. more attachments.

____ 23. McDonald's runs advertisements featuring children, senior citizens, and minority groups. These ads indicate that the company
a. is production-oriented.
b. considers only environmental factors.
c. has several tartet markets.
d. lacks focus.
e. has not adopted the marketing concept.

_____ 24. If Merrill Lynch were to perceive that consumers within a particular group were becoming more conservative in their investing, and thus developed more products with lower risk, it would be
  a. responding to the marketing environment.
  b. changing its target market.
  c. developing a sales orientation.
  d. changing its organization structure.
  e. responding to changes in technology.

_____ 25. B-Mart, a chain of grocery stores located in the northwestern United States, practices and is very committed to the marketing concept. Because of its emphasis on customer satisfaction and the marketing concept, one could say that B-Mart is
  a. market aware.
  b. market-oriented.
  c. satisfaction-oriented.
  d. customer focused.
  e. concept-oriented.

MINICASE: DADE ELECTRONICS DISCONTINUES DIGITAL WATCHES

Dade Electronics is a major producer of computers, defense electronics, and consumer electronics. Several years ago, Dade management laid off nearly two thousand employees and decided to drop its line of digital watches. At the time, company spokespersons stated that these moves were part of Dade's plans to restructure its business priorities. Industry analysts viewed the moves as a sign that Dade's management systems had fallen apart, and competitors claimed that the company's past marketing and technological improprieties were finally catching up with the firm. Company insiders and former employees saw the moves as adjustments to a precision machine. In reality, the truth was somewhere in between. Dade was not changing its business priorities, for its goal remained to sell $15 billion of computers, and defense and consumer electronics.

Technology is the key to Dade's strategy, but management realized that it had to deal with costly failures. The failure to listen to the marketplace was the major reason for Dade's defeat in the digital watch business. In an aggressive selling campaign, Dade kept pushing the utility and low prices of its watches when consumers wanted more fashion and more features. Dade did not adapt its product to meet consumers' demands.

As a company founded on technology, Dade tends to have an engineering orientation. Most managers have engineering, not business, degrees. Management energies are often focused on the design and manufacturing processes rather than on customers' needs. Moreover, management has been unable to develop a long-term strategy that integrates the resources to design, make, and bring a product to market. Executives frequently neglect to consider how much money it costs to market a new product until after it has been developed and produced.

Questions

_____   1. Which of the following statements is true?
  a. Dade is practicing the marketing concept.
  b. Dade is not practicing the marketing concept.
  c. Dade is practicing some parts of the marketing concept.
  d. Dade should have kept its digital watch line.
  e. Dade should merge with another company.

_____   2. Dade's business philosophy can best be described as a _____ orientation.
  a. product
  b. sales
  c. customer
  d. marketing
  e. distribution

_____   3. What problem(s) might Dade's management anticipate if they adopt the marketing concept?
  a. Maintaining employee morale
  b. Contributing to the dissatisfaction of some segments of the market
  c. Maintaining employee morale and contributing to the dissatisfaction of some segments of the market
  d. There should be no problems.
  e. Widespread dissatisfaction among current customers

_____   4. What change(s) might be necessary when Dade adopts the marketing concept?
  a. Establishment of an information system
  b. Organization restructuring
  c. Establishment of totally new business priorities
  d. Organization restructuring and establishment of new business priorities
  e. Establishment of an information system and organization restructuring

PROGRAMMED COMPLETION EXERCISES

activities, facilitating, expediting, dynamic environment

1. Marketing is a set of _Activities_ that are aimed at _facilitating_ and _expediting_ satisfying exchange relationships in a _Dynamic environment_ through the creation, distribution, promotion, and pricing of goods and services, and ideas.

somethings of value, products

2. The ___somethings of value___ that two exchange parties hold are usually ___products___ or financial resources such as money or credit.

human, mechanical

3. Services result from the application of ___Human___ and ___Mechanical___ efforts to people or objects.

concepts, philosophies, images, issues

4. Products in the form of ideas include ___Concepts, Philosophies, images___, and ___issues___.

marketing concept, customers', clients', coordinated

5. The ___Mktg Concept___ is a philosophy that a business organization should try to satisfy ___Customers___ or ___Clients___ needs through a ___coordinated___ set of activities that allows the organization to achieve its goals.

alter, adapt

6. To be customer-oriented, a firm must _____ and _____ current product offerings to keep pace with changes in consumers' needs and preferences.

customer satisfaction, coordinated activities

7. The marketing concept stresses the point that a business organization can achieve its goals by providing _____ _____ through _____ _____.

satisfying exchange relationships

8. Organizations that rely on repeat business must develop _____ _____ _____.

philosophy, activities, top management

9. Because the marketing concept is a management _____ that affects all types of business activities rather than just marketing _____, it must be implemented by _____ _____ in the organization.

information system,
satisfying products

10. Management must establish an _____ _____ that allows the firm to obtain information about customers' needs and to use that information internally to create _____ _____.

top management,
individuals,
organization

11. To be implemented, the marketing concept philosophy must receive the support not only of _____ _____ but of all the other _____ within the _____.

management,
product needs

12. To provide customer satisfaction, _____ must be able to determine customers' _____ _____.

department,
restructuring

13. To properly coordinate the actions of a _____ in a business organization, a _____ of the organization may be required.

controllable,
marketing managers

14. Even though marketing mix variables can be altered, they are not totally _____ because _____ _____ are limited in the degree to which they can change them.

pricing policies,
product prices

15. In dealing with the price variable, marketing managers usually are concerned with establishing _____ _____ and determining _____ _____.

quantities, inventory,
transportation,
storage

16. When dealing with the distribution variable, marketing managers attempt to make products available in the _____ necessary, to as many customers as possible, and to keep total _____, _____, and _____ costs as low as possible.

informing, organization, products

17. The promotion variable in the marketing mix is directed

toward _____ one or more groups of people about

an _____ and its _____.

marketing manager's, buyers' reactions

18. Environmental forces may affect a _____

_____ decisions and actions by influencing

_____ _____ to the firm's marketing mix or

mixes.

variables, buyer, marketing mix

19. The marketing environment consists of several _____

and surrounds both the _____ and the

_____ _____.

ANSWERS TO OBJECTIVE QUESTIONS

Matching		*True or False*		*Multiple-Choice*		*Minicase*
1. l	11. d	1. T	15. T	1. a	14 b	1. b
2. j	12. p	2. T	16. F	2. c	15. b	2. d
3. m	13. a	3. F	17. F	3. b	16. e	3. b
4. k	14. q	4. F	18. T	4. c	17. a	4. a
5. f	15. n	5. T	19. T	5. e	18. d	
6. s	16. e	6. T	20. T	6. c	19. e	
7. c	17. h	7. T	21. T	7. b	20. e	
8. t	18. i	8. T	22. F	8. a	21. a	
9. g	19. b	9. F	23. T	9. b	22. d	
10. o		10. T	24. F	10. e	23. c	
		11. T	25. F	11. b	24. a	
		12. F	26. T	12. b	25. b	
		13. F	27. F	13. e		
		14. T	28. T			

2 THE MARKETING ENVIRONMENT

CHAPTER OUTLINE

Examining and responding to the marketing environment
Environmental scanning and analysis
Responding to environmental forces
Political forces
Legal forces
Procompetitive legislation
Consumer protection legislation
Interpreting laws
Regulatory forces
Federal regulatory agencies
State and local regulatory agencies
Nongovernmental regulatory forces
Deregulation
Societal forces
Living standards and quality of life
Cultural diversity as a societal force
Consumer movement forces
Economic and competitive forces
General economic conditions
Consumer demand and spending behavior
Assessment of competitive forces
Technological forces
The impact of technology
Adoption and use of technology

CHAPTER SUMMARY

The marketing environment consists of external forces that directly or indirectly influence an organization's acquisition of inputs and generation of outputs. The environment is capable of producing both threats to and opportunities for organizations. For the organization to survive and achieve its long-term goals, the environment must be closely monitored.

To monitor the changing environment effectively, marketers must engage in environmental scanning and analysis. Environmental scanning is the collection of information about the forces in the marketing environment. Environmental analysis is the process of assessing and interpreting the information gathered through scanning.

Marketing managers use two approaches to respond to environmental forces. One approach is passive; it assumes that environmental forces are totally uncontrollable and difficult to predict. The other approach is proactive; it attempts to influence and shape environmental forces. The selection of a passive or an aggressive approach to the environment is determined by many variables, including the organization's management philosophies, objectives, financial resources, markets, and human skills and the composition of the set of environmental forces in which the organization operates.

Political, legal, and regulatory forces are closely interrelated aspects of the marketing environment. Elected officials strongly influence the strength and effectiveness of the legal forces with which marketers must deal. They also can influence how much and from whom the government purchases, and they can play key roles in helping the organization secure foreign markets.

For purposes of analysis, laws that directly affect marketing practices can be divided into two categories: procompetitive legislation and consumer protection laws. The procompetitive laws were enacted to preserve competition and include the Sherman Act, the Clayton Act, the Federal Trade Commission Act, and the Robinson-Patman Act. Consumer protection legislation deals with product safety, product standards, and disclosure of information; examples are the Pure Food and Drug Act, the Flammable Fabrics Act, and the Cigarette Labeling Act. Although the laws themselves provide the legal framework that has the potential to influence many marketing activities, it is the actual interpretations of the laws by marketers, courts, and regulatory bodies that determine their influence. These interpretations vary over time as the makeup of the courts and regulatory agencies changes.

Regulatory forces are governmental or nongovernmental. Federal regulatory units usually have the power to enforce specific laws as well as to establish operating rules and regulations to guide industry practices. Of all the federal regulatory units, the Federal Trade Commission (FTC) has the broadest powers to influence marketing activities. Its functions include enforcing the laws and regulatory guidelines that fall under its jurisdiction, providing assistance and information so that businesses will know how to comply with those laws, and investigating industry trade practices. The FTC has no direct power or authority to imprison or fine. However, it can seek civil penalties in the courts for violation of its cease and desist orders. Other federal regulatory bodies are the Interstate Commerce Commission, the Federal Communications Commission, the Environmental Protection Agency, the Product Safety Commission, the Food and Drug Administration, and the Office of Consumer Affairs. In addition to federal agencies, many state and local agencies regulate such industries as banking, savings and loans, insurance, utilities, and liquor. Some state and local agencies also focus on consumers' interests.

In the absence of governmental regulatory forces and in an attempt to prevent governmental intervention, some businesses try to regulate themselves, often through trade associations and often as an indirect result of legal action or proposed legislation. Self-regulatory programs offer several advantages over governmental regulation. They are usually less expensive to establish, their guidelines are generally more realistic, and they reduce the need to expand government bureaucracy. The biggest problem facing these self-regulatory units is the enforcement of policies and guidelines. The Better

Business Bureau and the National Advertising Review Board are two examples of successful self-regulatory bodies.

Deregulation is the federal government's attempt to reduce the costs associated with enforcing regulations on various industries. The airline, railroad, trucking, and banking industries are the most heavily affected by deregulation. Opinions are mixed on the overall effects of deregulation, and future administrations may seek to reregulate these industries.

Societal forces include the structure and dynamics of individuals and groups and their issues of concern. Society expects marketers to provide a high standard of living and to protect the general quality of life. Because marketing activities are a vital part of the total business structure, marketers are responsible for providing what society wants and for minimizing what it does not want.

The changing values of society have increased pressure on marketers to act ethically. Ethics in marketing relates to a moral evaluation of decisions based on accepted principles of behavior that result in an action being judged right or wrong. Marketers should operate in accordance with sound moral philosophies based on ideals such as fairness, justice, and trust. Important ethical issues include conflict of interest, fairness and honesty, communication, and organizational relationships.

Such issues as racial injustice, human rights, and deceptive marketing behavior have led to increased public concern about the role of marketing in society. These issues have taken on increased importance in recent years as the U.S. population becomes more cuturally diverse. Some businesses are recognizing that ethical issues and social responsibility must be grounded in their daily decisions, that they are not abstract ideals. To combine ethical and socially responsible behavior with their marketing strategy, firms must monitor changes and trends in society's values, and they must control organization procedures. Socially responsible marketers face major problems: They must determine what society wants and then predict what the long-run effects of their decisions will be. Neither is an easy task, and in trying to satisfy the desires of one group, they may contribute to the dissatisfaction of other groups. Then too there is the question of cost. Much of what society demands it is not willing to pay for.

The consumer movement is made up of independent individuals, groups, and organizations working to protect the rights of consumers. The major issues of the consumer movement fall into three categories: environmental protection, product performance and safety, and information disclosure. Individual consumer advocates, consumer organizations, consumer education, and consumer laws are the major forces of the consumer movement.

Fluctuations in the overall state of the economy have a broad impact on the success of an organization's marketing strategy. The business cycle consists of four stages: prosperity, recession, depression, and recovery. Unemployment is low and aggregate income is relatively high during prosperity. In a recession, unemployment rises, which causes total buying power to decline. A depression is a period in which unemployment is extremely high, wages are very low, total disposable income is at a minimum, and consumers lack confidence in the economy. During recovery, the economy moves from recession to prosperity. The marketer must adapt the marketing strategy to the general state of the economy at any given time.

Consumer demand is influenced by consumers' buying power and willingness to spend. The resources that make up buying power are goods, services, and financial holdings. The major financial sources of buying power are income, credit, and wealth. Buying power, the absolute price of a product and its price relative to that of substitute products, and the amount of satisfaction currently received or expected in the future from a product already owned, all influence the willingness to spend. Other factors that affect willingness to spend are expectations about future employment, income levels, prices, family size, and general economic conditions. To better understand buying behavior, marketers must analyze consumer spending patterns—how consumers actually use their disposable and discretionary incomes, and credit.

A business views competition as those firms that market products similar to or that could substitute for its products in the same geographic area. Several factors influence the level of a firm's competitive forces. The number of firms that control the supply of a product is one important factor. A monopoly exists when a firm produces a product that has no close substitute, when the organization has complete control over the supply of a product. An oligopoly exists when a few sellers control most of the supply of a product. Monopolistic competition exists when a firm with many potential competitors develops a differential marketing strategy to establish its own market share. Perfect competition, if it existed, would entail a large number of sellers, no one of which could significantly influence price or supply. The number and types of competitive tools used by competitors is another factor that influences the level of competition. Among those tools is competitive pricing, focusing on a specific market segment, differentiating product offerings, services, and promotional methods. It is the responsibility of each firm to monitor its competitors so as to remain competitive. By monitoring other firms, marketing managers are able to assess the strengths and weaknesses of their own marketing strategies.

Technology is the knowledge of how to accomplish tasks and goals. Technology affects marketing activities in two ways: First, it influences consumers and society in general. Second, it influences what, how, when, and where products are marketed. Product development, promotion, price, and distribution systems are all affected directly by technology.

Technology determines how consumers satisfy their physiological needs. It has improved the standard of living, but its sometimes undesirable side effects have also detracted from the quality of life. Technology has improved production processes, communications, and distribution channels. Through technology assessment, managers foresee the effects of new products and processes on their firm's operation.

MATCHING EXERCISES

Use the following set of terms to identify the sentences and phrases below. On the blank line next to each sentence or phrase, place the letter of the term that the sentence or phrase describes. Do not use a term more than once.

a. Wheeler-Lea Act
b. Oligopoly
c. Consumer protection legislation
d. Wealth
e. Sherman Act
f. Consumer movement

g. Discretionary income
h. Consumer Goods Pricing Act
i. Federal Trade Commission
j. Buying power index
k. Prosperity
l. Environmental scanning

m. Marketing environment
n. Quality of life
o. Monopolistic competition
p. Procompetitive legislation
q. Better Business Bureau
r. Recovery
s. Willingness to spend
t. Federal Trade Commission Act
u. Pure Food and Drug Act
v. Product-specific spending pattern
w. Technology assessment
x. Consumer spending patterns
y. Competition
z. Societal forces
aa. Economic forces
bb. Technological forces
cc. Income
dd. Clayton Act
ee. Exclusive dealing contracts

ff. Effective buying income
gg. Perfect competition
hh. Robinson-Patman Act
ii. Recession
jj. Legal forces
kk. Celler-Kefauver Act
ll. National Advertising Review Board
mm. Disposable income
nn. Depression
oo. Comprehensive spending patterns
pp. Monopoly
qq. Buying power
rr. Technology
ss. Inflation
tt. Consumer credit
uu. Regulatory forces
vv. Political forces
ww. Cultural diversity

_p_ 1. A group of laws that were enacted to preserve competition. *Procompetitive Legis.*

_e_ 2. Passed in 1890 to prevent businesses from restraining trade and monopolizing markets. *Sherman Act*

_ll_ 3. A self-regulatory unit that screens national advertisements to check for honesty and that processes complaints about deceptive advertisements. *Nat'L Advert. Review Board*

_a_ 4. An amendment to the Federal Trade Commission Act that makes unfair and deceptive acts or practices unlawful regardless of whether they injure competition. *Wheeler-Lea A*

_q_ 5. A local regulatory agency that is supported by local businesses; it helps settle problems between consumers and specific business firms. *Better Business Bureau*

_hh_ 6. A law that prohibits price discrimination that lessens competition among wholesalers or retailers and prohibits producers from giving disproportionate services or facilities to large buyers. *Robinson-Patman A*

_aa_ 7. Forces that determine the strength of a firm's competitive atmosphere and affect the impact of marketing activities because they determine the size and strength of demand for products.

_t_ 8. Legislation that established the Federal Trade Commission.

_dd_ 9. A law that prohibits price discrimination, tying and exclusive agreements, and the acquisition of stock in another corporation "where the effect may be to substantially lessen competition or tend to create a monopoly."

_c_ 10. A category of regulatory laws that are aimed at providing consumer safety and information.

22 Chapter 2

_____ 11. Forces that arise from regulations and guidelines established by government regulatory units and self-regulation efforts; they are part of the marketing environment.

_____ 12. A federal regulatory agency that enforces laws and regulatory guidelines, provides assistance and information so that businesses will know how to comply with those laws and regulations, and investigates industry trade practices.

_____ 13. The collection of information about the forces in the marketing environment.

_____ 14. The annual dollar amounts families spend for specific products within a general product class.

_____ 15. The amount of money an individual receives from various sources; it is used for paying taxes, spending, and saving.

_____ 16. A competitive relationship in which there are a large number of sellers, no one of which can significantly influence price or supply.

_____ 17. Used by marketers to compare the buying power of one area with that of another area; also used to analyze buying power trends for a particular area.

_____ 18. The accumulation of past income, natural resources, and financial resources.

_____ 19. Exists when a firm with many potential competitors attempts to develop a differential marketing strategy to establish its own market share.

_____ 20. Includes salaries, wages, dividends, interest, profit, and rents less federal, state, and local taxes.

_____ 21. A period of high unemployment, low wages, and lack of confidence in the economy.

_____ 22. An indication of the actual amount of money that a family spends on certain kinds of goods and services.

_____ 23. After-tax income; used for spending and/or saving.

_____ 24. The stage of the business cycle in which the economy moves from recession to prosperity.

_____ 25. The competitive structure that exists when a firm produces a product that has no close substitutes.

_____ 26. From the viewpoint of a business, those firms that market products similar to or that substitute for its products in the same geographic area.

_____ 27. The knowledge of how to accomplish tasks and goals.

_____ 28. The stage of the business cycle in which unemployment is low and aggregate income is relatively high.

_____ 29. A diverse group of independent individuals, groups, and organizations attempting to protect the rights of consumers.

_____ 30. Technical forces that influence marketing decisions and activities because they affect people's lifestyles and standards of living, influence people's desire for products and their reaction to marketing mixes, and have a direct impact on maintaining a marketing mix by influencing all its variables.

_____ 31. Forces that pressure marketers to provide high living standards and enjoyable lifestyles through socially responsible decisions and activities; the structure and dynamics of individuals and groups and the issues of concern to them.

_____ 32. That part of the income that is available for spending and saving after an individual has purchased the basic necessities.

_____ 33. The procedure through which managers try to foresee the effects of new products and processes.

_____ 34. The phase of the business cycle in which unemployment rises and total buying power declines.

_____ 35. Made up of goods, services, and financial holdings that give an individual the ability to purchase.

_____ 36. The general condition that surrounds a society and adds to the well-being of its citizens.

_____ 37. The competitive structure that exists when a few sellers control the supply of a large proportion of a product.

_____ 38. The desire to use one's buying power.

_____ 39. Consists of external forces that directly or indirectly influence an organization's acquisition of inputs and generation of outputs.

_____ 40. A law that prohibits any corporation engaged in commerce from acquiring the whole or any part of the stock or other share of the capital or assets of another corporation when the effect lessens competition or tends to create a monopoly.

_____ 41. A law that prohibits the use of price maintenance agreements among manufacturers and resellers in interstate commerce.

_____ 42. Forces that arise from legislation and the interpretation of laws.

_____ 43. Changes in the demographic mix of the U.S. population.

TRUE OR FALSE STATEMENTS

T   F   1. It is possible to generalize and say that a reactive approach to the environment is superior to a passive approach.

T F 2. Environmental analysis is the process of assessing and interpreting the information gathered through scanning.

T F 3. When political officials have positive feelings toward particular firms or industries, they are more likely to create and enforce laws that are unfavorable to business organizations.

T F 4. Many marketers view political forces as being beyond their control; therefore they try to adjust to conditions that result from these forces.

T F 5. Political forces strongly influence the strength and effectiveness of legal forces.

T F 6. The Sherman Act can be categorized as a pricing law.

T F 7. The Sherman Act does not apply to U.S. firms operating in foreign commerce.

T F 8. The Clayton Act prohibits price discrimination, tying agreements, and interlocking directorates.

T F 9. The Federal Trade Commission Act of 1914 specifically prohibits false advertising of foods, drugs, therapeutic devices, and cosmetics.

T F 10. Farm cooperatives and labor organizations are exempt from antitrust laws.

T F 11. The Robinson-Patman Act originated to control suppliers who were providing chain stores with lower prices than independent stores.

T F 12. The Wheeler-Lea, Celler-Kefauver, and Consumer Goods Pricing acts all deal with providing product safety.

T F 13. Some marketers interpret regulations and statutes very conservatively to avoid violating a vague law.

T F 14. All regulatory forces are sponsored by the government.

T F 15. The goal of most federal regulatory units is to enforce the laws and guidelines to the letter to establish a precedent for business persons to follow in their business activities.

T F 16. It is impossible to have both a high standard of living and a high quality of life.

T F 17. Although the FTC has no direct power or authority to imprison or fine, it can seek civil penalties of up to $10,000 a day for each violation if a cease and desist order is violated.

T F 18. The powers of regulatory units other than the FTC generally are limited to specific products, services, and business activities.

T F 19. Regulatory agencies at the state and local levels enforce specific laws dealing with the production and/or sale of particular goods and services.

T F 20. Technology affects all aspects of our lives.

T   F   21. Marketers can employ price differentials when they do not injure or lessen competition.

T   F   22. The four stages of the business cycle are prosperity, recession, depression, and inflation.

T   F   23. During a recession, firms may make the mistake of cutting back their marketing efforts.

T   F   24. Any channel structure that tends to restrain trade may be ruled a violation of the Sherman Act.

T   F   25. Firms' compliance with consumer laws is aided by the vagueness of the laws.

T   F   26. Court interpretations of laws change over the years, making it difficult for marketers to comply with laws.

T   F   27. Firms can influence legislation affecting marketing practices by attempting to cooperate with government agencies.

T   F   28. Disposable income is used to purchase vacations and automobiles.

T   F   29. It is possible to have a high income and very little wealth.

T   F   30. Effective buying income and disposable income are virtually the same thing.

T   F   31. Consumer spending patterns are difficult to analyze and therefore are of little value to marketers.

T   F   32. The overall state of the economy is relatively stable.

T   F   33. Much of the research that produces technology is funded by the government.

T   F   34. The effects technology has on society are determined by how it is applied.

T   F   35. Consumer spending patterns indicate the relative proportions of annual family income or the actual dollar amounts spent on certain types of products.

T   F   36. Determining exactly what society wants and does not want is a difficult task for marketers.

T   F   37. Consumer education is an important force in the consumer movement because it prepares consumers to make wiser purchasing decisions.

T   F   38. In perfect competition, entry into a market is difficult.

T   F   39. Price is the most obvious competitive tool.

T   F   40. Buying power is directly influenced by the state of the economy.

T   F   41. The increased diversity of the U.S. population means marketers will enjoy the benefits of a less diverse customer base.

MULTIPLE-CHOICE QUESTIONS

_____ 1. The selection of an organization's approach to the environment is affected *least* by which of the following?
   a. Financial resources
   b. Managerial philosophies
   c. Human skills
   d. Markets
   e. Price of products

_____ 2. If IBM were concerned about the interest rate it must pay in the next quarter to acquire needed finacial resources, this concern would involve which of the following?
   a. A marketing environment
   b. Its marketing mix
   c. Its marketing concept
   d. A marketing environment output
   e. Its marketing approach

_____ 3. Which of the following represents an output from the marketing environment?
   a. People hired by Procter & Gamble to be part of its sales force
   b. Money borrowed by the St. Louis Cardinals to help finance operations
   c. Nike's television advertising campaign featuring Michael Jordan
   d. Information on shoppers' attitudes purchased by Dillard's Department Stores
   e. Steel purchased by General Motors to be used in producing cars

_____ 4. Smith's is a small retail chain in a large southern city. When considering changes in its marketing strategy, the firm's management looks only at changes in shopper attitudes and spending patterns. With regard to responding to environmental forces, Smith's approach can best be described as
   a. passive and proactive.
   b. aggressive and proactive.
   c. dominant and proactive.
   d. passive and reactive.
   e. dominant and reactive.

_____ 5. Many marketers view political forces as
   a. extremely helpful to businesses.
   b. easily influenced.
   c. simple to recognize.
   d. beyond their control.
   e. easily ignored.

_____ 6. The Sherman Act was created primarily to
   a. establish a means of controlling unfair advertising activities.
   b. prevent businesses from restraining trade and monopolizing markets.
   c. stop the price fixing that was a common tactic of big business at the time.

    d. amend and strengthen the Federal Trade Commission Act.

    e. amend and strengthen the Robinson-Patman Act.

7. The Clayton Act prohibits all the following *except*
   a. price discrimination.
   b. tying agreements.
   c. interlocking directorates.
   d. buying stock in another corporation so as to lessen competition or create a monopoly.
   e. actions by labor organizations in restraint of trade.

8. The Clayton Act
   a. supplements the Sherman Act and prohibits price discrimination, tying contracts, and exclusive agreements.
   b. amends the Robinson-Patman Act and prohibits price discrimination among different purchasers of commodities of like grade and quality when the effect substantially lessens competition.
   c. exempts vertical price fixing from antitrust laws.
   d. supplements the Federal Trade Commission Act, prohibits unfair and deceptive practices regardless of their effects on competition, and places advertising of food and drugs under the jurisdiction of the FTC.
   e. deals mainly with consumer protection.

9. The Robinson-Patman Act
   a. prohibits any corporation engaged in commerce from acquiring all or any part of the stock or other share of the capital assets of another corporation when the effect substantially lessens competition or tends to create a monopoly.
   b. extends the Miller-Tydings Act to make the nonsigner's clause enforceable in interstate commerce among states that have nonsigner's clauses in their fair trade laws.
   c. prohibits contracts, combinations, or conspiracies to restrain trade and designates monopolizing or attempts to monopolize as a misdemeanor.
   d. created the Federal Trade Commission, giving it investigatory powers to be used in preventing unfair methods of competition.
   e. prohibits price discrimination that lessens competition among wholesalers or retailers and prohibits producers from giving disproportionate services or facilities to large buyers.

10. Bob Roberts operates an industrial supply company in a large northwestern city. One of his competitors accuses him of having contracts with his customers that restrain trade. From which one of the following acts is the competitor most likely to seek enforcement?
    a. Sherman Antitrust Act
    b. Ferrell Act
    c. Unfair Trade Practices Act
    d. Federal Trade Commission Act
    e. Robinson-Patman Act

_____ 11. The Sherman Act is enforced by the
a. Antitrust Division of the Department of Justice.
b. Interstate Commerce Commission.
c. Internal Revenue Service.
d. Federal Trade Commission.
e. Office of Consumer Affairs.

_____ 12. Which one of the following acts influences the regulation of the greatest number of marketing practices?
a. Clayton Act
b. Celler-Kefauver Act
c. Federal Trade Commission Act
d. Sherman Act
e. Robinson-Patman Act

_____ 13. If a small appliance manufacturer offers to sell its products to K mart for substantially less than it would sell to Wal-Mart to keep K mart as a customer, the manufacturer might be considered in violation of which one of the following procompetitve acts?
a. Sherman Act
b. FTC Act
c. Robinson-Patman Act
d. Wheeler-Lea Act
e. Clayton Act

_____ 14. Which of the following statements is false?
a. Generally, marketers try to cope with political and legal forces either by complying with their demands or by trying to influence their creation or change.
b. A few marketers sometimes deal with legal pressures by violating laws and regulatory rules.
c. It is difficult to comply with all the laws and regulatory guidelines simply because there are so many of them.
d. Legal compliance is complicated by the vagueness of laws and regulatory guidelines.
e. Marketers may not know how to comply because the laws change over the years, but the interpretations of legal provisions do not change.

_____ 15. Federal regulatory units
a. when created are usually given power to enforce specific laws.
b. usually are given little discretion in establishing their own operating rules and in creating regulations to guide certain types of industry practices.
c. are characterized as being controlled by but in reality are independent of the president and Congress.
d. seldom overlap jurisdictions with regard to specific types of marketing activities.
e. are little influenced by public opinion.

_____ 16. The Federal Trade Commission
   a. consists of five commissioners, each appointed for a term of seven years by the president with the consent of the U.S. Senate.
   b. is set up so that no more than three of the commissioners may be from the same state.
   c. consists of commissioners who are appointed every four years; the commission head, however, is appointed in staggered terms to ensure continuity in the judgment of cases.
   d. was established under the Sherman Act to help strengthen that law.
   e. does not vary in its decisions over the years because the laws that give it its powers do not vary and because staggered terms give it continuity of experience.

_____ 17. The Federal Trade Commission
   a. by considering each case on its own merits, establishes guidelines for specific firms.
   b. is intended to be a lawmaking agency rather than a law enforcement agency, and as such has little power to enforce its decisions.
   c. has as a major goal the provision of assistance and information to businesspeople to help them understand and comply with laws.
   d. seldom tries to explain to business what is considered unfair, deceptive, or illegal but instead lets the courts determine this.
   e. has the direct power and authority to imprison and can fine up to $10,000 a day for violation of its cease and desist orders.

_____ 18. Marketers find it difficult to comply with some laws because of the sheer number and vagueness of different regulations and also because
   a. what marketers easily get away with at one time they may be fined for at another time.
   b. government intervention is inconsistent with the concept of free enterprise.
   c. the courts' interpretations of laws change over the years.
   d. most marketers refuse to be regulated.
   e. the continual turnover in public officials makes for an unstable political environment.

_____ 19. Which of the following is *not* a federal regulatory force?
   a. Federal Trade Commission
   b. Food and Drug Administration
   c. Federal Power Commission
   d. National Consumer Products Office
   e. Environmental Protection Agency

_____ 20. State regulatory agencies
   a. usually regulate such industries as banking, savings and loans, insurance, utilities, and liquor.
   b. usually act in a consulting role and leave enforcement of specific laws to national regulatory agencies and the governor.

c. often establish regulations that conflict with the actions of regulatory agencies at the national level because officials in many state governments feel their authority is being usurped by the federal government.
d. have no advantages in relation to the national government with regard to consumer protection, leaving this area to the federal government for enforcement.
e. usually are located in the office of the secretary of state.

_____ 21. Which of the following is *not* an advantage of self-regulatory programs?
a. Many self-regulatory programs do not have the tools or authority to enforce guidelines.
b. Self-regulatory guidelines are more realistic and operational.
c. Self-regulatory programs are usually less expensive to establish and implement.
d. Self-regulatory programs can reduce the need to expand government bureaucracy.
e. Managers prefer to have the opportunity to regulate themselves rather than having a government agency regulate them.

_____ 22. The main task of the National Advertising Review Board is to
a. handle the advertising campaigns of the Better Business Bureaus.
b. screen national advertisements, check for honesty, and process complaints about deceptive advertisements.
c. replace deceptive advertisements with more informative and honest advertisements.
d. fine firms that use deceptive advertising.
e. enforce regulations regarding deceptive trademarks.

_____ 23. The Better Business Bureau
a. provides consumers with point-of-sale information about maintenance costs of automobiles and major appliances.
b. sponsors meetings among local business leaders to facilitate the development of self-regulatory programs.
c. is a local regulatory agency that is financially supported by local businesses.
d. has strong enforcement tools to use in dealing with firms that use questionable business practices.
e. is a governmental regulatory group.

_____ 24. Price differences are ruled discriminatory and are prohibited if they
a. increase competition.
b. lessen competition.
c. exist because of differences in the costs of selling to various customers.
d. are charged to customers who are not competitors.
e. arise because the firm has to cut its price to a particular buyer to meet competitors' prices.

_____ 25. Any channel structure that tends to restrain trade may be ruled a violation of the
  a. McGuire Act.
  b. Sherman Act.
  c. Miller-Tydings Act.
  d. Robinson-Patman Act.
  e. Wheeler-Lea Act.

_____ 26. One factor that contributes to the high quality of life is
  a. the amount of effort required to achieve a certain living standard.
  b. the unwillingness of marketers to provide products.
  c. political payoffs.
  d. pollution.
  e. legal restrictions on business operations.

_____ 27. Society wants
  a. high living standards.
  b. a high quality of life.
  c. high living standards and a high quality of life.
  d. total utilization of technology.
  e. more regulation of television programming.

_____ 28. Which of the following is *not* usually a concern of forces in the consumer movement?
  a. False advertising
  b. Product safety
  c. Consumer education
  d. Pollution
  e. Equal protection

_____ 29. Bayer aspirin operates in what type of competitive structure?
  a. Oligopolistic competition
  b. Monopoly
  c. Perfect competition
  d. Oligopoly
  e. Monopolistic competition

_____ 30. According to the authors' definition of the *quality of life*, which of the following products represents an improvement in the quality of life?
  a. The supersonic jet
  b. Gasoline
  c. Solar cells
  d. Aerosol deodorants
  e. Cigarettes

_____ 31. Which of the following is *not* a characteristic of a monopoly?
  a. There is only one competitor in the market.
  b. Entry into the market is difficult.
  c. Several substitutes for the product exist.
  d. Knowledge of the market is perfect.
  e. Competition is very restricted.

_____ 32. One resource that makes up buying power is
   a. income.
   b. goods.
   c. wealth.
   d. wages.
   e. credit.

_____ 33. After-tax income is known as
   a. discretionary income.
   b. wealth.
   c. buying power.
   d. disposable income.
   e. consumer income.

_____ 34. Discretionary income can be used for which of the following?
   a. To pay taxes
   b. To buy food
   c. To increase current buying power and reduce future buying power
   d. To buy shelter
   e. To buy an automobile

_____ 35. Effective buying income is similar to
   a. disposable income.
   b. consumer income.
   c. wealth.
   d. buying power.
   e. discretionary income.

_____ 36. Income left over after an individual pays taxes and purchases the basic necessities of food, clothing, and shelter is called
   a. disposable income.
   b. taxable income.
   c. accounting income.
   d. discretionary income.
   e. credit.

_____ 37. One's willingness to purchase a product; the satisfaction one receives from the product; and one's expectations of future employment, income level, and prices determine one's
   a. propensity to buy.
   b. ability to obtain credit.
   c. buying power.
   d. patronage motives.
   e. expected accumulation of wealth.

_____ 38. All the following affect a consumer's willingness to spend *except*
   a. a lack of substitute products.
   b. the product's absolute price.
   c. buying power.
   d. the price of a product relative to the price of substitute products.
   e. satisfaction derived from using a product.

_____ 39. Comprehensive spending patterns
   a. show the percentages of family income allotted to annual expenditures for general classes of goods and services.
   b. indicate the annual dollar amounts families spend for specific products within a general product class.
   c. are difficult to analyze and therefore are of little value to marketers.
   d. consist of effective buying income and retail sales data.
   e. are most useful for comparative purposes.

_____ 40. Which of the following is one of the four stages of the business cycle?
   a. Decline
   b. Inflation
   c. Wealth
   d. Shortage
   e. Prosperity

_____ 41. During recession,
   a. unemployment is low.
   b. consumers are more concerned about the functional value of products.
   c. buying power is high.
   d. consumers are willing to buy.
   e. marketers sometimes make the mistake of increasing their marketing efforts.

_____ 42. American Airlines operates in a competitive environment in which it must consider the reaction of other airlines to its marketing activities and in which many customers see the services offered as homogeneous. The cost of airplaines and maintenance facilities form sizable entry barriers. American's competitive environment is best characterized as
   a. a monopoly.
   b. an oligopoly.
   c. monopolistic competition.
   d. perfect competition.
   e. stiff competition.

_____ 43. This type of competitive structure that eists when a firm with many potential competitors attempts to develop a differential marketing strategy to establish its own market share is
   a. a monopoly.
   b. an oligopoly.
   c. monopolistic competition.
   d. heterophilous competition.
   e. perfect competition.

_____ 44. Technology
   a. has little impact on buyers' or marketers' decisions.
   b. has only a positive influence on our lives.
   c. is the result of research conducted by businesses, universities, and nonprofit organizations.
   d. does not influence our standard of living.
   e. is always beneficial.

_____ 45. Technology influences marketing activities in all but which one of the following ways?
   a. It can lessen the competitive pressures with which marketers must deal.
   b. It can lead to higher-quality, lower-priced products.
   c. It helps salespeople be more efficient.
   d. It has allowed marketers to communicate with larger masses of people.
   e. It determines the types of products that marketers can offer for sale.

_____ 46. If RCA developed a new technology that made 3-D imagery possible through the use of videotape played on an advanced television set, it would be more likely to market this innovation if it could obtain a
   a. competitive advancement.
   b. patent.
   c. promotional campaign.
   d. low-price advantage.
   e. technological assessment.

MINICASE: CHANGES IN ENVIRONMENTAL FORCES AFFECT THE TELEPHONE EQUIPMENT INDUSTRY

As a result of a ruling by the Federal Communications Commission (FCC), there have been widespread changes in the marketing of telephone equipment and services. Before this ruling, customers were required to pay a telephone equipment rental charge to the local telephone company, which was the only provider, but now individuals are allowed to purchase and connect their own FCC-registered telephone products without paying monthly equipment rental charges.

Because of this ruling there are now numerous retail facilities that offer new telephone products. These retailers provide an array of brands with a variety of features that cater to consumers' diverse needs. Many of these features have resulted from new technological developments. Consumers can usually save money by purchasing their own phone equipment. How much they save depends on the type of phone purchased and on the charges of the telephone company supplying rental equipment.

Questions

_____ 1. What market structure existed for telephone equipment before the FCC ruling?
   a. Perfect competition
   b. Oligopoly
   c. Monopoly
   d. Monopolistic competition
   e. Monopolistic oligopoly

_____ 2. Since the FCC ruling, the market structure has changed. Today the market for telephone equipment can be characterized as being
   a. a monopoly.
   b. perfect competition.
   c. an oligopoly.
   d. monopolistic competition.
   e. pure competition.

_____ 3. Which environmental force(s) probably had the *strongest* impact on the changes that occurred in the structure of the market for telephone equipment?
   a. Economic
   b. Procompetitive legislation
   c. Consumer protection legislation
   d. Political, legal, and regulatory forces
   e. Societal

_____ 4. The new cellular telephone equipment and services available to customers are the result of
   a. inflation.
   b. technology.
   c. competition.
   d. technology assessment.
   e. market structure.

PROGRAMMED COMPLETION EXERCISES

enactment,
interpretation,
regulatory agencies

1. Political and legal forces are closely interrelated aspects of the marketing environment because the _____ and _____ of laws and the creation and effectiveness of _____ _____ are determined mainly by persons who occupy government positions.

political forces,
influence, political
element

2. Many marketers view _____ _____ as being beyond their control and therefore try to adjust to the conditions that result from these forces. However, some firms attempt to _____ the _____ _____ by helping to elect certain individuals to political office.

monitor, environmental scanning, analysis

3. To effectively _____ changes in the marketing environment, marketers engage in _____ _____ and _____.

procompetitive, consumer protection laws

4. For purposes of analysis, laws that directly affect marketing practices can be categorized as _____ and _____ _____ _____.

Sherman Act, restraining trade, monopolizing markets

5. The first procompetitive law, the _____ _____, was created in 1890 to prevent business from _____ _____ and _____ _____.

interstate commerce, U.S. firms, foreign commerce

6. The Sherman Act applies to firms operating in _____ _____ and to _____ _____ operating in _____ _____.

Sherman Act, Clayton Act, stock, farm cooperatives, labor organizations

7. Partly because of weaknesses in the _____ _____ and partly because of weaknesses in its interpretation, the _____ _____ was passed in 1914. It prohibits price discrimination that is based on tying and exclusive agreements and the acquisition of another company's _____ when the effect may substantially lessen competition or tend to create a monopoly. In addition, interlocking directorates are deemed unlawful. The act exempts _____ _____ and _____ _____ from antitrust laws.

Federal Trade Commission Act

8. The _____ _____ _____ _____ regulates the greatest number of marketing practices.

Wheeler-Lea Act, deceptive, false advertising

9. The Federal Trade Commission Act was amended by the _____ _____, which also makes it unlawful to use _____ acts or practices; it specifically prohibits _____ _____ of foods, drugs, therapeutic devices, and cosmetics, and provides penalties for violations and procedures for enforcement.

price discrimination

10. The Robinson-Patman Act prohibits _____ _____ among different purchasers of commodities of like grade and quality when it substantially lessens competition or creates a monopoly.

safety, standards, information disclosure

11. Many laws and regulatory guidelines that concern marketers deal with product _____, product _____, and _____ _____.

vague, counseling

12. Many laws and regulations that affect marketing are stated in _____ terms, often forcing marketers to resort to legal _____ rather than rely on their own interpretations.

governmental, nongovernmental

13. Regulatory forces can be either _____ or _____, and local, state, or national in character.

five, seven, president, the Senate

14. The Federal Trade Commission consists of _____ members, each appointed for a term of _____ years by the _____ with the advice and consent of _____ _____.

three

15. No more than _____ commissioners may be from the same political party.

assistance,
information

16. One major goal of the FTC is to provide _____ and _____ so that businesses will know how to comply with laws.

FTC, complaint,
cease and desist

17. The _____ issues a _____ when it has reason to believe that a law has been violated. The FTC can issue a _____ _____ _____ order to stop whatever caused the condition in the first place.

banking, savings
and loans, insurance,
utilities, liquor

18. Industries that are commonly regulated by state agencies include _____, _____ _____ _____, _____, _____, and _____.

trade associations,
legal action, proposed
legislation

19. Firms in a number of industries develop self-regulatory programs through _____ _____ or as an indirect result of _____ _____ or _____ _____.

National Advertising
Review Board

20. The _____ _____ _____ _____ screens advertisements to check for honesty and processes complaints about deceptive advertisements.

expensive, realistic,
reduce

21. The advantages of self-regulatory programs over laws and guidelines are that they are less _____, their programs are _____ and operational, and they _____ the need to expand government bureaucracy.

vagueness, change
over the years

22. It is difficult to comply with all the laws and regulatory guidelines because of their _____ and because the courts' interpretations of them _____ _____ _____ _____.

high standard of living, high quality of life

23. People in our society want not only a _____ _____ _____ _____ but also a _____ _____ _____ _____ .

Environmental protection, product performance, safety, information disclosure

24. _____ _____, _____ _____ and _____, and _____ _____ are the major issues of the consumer movement.

desires, long-run effects

25. In being socially responsible, marketers face the problem of determining the _____ of society and predicting the _____ _____ of their decisions on society.

economic, competitive forces, marketers', customers'

26. The _____ and _____ _____ in the marketing environment influence both _____ and _____ decisions and activities.

competition, geographic area

27. From the viewpoint of a business, _____ is those firms that market products similar to or that substitute for its products in the same _____ _____ .

supply, strength of competition

28. The number of firms that control the _____ of a product may affect the _____ _____ _____ .

monopoly, perfect competition

29. In a _____, there is only one competitor in the market; in _____ _____, the number of competitors is unlimited.

oligopoly

30. When a few sellers control the supply of a large proportion of a product, an _____ exists.

number, type,
competitive tools

31. The _____ and _____ of _____ _____ used by competitors influence the level of competition.

Price

32. _____ is one of the most recognizable competitive tools.

specific market
segment

33. A marketer may gain a competitive advantage by focusing on a _____ _____ _____.

Buying power,
resources, state,
economy

34. _____ _____ is influenced by the size of the _____ that enable a person to purchase and by the _____ of the _____.

Income, paying
taxes, spending

35. _____ is used for _____ _____, _____, and saving.

disposable income,
spending, saving

36. After-tax income is called _____ _____ and is used for _____ and _____.

Buying power, trade
associations,
research agencies

37. _____ _____ information can be obtained from government sources, _____ _____, and _____ _____.

Income, wealth,
credit

38. _____, _____, and _____ enable consumers to purchase goods and services.

willingness to spend,
absolute price

39. A person's _____ _____ _____ is influenced by his or her buying power and by a product's _____ _____.

business cycle,
prosperity, recession,
depression, recovery

40. The _____ _____ consists of four stages: _____, _____, _____, and _____.

unemployment,
aggregate income

41. During prosperity, _____ is low and _____
_____ is relatively high.

Total buying power

42. _____ _____ _____ declines
during a recession because of increased unemployment.

Technology, tasks,
goals

43. _____ is the knowledge of how to accomplish
_____ and _____.

technology
assessment,
operation, other
business
organizations,
society

44. Through _____ _____, managers try to
foresee the effects of new products and processes on the
firm's _____, on _____ _____
_____, and on _____ in general.

ANSWERS TO OBJECTIVE QUESTIONS

Matching		*True or False*		*Multiple-Choice*		*Minicase*
1. p	23. mm	1. F	22. F	1. e	24. b	1. c
2. e	24. r	2. T	23. T	2. a	25. b	2. d
3. ll	25. pp	3. F	24. T	3. c	26. a	3. d
4. a	26. y	4. T	25. F	4. d	27. c	4. b
5. q	27. rr	5. T	26. T	5. d	28. e	
6. hh	28. k	6. F	27. T	6. b	29. d	
7. aa	29. f	7. F	28. F	7. e	30. c	
8. t	30. bb	8. T	29. T	8. a	31. c	
9. dd	31. z	9. F	30. T	9. e	32. b	
10. c	32. g	10. T	31. F	10. a	33. d	
11. uu	33. w	11. T	32. F	11. a	34. e	
12. i	34. ii	12. F	33. T	12. c	35. a	
13. l	35. qq	13. T	34. T	13. c	36. d	
14. v	36. n	14. F	35. T	14. e	37. a	
15. cc	37. b	15. F	36. T	15. a	38. a	
16. gg	38. s	16. F	37. T	16. a	39. a	
17. j	39. m	17. T	38. F	17. c	40. e	
18. d	40. kk	18. T	39. T	18. c	41. b	
19. o	41. h	19. T	40. T	19. d	42. b	
20. ff	42. jj	20. T	41. F	20. a	43. c	
21. nn	43. ww	21. T		21. a	44. c	
22. x				22. b	45. a	
				23. c	46. b	

3 MARKETING ETHICS AND SOCIAL RESPONSBILITY

CHAPTER OUTLINE

CHAPTER SUMMARY

Marketing ethics are moral principles that define acceptable and unacceptable behavior in marketing. Most marketing decisions can be judged as ethical or unethical. Ethics are an important concern in marketing decisions, yet ethics may be one of the most misunderstood and controversial concepts in marketing. Many people believe that marketing ethics are a personal matter, but this chapter points out that marketers must take responsibility for ethical behavior in their organization.

Personal moral philosophies, organizational factors, and opportunity are three important components of ethical decision making. Moral philosophies are principles or rules that individuals use to determine the right way to behave. They provide guidelines for resolving conflicts and ensuring mutual benefit for all members of society. Utilitarian moral philosophies are concerned with maximizing the greatest good for the greatest number of people. Ethical formalism philosophies, on the other hand, focus on general guidelines for behavior and on the rights of the individual. Organizational relationships with one's peers, subordinates, or superiors create ethical problems such as maintaining confidentiality in personal relations; meeting obligations, responsibilities, and mutual agreements; and avoiding undue pressure that may force others to behave unethically. Opportunity—a favorable set of conditions that limit barriers or provide internal or external rewards—to engage in unethical behavior provides another pressure that may determine whether a person behaves ethically. It is obvious that ethical decision making is a complex cognitive process, and simple statements or conclusions about why someone is ethical or unethical reveal limited understanding about the ethical decision-making process.

An ethical issue is an identifiable problem, situation, or opportunity requiring an individual or organization to choose from among alternatives that must be evaluated as ethical or unethical. Product-related ethical issues may develop when marketers fail to disclose risks associated with the product or information that relates to understanding the function, value, or use of the product. The promotion process gives rise to situations that can result in ethical issues, such as false and misleading advertising and deceptive sales tactics. Sales promotions and publicity that use deception or manipulation also create significant ethical issues. Bribery may be an ethical issue in some selling situations. Price fixing, predatory pricing, and failure to disclose the full price associated with a purchase are typical price-related ethical issues. Ethical issues in distribution relate to relationships and conflicts among producers and marketing middlemen.

Eliminating unethical individuals and improving an organization's ethical standards may help to improve ethical behavior in that organization. Codes of ethics, which formalize what an organization expects of its employees, eliminate the opportunity for unethical behavior because they provide rules to guide conduct and punishments for violating the rules. If the number of employees making ethical decisions on a regular basis is not satisfactory, the company needs to determine why and take corrective action through enforcement. Enforcement of standards is what makes codes of ethics effective. Enforcement eliminates opportunity and provides social pressure for ethical behavior.

Social responsibility in marketing refers to an organization's obligation to maximize its positive impact and minimize its negative impact on society. Marketing managers try to determine what accepted relationships, obligations, and duties exist between the business organization and society. Ethical behavior should be consistent with socially responsible behavior.

To be successful, a business must determine what customers, government regulators, and competitors, as well as society in general, want or expect in terms of social responsibility. Major categories of social responsibility issues include consumerism, community relations, and green marketing. Consumerism refers to the activities of independent individuals, groups, and organizations in trying to protect the rights of consumers. Of great importance to the consumer movement is the consumer "bill of rights," which includes the right to safety, the right to be informed, the right to choose, and the right to be heard. Communities expect a marketer to contribute to their satisfaction and growth. Green marketing is the specific development, pricing, promotion, and distribution of products that do not harm the environment.

Four approaches for dealing with social responsibility issues are reaction, defense, accommodation, and proaction. A business adopting a reaction strategy allows a condition or potential problem to go unresolved until the public learns about it. A business using the defense strategy tries to minimize or avoid additional obligations associated with a problem or problems. In the accommodation strategy, a business assumes responsibility for its actions. A business that uses the proactive strategy assumes responsibility for its actions and responds to accusations made against it without outside pressure or the threat of government intervention.

Marketing ethics and social responsibility work together because a company that has a corporate culture built on socially acceptable moral philosophies with individuals who have ethical personal values will generally make decisions that have a positive impact on society. If other persons in an organization approve of an activity and it is legal and customary within the industry, chances are the activity is acceptable from both an ethical and a social responsibility perspective.

MATCHING EXERCISES

Use the following set of terms to identify the sentences and phrases below. On the blank line next to each sentence or phrase, place the letter of the term that the sentence or phrase describes. Do not use a term more than once.

a. Green marketing
b. Moral philosophies
c. Defense strategy
d. Codes of ethics
e. Accommodation strategy
f. Marketing ethics
g. Consumerism

h. Utilitarianism
i. Reaction strategy
j. Ethical issue
k. Social responsibility
l. Proactive strategy
m. Ethical formalism
n. Marketing concept

_C_ 1. A strategy in which a business tries to minimize or avoid additional obligations linked to a problem or problems. *Defense Strategy*

_l_ 2. A strategy in which a business assumes responsibility for its actions and responds to accusations made against it without outside pressures or the threat of government intervention. *Proaction Strategy*

_f_ 3. Moral principles that define right and wrong behavior in marketing. *Mktg Ethics*

_a_ 4. The specific development, pricing, promotion, and distribution of products that do not harm the environment. *Green Marketin*

_d_ 5. Formalized rules and standards that describe what a company expects of its employees. *Code of Ethics*

_m_ 6. Moral philosophies that focus on the intentions associated with a particular behavior and on the rights of the individual. *Ethical Formalism*

_l_ 7. A strategy in which a business allows a condition or potential problem to go unresolved until the public learns about it. *Reaction Strategy*

_j_   8. An identifiable problem, situation, or opportunity requiring a person or organization to choose from among several actions that must be evaluated as ethical or unethical. *Ethical Issue*

_b_   9. Principles or rules that individuals use to determine the right way to behave. *Moral Philosophies*

_e_   10. A strategy in which a business assumes responsibility for its actions. *Accomodation Strategy*

_k_   11. An organization's obligation to maximize its positive impact and minimize its negative impact on society. *Social Responsibility*

_h_   12. Moral philosophies that are concerned with maximizing the greatest good for the greatest number of people. *Utilitarianism*

TRUE OR FALSE STATEMENTS

T **F̸** 1. Marketing ethics are well understood and noncontroversial.

T̸ F 2. A company that supports both socially acceptable moral philosophies and individuals who act ethically will probably make decisions that have a positive impact on society.

T̸ F 3. Most marketing decisions can be judged as ethical or unethical.

T̸ F 4. An oil company that accepts liability and responsibility for an oil spill from one of its tankers and that offers to clean it up and make restitution to people whose livelihoods were hurt by the spill without pressure from those people, the government, or the public, is taking a proactive strategy.

T **F̸** 5. Utilitarian moral philosophies focus on the intentions associated with a particular behavior and on the rights of the individual.

T̸ F 6. The specific development, pricing, promotion, and distribution of products that do not harm the environment is called green marketing.

T **F̸** 7. The Golden Rule is an example of utilitarianism.

T **F̸** 8. The right to be heard means that marketing organizations must listen to consumers' concerns.

T **F̸** 9. Personal moral philosophies are the central component that guides an organization's decisions and activities.

T̸ F 10. There are costs associated with being socially responsible and satisfying society's demands.

T̸ F 11. Top management may affect employees' activities and influence their behavior by putting into practice the company's standards of ethics.

T **F̸** 12. The concepts of ethics and social responsibility refer to the impact of individuals' decisions.

T   F   13. If a person is rewarded, either internally or externally, for developing a deceptive advertisement, he or she will probably continue such behavior in the future.

T   F   14. Codes of ethics encourage ethical behavior by eliminating opportunities for unethical behavior because employees know what is expected of them and what the punishment will be if they violate the codes.

T   F   15. Ethical issues may stem from conflicts between a marketer's attempts to achieve organizational objectives and customers' desires for safe and reliable products.

T   F   16. A bribe offered to benefit one's company is usually considered acceptable.

T   F   17. Exaggerated claims and concealed facts in advertising are generally accepted practices that foster consumer trust.

T   F   18. Competitive pressures do not result in ethical issues.

T   F   19. The emotional and subjective nature of price creates many situations in which misunderstandings between the seller and buyer cause ethical problems.

T   F   20. Codes of ethics and ethics-related corporate policy influence ethical behavior by prescribing what behaviors are acceptable.

T   F   21. Establishing a code of ethics guarantees that an organization's employees will act ethically.

T   F   22. The more a person is exposed to ethical behavior in his or her organization, the more likely he or she will behave unethically.

T   F   23. To preserve socially responsible behavior while achieving organizational goals, organizations must monitor changes and trends in society's values.

T   F   24. People learn to act unethically only by observing their peers at work.

T   F   25. Ralph Nader drafted the consumer "bill of rights."

T   F   26. The idea of consumer choice is consistent with ethical formalism.

T   F   27. Individual communities generally expect a marketing firm to contribute to their satisfaction and growth.

T   F   28. A company's decision to dump toxic chemicals into a stream to save money and preserve thousands of jobs for the local economy is an example of ethical formalism.

T   F   29. A business adopting a reaction strategy attempts to minimize or avoid additional obligations linked to a problem or problems.

T   F   30. Moral philosophies provide guidelines for resolving conflicts and ensuring mutual benefit for society.

T   F   31. A tuna fish marketer who agrees to stop purchasing tuna products from companies using fishing techniques that harm endangered wildlife after consumers boycott the company in protest is using an accommodation strategy.

T   F   32. Marketing ethics relate to legal issues and are the only rules with which marketers need be concerned.

MULTIPLE-CHOICE QUESTIONS

_____   1. Which of the following is *not* one of the factors that interact to determine ethical decisions in marketing?
    a. Organizational relationships
    b. Opportunity
    c. Marketing strategy
    d. Personal moral philosophies
    e. All of the above are factors in the ethical decision-making process.

_____   2. Which of the following statements about marketing ethics is *not* true?
    a. Marketing ethics are principles or rules that people use to determine the right way to behave.
    b. Marketing ethics are moral principles that define right and wrong behavior in marketing.
    c. Marketing ethics are highly controversial.
    d. Marketing ethics foster mutual trust among individuals and in marketing relationships.
    e. Marketing ethics relate to personal judgments about what is ethical or unethical in a particular marketing decision situation.

_____   3. Moral philosophies that develop specific rules for behavior by determining whether an action can be taken consistently as a general rule without concern for alternative results are known as
    a. utilitarianism.
    b. marketing ethics.
    c. social responsibility.
    d. ethical realism.
    e. ethical formalism.

_____   4. Which of the following statements is false?
    a. Social responsibility and marketing ethics work together.
    b. A company that supports both socially acceptable moral philosophies and individuals who act ethically is likely to make decisions that have a positive impact on society.
    c. If people in an organization approve of an activity, and it is legal and customary within the industry, the activity is probably ethical and socially responsible.

    d. Once a final solution is reached on an ethical issue, everyone will share the same viewpoint about the issue.

    e. If an ethical or social responsibility issue can withstand open discussion and result in agreement or limited debate, an acceptable solution may exist.

_____ 5. Which one of the following moral philosophies evaluates the ethicality of a particular marketing activity on the basis of its consequences?
    a. Marketing ethics
    b. Practicalism
    c. Ethical formalism
    d. Utilitarianism
    e. Ethical informalism

_____ 6. Maximizing the greatest good for the greatest number of people is the basic concept behind _____ moral philosophies.
    a. pluralistic
    b. egalitarian
    c. humanitarian
    d. practical
    e. utilitarian

_____ 7. As a new employee, John is most likely to look to which one of the following to learn the ethical culture of his new organization?
    a. Coworkers
    b. Customer contact employees
    c. Other new hires
    d. The legal department
    e. Top management

_____ 8. After reading Chapter 3 in the text, you go to a company meeting and point out that moral philosophies, organizational relationships, and _____ are three factors that interact to determine ethical decisions in marketing.
    a. personal feelings
    b. opportunity
    c. personal formalism
    d. corporate culture
    e. the game of marketing

_____ 9. Which of the following represents an internal reward that might influence a person's ethical decision-making process?
    a. A demotion for failing to follow the firm's ethical standards
    b. A promotion for winning a big contract
    c. Praise from superiors for refusing to offer a bribe
    d. A feeling of satisfaction after refusing the temptation of a bribe
    e. A bonus for using manipulative sales tactics to win a large sale

_____ 10. A company that installs more efficient scrubbers and other emission-control devices on a chemical-processing plant while public interest groups are lobbying Congress to pass tougher pollution-control standards to halt acid rain is using the
   a. reaction strategy.
   c. accommodation strategy.
   d. proactive strategy.
   e. smart strategy.

_____ 11. Offering a prospect a lavish trip to a foreign country to secure an important sales contract is
   a. a product-related ethical issue.
   b. a promotion-related ethical issue. _sales bro_
   c. a pricing-related ethical issue.
   d. a distribution-related ethical issue.
   e. not an ethical issue.

_____ 12. A company that stops dumping its chemical wastes, which contain high levels of mercury, into a popular recreation lake after the public learns about it and protests is using the
   a. reaction strategy.
   b. defense strategy.
   c. accommodation strategy.
   d. proactive strategy.
   e. offense strategy.

_____ 13. Which of the following statements about social responsibility is false?
   a. Social responsibility refers to a company's obligation to maximize its positive impact and minimize its negative impact on society.
   b. Social responsibility can be viewed as a contract with society.
   c. Social responsibility is not an easy endeavor.
   d. Social responsibility relates to individual decisions.
   e. Social responsibility relates to the accepted relationships, obligations, and duties that exist between a marketer and society.

_____ 14. When marketers fail to disclose the risks associated with a product or information about a product's function, value, or use, there exists the possibility of a
   a. distribution-related ethical issue.
   b. pricing-related ethical issue.
   c. product-related ethical issue.
   d. advertising-related ethical issue.
   e. personal-selling-related ethical issue.

_____ 15. Ethical behavior in marketing requires all of the following *except*
   a. a strong moral foundation, including personal moral development.
   b. an organizational culture that encourages and rewards desired ethical action.
   c. codes of ethics that are very detailed and take into account every possible situation.

d. an understanding of competitive pressures.

e. an effective control system.

16. Which of the following is a social responsibility issue related to local development and charitable activities?
a. Green marketing
b. Cause-related marketing
c. Consumerism
d. Benevolence
e. Community relations

17. The efforts of independent individuals, groups, and organizations to protect the rights of consumers is often called
a. consumerism.
b. social responsibility.
c. ethics.
d. consumer responsibility.
e. the marketing concept.

18. In Kennedy's consumer bill of rights, marketers' obligation not to knowingly market a product that could harm consumers is known as
a. let the seller beware.
b. the right to live and let live.
c. the right to health and welfare.
d. the right to safety.
e. the right to quality products.

19. Which of the following "rights" requires that all products be safe for their intended use, include thorough and explicit instructions for proper and safe use, and be tested to ensure reliability and quality?
a. The right to be heard
b. The right to safety
c. The right to buy quality products
d. The right to be informed
e. The right to choose

20. Which of the following "rights" requires that consumers have access to and the opportunity to review all relevant information about a product before buying it?
a. The right to a fair price
b. The right to choose
c. The right to be heard
d. The right to safety
e. The right to be informed

21. A restaurant that announces that it will no longer package its take-out meals in Styrofoam containers and plastic cups is using
a. social responsibility.
b. marketing ethics.
c. green marketing.
d. consumerism.
e. community relations.

_____ 22. Which of the following activities will *not* help improve the ethical behavior of a marketing firm?
a. Establishing and enforcing a code of ethics
b. Eliminating "bad apples" from the firm
c. Rewarding employees who use questionable business tactics
d. Redesigning the company's culture to foster more ethical practices
e. Helping employees become aware of and sensitive toward ethical issues

_____ 23. The Carter Company voluntarily offered to recall thousands of defective lawn mowers without threats from the public or the government. None of the defective mowers caused any injuries or deaths. Which of the following social responsibility strategies is the Carter Company using?
a. Good-guy strategy
b. Reaction strategy
c. Defense strategy
d. Accommodation strategy
e. Proactive strategy

_____ 24. A company's failure to inform consumers about changes in the ingredients of one of its products is
a. a product-related ethical issue.
b. a promotion-related ethical issue.
c. a pricing-related ethical issue.
d. a distribution-related ethical issue.
e. not an ethical issue.

_____ 25. A fast-food company's decision to make foam packages into playground equipment only after local laws were passed and consumers staged boycotts is consistent with which of the following strategies for dealing with social responsibility issues?
a. Reaction
b. Accommodation
c. Proaction
d. Ethical consciousness
e. Arbitration

_____ 26. A company that lobbies Congress to restrict the number of microwave ovens imported from Korea in an effort to stem the sales decline of its own microwave ovens is using the
a. reaction strategy.
b. defense strategy.
c. accommodation strategy.
d. proactive strategy.
e. wimp strategy.

_____ 27. Which of the following is *not* an organizational relationship that may create ethical problems within the organization?
a. Employee and coworkers
b. Employee and family members
c. Employee and superiors

d. Employee and subordinates

e. Employee and the firm's top management

_____ 28. From which of the following do people learn personal moral philosophies, and therefore, ethical behavior?

a. Society in general

b. Social groups and relationships

c. Coworkers

d. Superiors

e. All of the above

_____ 29. Social responsibility is the obligation of an organization to maximize its positive impact and minimize its negative impact on society. Marketing ethics are

a. the same thing.

b. related to the impact of individual marketing decisions on society.

c. concerned with the total effect of marketing decisions on society.

d. related to individuals' moral evaluations of what is right or wrong in a particular marketing situation.

e. related to industry evaluations of what is right or wrong in a particular marketing situation.

_____ 30. Recently, the Hughes Corporation contacted several consumer groups, industry associations, and government regulatory groups about a particular social responsibility issue. The Hughes Corporation was most likely trying to determine

a. how liable it may be for an unethical action.

b. the amount of negative publicity that will be created by the company's action.

c. whether a specific behavior is ethical and socially responsible.

d. the negative impact on society that could result from the company's actions.

e. how often competitors engage in unethical behaviors related to the issue.

MINICASE: A CASE OF BRIBERY

Acme Construction Co. is a medium-sized company that builds and repairs roads and highways, primarily for the federal government and for five state governments. However, federal and state budget cuts have hurt the company's profits in recent years. The company was recently offered the opportunity to bid on a multimillion-dollar project to rebuild a hurricane-damaged highway in Mexico. The project not only will earn millions of dollars for the firm but also will give the firm its first international exposure, possibly leading to other lucrative international construction projects.

Drew Garcia, one of Acme's senior managers, has been sent to Mexico City to facilitate the bidding process. Oscar Villarreal, a Mexican administrator who oversees highway building and repair, has told Garcia that Acme has a very good chance of winning the contract because it has one of the lowest bids and is most qualified to handle the project. However, Villarreal tells Garcia that he will not award Acme the contract unless it gives him *la mordida,* a bribe, of $25,000.

Drew Garcia knows that offering bribes to secure business is a violation of U.S. law. On the other hand, he knows that winning this contract is very important to Acme's future. Furthermore, lacking international experience, Acme does not have a corporate policy prescribing how to act in such a situation. He therefore asks Acme's president, Al Wilson, what he should do. Wilson tells Garcia that he must do whatever is necessary to win the contract because Acme needs the business. In fact, Wilson tells Garcia that if Acme does not win the contract, it will probably have to lay off 100 employees, including Garcia, because there will not be enough work for them.

Garcia decides that the greatest good would be served by violating the law and thereby saving 100 jobs (including his own). He therefore agrees to pay Villarreal the $25,000, listing the sum on his expense report as a cost of securing the contract. Acme wins the contract, and Garcia is awarded a bonus of $10,000.

Questions

_____ 1. Which moral philosophy does Drew Garcia appear to be using to resolve his ethical issue?
  a. Utilitarianism
  b. Ethical formalism
  c. The Golden Rule
  d. Kant's categorical imperative
  e. Marketing ethics

_____ 2. Which of the following elements of the ethical decision-making process did *not* influence Drew Garcia's decision?
  a. His personal moral philosophy
  b. His relationship with his superior
  c. The opportunity to earn external rewards (e.g., to save his and others' jobs, to earn a bonus)
  d. Acme's code of ethics
  e. All of the above influenced his decision.

_____ 3. Because Drew Garcia was awarded a bonus for winning the contract, when faced with a similar situation in the future, he may offer a bribe to secure another contract because of which of the following elements of the ethical decision-making process?
  a. His personal moral philosophy
  b. Pressure exerted through organizational relationships
  c. The opportunity to earn another large bonus
  d. U.S. laws
  e. His company's code of ethics

PROGRAMMED COMPLETION EXERCISES

Marketing ethics

1. _____ _____ are moral principles that define right and wrong behavior in marketing.

legal issues,
mutual trust

2. Marketing ethics go beyond _____ _____; they foster _____ _____ among individuals and in marketing relationships.

ethical, unethical

3. Most marketing decisions can be judged as _____ or _____.

Personal moral
philosophies,
organizational rela-
tionships, opportunity

4. _____ _____ _____, _____ _____, and _____ are three factors that interact to determine ethical decisions in marketing.

Utilitarian moral
philosophies,
Ethical formalism

5. _____ _____ _____ are concerned with maximizing the greatest good for the greatest number of people. _____ _____ focuses on the intentions associated with a particular behavior and on the rights of the individual.

moral philosophy

6. Research has shown that most businesspersons use one _____ _____ at work and a completely different one outside of work.

war, game

7. Some businesspersons view marketing as _____, adopting tactics such as "guerrilla warfare"; others view marketing as a _____ in which ordinary rules and morality do not apply.

employees, coworkers,
superiors

8. Relationships with one's _____, _____, or _____ create ethical problems, such as maintaining confidentiality in personal relations; meeting obligations,

responsibilities, and mutual agreements; and avoiding undue pressure that may force others to behave unethically.

opportunity, rewarded, penalty

9. If a marketer takes advantage of an _____ to act unethically and is _____ or suffers no _____, he or she may repeat such acts as other opportunities arise.

codes of ethics, ethics-related corporate policy

10. Professional _____ _____ _____ and _____ _____ _____ influence opportunity by prescribing what behaviors are acceptable.

ethical issue

11. An _____ _____ is an identifiable problem, situation, or opportunity requiring an individual or organization to choose from among several actions that must be evaluated as ethical or unethical.

Product-related ethical issues

12. _____ _____ _____ may arise when marketers fail to disclose risks associated with the product or information regarding the function, value, or use of the product.

communication process, advertising, sales promotions, publicity

13. The _____ _____ provides a variety of situations that can create ethical issues, such as false and misleading _____ and manipulative or deceptive _____ _____, tactics, or _____ efforts.

bribery

14. When payments, gifts, or special favors are granted to obtain a sale or for some other reason, there is always some question of _____.

price

15. The emotional and subjective nature of _____ creates many situations in which misunderstandings between the seller and buyer cause ethical problems.

distribution, middlemen

16. Ethical issues in _____ relate to relationships among producers and marketing _____.

ethical, eliminating, improving, ethical

17. It is possible to improve _____ behavior in an organization by _____ unethical individuals and _____ the organization's _____ standards.

Codes of ethics

18. _____ _____ _____ are formalized rules and standards that describe what the company expects of its employees.

policies, rules, standards, control

19. If a company is to maintain ethical behavior, its _____, _____, and _____ must be worked into its _____ system.

Social responsibility, maximize, minimize

20. _____ _____ in marketing refers to an organization's obligation to _____ its positive impact and _____ its negative impact on society.

relationships, obligations, duties

21. Marketing managers try to determine what accepted _____, _____, and _____ exist between the marketing organization and society.

consumerism, community relations, green marketing

22. Three important social responsibility issues are _____, _____ _____, and _____ _____.

safety, informed, choose, heard

23. The consumer "bill of rights" drafted by John F. Kennedy includes the right to _____, the right to be _____, the right to _____, and the right to be _____.

satisfaction, growth

24. Individual communities expect marketers to contribute to the _____ and _____ of their communities.

green marketing

25. The specific development, pricing, promotion, and distribution of products that do not harm the environment is called

_____ _____.

reaction, defense, accommodation, proaction

26. Four approaches for dealing with social responsibility issues are _____, _____, _____, and _____.

Ethics, social responsibility, moral philosophies, ethically

27. _____ and _____ _____ work together because a company that supports both socially acceptable _____ _____ and individuals who act _____ is likely to make decisions that have a positive impact on society.

organization, industry, acceptable

28. If other people in the _____ approve of the activity and it is legal and customary in the _____, chances are the activity is _____ from both an ethical and a social responsibility perspective.

ANSWERS TO OBJECTIVE QUESTIONS

Matching		*True or False*		*Multiple-Choice*		*Minicase*
1. c	7. i	1. F	17. F	1. c	16. e	1. a
2. l	8. j	2. T	18. F	2. a	17. a	2. d
3. f	9. b	3. T	19. T	3. e	18. d	3. c
4. a	10. e	4. T	20. T	4. d	19. b	
5. d	11. k	5. F	21. F	5. d	20. e	
6. m	12. h	6. T	22. F	6. e	21. c	
		7. F	23. T	7. e	22. c	
		8. F	24. F	8. b	23. e	
		9. F	25. F	9. d	24. a	
		10. T	26. T	10. c	25. a	
		11. T	27. T	11. b	26. b	
		12. F	28. F	12. a	27. b	
		13. T	29. F	13. d	28. e	
		14. T	30. T	14. c	29. d	
		15. T	31. T	15. c	30. c	
		16. F	32. F			

4 TARGET MARKETS: SEGMENTATION AND EVALUATION

CHAPTER OUTLINE

What are markets?
  Requirements for a market
  Types of markets
Selecting target markets
  Total market, or undifferentiated, approach
  Market segmentation approach
  Market segmentation strategies
  Conditions for effective segmentation
Choosing segmentation variables
  Variables for segmenting consumer markets
  Variables for segmenting organizational markets
  Single-variable versus multivariable segmentation
Evaluating markets and forecasting sales
  Market and sales potentials
  Developing sales forecasts
  Using multiple forecasting methods

CHAPTER SUMMARY

A market is an aggregate of people who, as individuals or as organizations, have a need for products in a product class and the ability, willingness, and authority to purchase those products. There are two major types of markets: consumer and organizational. A consumer market consists of purchasers and/or individuals in their households who intend to consume or benefit from the purchased products and who do not buy products for the main purpose of making a profit. Organizational, or industrial, markets consist of individuals or groups that buy products for resale, for direct use in producing other products, or for use in the daily operation of the organization. Organizational markets can be divided into four categories: producer, reseller, government, and business-to-business.

The two general ways marketers identify target markets are the total market approach and the market segmentation approach. When a firm designs a single marketing mix and directs it at an entire market for a particular product, the firm is using a total market, or undifferentiated, approach. This method is effective only when a large proportion of individuals in the total market have similar product needs and when the organization is capable of developing and maintaining a single marketing mix that satisfies these people's needs.

Sometimes a firm cannot satisfy the total market with a single marketing mix because the individuals within the market have diverse needs. This kind of market is called a heterogeneous market. Here, a marketer must use a market segmentation approach to divide the total market into market segments, or groups of individuals who have relatively similar product needs. Then the marketer can design a marketing mix (or mixes) that better fits the product needs of the selected segment (or segments).

There are two major market segmentation strategies: (1) the concentration strategy and (2) the multisegment strategy. When a firm focuses its marketing efforts on a single market segment through one marketing mix, it is using a concentration strategy. The primary advantage of this strategy is that it allows the firm to specialize—to direct all its efforts toward satisfying a specific need. The major drawback of a concentration strategy is that if demand in the segment falls, total sales will decline. A firm using a multisegment strategy designs a marketing mix for each of two or more selected segments. Although the costs of a multisegment strategy are high, the potential buyer population is much larger than a single market segment.

For segmentation to be effective, five conditions must exist: (1) consumers' needs must be heterogeneous; (2) the segments must be identifiable and divisible; (3) the estimated sales potential, cost, and profits for each segment must be measurable; (4) at least one segment must have enough profit potential to support a special marketing mix; and (5) the firm must be able to reach a chosen segment with a particular marketing mix.

Segmentation variables are the dimensions, or characteristics, of individuals, groups, or organizations that are used for dividing the total market into segments. The four general categories of segmentation variables for consumer markets are demographic (for example, age, gender, income, education), geographic (climate, terrain, population, market density), psychographic (personality, motives, lifestyle), and behavioristic (users, uses, benefits).

Organizational markets too can be segmented to satisfy product needs. Segmentation variables for organizational markets are geographic location, type of organization, customer size, and product use.

A marketer can divide a market in terms of one variable or several. Single-variable segmentation is the easiest form of segmentation to use, but it gives marketers only moderate precision in designing a marketing mix to satisfy individuals in a specific segment. Multivariable segmentation, which uses more than one characteristic to divide a total market, provides more information about the individuals in each segment, allowing marketers to develop a marketing mix that will satisfy customers in a given segment more precisely.

The sales potential of a segment or segments must justify the cost of developing and maintaining one or more marketing mixes. *Market potential* is the total amount of a product that customers will purchase within a specified time period at a specific intensity of industrywide marketing activity. *Sales potential* is the maximum percentage of market potential that an individual firm within an industry can expect to obtain for a specific product. In measuring sales potential, a marketer can use either the breakdown approach or the buildup approach.

A sales forecast is the amount of a product that the company actually expects to sell during a specific period at a specified level of marketing activity. Marketers have five methods at their disposal for developing sales forecasts: (1) executive judgment, which is based on the intuition of executives; (2) surveys of customers, the sales force, or experts; (3) time series analysis, which relies on historical data; (4) correlation methods, which are used to develop a mathematical relationship between past sales and one or more selected variables; and (5) market tests, which measure actual consumer purchases and consumer responses to promotion, price, and distribution efforts. Most firms use a combination of two or more of these methods.

MATCHING EXERCISES

Use the following set of terms to identify the sentences and phrases below. On the blank line next to each sentence or phrase, place the letter of the term that the sentence or phrase describes. Do not use a term more than once.

a.	Customer forecasting survey	v.	Executive judgment
b.	Advertising	w.	Marketing intelligence
c.	Sales-force forecasting survey	x.	Consumer markets
d.	Trend analysis	y.	Product deletion
e.	Correlation methods	z.	Breakdown approach
f.	Market	aa.	Buildup approach
g.	Single-variable segmentation	bb.	Total market (undifferentiated) approach
h.	Market test		
i.	Time series analysis	cc.	Organizational or industrial market
j.	Sales forecast		
k.	Channel strategy	dd.	Sales potential
l.	Advertising platform	ee.	Seasonal analysis
m.	Cycle analysis	ff.	Motive
n.	Random factor analysis	gg.	Group market analysis
o.	Heterogeneous market	hh.	Focused market orientation
p.	Product differentiation strategy	ii.	Concentration strategy
q.	Market potential	jj.	Multisegment strategy
r.	Multivariable segmentation	kk.	Segmentation variable
s.	Market segment	ll.	Benefit segmentation
t.	Market segmentation	mm.	Market density
u.	Expert forecasting survey	nn.	Accumulation

_____ 1. An aggregate of people who, as individuals or as organizations, have needs for products in a product class and the ability, willingness, and authority to purchase those products.

_____ 2. A market made up of individuals with diverse product needs for a product in a specific product class.

_____ 3. A sales forecasting method that involves making a product available to buyers in one or more test areas and measuring purchases and consumer responses to promotion, price, and distribution efforts.

_____ 4. A market segmentation approach in which an organization directs marketing efforts at two or more market segments by developing a marketing mix for each segment.

_____ 5. A general approach to measuring sales potential in which the analyst initially estimates how much the average purchaser of a product will buy in a specified time period and then multiplies that figure by the number of potential buyers; estimates generally are calculated by individual geographic areas.

_____ 6. Purchasers or individuals in their households who intend to consume or benefit from the purchased products and who do not buy products for the main purpose of making a profit.

_____ 7. An estimate by members of a firm's sales force of the anticipated sales in their territories for a specified period.

_____ 8. The total amount of a product that customer groups will purchase within a specified period at a specific level of industrywide marketing activity.

_____ 9. A market division achieved by using more than one characteristic to divide the total market; this approach provides more information about the individuals in each segment than does single-variable segmentation.

_____ 10. A method of forecasting sales in which an analyst studies daily, weekly, or monthly sales figures to evaluate the degree to which climate and holiday activities influence the firm's sales.

_____ 11. A group of individuals, groups, or organizations that share one or more similar characteristics that give them relatively similar product needs.

_____ 12. A market segmentation approach in which one marketing mix is directed toward a single market segment.

_____ 13. A method of forecasting sales in which an attempt is made to attribute erratic sales variations to random, nonrecurrent events, such as regional power failures or natural disasters.

_____ 14. Questioning customers about the types and quantities of products they intend to buy during a specified period.

_____ 15. Methods used to develop sales forecasts in which the forecaster attempts to find a relationship between past sales and one or more variables, such as population, per capita income, or gross national product.

_____ 16. The process of dividing a total market into groups of people with relatively similar product needs for the purpose of designing a marketing mix (or mixes) that more precisely matches the needs of individuals in the selected segment (or segments).

_____ 17. The amount of a product that a firm actually expects to sell during a specific period at a specified level of company marketing activity.

_____ 18. An approach in which an organization designs a single marketing mix and directs it at an entire market for a specific product category.

_____ 19. A dimension or characteristic of individuals, groups, or organizations that is used to divide a total market into segments.

_____ 20. A general approach for measuring sales potential based on a general economic forecast—or other aggregate data—and the sales potential derived from it.

_____ 21. An analysis that focuses on aggregate sales data, such as a company's annual sales figures, over a period of many years to determine whether annual sales generally are rising, falling, or staying about the same.

_____ 22. The maximum percentage of market potential that an individual firm can expect to obtain for a specific product.

_____ 23. The number of potential customers within a unit of land area, such as a square mile.

_____ 24. A method of predicting sales in which a forecaster analyzes sales figures for a period of three to five years to ascertain whether sales fluctuate in a consistent, periodic manner.

_____ 25. A market consisting of individuals or groups that purchase specific kinds of products for one of three purposes: resale, direct use in producing other products, or use in day-to-day operations.

_____ 26. A technique in which the forecaster, using the firm's historical sales data, tries to discover patterns in the firm's sales volume over time.

_____ 27. A sales forecast prepared by economists, management consultants, advertising executives, college professors, or other persons outside the firm.

_____ 28. The division of a market according to the benefits that customers want from the product.

_____ 29. The simplest form of segmentation; it is achieved by using only one characteristic to divide—or segment—a market.

_____ 30. A sales forecasting method based on the intuition of one or more executives.

TRUE OR FALSE STATEMENTS

T   F   1. An individual who has the desire, the buying power, and the willingness to purchase certain products may certainly do so.

T   F   2. The consumer market is composed of persons who do not buy products to resell at a profit.

T   F   3. A person cannot be categorized neatly into only a single market but is part of numerous consumer markets.

T   F   4. The segmentation approach is most appropriate for use in a homogeneous market.

T F 5. A company sometimes defines the total market as its target market.

T F 6. A concentration strategy allows a firm to analyze carefully the needs of a specific group of customers.

T F 7. A multisegment strategy is one in which the organization directs its marketing efforts at two or more segments by developing one marketing mix to be used in all selected segments.

T F 8. For market segmentation to be effective, a firm must be able to reach a chosen segment with a particular marketing mix.

T F 9. The demographic characteristics of a market can be measured readily through observation or surveys.

T F 10. *Target market* refers to the number of potential customers within a unit of land area.

T F 11. Psychographic segmentation variables are being used more often because they are relatively easy to measure.

T F 12. A market can be divided according to the benefits that customers want from a particular product.

T F 13. The analysis of sales potential should be limited to one specific level of marketing activity.

T F 14. A sales forecast must be specific in terms of time.

T F 15. The customer survey is the most feasible sales forecasting method for a soft-drink company.

T F 16. The customer survey method generally is easier to use with industrial customers than with customers in consumer markets.

T F 17. Time series analysis seeks a pattern in a firm's sales volume based on historical data.

T F 18. Correlation methods are the most useful methods for forecasting the sales of a new product.

MULTIPLE-CHOICE QUESTIONS

_____ 1. Which of the following is *not* a requirement for a market?
a. Ability to purchase
b. Measurable relationship between supply and demand
c. Need for a product
d. Authority to buy
e. Willingness to purchase

_____ 2. All the following are types of organizational markets *except*
a. reseller.
b. government.
c. business-to-business.
d. producer.
e. all the above.

_____ 3. The two major groups of markets are
a. business-to-business and reseller.
b. consumer and producer.
c. consumer and organizational.
d. business-to-business and consumer.
e. consumer and reseller.

_____ 4. A market consisting of individuals, groups, or organizations that purchase a specific kind of product for direct use in producing other products or for use in day-to-day operation is a(n)
a. consumer market.
b. institutional market.
c. producer market.
d. business-to-business market.
e. reseller market.

_____ 5. A total market approach can be effective when
a. many individuals have similar needs and are satisfied by several marketing mixes.
b. many individuals have diverse product needs but are satisfied by a single marketing mix.
c. used only in the consumer market.
d. many individuals have diverse product needs that can be satisfied by a single marketing mix.
e. many individuals have similar product needs that can be satisfied by a single marketing mix.

_____ 6. The marketing mix consists of
a. price, product, promotion, and package.
b. promotion, package, distribution, and product.
c. price, promotion, distribution, and product.
d. price, distribution, advertising, and product.
e. product, package, selling, and distribution.

_____ 7. Markets made up of individuals with diverse product needs are called
a. homogeneous markets.
b. heterogeneous markets.
c. differentiated markets.
d. segmented markets.
e. market segments.

_____ 8. The preceding diagram illustrates what marketing strategy?
   a. Undifferentiated
   b. Multisegment
   c. Concentration
   d. Product differentiation
   e. Total market

_____ 9. One major difference between a total market approach and a multi-segment approach is the
   a. number of product modifications.
   b. number of marketing mixes required.
   c. relative size of the marketing mix.
   d. number of prices used.
   e. homogeneity of the target group.

_____ 10. A firm with limited resources can compete with much larger organizations by
   a. concentrating its efforts on a single segment.
   b. using a multisegment strategy.
   c. using a geographical segmentation variable.
   d. using multivariable segmentation.
   e. concentrating its efforts on the total population.

_____ 11. Consequences that may be associated with the multisegment strategy are
   a. an increase in sales and a decrease in total marketing costs.
   b. the use of excess production capacity and a decrease in total marketing costs.
   c. an increase in sales and the use of excess production capacity.
   d. a decrease in production costs and a decrease in total marketing costs.
   e. an increase in sales and a decrease in total production costs.

_____ 12. Firms in the automobile industry generally use which of the following marketing strategies?
   a. Product differentiation
   b. Total market
   c. Multisegment
   d. Concentration
   e. Mass marketing

_____ 13. All the following are necessary conditions for effective segmentation *except*
   a. consumers' needs must be homogeneous
   b. the segments must be divisible.
   c. the estimated sales potential of the segments must be measurable.

d. at least one segment must provide enough profit to support a special marketing mix.
e. the segments must be accessible.

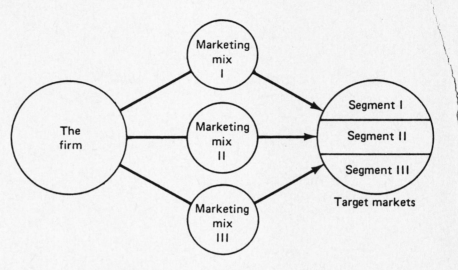

_____ 14. The type of segmentation illustrated in the preceding diagram
a. is effective when customers' needs are homogeneous.
b. is used when a firm directs its efforts at the market with a particular product.
c. is used when a firm attempts to differentiate a particular product in customers' minds.
d. ordinarily entails higher marketing costs than a concentration strategy.
e. is used by all producers of staple food items.

_____ 15. The segmentation variables that are measured most easily are
a. product benefits.
b. demographic characteristics of buyers.
c. buyer behavior.
d. buyer motives.
e. buyer personality.

_____ 16. The number of potential customers within a unit of land area is referred to as the
a. target market.
b. market objective.
c. market density.
d. market segment.
e. total market.

_____ 17. Personality characteristics, motives, and lifestyles are
a. product-related customer characteristics.
b. variables for segmenting institutional markets.
c. demographic characteristics.
d. psychographic dimensions for segmenting markets.
e. behavioristic variables.

18. If a market is divided into heavy users and light users of a particular product, the market has been segmented by
    a. psychological dimensions.
    b. geographic variables.
    c. types of organizations.
    d. product uses.
    e. behavioristic variables.

19. Georgia Pacific provides lumber to various manufacturers in the northwestern United States. Georgia Pacific would most likely segment markets based on which one of the following variables?
    a. Demographics
    b. Psychographics
    c. Type of organization
    d. Branch loyalty
    e. Population

20. The segmentation variable that would most likely be used to segment magazines such as *Mademoiselle, Glamour,* and *Vogue* is
    a. geographic location.
    b. religion.
    c. age.
    d. rate of usage.
    e. personality.

21. Geographic segmentation variables include
    a. climate, citizenship, and terrain.
    b. natural resources, lifestyles, and climate.
    c. population density, social class, and subcultural values.
    d. subcultural values, motives, and lifestyles.
    e. terrain, natural resources, and regional subcultural values.

22. Coppertone Suncare focuses more of its marketing efforts on Miami than Portland despite their similarity in size. Here the firm is responding to differences in
    a. family life cycle.
    b. gender.
    c. market density.
    d. demographics.
    e. psychographics.

23. The three psychographic dimensions most commonly used in market segmentation are
    a. personality, perception, and learning.
    b. personality, perception, and behavior.
    c. motives, attitudes, and lifestyles.
    d. attitudes, personality, and perception.
    e. personality, motives, and lifestyles.

_____ 24. Through a program called Club Rewards, Diners Club International, the entertainment credit card, allows cardholders to purchase merchandise and trips using points earned based on dollar volume charging. Diners' program is based on which one of the following variables?
a. Lifestyle
b. Demographic
c. Behavioristic
d. Psychographic
e. Benefit

_____ 25. By offering Crest for Kids (attractive taste for children), Regular Crest for cavity control, and Tartar Control Crest toothpastes, Procter & Gamble is segmenting the market based on
a. benefits.
b. psychographics.
c. lifestyle.
d. demographics.
e. behavioristics.

_____ 26. Marketers of several Procter & Gamble products define markets on the basis of both volume usage of the product and annual family income. This is an example of which market segmentation approach?
a. Homogeneous
b. Multisegment
c. Variable
d. Benefit
e. Multivariable

_____ 27. The amount of a product that specific customer groups would purchase within a specified time period at a specific level of industrywide marketing activity is
a. sales potential.
b. market potential.
c. consumer buying potential.
d. a sales forecast.
e. marketability.

_____ 28. The maximum percentage of market potential that an individual firm can expect to obtain for a specific product is
a. sales potential.
b. market potential.
c. a sales forecast.
d. the profitability margin.
e. a sales breakdown schedule.

_____ 29. The company sales forecast
a. is not affected by the industry's activities.
b. should be based on the assumption that the company will operate at a certain level of marketing effort.
c. is the amount of a product that could be sold.

    d. can be determined accurately only through mathematical models.

    e. considers what sales levels are possible at various intensities of company marketing activities.

_____ 30. Through a customer survey, the forecaster gains information about consumers'
   a. past purchases.
   b. actual purchases.
   c. intended purchases.
   d. buying power.
   e. minimum purchases.

_____ 31. A major justification for a firm's surveying its own salespeople is that they are
   a. least biased.
   b. least likely to be overly pessimistic.
   c. able to devote more time to the study.
   d. the best at setting reasonable quotas.
   e. closer to customers.

_____ 32. The sales forecasting method that relies specifically on historical data is
   a. market tests.
   b. executive judgment.
   c. expert surveys.
   d. time series analysis.
   e. forecasts of sales personnel.

_____ 33. A disadvantage of using expert surveys is that the experts
   a. seldom have the needed experience.
   b. often lack necessary information.
   c. are not expedient.
   d. may not be motivated.
   e. are too expensive.

_____ 34. Through a market test, the forecaster gains information about consumers'
   a. past purchases.
   b. actual purchases.
   c. intended purchases.
   d. estimated purchases.
   e. minimal purchases.

_____ 35. A market test can be effective for estimating the sales of an existing product in new geographic areas because
   a. it correlates new sales with those in existing markets.
   b. it is not dependent on historical data.
   c. it can measure consumers' intended purchases accurately.
   d. it is the least expensive method available.
   e. the product demand will stabilize quickly.

_____ 36. Which one of the following is the first step in the breakdown approach to forecasting?
   a. Developing a general forecast of demand
   b. Developing a general economic forecast for a specific time period
   c. Estimating market sales potential
   d. Estimating company sales potential
   e. Developing a sales forecast

_____ 37. The amount of a product that a firm actually epxects to sell during a specific time period at a specified level of marketing activity is called the
   a. marketing density.
   b. market potential.
   c. sales forecast.
   d. sales potential.
   e. market opportunity.

_____ 38. Suppose Kathleen Day is a marketer for Nestlé. To create a company sales forecast, she questioned customers and sales personnel. Kathleen was using which sales forecasting technique?
   a. Surveys
   b. Executive judgment
   c. Time series analysis
   d. Market tests
   e. Correlation methods

_____ 39. If a marketer for Coca-Cola measured purchases and consumer responses to price, promotion, and distribution of its new product, Raspberry Coke, it would be using which sales forecasting technique?
   a. Surveys
   b. Executive judgment
   c. Time series analysis
   d. Market tests
   e. Correlation method

MINICASE: CRIBS AND DRESSERS FOR LEISURE ENJOYMENT

Cribs and Dressers for Leisure Enjoyment (Cradle) was established thirty years ago. It is the largest supplier of specialty baby furniture in the United States. Each year the firm's marketing department prepares both long-range and short-range forecasts of demand for its products. Currently, a short-range forecast is being developed to cover all twenty-five products the firm manufactures and distributes.

Duane Norton has been given the responsibility of forecasting next year's sales for the specialty baby cribs Cradle produces. He has been with the company for only eighteen months but is considered capable of performing the assigned task because he graduated from a well-known state university with a major in marketing.

Norton has decided to use a variety of forecasting methods rather than rely on one technique. Before determining the sales forecast for the specialty cribs, he wants to project an industry sales forecast for cribs of this type. From this estimate he will predict Cradle's expected share of the market. He has decided to use an executive jury, sales-force estimates, trend analysis, and correlation analysis.

The jury consists of five executives from various functional areas of the firm. All have received company awards for outstanding work. This fact, along with the executives' tremendous enthusiasm, have convinced Norton that they are the obvious choices for the executive jury. He also has requested a forecast from a sample of the sales force that sells the cribs to retail stores. Eight salespersons have been selected.

Norton has analyzed industry sales over the last ten years from information provided by the industry trade association. The sales figures are shown below. From these data, he projected a trend and then used it to estimate sales for the industry.

Industry Sales over the Last Ten Years

Year	Sales (thousands)
1983	560
1984	480
1985	600
1986	680
1987	720
1988	600
1989	550
1990	560
1991	620
1992	710

A summary of the sales forecasts for the four approaches used is shown below. Norton must now evaluate the predictions and decide on a single estimate that represents the final projection.

Industry Sales Forecast by Technique Used

Techniques	Forecasts (units)
Executive jury	800,000
Trend analysis	750,000
Sales-force estimate	850,000
Correlation method	700,000

Questions

_____ 1. Once Norton settles on a final projection for industrywide sales, his next step will be to
   a. develop a general economic forecast.
   b. assign sales quotas to company sales representatives.
   c. multiply that amount by the total number of potential buyers in the area.
   d. determine what proportion of the total market potential the company can obtain at specific levels of marketing activity.
   e. adjust the company's marketing mix.

_____ 2. Norton's approach to measuring company sales potential is a(n)
   a. buildup approach.
   b. segmentation approach.
   c. arbitrary approach.
   d. total market approach.
   e. breakdown approach.

_____ 3. A sales forecast is the amount of a product that
   a. specific customer groups would purchase within a specified period at a specific level of industrywide marketing activity.
   b. the company actually expects to sell during a specified period at a specific level of marketing activity.
   c. an organization could sell during a specified period.
   d. an industry can sell in a specified time period.
   e. a potential buyer in a specific sales territory will purchase in a given period.

_____ 4. The advantage of Norton's use of executive judgment to forecast sales is that
   a. this method reflects actual purchases.
   b. this method is scientific.
   c. this method is inexpensive.
   d. executives are close to customers.
   e. executives are highly motivated.

_____ 5. Norton has decided against test-marketing the company's cribs because market tests
   a. are useful only for new products.
   b. would be too expensive and time-consuming for the preparation of a short-range forecast.
   c. are useful only in new geographic areas.
   d. require extensive historical sales data.
   e. measure consumers' intentions, not their actual purchases.

PROGRAMMED COMPLETION EXERCISES

ability, willingness, authority to buy

1. For an aggregate of people to be a market, the people must have a need for a product, as well as the _____, _____, and _____ _____ _____ it.

consumer, organizational, industrial

2. The two major types of markets are _____ and _____ or _____ markets.

Consumer, organizational

3. _____ markets are those in which the purchaser intends to reap the utility of the product; _____ markets are those in which the product can be used to create another product.

total market, market segmentation

4. The two approaches to finding target markets are the _____ _____ approach and the _____ _____ approach.

total market

5. A _____ _____ approach is effective if many individuals have similar product needs that can be satisfied by a single marketing mix.

segmentation variable

6. A _____ _____ is a basis on which a marketer divides a total market into segments.

concentration

7. A disadvantage of the _____ strategy is that by developing strong brand recognition in one market segment, a firm may be prevented from successfully entering another segment.

multisegment strategy

8. A _____ _____ is employed when a firm directs its marketing efforts at two or more segments by developing a market mix for each segment.

heterogeneous

9. Market segmentation is used when consumers' needs are _____.

family life cycle

10. Characteristics such as marital status and the presence and age of children are combined into the single dimension of the _____ _____ _____.

climate

11. Producers of air conditioners often use _____ as a segmentation variable.

market density

12. The number of potential customers per unit of land is referred to as _____ _____.

personality dimensions

13. Competitiveness, ambitiousness, and aggressiveness are _____ _____.

Single-variable segmentation

14. _____ _____ is the simplest form of segmentation and the easiest to perform.

Market potential, Sales potential

15. _____ _____ is the total amount of a product that customers will purchase within a specified period of time at a specific intensity of industrywide marketing activity. _____ _____ is the maximum percentage of market potential that an individual firm within an industry can expect to obtain for a specific product.

breakdown, buildup

16. The _____ approach and the _____ approach are used to measure company sales potential.

executive judgment, time series analysis, correlation, market tests

17. The most commonly used forecasting techniques are (a) surveys, (b) _____ _____, (c) _____ _____ _____, (d) _____, and (e) _____ _____.

expedient,
inexpensive,
stable, experience

18. The advantages of the sales forecast method based on executive judgment are that it is _____ and _____. This method works reasonably well when product demand is _____ and when the forecaster has extensive _____.

relatively small

19. The customer survey can be useful to a firm that has a _____ _____ number of customers.

actual, intended

20. Through a market test, a forecaster gains information regarding consumers' _____ purchases rather than their _____ purchases.

promotion, price,
distribution

21. A market test can be used to measure consumers' responses to _____, _____, and _____ efforts.

ANSWERS TO OBJECTIVE QUESTIONS

Matching		*True or False*		*Multiple-Choice*		*Minicase*
1. f	16. t	1. F	10. F	1. b	21. e	1. d
2. o	17. j	2. T	11. F	2. e	22. c	2. e
3. h	18. bb	3. T	12. T	3. c	23. e	3. b
4. jj	19. kk	4. F	13. F	4. d	24. c	4. c
5. aa	20. z	5. T	14. T	5. e	25. a	5. b
6. x	21. d	6. T	15. F	6. c	26. e	
7. c	22. dd	7. F	16. T	7. b	27. b	
8. q	23. mm	8. T	17. T	8. c	28. a	
9. r	24. m	9. T	18. F	9. b	29. b	
10. ee	25. cc			10. a	30. c	
11. s	26. i			11. c	31. e	
12. ii	27. u			12. c	32. d	
13. n	28. ll			13. a	33. d	
14. a	29. g			14. d	34. b	
15. e	30. v			15. b	35. b	
				16. c	36. b	
				17. d	37. c	
				18. e	38. a	
				19. c	39. d	
				20. c		

5 CONSUMER BUYING BEHAVIOR

CHAPTER OUTLINE

Types of consumer buying behavior
The consumer buying decision process
  Problem recognition
  Information search
  Evaluation of alternatives
  Purchase
  Postpurchase evaluation
Personal factors influencing the buying decision process
  Demographic factors
  Situational factors
  Level of involvement
Psychological factors influencing the buying decision process
  Perception
  Motives
  Ability and knowledge
  Attitudes
  Personality
Social factors influencing the buying decision process
  Roles and family influences
  Reference groups
  Social classes
  Culture and subculture
Understanding consumer buying behavior

CHAPTER SUMMARY

Marketers must understand consumer buying behavior for several reasons. First, buyers' reactions to a firm's marketing strategy have great impact on the firm's success. Second, to implement the marketing concept, a firm must understand how consumers make purchasing decisions so that it can create a marketing mix to satisfy its customers. Third, by understanding the factors that influence consumers, marketers are in a better position to predict how consumers will respond to marketing strategies.

Consumers make purchasing decisions to create and maintain assortments of products that provide current and future satisfaction. A buyer's decision behavior can be classified

76

into one of three broad categories: routine response behavior (involved in the purchase of low-priced, frequently used products); limited decision making (used in the occasional purchase of particular products and to acquire information about unfamiliar brands in a familiar product category); and extensive decision making (used to purchase a product for the first time or to purchase an expensive, infrequently bought item). Impulse buying involves no conscious planning but rather a powerful, persistent urge to buy something immediately.

The decision process consumers use to make purchases is a major part of buying behavior. A simplified model of the consumer buying decision process consists of five stages: (1) problem recognition, (2) information search, (3) evaluation of alternatives, (4) purchase, and (5) postpurchase evaluation.

Problem recognition occurs when a buyer becomes aware that there is a difference between a desired state and an actual condition. Sometimes a problem or a need exists, but the person is not aware of it. Marketers can use sales promotion, advertising, or packaging to help trigger an awareness of the need or problem.

After becoming aware of a problem or need, the consumer searches for information, using an internal search and/or an external search. The duration and intensity of information search efforts depend on the consumer's experience in purchasing the product and how important the product is to the consumer. There are several major sources of information: direct experience, personal contacts, marketer-dominated sources, and public sources. The end product of the information search is an evoked set, or group, of products.

Next, the consumer establishes a set of criteria against which to compare product characteristics and evaluate the products in the evoked set. The buyer rates and eventually ranks the brands in the evoked set.

After evaluating the alternatives, the consumer selects the product or brand he or she will buy. Product availability, the choice of a particular seller, or the terms of sale can influence the final selection and purchase.

After the purchase, the buyer begins to evaluate the product. As the product is used, the consumer evaluates it to determine if its actual performance meets expected performance labels. The satisfaction or dissatisfaction that results influences the buyer's future purchases. Cognitive dissonance is dissatisfaction that may occur when the buyer questions whether the purchase should have been made or whether another brand should have been purchased.

To understand the consumer buying decision process, marketers must analyze the three major categories of factors that influence that decision process: personal, psychological, and social.

A personal factor is one that is unique to a particular individual. There are two categories of personal influences: demographic factors, which are individual characteristics (age, sex, race), and situational factors, which are external circumstances or conditions that exist when a consumer is making a purchase decision. Level of involvement is the importance and intensity of interest in a particular product in a particular situation.

Psychological factors operating within individuals partially determine their general behavior and thus influence their behavior as consumers. The primary psychological influences on consumer behavior are perception, motives, ability, knowledge, attitudes, and personality. Perception is the process of selecting, organizing, and interpreting information inputs to produce meaning. A motive is an internal energizing force that orients a person's activities toward a goal. Ability refers to an individual's competency and efficiency in performing tasks. Knowledge is familiarity with a product and an individual's ability to apply the product. An attitude refers to knowledge and positive or negative feelings about an object or activity. Personality is all the traits and behaviors that make a person unique.

The forces that other people exert on buying behavior are called social factors. The four major groups of social factors are roles and family influences, reference groups, social classes, and culture and subcultures. A role is a set of actions and activities that a person in a particular position is supposed to perform, based on the expectations of both the individual and the persons around the individual. A reference group is a group with which an individual identifies so much that she or he takes on the values, attitudes, or behaviors of group members. A social class is an open grouping of individuals who have similar social ranking. Culture is everything in our surroundings made by human beings. A culture can be divided into subcultures on the basis of geographic differences or human characteristics. Both cultural and subcultural factors influence buying behavior.

MATCHING EXERCISES

Use the following set of terms to identify the sentences and phrases below. On the blank line next to each sentence or phrase, place the letter of the term that the sentence or phrase describes. Do not use a term more than once.

a. Internal search
b. Subculture
c. Buying behavior
d. Psychological factors
e. Knowledge
f. External search
g. Cognitive dissonance
h. Appropriation
i. Culture
j. Routine response behavior
k. Perception
l. Impulse buying
m. Gatekeepers
n. Evoked set
o. Limited decision making
p. Social class
q. Reference group
r. Advertising platform
s. Extensive decision making
t. Information inputs
u. Level of involvement
v. Demographic factors

w. Personal factors
x. Projective technique
y. Role
z. Selective exposure
aa. Consumer buying decision process
bb. Attitude
cc. Situational factors
dd. Consumer buying behavior
ee. Social factors
ff. Selective distortion
gg. Group interview
hh. Motive
ii. Personality
jj. Depth interview
kk. Segmentation
ll. Attitude scale
mm. Patronage motives
nn. Ability
oo. Straight-rebuy purchase
pp. Learning
qq. Selective retention
rr. Self-concept

_____ 1. Making purchase decisions quickly, with very little mental effort.

_____ 2. The sensations we receive through our sense organs.
Routine response behavior
Information Inputs

_____ 3. Motives that influence where a person purchases products on a regular basis. *Patronage Motives*

_____ 4. A division of a culture based on geographic region or human characteristics, such as age and ethnic background.
Subculture

_____ 5. A method to uncover people's motives relating to some issue, such as product usage, with an interviewer generating discussion on one or several topics among the six to twelve people in the group. *group interviews*

_____ 6. A powerful, persistent urge to buy something immediately.
Impulse buying

q 7. The dissatisfaction that occurs when the buyer questions whether the right decision was made in purchasing the product. *cognitive dissonance*

v 8. Individual characteristics such as age, sex, race, income, and occupation.
Demographic factors

cc 9. External circumstances or conditions that exist when a consumer is making a purchase decision. *Situational factors*

_____ 10. The changing or twisting of currently received information. *Selective Distortion*

X 11. A test in which subjects are asked to perform specific tasks for particular purposes while in fact they are being evaluated for other purposes; it assumes that subjects unconsciously "project" their motives as they perform the tasks. *Projective technique*

bb 12. Knowledge and positive or negative feelings about an object. *Attitude*

k 13. The process by which an individual selects, organizes, and interprets information to create a meaningful picture of the world. *Perception*

y 14. A set of actions and activities that a person in a particular position is supposed to perform, based on the expectations of both the individual and the persons around her or him. *Role*

ll 15. A measurement instrument that usually consists of a series of adjectives, phrases, or sentences about an object; subjects are asked to indicate the intensity of their feelings toward the object by reacting to the statements in a certain way. *Attitude Scale*

gg 16. When one remembers information inputs that support one's own feelings but forgets inputs that do not. *Selective Retention*

ee 17. The forces that other people exert on one's buying behavior.

c 18. The decision processes and acts of people involved in buying and using products. *Social factor*

jj 19. A meeting of up to several hours in which the researcher tries to create an open, informal atmosphere; used to study motives. *Depth interview*

n 20. A group of brands that a buyer views as possible purchase alternatives.
Evoked Set

_hh_   21. An internal energizing force that directs a person's behavior toward his or her goals. _Motive_

_i_   22. Everything in our surroundings made by human beings, consisting of tangible items as well as intangible concepts and values. _Culture_

_s_   23. Considerable time and effort spent by a buyer in seeking out alternative products, searching for information about them, and then evaluating them to determine which one will be most satisfying. _Extensive decision making_

_d_   24. Factors that operate within individuals to determine in part their general behavior and thus influence their behavior as consumers. _Psychological factors_

_rr_   25. The buyer's self-perception. _Self-concept_

_ii_   26. All the traits and behaviors that make a person unique. _Personality_

_p_   27. An open group of people with similar social ranking. _Social Class_

_z_   28. The selection of some inputs to reach awareness while ignoring many others because of the inability to be conscious of all inputs at one time. _Selective Exposure_

_q_   29. A group with which an individual identifies so much that he or she takes on many of the values, attitudes, and/or behaviors of group members. _Reference group_

_pp_   30. A change in an individual's behavior that is caused by information and experience. _Learning_

_w_   31. Characteristics unique to a particular individual. _Personal Factors_

_dd_   32. The decision processes and acts of people buying products for personal or household use, not for business purposes. _Consumer Buying Behavior_

TRUE OR FALSE STATEMENTS

T ~~F~~   1. Consumer behavior is highly predictable.

T **F**   2. By studying the laws and principles of human behavior, marketers have learned to control the consumer buying decision process.

T ~~F~~   3. Consumer buying behavior refers to the buying behavior of persons who purchase products for business purposes.

T F   4. When buying a frequently purchased, low-cost item that requires little search and purchase effort, a consumer uses a routine response behavior.

T F   5. Limited decision making requires a moderate amount of time for information gathering and deliberation.

T ~~F~~   6. Extensive decision making is used when an individual purchases a familiar, inexpensive product.

T ~~F~~   7. The first stage in the consumer buying decision process is information search.

T ~~F~~ 8. An example of a marketer-dominated source of information is personal friends and relatives.

~~T~~ F 9. A group of brands that a buyer views as possible purchase alternatives is the buyer's evoked set.

T ~~F~~ 10. Cognitive dissonance is the satisfaction that occurs after a purchase because the buyer is confident of the purchase decision.

T ~~F~~ 11. A personal factor is one that is not unique to a particular individual.

T ~~F~~ 12. Psychological factors operate independently of external forces.

~~T~~ F 13. A person becomes aware of only a small number of the information inputs he or she receives.

~~T~~ F 14. If an event is anticipated, inputs regarding that event are more likely to reach one's awareness.

T ~~F~~ 15. If the intensity of an input changes significantly, it is not likely to reach awareness.

~~T~~ F 16. An individual is influenced by a set of motives rather than just one motive.

T ~~F~~ 17. Personality is the internal energizing force that directs a person toward goals.

T ~~F~~ 18. Motives that influence where a person purchases products on a regular basis are called purchase motives.

~~T~~ F 19. Consumers learn about products directly by experiencing them and indirectly through information from salespeople, advertisements, friends, and relatives.

T ~~F~~ 20. Direct questioning about their motives is an effective way for marketers to determine consumers' motives.

T ~~F~~ 21. Projective techniques are tests in which subjects are asked to project their motives through a depth interview.

T ~~F~~ 22. Learning refers to the effects of direct and indirect experiences, such as hunger and fatigue, on future behavior.

T ~~F~~ 23. Attitudes are hereditary and therefore cannot be changed.

~~T~~ F 24. Personality is an internal structure in which experience and behavior are related in an orderly way.

~~T~~ F 25. Researchers have not been able to prove conclusively that a person's personality strongly affects buying behavior.

~~T~~ F 26. A role is a set of actions and activities that a person in a particular position is supposed to perform.

~~T~~ F 27. The degree to which a reference group influences a purchase decision depends on an individual's susceptibility to reference-group influence and strength of involvement with the group.

T F 28. The decisions to buy cigarettes and which brand to buy are influenced by one's reference group.

T F 29. A social class is a closed aggregate of individuals with similar social ranking.

T F 30. One's social class influences the type, quality, and quantity of products one consumes.

T F 31. Culture consists only of tangible manmade items in our society, such as furniture, buildings, and clothes.

T F 32. Subcultures are divisions of a culture based on geographic region or human characteristics.

T F 33. Consumer dissatisfaction exists because all marketers have adopted the marketing concept.

MULTIPLE-CHOICE QUESTIONS

_____ 1. Marketers are concerned with consumer behavior because
   a. consumers are predictable.
   b. the way consumers behave toward an organization's marketing strategies has a great impact on the firm's success.
   c. consumer behavior is influenced by many factors.
   d. marketers are able to control consumer behavior.
   e. a consumer must make purchasing decisions.

_____ 2. Which of the following statements concerning purchasing decisions is *most* correct?
   a. Brand loyalty would be expected to play a much greater role in the selection of expensive items because the cost of making a wrong decision is greater.
   b. As the price of an item increases, the amount of time spent making a purchasing decision increases proportionally.
   c. The amount of satisfaction a product gives a consumer when it is purchased determines whether the selection process will be routine or extensive.
   d. A homemaker would be expected to make more routine purchases than a wife who works outside the home.
   e. A consumer may use extensive decision making when a product that was purchased routinely in the past no longer satisfies the consumer's needs.

_____ 3. A product that is purchased quickly with little mental effort is thought to reflect
   a. impulse buying.
   b. limited decision making.
   c. routine response behavior.

    d. intensive decision making.

    e. extensive decision making.

_____ 4. Which of the following products would probably require extensive decision making before they are bought?

    a. Products purchased frequently

    b. Products to be purchased in the future

    c. Products that are purchased routinely

    d. Expensive products

    e. Products purchased as a result of social influences

_____ 5. Marsha went to the store to buy toothpaste. She will most likely use a(n) _____ decision-making process in making her purchase.

    a. extensive

    b. routine

    c. intensive

    d. comparative

    e. comprehensive

_____ 6. In switching to a new brand after routinely purchasing a brand that once was but no longer is satisfying, the consumer probably will use

    a. limited decision making.

    b. selective decision making.

    c. routine response behavior.

    d. intensive decision making.

    e. extensive decision making.

_____ 7. The first stage in the consumer buying decision process is

    a. evaluation of alternatives.

    b. problem recognition.

    c. purchase.

    d. information search.

    e. postpurchase evaluation.

_____ 8. Before hosting a dinner party, Jan notices that she does not have enough dishes and decides to look for another set. Jan has gone through which stage of the consumer decision-making process?

    a. Problem recognition

    b. Information search

    c. Evaluation of alternatives

    d. Purchase

    e. Cognitive dissonance

_____ 9. Marriott Hotels places an advertisement with a coupon in the travel section of the Sunday newspaper. This ad is primarily intended to help consumers in which phase of the decision-making process?

    a. Internal search

    b. Cognitive dissonance

    c. Purchase

    d. External search

    e. Framing

_____ 10. The source of information in a consumer's information search that stems from friends and relatives is
a. individual sources.
b. personal sources.
c. marketer-dominated sources.
d. direct sources.
e. organizational sources.

_____ 11. Tom Ingram is trying to close a major sale with a customer who is a trout fishing enthusiast. Tom starts reading fishing catalogs and going to sporting goods stores to learn as much as he can about fly rods, waders, and other related products. His interest in such products would be best classified as _____ involvement.
a. low
b. enduring
c. high
d. perceived
e. situational

_____ 12. All the following are marketer-dominated sources of information *except*
a. salespersons.
b. advertising.
c. packaging.
d. associates.
e. displays.

_____ 13. Which of the following statements about perception is *least* correct?
a. All the inputs of information to which an individual is exposed are used in forming a perception of the world.
b. Perception is a process by which an individual selects, organizes, and interprets information into a meaningful picture of the world.
c. A person selects only a small number of inputs to reach awareness.
d. A person is likely to allow an input to reach consciousness if the information helps satisfy current needs.
e. If the intensity of an input changes significantly, the input is more likely to reach awareness.

_____ 14. Perception is
a. the major factor within the individual that influences both general behavior and consumer behavior.
b. the selection of a small number of inputs and the disregard of many other inputs.
c. the organization of inputs that a person receives.
d. the interpretation of inputs that allows an individual to avoid mental confusion.
e. a process through which an individual selects, organizes, and interprets inputs to create a meaningful picture of the world.

_____ 15. Which of the following statements about the organization of inputs that reach awareness is *most* correct?
   a. Generally, inputs are organized by individuals to produce meaning, and this organizational process is usually a slow one.
   b. The organization of information inputs is not always needed to produce meaning.
   c. Inputs that reach awareness are organized and interpreted in pretty much the same way by all consumers.
   d. Because a person interprets information in terms of what is familiar, only one interpretation of organized inputs usually is possible.
   e. Inputs that reach awareness are organized to produce meaning, and this meaning is interpreted in light of what is familiar to the individual.

_____ 16. As Randy drives his car through town, he is bombarded by hundreds of signs, billboards, and other forms of outdoor advertising. It is impossible for Randy to be conscious of all of these inputs at one time. Randy is thus experiencing a phenomenon known as selective
   a. exposure.
   b. distortion.
   c. retention.
   d. information.
   e. organization.

_____ 17. As Michaela watches commercials on television, she is more likely to perceive the information contained in the ads when it is
   a. familiar and consistent with current beliefs.
   b. unfamiliar and inconsistent with current beliefs.
   c. familiar and inconsistent with current beliefs.
   d. unfamiliar and consistent with current beliefs.
   e. new information.

_____ 18. The best definition of a motive is
   a. behavior that reduces tension.
   b. an internal behavioral factor that operates within people and determines their behavior as consumers.
   c. a determinant of consumer behavior.
   d. an internal force that directs one's behavior toward goals.
   e. an internal structure in which experience and behavior are related.

_____ 19. Studies dealing with internal forces that direct one's behavior toward goals are called
   a. motivation research.
   b. attitude research.
   c. personality research.
   d. internal search.
   e. reflective introspection.

_____ 20. The interview technique that tries to generate discussion among people regarding one or more topics is known as the
   a. projective interview.
   b. group interview.
   c. depth interview.
   d. conversation technique.
   e. sentence-completion test.

_____ 21. Word-association tests and sentence-completion tests are research methods used by some firms. Such firms attempt to understand more fully the major motives that influence whether or not customers buy their products. What type of motivational research method is this?
   a. Motivational specification techniques.
   b. Projective techniques
   c. Group interviews
   d. Depth interviews
   e. Patronage clarification techniques

_____ 22. Learning
   a. refers to the effects of direct and indirect experience on future behavior.
   b. is a change in an individual's behavior that arises from physiological conditions, such as hunger, fatigue, and growth.
   c. is knowledge and positive or negative feelings about an object.
   d. is seldom influenced by attitudes and motives.
   e. has no bearing on consumers' behavior.

_____ 23. Which of the following is an example of a consumer's direct experience of a product?
   a. A consumer receives a letter that explains the features of the product.
   b. A salesperson gives a consumer a sales pitch about a particular product.
   c. A consumer test-drives an automobile.
   d. A consumer hears a friend tell about using a product and how he or she was satisfied with the product.
   e. A consumer reads an advertisement for a particular product.

_____ 24. Attitudes
   a. are learned and therefore cannot be changed.
   b. possessed by a person at a particular time are all of equal strength.
   c. of consumers toward a particular firm have no influence on the firm's marketing strategy.
   d. are acquired through experience and interaction with other people.
   e. have little influence on consumer behavior.

_____ 25. Which of the following statements regarding personality is true?
   a. Only outgoing people have personalities.
   b. Personality is all the traits and behaviors that make a person unique.

c. Studies have shown that buying behavior reliably reflects personality characteristics.

d. All types of personalities are represented, when possible, in advertising campaigns.

e. Personality is a structure in each individual that operates independently of other people.

26. Social influences can be grouped into four major areas:
    a. roles and family influences, psychographics, reference groups, and social class.
    b. roles and family influences, reference groups, social class, and culture and subcultures.
    c. roles and family influences, psychographics, social class, and personality structures.
    d. roles and family influences, reference groups, social class, and personality structures.
    e. roles and family influences, reference groups, social class, and dissonant groups.

27. If an individual purchases a certain product, she or he may be fulfilling another person's expectations for her or his behavior. This best illustrates the influence of
    a. roles.
    b. product attractiveness.
    c. motives.
    d. personality influence.
    e. personal autonomy.

28. Roles
    a. are associated with positions that only leaders occupy.
    b. are unchanging.
    c. influence only general behavior, not consumer behavior.
    d. are numerous, but each individual has only one role.
    e. consist of a set of actions and activities that are supposed to be performed by a person in a particular position.

29. Which of the following would *not* be considered a reference group?
    a. A consumer's family
    b. The American Medical Association
    c. A group from which a consumer derives information
    d. An organization that has little influence on the individual
    e. A church group

30. A marketer uses reference-group influence in advertisements
    a. to promote the message that people in a specific group buy the product and are highly satisfied with it.
    b. to show general satisfaction with the product regardless of reference-group size or the number of people who identify with it.
    c. because reference-group influence is more effective than all other influences in advertisements.

    d. because most people have only one reference group that influences them significantly.

    e. to determine which product satisfies a particular reference group.

_____ 31. Such factors as income level, occupation, religion, and education are used to
   a. influence consumer behavior.
   b. measure personality traits.
   c. group people into various social classes.
   d. group people into various reference groups.
   e. determine an individual's personality characteristics.

_____ 32. Culture is defined as
   a. the characteristics of various social classes.
   b. everything in our surroundings that is manmade.
   c. a set of actions and activities that an individual is expected to perform.
   d. an open aggregate of people with similar social ranking.
   e. a group with which an individual identifies.

_____ 33. Consumer dissatisfaction still exists for several reasons: (1) marketers cannot accurately determine what is highly satisfying to consumers, (2) marketers may not be capable of providing what satisfies consumers, and (3)
   a. consumers' actions strongly influence the success or failure of a marketing program.
   b. the consumer movement is becoming widespread.
   c. some marketers have not adopted the marketing concept.
   d. consumer behavior is unimportant to marketers.
   e. consumers are not viewed as decision makers.

MINICASE: THE "NOISELESS" BLENDER

Each month the department heads of Easy-Cook Company meet with the firm's New-Product Committee to evaluate and either accept or reject the committee's new product ideas. The committee was activated five years ago to give a preliminary screening to all new product ideas. It has been very successful, as indicated by the company's present line of home appliances. About 65 percent of the products in that line have resulted from the committee's recommendations.

This month the committee has six product ideas to recommend. Among them is a unique kitchen blender that has been engineered to operate without any noise. It accomplishes this feat with no increase in size or weight over blenders currently on the market. The committee believes this blender will be an excellent item to complement the other products in the company's line of small kitchen appliances.

The committee has suggested a retail price of $89.95 and has recommended that the new blender be targeted at consumers who are furnishing newly built homes. The department heads are pleased with this recommendation and vote to initiate an all-out effort to begin production as soon as possible.

Questions

_____ 1. Knowledge and positive or negative feelings make up one's _____ and could influence the purchase of a blender.
   a. motives
   b. attitudes
   c. culture
   d. drives
   e. personality

_____ 2. One problem in marketing the noiseless blender could arise because consumers, through the process of interpretation, might consider a noiseless blender less effective than other types of blenders. This situation would relate most directly to
   a. information inventory.
   b. learning.
   c. personality.
   d. perception.
   e. behavior.

_____ 3. When a consumer buys a noiseless blender because of the values, behaviors, or attitudes of group members, the purchasing decision may be a result of
   a. socialization forces.
   b. cultural influences.
   c. reference groups.
   d. perception.
   e. family roles.

_____ 4. Before production of the noiseless blender begins, Easy-Cook must
   a. conduct consumer research.
   b. check out production lines.
   c. redefine the target market.
   d. develop additional products.
   e. increase the size of the blender.

_____ 5. Purchase of a noiseless blender would most likely involve _____ decision making.
   a. routine
   b. extensive
   c. learning
   d. limited
   e. fast

PROGRAMMED COMPLETION EXERCISES

marketing mix

1. A major component of the marketing concept is the belief that a firm should create a _____ _____ that satisfies consumers.

behavioral sciences

2. Even though some social critics give marketers credit for being able to manipulate consumers, marketers depend on information from the _____ _____ to understand consumer behavior.

routine, frequently, limited, occasional, unfamiliar brands, extensive, expensive, infrequently

3. In making decisions, a buyer generally uses one of three decision-making processes: _____ decision making for low-priced, _____ bought items; _____ decision making for _____ purchases and purchases of _____ _____; and _____ decision making for _____, _____ bought items.

difference, desired, actual

4. Problem recognition occurs when a buyer becomes aware that there is a _____ between a _____ state and an _____ condition.

searches for information

5. After becoming aware of a problem or need, the consumer _____ _____ _____.

direct experience, personal sources, marketer-dominated sources, public sources

6. The four major categories of information are _____ _____, _____ _____, _____ _____, and _____ _____.

personal, psychological, social

7. Three major categories of factors that influence the consumer buying decision process are _____, _____, and _____.

demographic, situational

8. Two classes of personal factors are _____ and

_____.

perception, motives, ability and knowledge, attitudes, personality

9. The primary psychological influences on consumer behavior

are _____, _____, _____

_____ _____, _____, and

_____.

Perception

10. _____ is the process by which an individual selects, organizes, and interprets information.

aware, inputs

11. A person becomes _____ of only a small portion of the information _____ that are received at any given time.

anticipated event, satisfying, current, intensity

12. An input is more likely to reach awareness if it is related to an _____ _____, if the information is useful in _____ one's _____ needs, and if the input changes significantly in _____.

motives, motive

13. A buyer's actions at any given time are affected by a set of _____, not just one _____.

interviews, projective techniques

14. Motivation research is performed through either _____ or _____ _____.

Learning, Free samples, directly, indirectly

15. _____ refers to the effects of direct and indirect experiences on future behavior. _____ _____ are used by a marketer to get potential consumers to experience a product _____. Consumers' learning also is affected _____ by experiencing products through information from salespeople, advertisements, friends, and relatives.

acquires attitudes

16. Through experience and interaction with other people, an individual _____ _____.

Consumers' attitudes, strongly influence

17. _____ _____ toward a firm and its products _____ _____ the success or failure of the organization's marketing program.

long, expensive, difficult

18. Changing people's attitudes is generally a _____, _____, and _____ task.

social factors, roles, family influences, reference groups, social class, culture, subcultures

19. Consumers' buying decisions are affected partially by the persons around them. These persons and the forces they exert on a buyer are called _____ _____ and can be grouped into four major areas: _____ and _____ _____, _____ _____, _____ _____, and _____ and _____.

general behavior, consumers

20. Numerous expectations are placed on people's behavior by both themselves and the people around them. People's roles influence not only their _____ _____ but to some extent their behavior as _____.

role

21. Each person occupies positions within groups, organizations, and institutions. The set of actions that a person is expected to perform within a position is called a _____.

roles

22. Because a person occupies numerous positions, she or he has many _____.

buying behavior, who,
buying, purchasing
decision

23. Marketers need to be aware of how roles affect
_____ _____. They need to know not only
_____ does the _____ but also who,
because of his or her roles, influences the _____
_____.

buy, brand

24. Reference-group influence can affect the decision to
_____ and the choice of a _____,
depending on the type of product being purchased.

involvement

25. The degree to which a reference group influences a purchasing decision depends on the strength of the individual's
_____ with the group.

reference group,
reference-group,
advertisements

26. A group is a _____ _____ when an
individual identifies with the group so much that she or he
takes on many of the values, attitudes, or behaviors of group
members. A marketer sometimes uses _____
influence in _____ to promote the message that
people in a specific group buy the product and are highly
satisfied with it.

information,
comparison

27. A reference group is a source of _____ and a point
of _____ for the individual.

Culture, Cultural,
buying behavior,
subcultural differences

28. _____ is everything in our surroundings that is
manmade. _____ influences have broad effects on
_____ _____ because they touch so many
aspects of our daily lives. When trying to create a satisfying
marketing mix, marketers must recognize that even though
their operations may be confined to the United States, to one
state, or to one city, _____ _____ can result
in considerable variations in what, how, and when people buy.

social class

29. A _____ _____ is an open aggregate of people with similar social ranking.

susceptibility

30. When a marketer uses reference-group influence in advertising, the success of the advertising depends on how effective the advertisement is, the type of product, and an individual's _____ to reference-group influence.

common patterns of behavior

31. Individuals within social classes to some degree develop _____ _____ _____ _____.

criteria

32. The _____ used to group people into classes vary from one society to another.

determines

33. Marketers need to be aware of the impact of social class on a person's behavior as a consumer. An individual's social class to some extent _____ the type, quality, and quantity of products consumed.

purchased, used

34. Because culture to some degree determines the ways products are _____ and _____, it in turn affects the development, distribution, pricing, and promotion of products.

marketing mixes

35. International marketers find that people in other cultures have different attitudes, values, and needs, which in turn call for different methods of doing business as well as different types of _____ _____.

subcultures

36. On the basis of geographic differences or human characteristics, such as age and ethnic background, a culture can be divided into _____.

ANSWERS TO OBJECTIVE QUESTIONS

Matching			
1. j	17. ee		
2. t	18. c		
3. mm	19. jj		
4. b	20. n		
5. gg	21. hh		
6. l	22. i		
7. g	23. s		
8. v	24. d		
9. cc	25. rr		
10. ff	26. ii		
11. x	27. p		
12. bb	28. z		
13. k	29. q		
14. y	30. pp		
15. ll	31. w		
16. qq	32. dd		

True or False	
1. F	18. F
2. F	19. T
3. F	20. F
4. T	21. F
5. T	22. F
6. F	23. F
7. F	24. T
8. F	25. T
9. T	26. T
10. F	27. T
11. F	28. T
12. F	29. F
13. T	30. T
14. T	31. F
15. F	32. T
16. T	33. F
17. F	

Multiple-Choice	
1. b	18. d
2. e	19. a
3. c	20. b
4. d	21. b
5. b	22. a
6. e	23. c
7. b	24. d
8. a	25. b
9. d	26. b
10. b	27. a
11. e	28. e
12. d	29. d
13. a	30. a
14. e	31. c
15. e	32. b
16. a	33. c
17. a	

Minicase
1. b
2. d
3. c
4. a
5. b

6 ORGANIZATIONAL MARKETS AND BUYING BEHAVIOR

CHAPTER OUTLINE

Types of organizational markets
Producer markets
Reseller markets
Government markets
Institutional markets

Dimensions of organizational buying
Characteristics of organizational transactions
Attributes of organizational buyers
Primary concerns of organizational buyers
Methods of organizational buying
Types of organizational purchases
Demand for industrial products

Organizational buying decisions
The buying center
Stages of the organizational buying decision process
Influences on organizational buying

CHAPTER SUMMARY

An organizational market consists of individuals or groups that purchase a product for resale, for use in producing other products, or for use in day-to-day operations. The four major organizational markets are (1) producers, who purchase products for the purpose of making a profit by using them to produce other products or by using them in their operations; (2) resellers, who are intermediaries—such as wholesalers and retailers—who buy finished goods and resell them for profit; (3) government units; and (4) institutions, which are organizations whose goals are not the normal business goals.

Organizational transactions differ from consumer sales in several ways. They tend to be much larger than consumer sales, they are negotiated less frequently, and they usually involve several individuals or departments in the transaction, which lengthens the negotiating period. Reciprocity, an arrangement whereby two organizations agree to buy from each other, is another factor in a limited number of cases. Organizational buyers also tend to be better informed than their consumer counterparts.

Several factors are of primary importance to organizational buyers. First, buyers try to achieve and maintain a specific level of quality in the products they buy and then offer their target markets. Services such as market information, inventory maintenance, on-time delivery, repair services and replacement parts, and credit are also important to buyers. Price affects operating costs and costs of goods sold, and thus selling price and profit margin. Although organizational buyers are likely to compare the price of equipment with the value of benefits, they do not buy strictly according to price; quality and services are also important elements in the purchase decision.

Four common methods of organizational buying are description, inspection, sampling, and negotiation. Description is used when the products being purchased are standardized on the basis of size, shape, weight, color, or other characteristics. Inspection is relied on when the products are unique or of uncertain condition. Sampling is used to test large, homogeneous products, such as grain, on the basis of a representative sample. Negotiation involves the submission of bids by sellers. Most organizational purchases are one of three types: new-task purchases, modified-rebuy purchases, and straight-rebuy purchases.

Organizational demand differs from consumer demand in that it is (1) derived, (2) inelastic, (3) joint, and (4) more fluctuating. Derived demand means that demand for industrial products ultimately depends on the demand for consumer products. Inelasticity of demand means that a price increase or decrease does not significantly affect demand for that item. This applies to overall industry demand for a product, however, not to demand for an item produced by an individual supplier. Joint demand occurs when two or more items are used in combination to produce a product. A shortage of one item thus jeopardizes sales of all the jointly demanded products. Demand fluctuations are caused by changes in the demand for consumer products, changes in customers' inventory policies, or price changes.

Organizational purchases are seldom made by a single person; they are made through a buying center, which involves users, influencers, buyers, deciders, and gatekeepers in the buying process. Users are those who actually use the product being acquired. Influencers affect the purchase decision process by developing product specifications and evaluating alternative products for possible use. Buyers select the supplies and negotiate the terms of the purchase, but deciders actually choose the products and vendors. Gatekeepers control the flow of information to and among participants in the buying center.

The stages in the organizational buying decision process are similar to those in the consumer buying decision process. In the first stage, one or more individuals in the organization recognize that a problem or need exists. In the next stage—the development of product specifications—organizational participants must assess the problem or need and determine what can satisfy it. Searching for possible products to solve the problem and locating suppliers of those products is the third stage in the decision process. The fourth stage is evaluating the products on the list generated in the search stage to determine which ones meet the product specifications developed in the second stage. In the fifth stage, the product is actually ordered. During the sixth stage, the product's performance is evaluated.

Four major factors appear to influence the organizational buying decision: environmental, organizational, interpersonal, and individual dimensions. Environmental factors are uncontrollable forces such as laws and regulatory actions. Organizational factors include the buying organization's objectives and resources. Interpersonal factors refer to the relationships among people in the buying centers. Individual factors are the personal characteristics of individuals in the buying center.

MATCHING EXERCISES

Use the following set of terms to identify the sentences and phrases below. On the blank line next to each sentence or phrase, place the letter of the term that the sentence or phrase describes. Do not use a term more than once.

a. Elastic demand
b. Producer market
c. Reseller market
d. Institutional market
e. Influencers
f. Reciprocity
g. New-task purchase
h. Purchase decision
i. Users

j. Modified-rebuy purchase
k. Straight-rebuy purchase
l. Derived demand
m. Inelastic demand
n. Organizational market
o. Joint demand
p. Organizational buying behavior
q. Buying center
r. Environmental factors

_____   1. Consists of individuals or groups that purchase a specific type of product to resell it, to use it for producing other products, or to use it in day-to-day operations.

_____   2. Individuals or business organizations that purchase products for use in producing other products.

_____   3. Organizations whose goals are not the normal business goals of profit making, market share, return on investment, or the like.

_____   4. Intermediaries, such as wholesalers and retailers, who buy finished goods and resell them to make a profit.

_____   5. An arrangement whereby two organizations agree to buy from each other.

_____   6. A purchase in which an organization is buying an item for the first time.

_____   7. A purchase in which the requirements of a straight-rebuy purchase are modified.

_____   8. A purchase in which the same products are reordered routinely.

_____   9. A demand that is not affected by price fluctuations.

_____   10. A demand that is generated because of the production of goods and services to satisfy consumers' needs.

_____   11. Occurs when two or more items are used in combination to produce a product.

_____   12. Consists of individuals who participate in the purchase decision process.

_____   13. Organizational participants who actually utilize the product being acquired.

_____   14. Technical personnel who develop product specifications and evaluate alternative products for possible use.

TRUE OR FALSE STATEMENTS

T   F   1. The federal government spends more than three-fourths of the total amount spent by the government sector.

T   F   2. Organizational purchases tend to be larger than consumer purchases.

T   F   3. Institutional markets may require special types of marketing activities.

T   F   4. Inelastic demand means that a change in price results in a significant change in the demand for a product.

T   F   5. The fact that industrial demand is derived from consumer demand may contribute significantly to demand fluctuations.

T   F   6. Producer markets are groups that buy finished goods and resell them.

T   F   7. Resellers do not consider the level of demand in their decision making.

T   F   8. Organizational transactions differ only slightly from consumer sales.

T   F   9. Reciprocity is a safeguard against less than optimal transactions.

T   F   10. Organizational customers consider service an important decision variable.

T   F   11. New-task purchases involve a routine buying process.

T   F   12. Joint demand offers an aggressive marketer no opportunities.

T   F   13. A buying center consists of individuals who participate in the purchase decision process.

T   F   14. Some industrial purchases rely on negotiated contracts.

T   F   15. The three types of organizational purchases are new-task, straight rebuy, and modified rebuy.

T   F   16. Modified-rebuy purchases can be the result of a modified new-task purchase.

T   F   17. Organizational buyers sometimes get involved in developing specifications.

MULTIPLE-CHOICE QUESTIONS

_____   1. The stage in the organizational buying decision process that requires participants to assess a problem or need and determine what can satisfy that need is
  a. problem recognition.
  b. development of product specifications.
  c. search activities.
  d. product evaluation.
  e. product selection.

_____ 2. All the following are individual influences on the organizational buying process *except*
   a. age.
   b. educational level.
   c. power relationships.
   d. personality.
   e. job status.

_____ 3. Which of the following best explains the behavior of organizational buyers?
   a. They are careless about details in their jobs.
   b. They are characteristically cold, unfeeling people.
   c. They are highly ambitious and may be persuaded to sacrifice integrity for personal gain.
   d. They often seek to fulfill personal goals by helping their firms achieve organizational objectives.
   e. They have social and psychological difficulties adjusting to their roles as purchasers.

_____ 4. When a buyer purchases the same products routinely under approximately the same terms of sale, the purchase is a
   a. new-task purchase.
   b. negotiated purchase.
   c. continuing purchase.
   d. homogeneous purchase.
   e. straight-rebuy purchase.

_____ 5. Jean, a purchasing agent, visits a warehouse containing the inventory of a product her organization is considering buying. During her visit, Jean opens a carton and takes a representative product from the inventory and evaluates it. What method of organizational buying is Jean using?
   a. Homogeneous selection
   b. Description
   c. Trust
   d. Negotiated inspection
   e. Sampling

_____ 6. A grocery store wants to order several dozen large grade A eggs from its local supplier. The store's buyer will most likely use which method of organizational buying?
   a. Description
   b. Inspection
   c. Sampling
   d. Negotiation
   e. Blind

_____ 7. When a buyer purchases the same products routinely under approximately the same terms of sale, this is called a
   a. straight-rebuy purchase.
   b. reciprocal purchase.

    c. delayed purchase.

    d. new-task purchase.

    e. modified-rebuy purchase.

8. Reseller markets consist mainly of
    a. consumers.
    b. retailers.
    c. wholesalers and retailers.
    d. manufacturers.
    e. industrial users.

9. Reciprocity refers to
    a. two organizations that agree to buy from the same supplier.
    b. two suppliers who agree to sell to the same customers.
    c. two organizations that agree to buy from each other.
    d. two suppliers who provide products that are in joint demand.
    e. an organization that agrees to buy from its customers' other suppliers.

10. Which of the following statements relating to industrial demand is true?
    a. The demand for industrial products derives from the demand for raw materials.
    b. In the long run, industrial demand is independent of consumer demand.
    c. The derived nature of industrial demand is unilevel, in that it affects only industrial sellers who are closest to consumers in the marketing channel.
    d. Changes in derived demand can be traced to the types of channels used for distribution.
    e. Derived demand may change as the result of a chain reaction.

11. For an individual industrial supplier, demand is most likely to
    a. fluctuate.
    b. be inelastic.
    c. be elastic.
    d. be joint.
    e. increase steadily.

12. The use of two or more items in combination to produce a product creates
    a. joint demand.
    b. derived demand.
    c. fluctuating demand.
    d. inelastic demand.
    e. cooperative demand.

13. After automobile manufacturers' sales of new cars significantly increased, tire producers noticed an increase in sales. This example suggests that the demand for tires is
    a. derived.
    b. inelastic.
    c. unitary.

    d. fluctuating.

    e. elastic.

_____ ·14. South Side Industrial Supply calls its local Michelin representative to place an order for truck tires, because Arnold Distributors just bought fifteen sets of tires for its delivery trucks. This is an example of _____ demand for industrial products.

    a. derived

    b. inelastic

    c. joint

    d. fluctuating

    e. sporadic

_____ 15. Suppose marketers at Nucor Steel decided to raise the price of sheet metal sold to factories. However, they found that sales dropped significantly. This example suggests that the demand for the company's steel is

    a. derived.

    b. inelastic.

    c. joint.

    d. fluctuating.

    e. elastic.

_____ 16. Which of the following is *not* one of the four major kinds of organizational markets?

    a. Producer markets

    b. Consumer markets

    c. Reseller markets

    d. Government markets

    e. Institutional markets

_____ 17. Which of the following markets includes buyers of raw materials as well as purchasers of semifinished and finished items?

    a. Producer markets

    b. Reseller markets

    c. Government markets

    d. Institutional markets

    e. All of the above

_____ 18. Which of the following markets includes intermediaries who buy finished goods and resell them to make a profit?

    a. Institutional markets

    b. Government markets

    c. Producer markets

    d. Reseller markets

    e. All of the above

_____ 19. Which of the following factors do resellers *not* always consider when making a purchase decision?
    a. Level of demand for the product
    b. Amount of space required to handle the product
    c. The supplier's ability to provide adequate quantities
    d. Ease of placing orders
    e. The bidding process for government contracts

_____ 20. One characteristic of government markets is that
    a. they are not very lucrative.
    b. they work on a first come, first served basis.
    c. they are very vague in their requirements.
    d. their buying channels usually involve one person.
    e. they usually accept the lowest acceptable bid.

_____ 21. All the following are characteristics of organizational transactions *except*
    a. infrequent sales negotiations.
    b. long negotiation periods.
    c. expensive orders.
    d. large quantities.
    e. buyers usually are the sole purchase decision makers.

_____ 22. All of the following are examples of organizational buyers' concerns *except*
    a. a specific level of quality.
    b. consistent service.
    c. having a product meet specifications.
    d. competitors' inventory maintenance.
    e. on-time delivery.

_____ 23. Which of the following purchases is a type of organizational purchase?
    a. Modified sample purchase
    b. Associated-rebuy purchase
    c. Modified-rebuy purchase
    d. Straight channel purchase
    e. Buyer-modified purchase

_____ 24. The demand for industrial products is characterized *least* by which of the following?
    a. Derived demand
    b. Inverse demand
    c. Inelastic demand
    d. Joint demand
    e. Demand fluctuations

_____ 25. The typical buying center includes all the following individuals *except*
    a. users.
    b. gatekeepers.
    c. treasurers.
    d. influencers.
    e. deciders.

_____ 26. The receptionist at a doctor's office throws away certain product circulars mailed by pharmaceutical companies and keeps the ones on products that he believes are useful. The receptionist is performing which role in the buying center?
  a. User
  b. Influencer
  c. Buyer
  d. Decider
  e. Gatekeeper

_____ 27. Technical personnel who help develop the specifications and evaluate alternative products for possible use are called
  a. users.
  b. influencers.
  c. buyers.
  d. deciders.
  e. gatekeepers.

_____ 28. A production lineman at Gossner Cheese factory discovered that the slicing process could be speeded up if the machine had a certain type of arm attached. He consulted the supervisor about purchasing one. The lineman would be considered the _____ in the buying center.
  a. decider
  b. influencer
  c. buyer
  d. user
  e. gatekeeper

_____ 29. A vice-president for Ryder Truck Rental authorizes the purchase of a fleet of new trucks for the manager of the Denver center. The vice-president is performing which role in the buying center?
  a. User
  b. Influencer
  c. Buyer
  d. Decider
  e. Gatekeeper

_____ 30. In the typical buying center, gatekeepers usually
  a. develop specifications.
  b. negotiate price.
  c. decide the ultimate outcome.
  d. control the flow of information.
  e. select the suppliers.

_____ 31. All the following are major categories of factors that influence organizational buying decisions *except*
  a. environmental factors.
  b. organizational factors.
  c. atmospheric factors.
  d. interpersonal factors.
  e. individual factors.

MINICASE: BASIC FOODS INTERNATIONAL

Basic Foods International (BFI), a processor of a wide variety of corn and soybean products, is experiencing unparalleled sales growth. Due to the success of its dried soybean oil and the positive sales projections of its sales force, BFI is seriously considering expanding production facilities for this product.

Dried soy oil, which is used as a carrier and bulking agent in many packaged consumer foods, enhances mixing because of its capacity to carry sweeteners and other ingredients through a mixture evenly. Corn syrup is mixed with soy oil to help dry it. (Corn syrup also can add sweetness.) Additionally, soy oil is used in dry food mixes and nondairy whiteners because of its tendency to absorb moisture quickly.

BFI has been selling dried soy oil for many years. Recently, demand has increased so much that customers have been placed on an allocation program. BFI currently sells about 25 million pounds of soy oil annually and, with 11 percent of the market, is third among five competitors in market share. Note that most BFI soy oil customers are new users of the product and approximately 60 percent also purchase other BFI products.

Questions

_____   1. The textbook indicates that service factors often are a primary concern of organizational buyers. What service factor is likely to be the most important to BFI's customers?
   a. Market information
   b. Inventory maintenance
   c. On-time delivery
   d. Repair services
   e. Credit

_____   2. What method of buying would be most appropriate for BFI's products?
   a. Description
   b. Inspection
   c. Sampling
   d. Negotiation
   e. Reciprocity

_____   3. Given the profile of BFI's soy oil customers, what type of purchase decision would be most common?
   a. Infrequent
   b. New-task
   c. Rebuy
   d. Straight rebuy
   e. Modified rebuy

_____   4. Which of the following terms best characterizes the demand for BFI's dried soy oil?
   a. Derived
   b. Inelastic
   c. Joint
   d. Fluctuating
   e. Direct

PROGRAMMED COMPLETION EXERCISES

producer, reseller, government, institutional

1. The organizational category of markets includes

_____, _____, _____, and

_____ markets.

Reseller

2. _____ markets consist of intermediaries, such as wholesalers and retailers, who buy finished goods and resell them at a profit.

quality level, service, price

3. Many of the primary concerns of organizational buyers fall into three categories: _____ _____,

_____, and _____.

specifications

4. In an attempt to maintain a specific level of quality in their products, organizational buyers often buy products based on a set of characteristics called _____.

consistent

5. Organizational buyers look for industrial products whose level of quality is _____ in order after order.

larger

6. Organizational purchases are frequently much _____ than consumer purchases.

inelastic

7. When a price increase or decrease does not affect demand for an item significantly, demand is said to be _____.

Joint demand

8. _____ _____ occurs when two or more items are used in combination to produce a product.

description, inspection, sampling, negotiation

9. The four most common methods of organizational buying are

_____, _____, _____, and

_____.

bids

10. When buyers ask sellers to submit prices for industrial products, they are asking for _____.

new-task purchase, straight-rebuy purchase, modified-rebuy purchase

11. Most organizational purchases can be classified as one of three types: a _____ _____, a _____ _____, or a _____ _____.

users, influencers, buyers, deciders, gatekeepers

12. The five roles personnel in an organizational buying center assume are those of _____, _____, _____, _____, and _____.

environmental, organizational, interpersonal, individual

13. The four major influences that affect organizational buying decisions are _____, _____, _____, and _____ factors.

ANSWERS TO OBJECTIVE QUESTIONS

Matching		*True or False*		*Multiple-Choice*		*Minicase*
1. n	8. k	1. F	10. T	1. b	17. a	1. c
2. b	9. m	2. T	11. F	2. c	18. d	2. a
3. d	10. l	3. T	12. F	3. d	19. e	3. d
4. c	11. o	4. F	13. T	4. e	20. e	4. a
5. f	12. q	5. T	14. T	5. e	21. e	
6. g	13. i	6. F	15. T	6. a	22. d	
7. j	14. e	7. F	16. T	7. a	23. c	
		8. F	17. T	8. c	24. b	
		9. F		9. c	20. c	
				10. e	26. e	
				11. c	27. b	
				12. a	28. d	
				13. a	29. d	
				14. a	30. d	
				15. e	31. c	
				16. b		

7 MARKETING RESEARCH AND INFORMATION SYSTEMS

CHAPTER OUTLINE

Defining marketing research and marketing information systems
Information needs and decision making
The marketing research process
Defining and locating problems
Developing hypotheses
Collecting data
  Secondary data collection
  Primary data collection
Interpreting research findings
Reporting research findings
The importance of ethical marketing research

CHAPTER SUMMARY

Marketing research and systematic information gathering increase the probability of success in marketing activities, providing the insight for carrying out the marketing concept—the philosophy of customer orientation. Marketing research is the systematic design, collection, interpretation, and reporting of information to help marketers solve specific marketing problems or take advantage of marketing opportunities. Unlike marketing research, which is conducted on a special-project basis, a marketing information system (MIS) operates continually. It is the framework for the day-to-day managing and structuring of information gathered from sources both inside and outside the organization. The marketing databank is a file of the data collected through marketing research and the marketing information system.

The real value of marketing research and marketing information systems is measured by improvements in a marketer's ability to make decisions. Research and information systems provide critical customer feedback. Without that feedback, a marketer cannot understand the dynamics of the marketplace. And without that understanding, a marketer cannot develop objectives, assess opportunities, formulate strategies, or plan for implementation and control. Innovation is a key element of marketing research programs today, as buyers become more sophisticated.

Although uncertainty is inherent in the decision process, research can make the process more objective and systematic. The current increase in marketing research activities represents a transition from intuitive to scientific problem solving. Intuition involves personal knowledge and experience. Scientific decision making uses an orderly, logical approach to gathering information. Good decisions blend both intuition and research. Marketing research and information systems, then, are aids to sound management judgment, not substitutes for it. Global competition especially requires thorough marketing and information application. Although research provides an objective practical approach to making decisions, judgment and intuition also are important aspects of the process.

There are five steps in the marketing research process: (1) defining and locating problems, (2) developing hypotheses, (3) collecting data, (4) interpreting research findings, and (5) reporting research findings. Defining the nature and boundaries of a problem is a necessary first step in launching a research study. Refining a problem from an ambiguous state to a researchable and clearly defined statement permits the development of a hypothesis. A hypothesis is an assumption about a certain problem or set of circumstances.

To test a hypothesis, one must gather both primary and secondary data. Exploratory, descriptive, and causal studies are general designs for gathering these data. Primary data can be collected through experimentation or sampling. Secondary data collection involves the gathering of records, reports, and information presently available within the marketing information system or from outside sources (periodicals, government publications, syndicated data services).

Experimentation involves holding certain variables constant so that the effects of the experimental variables can be measured. In experimentation, an independent variable is manipulated and the resulting changes are measured in a dependent variable. Experiments can be conducted in the laboratory or in the field. Marketers must be able to design research procedures that produce reliable and valid data. Reliable research results can be reproduced almost exactly in repeated trials. Valid research measures what it is supposed to measure.

In marketing, the objective of sampling is to select representative units from a total population. Random sampling is basic probability sampling. Simple random, stratified, area, and quota sampling are the major sampling approaches used in developing estimates about population characteristics.

Surveys are a primary data collection method. They can be conducted by mail, by telephone, or through personal interviews. The selection of an interviewing approach depends on the nature of the problem, the data needed to test the hypothesis, and the resources (funding, personnel) available to the researcher. A mail survey is used most often when the individuals chosen for questioning are spread over a wide area and funds for the survey are limited. A telephone survey eliminates many of the disadvantages of mail surveys, but it has unique limitations too. Traditionally, marketing researchers have favored the face-to-face interview, primarily because of its flexibility. Today the shopping mall intercept interview is one of the most popular interview methods in use.

A well-constructed questionnaire elicits information that meets the study's data requirements. The composition of the questions depends on the nature and amount of detail demanded. Several kinds of questions can be designed: open-ended questions, dichotomous questions, and multiple-choice questions.

Various observation methods other than surveys can be used to collect primary data. In using an observation method, researchers record the overt behavior of respondents, taking note of physical conditions and events. Direct contact is avoided; instead, actions or phenomena are examined systematically and noted. Two major disadvantages of these methods are that they do not provide insights into causal relationships and that analyses of observations of behavior are subject to researcher bias.

Research findings must be carefully interpreted, through tabulation and statistical analysis. Last, research must be reported to the appropriate persons so that findings can contribute to decision making. It is important that marketing researchers establish ethical standards—that research is honest, that clients are treated fairly, and that results are kept confidential. These standards are essential to ensure that data inputs are accurate and can be used in making good marketing decisions.

MATCHING EXERCISES

Use the following set of terms to identify the sentences and phrases below. On the blank line next to each sentence or phrase, place the letter of the term that the sentence or phrase describes. Do not use a term more than once.

a. Observation method	o. Hypotheses
b. Validity	p. Mechanical observation devices
c. Primary data	q. Secondary data
d. Marketing research	r. Dependent variable
e. Survey methods	s. Quota sampling
f. Area sampling	t. Exploratory study
g. Population	u. Independent variable
h. Reliability	v. Random sampling
i. Problem definition	w. Causal study
j. Marketing databank	x. Marketing experimentation
k. Syndicated data services	y. Stratified sampling
l. Experimentation	z. Descriptive study
m. Sampling	aa. Statistical interpretation
n. Marketing information system (MIS)	

Stratified Sampling   1. y A sampling method in which <u>respondents or sample units are divided into</u> groups according to a common characteristic or attribute; then a probability sample is conducted within each group.

Secondary Data   2. q Information compiled inside or outside the organization for some <u>purpose other than the current investigation</u>.

Mktg Databank   3. j A file of data collected through both the marketing information system and marketing research projects.

Statistical interpretation   4. aa Analysis that focuses on what is typical or what deviates from average; it indicates how widely respondents vary and how they are distributed in relation to the variable being measured.

Mktg Research   5. d The systematic design, collection, interpretation, and reporting of information to help marketers solve specific marketing problems or take advantage of marketing opportunities.

_____ 6. All elements, units, or individuals of interest to researchers for a specific study. *Population*

_____ 7. The first step in the research process toward finding a solution or launching a research study; the researcher thinks about how best to discover the nature and boundaries of a problem or opportunity. *Problem Definition*

_____ 8. A system that establishes a framework for the day-to-day managing and structuring of information gathered regularly from sources both inside and outside the organization. *MIS*

_____ 9. A type of sampling in which all the units in a population have an equal chance of appearing in the sample; probability sampling. *Random Sampling*

_____ 10. A variable that is not influenced by or dependent on other variables. *Independent*

_____ 11. An accurate reflection of the entire market population; if the market is portrayed accurately and the data are gathered correctly, repeated trials produce almost identical results. *Reliability*

_____ 12. A type of research conducted when more information is needed about a problem and the tentative hypothesis has to be made more specific; it permits marketers to conduct ministudies with a very restricted database. *Exploratory Study*

_____ 13. Research in which those factors that are related to or may affect the variables under investigation are maintained as constants so that the effects of the experimental variables can be measured. *Experimentation*

_____ 14. External sources of information a marketer may use to study a marketing problem; they collect general information and sell it to subscribing clients. *Syndicated Data Services*

_____ 15. A set of rules and procedures under which the task of data gathering is organized to expedite analysis and interpretation. *Mktg Experimentation*

_____ 16. Selecting representative units from a total population. *Sampling*

_____ 17. A guess or assumption about a certain problem or set of circumstances; a reasonable supposition that may be right or wrong. *Hypotheses*

_____ 18. A variation of stratified sampling, with geographic areas serving as the segments, or primary units, used in random sampling. *Area Sampling*

_____ 19. Cameras, recorders, counting machines, and equipment to record movement, behavior, or physiological changes in individuals. *Mechanical Observation devices*

_____ 20. A method of data collection in which researchers systematically record the overt behavior of subjects, avoiding direct contact with them. *Observation method*

_____ 21. Include interviews by mail or by telephone and personal interviews. *Survey methods*

_____ 22. Said to exist when an instrument measures what it is supposed to measure. *Validity*

_____ 23. Information observed in and recorded or collected directly from subjects. *Primary data*

_____ 24. A variable contingent on, or restricted to, one or a set of values assumed by an independent variable. *Dependent Variable*

Descriptive Study 25. A type of study undertaken when marketers see that <u>knowledge of the characteristics of certain phenomena is needed</u> to solve a problem; may require statistical analysis and predictive tools.

Causal Study 26. <u>Research planned to prove or disprove that *x* causes *y*.</u>

TRUE OR FALSE STATEMENTS

T F 1. The value of research is measured by improvements in the marketer's ability to implement plans. *Better Decision*

T F 2. The feedback mechanism of the marketing information system is necessary to understand consumers and the dynamics of the marketplace.

T F 3. Formal marketing research departments have become less important in planning and strategy development in large organizations.

T F 4. In general, marketing research and information systems improve decision making and ~~increase the cost~~ of the product to consumers.

T F 5. Personal knowledge or experience is a source of decision making information.

T F 6. Limited research is valuable when, in terms of usefulness to decision makers, it is too expensive to gather complete data.

T F 7. The use of research in planning becomes more important as the alternative outcomes to a problem and the expected payoff increase.

T F 8. Usually either intuition or research, but not both, is necessary for successful marketing outcomes.

T F 9. The marketing information system within the organization is a fragmented process, generating an inconsistent flow of information about expenses, sales, and profits.

T F 10. In the MIS, the means of gathering data receive more attention than do the procedures for expediting the flow of information.

T F 11. Marketing research, unlike a marketing information system, does not involve specific investigations into problems related to marketing decisions.

T F 12. Descriptive studies involve the collection of data to clarify a research problem.

T F 13. Causal studies assume that an independent variable, *x*, is the cause of a dependent variable, *y*.

T F 14. Surveys, observation, and <u>secondary data</u> collection are <u>three basic</u> ways of gathering data for use in marketing research.

T F 15. Examples of <u>primary data</u> are surveys and observations.

T   F   16. A survey is valid if it actually measures what it is supposed to measure, not something else.

T   F   17. In area sampling, respondents or sample elements are separated into groups or strata according to socioeconomic characteristics.

T   F   18. If related variables are random, the effect of the experimental variables in the experimentation design can be measured.

T   F   19. Small organizations normally cannot afford to maintain the databank required for a marketing information system.

T   F   20. A variation of the personal interview technique focuses on groups rather than individuals.

T   F   21. A telephone survey is an example of a good ~~random~~ sample because people have an equal possibility of being selected; that is, most homes that have telephones are listed in a telephone directory.

T   F   22. Direct contact with respondents generally is avoided by using an observation method of data gathering.

T   F   23. The population for a particular marketing research design is that portion of the total market actually questioned or observed.

T   F   24. Random sampling requires that all members of a population have an equal chance of appearing in the sample.

T   F   25. The biggest disadvantage of mail surveys is the traditionally low response rate.

T   F   26. Syndicated data services offer a source of ~~primary~~ data for a particular company.

T   F   27. The company's own accounting records are not a valid source of data for decision making in the typical marketing division.

T   F   28. Although important to large businesses, marketing research is of little use to small businesses.

MULTIPLE-CHOICE QUESTIONS

_____ 1. Which of the following statements concerning marketing research and information systems is false?
   a. They help implement the marketing concept by providing adequate information about consumers.
   b. They increase the chances of success in performing marketing activities.
   c. They are used to plan and develop appropriate strategies.
   d. They provide important input into the development of the marketing mix.
   e. They increase the cost of the product to the consumer.

_____ 2. Marketing research and information systems
   a. represent an information gathering process for specific situations.
   b. lack a mechanism to provide feedback from consumers to organizations.
   c. provide valuable insights into consumer preferences.
   d. do not provide inputs into the development of consumer products.
   e. are most effectively utilized as selling techniques.

_____ 3. The first thing a marketer must think about when tackling a marketing research project is
   a. gathering data.
   b. developing a hypothesis.
   c. defining and locating the problem.
   d. interpreting research findings.
   e. how much the project will cost.

_____ 4. If Strike-King fishing lures knows that its market share in the southwest region has dropped 13 percent in the first quarter of the year but does not know what might have contributed to this decline, it is in which stage of the marketing research process?
   a. Hypothesis development
   b. Symptom identification
   c. Data collection
   d. Problem identification
   e. Data interpretation

_____ 5. If Shell notices that gasoline sales for its super-premium SU2000 brand have increased 30 percent in the past two months and cannot explain this good fortune, Shell is in the _____ phase of the marketing research process.
   a. problem definition
   b. hypothesis development
   c. data interpretation
   d. favorable results
   e. data collection

_____ 6. The marketing databank can be described as a(n)
   a. file of data collected through both the MIS and marketing research projects.
   b. establishment where money is received for the financial aspects of marketing.
   c. pool of external sources of marketing information.
   d. subscription to syndicated data services.
   e. file of data useful in bank studies.

_____ 7. Which of the following statements is false?
   a. Causal studies assume that a dependent variable, x, is the cause of an independent variable, y.
   b. The purpose of exploratory studies is to refine a tentative hypothesis or to acquire more information about a research problem.

    c. Descriptive studies are concerned with identifying the characteristics of certain phenomena and may require statistical analysis.

    d. Reliable research results can be reproduced almost exactly.

    e. Judgment is used in developing a nonprobability sample.

_____ 8. Marketing research is used in decision making

    a. as a substitute for judgment.

    b. as an objective and practical aid to judgment.

    c. as the number of alternative solutions to a problem decreases.

    d. as justification for a particular decision.

    e. when intuition fails to aid judgment.

_____ 9. In a laboratory experiment,

    a. the development of realism is not a problem.

    b. it is difficult to control independent variables.

    c. the setting is comparable to the real world.

    d. respondents are invited to react to experimental stimuli.

    e. animals are normally used to simulate human behavior.

_____ 10. If Hunts tests the effect of package labeling on ketchup purchases in an environment where advertising, couponing, shelf position, and pricing are controlled, Hunts is using

    a. experimentation.

    b. secondary data.

    c. exploratory research.

    d. survey research.

    e. dependent research.

_____ 11. A nonprobability sample chosen on the basis of an interviewer's own judgment is called a(n)

    a. intuitive sample.

    b. quota sample.

    c. stratified sample.

    d. area sample.

    e. random sample.

_____ 12. An example of a primary data source is

    a. the *Census of Business*.

    b. accounting records.

    c. the *Survey of Buying Power*.

    d. unpublished trade association data.

    e. a telephone interview.

_____ 13. The results of a research design are most reliable when

    a. the research techniques produce almost identical data in repeated trials.

    b. they actually measure what they are supposed to measure, not something else.

    c. the source of the data is trustworthy.

    d. measurements provide data that can be used to test a hypothesis.

    e. a personal computer is used on-site to tabulate results.

_____ 14. An example of a sampling design is
        a. cross-sampling.
        b. observation sampling.
        c. range sampling.
        d. stratified sampling.
        e. design sampling.

_____ 15. The University Book Store selects 200 of its more than 8,000 customers to participate in a study assessing the service quality of the store. The organization has established a(n) _____ for use in its research.
        a. population
        b. field setting
        c. dependent grouping
        d. sample
        e. experiment

_____ 16. Greg Bush of Quality Market Research, Inc., tells student intern Betsey Lee to go out and interview ten men and ten women. Greg is using _____ sampling for this phase of the research.
        a. random
        b. stratified
        c. quota
        d. area
        e. probability

_____ 17. A fault of the observation method of research is that
        a. direct contact between the researcher and respondent is not allowed.
        b. only demographic information can be gathered.
        c. it eliminates the need to motivate respondents to state their true feelings.
        d. it tends to be descriptive, failing to provide insights into causal relationships.
        e. consumers often get upset and attack the researcher.

_____ 18. Which of the following has *not* been a factor in the declining rate of response in personal survey research?
        a. Using a survey approach to sell a product
        b. Consumers' reluctance to talk to strangers
        c. Unethical survey tactics
        d. A general trend among the public to clam up on door-to-door solicitors
        e. The length and depth of face-to-face interviews

_____ 19. A characteristic of telephone surveys is that they
        a. provide a nonrepresentative sample.
        b. make it hard to get respondents to cooperate.
        c. are a time-consuming survey method.
        d. permit the interviewer to gain rapport with respondents and to ask them probing questions.
        e. create expensive phone bills.

____ 20. If Adidas needs a study addressing the attitudes of retailers toward the availability of product literature in athletic shoe stores and needs the results in four working days, Adidas should use the _____ survey for this study.
a. mail
b. telephone
c. mail intercept
d. personal interview
e. in-home survey

____ 21. Innovative Products, Inc., has recently developed a new gadget that prepares vegetables for party appetizers in novel and attractive ways. The firm want to measure potential customers' attitudes toward this product and other, existing vegetable peelers. In this situation, Innovative Products should use which one of the following methods to survey the selected sample?
a. Mail survey
b. Telephone survey
c. Computer-assisted telephone interviewing
d. Personal interview survey
e. Focus-group interviews

____ 22. If LizSport planned to get toether a small group of department store buyers to talk about their buying patterns and interests, the designer would be planning a(n)
a. experiment.
b. mail intercept.
c. personal interview.
d. questionnaire.
e. focus group.

____ 23. Which of the following statements about personal interviews is false?
a. They offer the interviewer a chance to probe certain questions in depth.
b. They enable the interviewer to develop lines of thought that were not anticipated.
c. They give the interviewer an opportunity to judge socioeconomic characteristics.
d. They allow follow-up studies about respondents.
e. They do not lend themselves well to group situations.

____ 24. One common mistake in constructing questionnaires is
a. developing the questionnaire after defining the specific objectives.
b. asking questions that interest the researcher but do not provide useful information for determining whether to accept or reject a hypothesis.
c. developing questions that are unbiased and objective.
d. asking questions that achieve the research objective.
e. asking questions that are boring.

_____ 25. If Pizza Hut asks survey participants if they have purchased a pizza for delivery in the last two weeks, this would be a(n) _____ question.
   a. open-ended
   b. dichotomous
   c. summed scale
   d. random
   e. multiple-choice

_____ 26. Syndicated data services
   a. provide researchers with primary data.
   b. are an example of an internal databank source.
   c. provide secondary data.
   d. collect specific information for a few clients.
   e. are supplied by the underground.

_____ 27. All the following are steps in the marketing research process *except*
   a. developing hypotheses.
   b. collecting data.
   c. interpreting research findings.
   d. surveying the population.
   e. defining the problem.

_____ 28. The sampling design that divides respondents into groups according to geographic divisions is called
   a. random sampling.
   b. area sampling.
   c. group sampling.
   d. stratified sampling.
   e. nonprobability sampling.

_____ 29. To set the price of a new dictionary, a book publisher wishes to know how many dictionaries can be sold at different prices. The dependent variable in this example would be
   a. competition.
   b. book publishers.
   c. sales.
   d. price.
   e. consumers.

_____ 30. In experimentation, the thing that is observed to see if it changes after something else is manipulated is called the
   a. independent variable.
   b. dependent variable.
   c. hypothesis.
   d. data.
   e. subject.

_____ 31. Which of the following is *not* a primary source of data for marketing research?
   a. Survey
   b. Interview
   c. Questionnaire
   d. Observation
   e. Government census

_____ 32. Which of the following is *not* a limitation of field experiences?
   a. The field can be influenced by inadvertent events.
   b. Gaining the cooperation of respondents can be difficult.
   c. Carryover effects are present from past experiments and may influence respondents.
   d. Many relevant variables cannot be controlled.
   e. Field experiences take place in natural surroundings.

MINICASE: SOUTHERN MUTUAL INSURANCE

Southern Mutual Insurance competes with many insurance companies, small and large, in the Deep South. When the firm was founded by a Louisiana farmer in 1943, its objective was to provide broad insurance coverage at a fair price for anyone who needed it. This is still Southern Mutual's primary objective, although the organization has changed considerably over the years to meet the needs of its policyholders.

Today, Southern Mutual services more than three million policyholders throughout the United States. The insurance needs of these individuals are many and diverse. To monitor those needs, the activities of competitors, and changes in the marketing environment (regulatory, economic, technological, and so on), the firm operates an ongoing research program.

Of major concern to Southern Mutual are rising household expenses, which have acted to lower discretionary income. Insurance, like energy, food, and housing, is a household expense. One research study showed that policyholders pay, on average, about $355 annually in automobile insurance premiums. It also indicated that about 45 percent of the policyholders surveyed feel their insurance premiums are so high they may not be able to continue paying them.

Southern Mutual is concerned about the affordability of insurance on two counts. First, increased costs of operation are going to require premium increases for the company to maintain an acceptable level of profitability. Second, there are the societal implications of more drivers operating vehicles without insurance—the result of drivers no longer being able to afford coverage.

To lessen the strain on household finances, Southern Mutual is considering several alternatives. One is to encourage policyholders to pay their premiums more often, perhaps monthly, as they do other household bills (utilities, house and rent payments, credit purchases). Currently, most companies, including Southern Mutual, encourage policyholders to pay premiums just twice a year (every six months). To determine the feasibility of an alternative payment plan, the company has formed a payment plan task force. It also has directed its research department to conduct a survey on policyholder attitudes toward insurance costs and payment plans. The survey results indicate that about 50 percent of the policyholders prefer to pay their premiums on an annual or semiannual basis, and 30 percent prefer a quarterly time schedule. Only 20 percent would prefer to pay a monthly insurance premium.

Questions

_____ 1. Southern Mutual's ongoing research program to monitor policyholders' needs, competition, and changes in the marketing environment is a type of marketing
a. intelligence.
b. research.
c. information system.
d. databank.
e. planning.

_____ 2. The survey the firm's research department conducted is a type of marketing
a. intelligence.
b. research.
c. information system.
d. databank.
e. planning.

_____ 3. Information concerning rising household expenses and falling discretionary income was most likely obtained through
a. survey methods.
b. observation methods.
c. internal records.
d. government records.
e. intuition.

_____ 4. Directing the firm's research department to conduct a survey on policyholders' attitudes toward insurance costs and to investigate alternative payment plans is an example of
a. primary exploratory research.
b. secondary exploratory research.
c. primary descriptive research.
d. secondary descriptive research.
e. primary causal research.

_____ 5. In which of the following stages of the research process is Southern Mutual's research department at this time?
a. Defining the problem
b. Developing hypotheses
c. Collecting data
d. Interpreting research findings
e. Reporting research findings

_____ 6. In regard to the survey conducted by the firm's research department, all policyholders constitute the
    a. target market.
    b. population.
    c. sample group.
    d. marketing group.
    e. research group.

PROGRAMMED COMPLETION EXERCISES

defining, developing, collecting, interpreting, reporting

1. The five basic steps in planning marketing research are
(1) _____ problems, (2) _____ hypotheses,
(3) _____ data, (4) _____ research findings,
and (5) _____ research findings.

Exploratory, descriptive, causal

2. _____ studies, _____ studies, and
_____ investigations are general designs for
gathering data.

surveys, observations, secondary

3. The three elementary techniques for obtaining data for marketing research are the primary data collection methods of
_____ and _____, and _____ data
collection.

Personal, telephone surveys, mail surveys

4. _____ interviews, _____ _____,
and _____ _____ are three types of survey
methods that can be used to obtain information for testing a
hypothesis.

Personal

5. _____ survey research is experiencing declining rates
of response because the public is clamming up on door-to-
door solicitors.

constructing a questionnaire, accept, reject

6. One of the most common mistakes in _____ _____ _____ is asking questions that are interesting to the researcher but do not provide information that can be used for deciding whether to _____ or _____ a hypothesis.

Dichotomous

7. _____ questions are frequently called "yes or no" questions because there are only two possible responses.

observation

8. In the _____ method of data gathering, direct contact is avoided; instead, action is examined systematically and noted.

descriptive, causal relationships

9. Two disadvantages of the observational method are that it tends to be _____ and may not provide insights into _____ _____ and that reliability is subject to researcher bias.

reliable, valid

10. Well-founded marketing data are _____, which means they can be duplicated, and _____, which means they measure what they are supposed to measure.

independent, dependent

11. Experimentation involves the manipulation of _____ variables to measure changes in a _____ variable.

intuitive, scientific

12. The increase in marketing research activities represents a transition from _____ to _____ problem solving.

specific situations

13. The marketing information system is a continuous process within the organization, whereas marketing research is an information gathering process for _____ _____.

intuitive

14. The _____ manager makes decisions based on personal knowledge and experience; the research approach to decision making is both orderly and logical.

marketing
information
system

15. The _____ _____ _____ is the framework for managing and structuring regularly gathered information.

realism

16. Laboratory experiments lack _____ and total comparability to the real world, but they simulate a real-world situation and offer the opportunity to control variables.

open-ended,
dichotomous,
multiple-choice

17. Several kinds of questions can be designed for use on questionnaires, including _____, _____, and _____ questions.

independent variable,
dependent variable

18. In causal relationship studies, it is assumed that a particular _____ _____, x, is the cause of variation in a _____ _____, y.

ANSWERS TO OBJECTIVE QUESTIONS

Matching		*True or False*		*Multiple-Choice*		*Minicase*
1. y	14. k	1. F	15. T	1. e	17. d	1. c
2. q	15. x	2. T	16. T	2. c	18. e	2. b
3. j	16. m	3. F	17. F	3. c	19. d	3. a
4. aa	17. o	4. F	18. F	4. d	20. b	4. c
5. d	18. f	5. T	19. F	5. a	21. d	5. d
6. g	19. p	6. T	20. T	6. a	22. e	6. b
7. i	20. a	7. T	21. F	7. a	23. e	
8. n	21. e	8. F	22. T	8. b	24. b	
9. v	22. b	9. F	23. F	9. d	25. b	
10. u	23. c	10. F	24. T	10. a	26. c	
11. h	24. r	11. F	25. T	11. b	27. d	
12. t	25. z	12. F	26. F	12. e	28. b	
13. l	26. w	13. T	27. F	13. a	29. c	
		14. T	28. F	14. d	30. b	
				15. d	31. e	
				16. c	32. e	

8 PRODUCT CONCEPTS

CHAPTER OUTLINE

What is a product?
Classifying products
    Consumer products
    Business-to-business products
Product line and product mix
Product life cycles
    Introduction
    Growth
    Maturity
    Decline
Product positioning and repositioning
Organizing to manage products

CHAPTER SUMMARY

Products are among a firm's most important and visible contacts with buyers. If a firm's products do not meet the buyers' needs and wants, the company will fail. The product's role in satisfying customers cannot be overstressed. Marketers must understand what a product means to consumers and know what consumers' expectations about products are.

A product is everything, both favorable and unfavorable, that one receives in an exchange. A product can be an idea, a service, a good, or any combination of these. Products fall into two general categories, depending on the buyers' intentions. Products purchased for the satisfaction of personal and family needs are consumer products; those bought for use in a firm's operations or to produce other products are business-to-business products. The classification of products as consumer or business-to-business is important in selecting target markets. Consumer products traditionally are broken down into four categories, based primarily on the characteristics of buyers' purchasing behavior. Convenience products are relatively inexpensive, frequently purchased items that buyers want to exert only minimal effort to obtain. Shopping products are items for which buyers are willing to put forth considerable effort in planning and making the purchase. Specialty products have one or more unique characteristics; they are products that buyers are willing to expend considerable effort to obtain. Unsought products are purchased when a sudden problem needs to be resolved or when aggressive selling is used to obtain a sale that otherwise would not be made.

Business-to-business products can be broken down into categories based on their characteristics and intended use. Business-to-business products include raw materials, major equipment, accessory equipment, component parts, process materials, consumable supplies, and industrial services.

No matter how large an organization is, there is a limit to the number and variety of products it can offer buyers. A product item is a specific version of a product that can be designated as a distinct offering among an organization's products. A product line, a group of closely related product items that are considered a unit, is developed on the basis of marketing or technical considerations. Specific items in a product line usually reflect the preferences or needs of different target markets. A product mix is the composite or total group of products that an organization makes available to customers. The depth of the product mix is measured by the number of different products offered in each product line. The width of the product mix measures the number of product lines in the company.

Products are like living organisms: They are born, they live, and they die. The product life cycle has four major stages. During the introduction stage, sales are just taking off and profits are negative. The company must make potential buyers aware of the product's features, uses, and advantages. During the growth stage, sales rise rapidly; profits reach a peak and then start to decline. In the maturity stage, the sales curve peaks and starts to fall as profits continue to decline. This stage is characterized by a high degree of competition. During the decline stage, sales fall rapidly. The marketer may cut promotional efforts, eliminate marginal distributors, and finally make plans for phasing out the product. Most enterprises have a product mix consisting of multiple products, and various products in the mix can be at different life cycle stages. Marketers must deal with the dual problems of prolonging existing products and introducing new ones to meet organizational sales goals.

When marketers introduce a product, they attempt to position it so that it seems to possess the characteristics most wanted by the target market. A product's position refers to the customers' concept of the product relative to their concept of competing brands. If a product has been developed properly, its attributes and brand image should give it the distinct appeal it needs. And where that appeal is missing, there is room for a new product or for the repositioning of an existing one.

Management must find an organizational form that accomplishes the tasks necessary for developing and managing products. Three of these forms are the product manager approach, the market manager approach, and the venture team approach. Product managers coordinate marketing efforts for a product, a product line, or a group of related products in all markets. Market managers focus on products for specific markets. Venture teams develop new products. Members of a venture team come from different functional areas within the organization. Unlike product managers and market managers, they are responsible for all aspects of a product's development.

MATCHING EXERCISES

Use the following set of terms to identify the sentences and phrases below. On the blank line next to each sentence or phrase, place the letter of the term that the sentence or phrase describes. Do not use a term more than once.

a. Product positioning
b. Product
c. Product life cycle
d. Width of product mix
e. Product manager
f. Consumer product
g. Introduction stage
h. Depth of product mix
i. Venture team
j. Business-to-business product
k. Growth stage
l. Product mix
m. Market manager
n. Convenience product
o. Maturity stage
p. Product line

q. Brand manager
r. Shopping product
s. Decline stage
t. Product item
u. Specialty product
v. Raw materials
w. Business-to-business services
x. Major equipment
y. Consumable supplies
z. Accessory equipment
aa. Product portfolio approach
bb. Process materials
cc. Component part
dd. Unsought product
ee. MRO items

Raw Materials 1. v Basic materials that become part of a physical product; they are obtained from mines, farms, forests, oceans, and recycled solid wastes.

Introduction 2. g The stage in a product's life cycle beginning with a product's first appearance in the marketplace, when sales are zero and profits are negative.

Product life Cycle 3. c The course of product development, consisting of introduction, growth, maturity, and decline. As a product moves through these stages, the strategies relating to competition, pricing, promotion, distribution, and market information must be evaluated and possibly changed.

Decline 4. s The stage in a product's life cycle in which sales fall rapidly and profits continue to decrease.

Brand Man 5. q A product manager who is responsible for a single brand.

Convenience 6. n A relatively inexpensive, frequently purchased item for which buyers want to exert only minimal effort.

Growth 7. k The product life cycle stage in which sales rise rapidly and profits reach a peak and then start to decline.

Venture teams 8. i An organizational unit comprised of members from different functional areas that is established to create new products.

Component Part 9. cc A finished item ready for assembly or a product that needs little processing before assembly that becomes a part of the physical product.

_____ 10. A specific version of a product that can be designated as a distinct offering among an organization's products. *Product item*

_____ 11. Items that facilitate an organization's production and operations but do not become part of the finished product. *Consumable supplies*

_____ 12. The composite of products that an organization makes available to consumers. *Product mix*

_____ 13. Materials used directly in the production of other products; unlike component parts, they are not readily identifiable. *Process material*

_____ 14. A product purchased for the ultimate satisfaction of personal and family needs. *Consumer good*

_____ 15. A person responsible for the marketing activities that serve a particular group or class of customers. *Mkt Mgr*

_____ 16. An item for which buyers are willing to put forth considerable effort in planning and making the purchase. *Shopping*

_____ 17. Everything (both favorable and unfavorable) that one receives in an exchange; it is a complex of tangible and intangible attributes, including functional, social, and psychological utilities or benefits. Includes goods, services, or ideas. *Product*

_____ 18. An intangible product that an organization uses in its operations, such as financial products and legal services. *Business to Business Service*

_____ 19. Measured by the number of different products in a firm's product lines that are offered to buyers. *Depth of Product mix*

_____ 20. An item that possesses one or more unique characteristics for which a significant group of buyers is willing to expend considerable purchasing effort. *Specialty*

_____ 21. A method of creating specific marketing strategies to achieve a balanced mix of products. *Product Portfolio approach*

_____ 22. A stage in the product life cycle in which the sales curve peaks and starts to decline as profits continue to decline. *maturity*

_____ 23. Measured by the number of product lines an organization offers. *Width of Product mix*

_____ 24. Equipment used in production or office activities; does not become a part of the final physical product. *Accessory equip*

_____ 25. A person who is responsible for a product, a product line, or several distinct products that are considered an interrelated group. *Product Mgr*

_____ 26. A group of closely related products that are considered a unit because of marketing, technical, or end-use considerations. *Product line*

_____ 27. A category of industrial products that includes large tools and machines used for production purposes. *Major Equip*

Product Positioning _____ 28.ᵃ The decisions and activities that are directed toward trying to create and maintain the firm's intended product concept in the customer's mind.

Business to Business Product _____ 29.ᵇ A product purchased to be used directly or indirectly to produce other products or in an organization's operations.

_____ 30.ᶜᶜ Consumable supplies used for maintenance, repair, and operating (or overhaul).   *MRO items*

_____ 31.ᵈᵈ Products purchased because of a sudden problem that needs to be solved or when aggressive selling is used to obtain a sale that otherwise would not take place.

Unsought goods

TRUE OR FALSE STATEMENTS

T F   1. The product is an important variable in the marketing mix.

T F   2. A product is a complex of tangible and intangible attributes, including functional, social, and psychological utilities or benefits.

T F   3. When people buy a product, they are also buying the benefits and satisfaction they believe the product will provide.

T F   4. Products bought for use in a firm's operations to produce other products are classified as consumer products.

T F   5. The classification of consumer products is based primarily on the characteristics of buyers' purchasing behavior.

T F   6. A consumer product can be classified as a convenience, shopping, specialty, or unsought good but cannot fit into more than one category.

T F   7. Whether a product is a business-to-business or a consumer product is important in determining marketing strategies.

T F   8. Because there are so many similar products on the grocery shelf, a creative label can act as a silent salesperson, attracting attention to a particular product.

T F   9. Electrical appliances are typical shopping products.

T F 10. Specialty products require consumers to expend considerable searching effort.

T F 11. Supplies are used indirectly in the production of other products.

T F 12. The product mix refers to a related group of products in the product line.

T F 13. A specific product in a product line should satisfy a definite target market.

T F 14. Lathes, cranes, and stamping machines are examples of business-to-business products classified as accessory equipment.

T F 15. A product may fail during its introductory stage because it does not provide benefits that consumers want.

T F 16. Profits are negative in the introductory stage of the product life cycle.

T F 17. Product positioning refers to the shelf space a reseller gives a product.

T F 18. Segmentation means that a firm is aiming a given brand at only a portion of the total market.

T F 19. Head-to-head positioning is critical when a firm is introducing a brand into market.

T F 20. A brand manager is a type of market manager.

T F 21. Venture teams are groups used to develop new products.

T F 22. Product planning tends to reduce the probability of product failure.

T F 23. A market manager has the responsibility of coordinating all product decisions for all target markets.

T F 24. A well-planned and managed product mix should not require alterations to maintain its effectiveness.

MULTIPLE-CHOICE QUESTIONS

_____ 1. An organization's products
   a. are not part of the marketing mix.
   b. represent visible contacts with consumers.
   c. are not information sources.
   d. are purchased for functional reasons only.
   e. include tangible products but not services.

_____ 2. Supercuts offers what types of product?
   a. Utility
   b. Good
   c. Service
   d. Functional
   e. Idea

_____ 3. The definition of a product includes all the following *except*
   a. functional utilities.
   b. supporting services.
   c. social utilities.
   d. psychological utilities.
   e. production techniques.

_____ 4. The four traditional categories of consumer products are
   a. convenience, shopping, specialty, and unsought.
   b. marketable, unsought, convenience, and mature.
   c. specialty, accessory, convenience, and spontaneous.
   d. emergency, intangible, convenience, and shopping.
   e. family, business, unsought, and specialty.

_____ 5. Consumer product classifications are based primarily on
  a. how consumers use the product.
  b. the characteristics of buyers' purchasing behavior.
  c. where the product is purchased.
  d. how consumers view the product.
  e. the cost of the product.

_____ 6. *The New York Times* would be classified as a(n) _____ product.
  a. unsought
  b. convenience
  c. intangible
  d. shopping
  e. specialty

_____ 7. Overnight mail service is an example of which type of product?
  a. Utility
  b. Service
  c. Symbolic
  d. Buyer-oriented
  e. Seller-oriented

_____ 8. In purchases of business-to-business products,
  a. organizational goals are often secondary.
  b. psychological considerations outweigh functional considerations.
  c. functional considerations outweigh psychological considerations.
  d. institutions constitute the largest market.
  e. most purchases are for raw materials.

_____ 9. Which of the following is *not* an example of a business-to-business product?
  a. Screws used to mount engine blocks on cars
  b. Steel used for manufacturing drill bits
  c. Gasoline for a salesperson's car
  d. A pencil used to write a weekly grocery list
  e. A chair used in a conference room

_____ 10. All the following are classes of business-to-business products *except*
  a. raw materials.
  b. semifinished supplies.
  c. accessory equipment.
  d. supplies.
  e. process materials.

_____ 11. The typewriters that Smith-Corona markets for office use would be classified as
  a. major equipment.
  b. component parts.
  c. process materials.
  d. accessory equipment.
  e. consumable supplies.

_____ 12. A. C. Spark Plug is a manufacturer of
    a. major equipment.
    b. component parts.
    c. process materials.
    d. accessory equipment.
    e. consumable supplies.

_____ 13. A flame-retardant solution produced by Du Pont used in the production of fabric for clothing would be classified as a(n)
    a. process material.
    b. MRO item.
    c. component part.
    d. raw material.
    e. consumable supply.

_____ 14. The classification of industrial products is useful in
    a. production.
    b. purchasing activities.
    c. understanding consumers' buying motives.
    d. developing a marketing mix.
    e. creating an advertising campaign.

_____ 15. The total group of products that a seller makes available to consumers is the
    a. product line.
    b. marketing mix.
    c. product mix.
    d. product items.
    e. market line.

_____ 16. Marketers measure a product mix by its
    a. scope and variability.
    b. age and marketability.
    c. variability and depth.
    d. width and scope.
    e. depth and width.

_____ 17. A product line refers to
    a. the composite of products that an organization makes available to consumers.
    b. a specific and unique version of a product.
    c. a group of closely related products that are considered a unit.
    d. product information a salesperson provides to a customer.
    e. the width of the product mix.

_____ 18. Each time Procter & Gamble introduces a new product line, it increases the _____ of its product mix.
    a. scope
    b. depth
    c. length
    d. width
    e. height

132   *Chapter 8*

_____ 19. Which of the following statements characterizes the maturity stage of the product life cycle?
   a. Sales fall rapidly, and new technology as well as social trends may cause profits to fall also.
   b. Sales are zero and profits are negative.
   c. Sales rise rapidly and profits reach a peak.
   d. The sales curve peaks and starts to decline as profits continue to decline.
   e. Minimal competition exists among sellers.

_____ 20. Which stage in the product life cycle is characterized by negative profits, zero sales, and an emphasis on communicating product benefits to buyers?
   a. Maturity stage
   b. Planning stage
   c. Decline stage
   d. Growth stage
   e. Introduction stage

_____ 21. Which of the following is a typical strategy in managing a product in the growth stage?
   a. Maintaining a constant price
   b. Concentrating on advertising and dealer-oriented promotion
   c. Encouraging strong brand loyalty to compete with aggressive product emulators
   d. Eliminating marginal distributors
   e. Making potential buyers aware of the product's features, uses, and advantages

_____ 22. A company's promotion of a new use for or feature of an old product can be used for
   a. cannibalization.
   b. brand extension.
   c. product repositioning.
   d. head-to-head positioning.
   e. product conception.

_____ 23. If a product's performance features are at least equal to those of its competitors, marketers may use which type of product positioning?
   a. Competition-avoidance
   b. High visibility
   c. Image oriented
   d. Head-to-head
   e. Target-oriented

_____ 24. Product positioning refers to
   a. distributing products in a good location.
   b. exaggerating product attributes.
   c. creating and maintaining the product concept in customers' minds.
   d. a product's shelf location.
   e. a product's hierarchy in the distribution channels.

___ 25. Perceptual maps are used by marketers to
   a. avoid a continuous reevaluation of numerous products.
   b. aim products at new markets.
   c. analyze product positions.
   d. plan marketing activities to achieve objectives by coordinating a mix of distribution, promotion, and price.
   e. determine a product's stage in its life cycle.

___ 26. The slogan "This is not your father's Oldsmobile" was used by General Motors to help to achieve
   a. target-oriented positioning.
   b. image-oriented positioning.
   c. brand extension.
   d. cannibalization.
   e. product repositioning.

___ 27. Advertisements for Sunsweet Prune Juice feature young, attractive people suggesting that consumers try the product as a breakfast drink and compare its taste to other popular juices. Sunsweet is attempting to
   a. relaunch.
   b. reposition.
   c. improve.
   d. diversify.
   e. rethink.

___ 28. Product managers are essentially
   a. salespeople.
   b. generators of creative ideas.
   c. planners and coordinators.
   d. financial managers.
   e. communications experts.

___ 29. Eric Stephens is responsible for the success or failure of Wholesome Foods' newest introduction—Sunsational Sunflower Seeds. Eric is a _____ manager.
   a. product
   b. brand
   c. line
   d. positioning
   e. market

___ 30. Unlike a product manager or market manager, a venture team
   a. is limited to planning and coordination.
   b. never manages a product following its development.
   c. seeks to modify existing products.
   d. is responsible for all aspects of a product's development, including research, engineering, finance, and marketing.
   e. is not highly flexible.

MINICASE: PERSONAL CARE PRODUCTS, INC.

Americans consume approximately $1.3 billion worth of soap annually. For nearly a century they have traditionally bought their soap in bar or cake form. In the early 1980s, a small Ohio firm named Personal Care Products, Inc., brought to market an innovative soap product: hand soap in liquid form. The liquid soap was packaged in an attractive plastic container with a pump dispenser and named Clean Cream. The product, which was backed by a $25 million advertising campaign, was such an immediate hit with consumers that there are now approximately fifty competing products available.

After grabbing a quick 9 percent of the $1 billion total soap market, the liquid soap market share has begun to stabilize at about 8 percent, and retailers have begun to react by reducing the number of brands they carry. Several liquid soap producers have started offering coupons, trade allowances, and price reductions to increase their individual shares of the market and to induce retailers to handle their brands.

Growth of the liquid soap market has not met the company's expectations. One reason that sales have fallen off from projections is that consumers use the liquid soap only for cleaning hands. The largest group of soap users, approximately 75 percent, is the tub and shower segment. As a result, the market potential for Clean Cream seems limited—and it will remain so as long as liquid soap sits on consumers' sinks. There is also evidence of consumer dissatisfaction with the price of Clean Cream.

To compound the company's troubles, several major competitors have been test-marketing their own versions of liquid soap. Of primary concern is these large firms' potential to overwhelm smaller competitors, including Personal Care Products, with their marketing skills, larger resources, strong channels of distribution, and well-established images.

Reacting to these problems, Personal Care Products has taken the offensive. It has launched a new product, called Clean Caddy, aimed at the tub and shower segment. The Clean Caddy package is designed to hang on a shower curtain rod or any similar horizontal rod/bar configuration. The firm is considering several other possibilities for liquid soap, including the following:

1. Liquid soap for children, in packages that resemble figures popular among children.
2. Liquid soap for "dirty hands."
3. Liquid soap for the health conscious, with properties that dermatologists might recommend for various groups of users (teenagers concerned about skin blemishes or older consumers concerned about excessive drying of the skin after washing hands).
4. Liquid soap for the beauty conscious, containing moisturizers and fragrances.

Questions

_____ 1. Why hasn't the growth of the liquid soap market met Personal Care Products's expectations?
   a. Consumers failed to recognize how liquid soap could be used.
   b. People are buying fewer health and beauty products.
   c. Too many products have stifled consumer demand.
   d. Industrial products are now being bought for the home.
   e. Consumers have lost interest in hand cleaners.

_____ 2. Clean Cream can be best classified as a(n)
   a. consumer product.
   b. industrial product.
   c. convenience product.
   d. shopping product.
   e. specialty product.

_____ 3. In what stage of the product life cycle is the liquid soap industry?
   a. Development
   b. Introduction
   c. Growth
   d. Maturity
   e. Decline

_____ 4. If Personal Care Products were to change Clean Cream's target market to industrial users, they would be engaging in a product _____ strategy.
   a. repositioning
   b. relocation
   c. extension
   d. focus
   e. branding

_____ 5. The launching of Clean Caddy does *not* involve
   a. adding a specialty product.
   b. extending the product line.
   c. expanding the product mix.
   d. adding depth to the product mix.
   e. offering a new product.

_____ 6. If Personal Care Products decides to promote liquid soap to industrial users, the product could be classified as
   a. a raw material.
   b. accessory equipment.
   c. a process material.
   d. a supply.
   e. a convenience product.

PROGRAMMED COMPLETION EXERCISES

product   1. The life expectancy of a _____ is based on buyers' wants, the availability of competing products, and other considerations.

good, service, idea   2. A product can be a _____, a _____, or an _____.

product, tangible, intangible

3. A _____ is a complex of _____ and _____ characteristics or attributes, including functional, social, and psychological utilities or benefits.

business-to-business, consumer

4. The functional aspects of a _____ product usually are considered more significant than the psychological rewards that sometimes are associated with _____ products.

raw materials, major equipment, accessory equipment, component parts, process materials, consumable supplies, business-to-business services

5. On the basis of their characteristics and intended uses, business-to-business products can be classified into several categories: _____ _____, _____ _____, _____ _____, _____ _____, _____ _____, _____, _____ _____, and _____ _____.

product

6. In multiproduct companies, the _____ manager, who holds a staff position, coordinates product efforts and becomes the strategy center for the product in all markets.

consumer, business-to-business

7. A product can be classified in one of two general categories, as a _____ product or as a _____ product, on the basis of its intended use.

shopping

8. Consumers purchase _____ products after going to several stores to compare price, quality, and service.

specialty

9. A _____ product has some unique attraction for which consumers are willing to make a special search effort; in general, economizing is not the major consideration.

Convenience

10. _____ products are relatively inexpensive, frequently purchased items for which buyers exert only minimal effort.

Unsought

11. _____ products are purchased because of a sudden problem that needs to be solved.

product mix

12. The _____ _____ is the composite of products that an organization makes available to consumers.

product line

13. A _____ _____ includes a group of closely related products that are considered a unit because of technical, marketing, or end-use considerations.

depth, width

14. The _____ of a product mix is measured by the number of different products offered to buyers in each product line; the _____ of the product mix is measured by the number of product lines in the company.

introduction, growth, maturity, decline

15. The four stages of a product's life cycle are _____, _____, _____, and _____.

life cycle

16. As a product moves through the product _____ _____, strategies must be evaluated continually, especially those relating to competition, promotion, distribution, and market information.

decline, phase

17. In the _____ stage of the product life cycle, the marketer may cut promotional efforts, eliminate marginal distributors, and finally make plans to _____ the product out of the market.

positioned, head-on, avoid competition

18. A product can be _____ to compete _____ with another brand or to _____ _____.

venture team, new products, new

19. A _____ _____ is an organizational structure established to create _____ _____ that may be aimed at _____ markets.

ANSWERS TO OBJECTIVE QUESTIONS

Matching		*True or False*		*Multiple-Choice*		*Minicase*
1. v	17. b	1. T	13. T	1. b	16. e	1. a
2. g	18. w	2. T	14. F	2. c	17. c	2. a
3. c	19. h	3. T	15. T	3. e	18. d	3. d
4. s	20. u	4. F	16. T	4. b	19. d	4. a
5. q	21. aa	5. T	17. F	5. a	20. e	5. a
6. n	22. o	6. F	18. T	6. b	21. c	6. d
7. k	23. d	7. T	19. F	7. b	22. c	
8. i	24. z	8. T	20. F	8. c	23. d	
9. cc	25. e	9. T	21. T	9. d	24. c	
10. t	26. p	10. T	22. T	10. b	25. c	
11. y	27. x	11. T	23. F	11. d	26. e	
12. l	28. a	12. F	24. F	12. b	27. b	
13. bb	29. j			13. a	28. c	
14. f	30. ee			14. d	29. a	
15. m	31. dd			15. c	30. d	
16. r						

9 DEVELOPING AND MANAGING PRODUCTS

CHAPTER OUTLINE

Modifying existing products
    Quality modifications
    Functional modifications
    Aesthetic modifications
Developing new products
    Idea generation
    Screening
    Concept testing
    Business analysis
    Product development
    Test marketing
    Commercialization
Managing products after commercialization
    Marketing strategy in the growth stage
    Marketing strategy for mature products
    Marketing strategy for declining products
Product elimination

CHAPTER SUMMARY

To provide products that satisfy the people in a firm's target market(s) and achieve the organization's objectives, a marketer must be able to improve the product mix. In strategic market planning, the management of the product mix is often referred to as the portfolio approach. Three ways of improving a product mix are modifying an existing product, developing a new product, and eliminating a product.

Product modification is changing one or more of a product's characteristics. It often is used in the maturity stage of the product life cycle to give a brand a competitive advantage. There are three major ways to change existing products: quality modifications, functional modifications, and aesthetic modifications. Quality modifications are changes that relate to a product's dependability and durability. They usually are accomplished by altering materials or the production process. Changes that affect a product's versatility, effectiveness, convenience, or safety are called functional modifications and usually

    139

require redesigning one or more parts of the product. Aesthetic modifications change the sensory appeal of a product by altering its taste, texture, sound, smell, or visual characteristics.

Developing new products is frequently expensive and risky. The process involves seven phases. The first phase is idea generation, which is a more or less systematic approach for producing new product ideas. Those ideas can come from internal sources or sources outside the firm. Next, ideas are screened. Those with the greatest potential are selected; those that do not match organizational objectives or those with limited potential are rejected. The third phase, concept testing, involves having a small sample of potential buyers review a brief description of a product idea in order to determine their initial buying intentions and attitudes toward the new product. The fourth phase is a business analysis that provides a tentative sketch of a product's compatibility with the market-place, including its probable profitability. The next phase is product development, the primary purpose of which is to determine if it is technically possible to produce the product and if the product can be produced at costs low enough to result in a reason-able price. Development here extends beyond the actual product, to promotion, distri-bution, and price. The sixth phase of new-product development is test-marketing, a limited introduction of a product in areas chosen to represent the intended market, to determine the reactions of probable buyers. The last phase is commercialization, during which plans for full-scale manufacturing and marketing are refined and settled and budgets for the project are prepared. It is at this point that the product is finally in-troduced into the market. Commercialization is significantly easier when customers accept a product rapidly. The stages of the product adoption process are (1) awareness, (2) interest, (3) evaluation, (4) trial, and (5) adoption. Most products are introduced in stages, starting in a set of geographic areas and gradually expanding into adjacent areas.

Most new products start off slowly, seldom generating enough sales to produce profits immediately. During this time, marketers should be alert for product weaknesses, cor-recting them quickly to prevent the early death or crippling of demand. As the sales curve moves upward and the breakeven point is reached, the growth stage begins. Mar-keting strategy at this point must support the momentum of the growth stage. Product offerings can be expanded to appeal to different market segments. Gaps in the distribu-tion network should be filled. Promotion should stress brand benefits. And prices, once development costs have been recovered, can be lowered.

In the maturity stage of the product life cycle, marketers may need to adjust a product's quality or otherwise modify the product. They also must encourage dealers to support the product. In this stage, advertising focuses on brand differentiation, and pricing strategies become more mixed.

In the decline stage, a product's sales curve turns downward and profits continue to fall. At this point, marketers must determine when to eliminate a product. Usually a declining product has lost its distinctiveness, and marketers do little to change its style or design. Outlets with core sales are maintained; unprofitable outlets are weeded out. Promotion becomes less important during decline. And the fact that a product returns a profit may be more important to a firm than maintaining a certain market share through repricing.

Most products do not satisfy target market customers or contribute to an organiza-tion's goals indefinitely. Product elimination is the process of deleting weak products. Although some organizations drop weak products only after they have become severe financial burdens, a better approach involves a systematic review, in which each product is evaluated periodically to determine its impact on the overall effectiveness of the firm's product mix. There are several ways to eliminate a product, but basically it can be phased out, run out, or dropped immediately.

MATCHING EXERCISES

Use the following set of terms to identify the sentences and phrases below. On the blank line next to each sentence or phrase, place the letter of the term that the sentence or phrase describes. Do not use a term more than once.

a. Test marketing
b   Business analysis
c. Product elimination
d. Commercialization
e. Idea screening
f. Aesthetic modification
g. Product adoption process

h. Functional modification
i. Idea generation
j. Quality modification
k. New-product development
l. Product modification
m. Product development
n. Concept testing

_____ 1. The multistep process through which a buyer comes to accept a product; the stages of awareness, interest, evaluation, trial, and adoption. *Product Adoption Process*

_____ 2. A stage in the product development process in which the ideas that do not match organizational objectives are rejected and those with the greatest potential are selected for further development. *Idea Screening*

_____ 3. The search by businesses and other organizations for product ideas to help them achieve their objectives. *Idea Generation*

_____ 4. A stage in the development of a new product in which a product idea is assessed to determine its potential contribution to the organization's sales, costs, and profits. *Business analysis*

_____ 5. A change in one or more of a product's characteristics. *Product Modification*

_____ 6. The elimination of a product that no longer satisfies the target market or contributes to achievement of the organization's overall goals. *Product Elimination*

_____ 7. A change in a product that relates to its dependability and durability; usually executed by altering materials or the production process. *Quality Modification*

_____ 8. A phase of new-product development in which plans for full-scale manufacturing and marketing are refined and settled and budgets for the project are prepared. *Commercialization*

_____ 9. A change that affects a product's versatility, effectiveness, convenience, or safety; it usually requires the redesign of one or more parts of the product. *Functional modification*

_____ 10. The limited introduction of a product in areas chosen to represent the intended market, to determine probable buyers' reactions to various parts of the marketing mix. *Test Mktg*

Aesthetic Modification   11. A modification that changes the sensory appeal of a product by altering its taste, texture, sound, smell, or visual characteristics.

Concept Testing   12. The phase of product development in which a sample of potential buyers evaluate the product idea.

TRUE OR FALSE STATEMENTS

T   F   1. For product modification to be successful, existing customers must be able to perceive that a change has been made.

T   F   2. Quality modifications are changes that affect a product's versatility, effectiveness, convenience, or safety. *(dependability & durability)*

T   F   3. Aesthetic modifications change the sensory appeal of a product.

T   F   4. A weak product can generate unfavorable images that rub off onto some of the firm's other products.

T   F   5. Weak products should be deleted only after they have become severe financial burdens.

T   F   6. Products often fail because companies have not adequately considered consumers' reasons for buying.

T   F   7. New-product introduction is neither costly nor risky.

T   F   8. Idea generation is the first stage in developing and introducing a new product.

T   F   9. One purpose of screening ideas is to assess the firm's overall ability to produce and market a new product.

T   F   10. The primary purpose of the development phase is to provide a tentative sketch of a product's compatibility with the marketplace, including its probable profitability.

T   F   11. Test-marketing is the widespread introduction of a product to determine if it will sell.

T   F   12. The product adoption model uses promotion to create widespread awareness of a new product and its benefits.

T   F   13. Commercialization means the rapid introduction of a product on a national basis.

T   F   14. Gradual product introduction lets competitors enter the target market quickly with similar products.

T   F   15. In the growth stage, the momentum of increasing sales must be supported by adjustments in the marketing strategy.

T   F   16. The goal during the growth stage of a product's life cycle is to establish the product's position and encourage brand loyalty.

T F   17. Price always falls during the maturity stage.

T F   18. Salespersons usually object when a product with a loyal core market is dropped.

MULTIPLE-CHOICE QUESTIONS

_____   1. According to the text, to adjust to competition, a firm may do all of the following *except*
  a. modify competitors' products.
  b. introduce a new product.
  c. expand its product mix.
  d. eliminate products that were once successful.
  e. modify its existing products.

_____   2. Which approach for managing the product mix creates specific marketing strategies to achieve a balanced mix of products?
  a. Product portfolio approach
  b. Marketing data approach
  c. Multidimensional approach
  d. Product niche approach
  e. Variable capacity approach

_____   3. Acme Toy Company has decided to add reinforcing braces to its miniature wind-up cars. This is an example of _____ modification.
  a. functional
  b. quality
  c. price
  d. cost
  e. product development

_____   4. Changes in consumers' wants and needs can best be met by
  a. advertising extensively.
  b. lowering prices.
  c. adopting the product manager system.
  d. altering the marketing mix.
  e. increasing personal selling efforts.

_____   5. AT&T phones now offer call memory and automatic redial in addition to standard touch-tone dialing. These are examples of _____ modifications.
  a. quality
  b. aesthetic
  c. cost
  d. functional
  e. product development

_____ 6. Aesthetic modifications are directed at changing a product's
a. sensory appeal.
b. convenience or safety.
c. durability.
d. price.
e. quality.

_____ 7. Granny's Pie Company recently developed a flaky pie crust to be used n its apple and cherry pies. This change is a(n) _____ modification.
a. aesthetic
b. product development
c. functional
d. quality
e. cost

_____ 8. One purpose of the business analysis stage of new-product development is to
a. provide an early projection of probable profitability.
b. ascertain whether it is technically feasible to produce the product.
c. determine whether similar marketing channels, outlets, and promotional resources can be used.
d. test-market the product.
e. commercialize the product.

_____ 9. Which of the following is *not* a means for developing new product ideas inside the organization?
a. Rewards
b. Brainstorming
c. Management consultants
d. Incentives
e. Venture teams

_____ 10. The marketing team at Ivan's Ice Cream is working on developing a new flavor. One of the team members suggests putting together a checklist of critical factors before continuing the development process. Ivan's is in the _____ phase of new-product development.
a. business analysis
b. product development
c. screening
d. idea generation
e. concept testing

_____ 11. One purpose of idea screening is to
a. brainstorm for new ideas.
b. provide an early projection of economic payoffs.
c. secure consultants to provide ideas.
d. determine a product's compatibility with the marketplace.
e. determine how a product will affect sales, costs, and profits.

_____ 12. Frosty D-Lite Root Beer is considering developing a diet version of its popular beverage. Before performing any business analysis of the product, Frosty D-Lite marketers would like an initial response from potential customers to determine interest in a new diet root beer. Frosty D-Lite will begin _____ to gather this information.
   a. screening
   b. concept testing
   c. product development
   d. idea generation
   e. test marketing

_____ 13. Concept testing is a phase of product development in which
   a. marketers develop a prototype for a potential new market.
   b. a new product is test-marketed in a limited geographical area.
   c. marketers engage in brainstorming sessions to develop product ideas.
   d. a small sample of potential buyers are presented with a product idea in order to determine their attitudes regarding the product.
   e. the organization finds out if it is technically feasible to produce the product at a reasonable cost.

_____ 14. Chrysler has just completed a prototype of a new car it plans to introduce. The company is in the _____ stage of new-product development.
   a. concept testing
   b. test marketing
   c. commercialization
   d. business analysis
   e. product development

_____ 15. During the latter part of the development phase, marketers begin to make decisions regarding
   a. the potential geographic locations for test-marketing the product.
   b. how consumers feel about a product and how they would use it.
   c. branding, packaging, labeling, and pricing.
   d. the next two phases of new product development, test marketing and commercialization.
   e. manufacturing and marketing.

_____ 16. In several different geographic areas, Narcissus Cosmetics is experimenting with different advertising, pricing, and packaging approaches for its proposed new line of lipsticks. Narcissus is in the _____ stage of new-product development.
   a. business analysis
   b. concept testing
   c. screening
   d. test marketing
   e. commercialization

_____ 17. Test-marketing
   a. helps guarantee a product's success.
   b. is the unlimited introduction of a product into a geographic area.

     c. is a sample launching of the entire marketing mix for a product.

     d. should be conducted for all products.

     e. is usually inexpensive.

18. Commercialization does *not* involve
    a. jamming.
    b. full-scale distribution.
    c. final budget preparation.
    d. scheduling and coordination.
    e. finalizing the marketing program.

19. What percentage of new products introduced to the marketplace fail?
    a. 90 percent
    b. 65 percent
    c. 50 percent
    d. 15 percent
    e. 60 to 90 percent, depending on the estimate

20. The product adoption process consists of all the following stages *except*
    a. awareness.
    b. interest.
    c. evaluation.
    d. adoption.
    e. rejection.

21. Walter is in the market for a new car. He spends his entire Sunday afternoon reading the new car advertisements in the paper to see what deals are available. Walter is in the _____ stage of the product adoption process.
    a. adoption
    b. interest
    c. awareness
    d. evaluation
    e. trial

22. Gradual product introduction is used because it
    a. prevents competitors from monitoring new-product introduction.
    b. reduces the risk associated with introducing a new product.
    c. is less expensive than rapid product introduction.
    d. prevents competitors from entering the market with similar products.
    e. maximizes the effectiveness of the product mix.

23. In which of the following stages of product development is a product transformed into a working model?
    a. Screening
    b. Development
    c. Testing
    d. Business analysis
    e. Commercialization

24. Sales of ABC Corporation's digital audio tapes are rising rapidly, industry profits are peaking, and competitors are entering the market. ABC is able to maintain its market lead. Based on this example, the digital audio tape is in the _____ stage of the product life cycle.
    a. decline
    b. introduction
    c. growth
    d. evaluation
    e. maturity

25. During which of the following life cycle stages should marketers establish a market position and encourage brand loyalty?
    a. Introductory stage
    b. Growth stage
    c. Maturity stage
    d. Decline stage
    e. Development stage

26. During which stage of the product life cycle does the competitive situation usually stabilize?
    a. Introductory stage
    b. Growth stage
    c. Maturity stage
    d. Decline stage
    e. Development stage

27. During which stage of the product life cycle is advertising kept at a minimum?
    a. Development stage
    b. Introductory stage
    c. Growth stage
    d. Maturity stage
    e. Decline stage

28. A phaseout approach to eliminating a product
    a. exploits any strengths left in the product.
    b. lets weak products be dropped only after they have become severe financial burdens.
    c. lets the product decline without a change in the marketing strategy.
    d. is very likely to be used by most businesses.
    e. is the best strategy when losses are too great to justify prolonging the product's life.

29. General Mills has decided to eliminate one of its unprofitable cereal lines by letting it decline without changing the marketing strategy. This approach is known as a(n)
    a. deletion.
    b. runout.
    c. phaseout.
    d. product review.
    e. immediate drop.

_____ 30. A runout approach to eliminating a product
   a. lets the product decline without changing the marketing strategy.
   b. exploits any strengths left in the product.
   c. involves the sudden termination of an unprofitable product.
   d. lets weak products be dropped only after they have become severe financial burdens.
   e. is not likely to be used by most businesses.

_____ 31. Branson Electronics wants to eliminate several of its older models of hand-held calculators that have become obsolete. The company will most likely use a(n)_____ approach to eliminate the items.
   a. immediate drop
   b. runout
   c. systematic
   d. product review
   e. phaseout

_____ 32. When several studies were published claiming that Vitamin E could dramatically reduce wrinkles, Ryland Pharmaceuticals began producing the vitamin in capsule form. Sales remained strong until the publication of evidence that the earlier studies had greatly overstated the merits of Vitamin E. Ryland now finds itself taking heavy losses on the capsules. Therefore, Ryland is likely to adopt a(n) _____ approach to the product.
   a. deletion
   b. phaseout
   c. product review
   d. immediate drop
   e. runout

MINICASE: MRS. SMITH'S POTATO CHIPS

The Smith Company had an innovative idea: to process a potato chip that would stay fresh longer, break less often, and travel and store more conveniently than conventional potato chips. Smith's breakthrough was a processing method that forms potatoes into chips in much the same way that paper is made from wood pulp. The chips were pressure-cooked, packaged in crush-resistant canisters, and called Mrs. Smith's.

   An excellent marketing program introduced the chips in 1978. The product attracted many new customers because of its packaging and its novelty. At one point, Mrs. Smith's led in national market share, forcing Frito-Lay and other competitors to test-market their own version. But Mrs. Smith's lost its lead within eighteen months. One reason was the Smith Company's concentration on a unique packaging idea instead of on product attributes, which are significantly more important than packaging to consumers of potato chips. John Grey, a consumer products consultant and former Smith Company brand manager, said, "Mrs. Smith's tasted more like tennis balls than potato chips."

Also, consumers did not believe that they received as many chips in a Mrs. Smith's can as they were getting in bags of competing potato chips. The Smith Company tried to offset this misperception with intensive advertising that showed that a can of Mrs. Smith's and a bag of chips would each completely fill a snack bowl. To fight consumers' perception that Mrs. Smith's was too expensive, the Smith Company stressed that few broken chips and prolonged freshness made the chips a "great value." Consumers also thought of Mrs. Smith's as "unnatural"—just when the country was becoming increasingly diet conscious and "natural" foods were becoming the vogue. A major competitor exploited this consumer attitude with advertising that called attention to preservatives and additives contained in Mrs. Smith's. By 1987, the Smith Company began selling a reformulated Mrs. Smith's. The "new" product contained no preservatives or artificial ingredients and was available in three forms: regular, light, and rippled.

The 1990 campaign theme, "I've got the fever for the flavor of new Mrs. Smith's," helped revive the chips. In the first three months after the new promotion began running, Mrs. Smith's share of the $2 billion potato chip market grew to 5.5 percent from 4.5 percent. This encouraging improvement in market position came only after the Smith Company had adjusted its product image by incorporating within it the environmental changes that affect consumer acceptance. Now, with 5.5 percent of the market, Mrs. Smith's needs proper management if it is going to remain profitable.

Questions

_____ 1. In 1987, the reformulated Mrs. Smith's contained no preservatives or artificial ingredients. This reformulation represents a(n)
   a. quality modification.
   b. functional modification.
   c. aesthetic modification.
   d. product modification.
   e. product line extension.

_____ 2. Introducing light and rippled Mrs. Smith's is an example of a(n)
   a. quality modification.
   b. functional modification.
   c. aesthetic modification.
   d. product modification.
   e. product line extension.

_____ 3. In terms of the product adoption process, Mrs. Smith's initially was successful through the _____ stage.
   a. awareness
   b. interest
   c. evaluation
   d. trial
   e. adoption

_____ 4. The quick decline of Mrs. Smith's market share illustrates failure at what stage in the product adoption process?
a. Awareness
b. Interest
c. Evaluation
d. Trial
e. Adoption

_____ 5. Mrs. Smith's now appears to be in what stage of the product life cycle?
a. Developmental stage
b. Introduction stage
c. Growth stage
d. Maturity stage
e. Decline stage

_____ 6. What distribution strategy would seem most appropriate for Mrs. Smith's at this time?
a. Obtaining new distribution outlets
b. Making sure the system is running efficiently
c. Encouraging dealers to support Mrs. Smith's
d. Weeding out unprofitable outlets
e. Eliminating entire channels that do not contribute to profits

PROGRAMMED COMPLETION EXERCISES

develop, alter, maintain, product mix

1. To provide products that satisfy the firm's target market(s) and to achieve the organization's objectives, a marketer must be able to _____, _____, and _____ an effective _____ _____.

modifiable, perceive, modification, consistent, desires

2. Product modification can be effective under certain conditions: The product must be _____; existing customers must be able to _____ that a _____ has been made; and the modification should make the product more _____ with customers' _____.

Quality modifications, functional modifications, aesthetic modifications

3. The three major ways to modify products are _____ _____, _____ _____, and _____ _____.

product development
personnel, product
attributes, product
benefits

4. The results of concept testing can be used by _____ _____ _____ to better understand the _____ _____ and _____ _____ that are most important to potential customers.

consumes, time, re-
sources, new
products,
unfavorable images

5. A weak product not only costs the firm financially but _____ too much of a marketer's _____, reduces time and _____ available for developing _____ _____, and may generate _____ _____ among customers.

phased out, run out,
dropped immediately

6. A product can be eliminated in several ways: It can be _____ _____, _____ _____, or _____ _____.

idea generation,
screening, concept
testing, business
analysis, product
development, test
marketing,
commercialization

7. The seven phases of new-product development are _____ _____, _____, _____ _____, _____, _____, _____ _____, _____ _____, and _____.

ideas

8. New product _____ can be obtained from sources outside the firm, such as advertising agencies, management consulting firms, and private research organizations.

new product ideas

9. Screening _____ _____ _____ involves a general assessment of the organization's resources and attempts, through forecasting techniques, to make an early projection of economic payoffs.

sales, costs, profits

10. During the business analysis stage of product development, the product idea is evaluated to _____, _____, and _____.

technically feasible, low, price

11. The primary purpose of the product development phase is to ascertain whether it is _____ _____ to produce a product at costs _____ enough to result in a reasonable _____ .

test-marketing

12. A competitor may try to jam the _____ program by increasing advertising, lowering prices, and developing special retailer incentives.

commercialization, marketing

13. The _____ phase is equivalent to the early introductory period of the product life cycle; it involves plans for full-scale _____ of the product.

Awareness, interest, evaluation, trial, adoption

14. _____, _____, _____, _____, and _____ are the stages that buyers go through in accepting a product.

growth, distribution network (marketing channels)

15. During the _____ stage, gaps in the _____ _____ should be filled.

profits, product mix

16. A business can justify maintaining a product as long as it contributes to _____ or enhances the overall effectiveness of a _____ _____ .

Phasing out, running out, dropping immediately

17. _____ _____ . _____ _____, or _____ _____ are the three basic ways to eliminate products.

growth

18. During the _____ period of the product life cycle, the tendency is to move from exclusive or selective exposure to a more extensive distribution network.

modification,
rejuvenation

19. The marketing strategy for a mature product can involve product _____ or _____ through packaging, new models, or style changes.

ANSWERS TO OBJECTIVE QUESTIONS

Matching		*True or False*		*Multiple-Choice*		*Minicase*
1. g	7. j	1. T	10. F	1. a	17. c	1. a
2. e	8. d	2. F	11. F	2. a	18. a	2. e
3. i	9. h	3. T	12. T	3. b	19. e	3. e
4. b	10. a	4. T	13. F	4. d	20. e	4. e
5. l	11. f	5. F	14. T	5. d	21. b	5. d
6. c	12. n	6. T	15. T	6. a	22. b	6. c
		7. F	16. T	7. a	23. b	
		8. T	17. F	8. a	24. c	
		9. T	18. T	9. c	25. b	
				10. c	26. c	
				11. b	27 e	
				12. b	28. c	
				13. d	29. c	
				14. e	33. b	
				15. c	31. b	
				16. d	32. d	

10 BRANDING AND PACKAGING

CHAPTER OUTLINE

Branding
    Benefits of branding
    Types of brands
    Selecting a brand name
    Protecting a brand
    Branding policies
    Brand licensing
Packaging
    Packaging functions
    Major packaging considerations
    Packaging and marketing strategy
    Criticisms of packaging
Labeling

CHAPTER SUMMARY

A brand identifies a seller's product and differentiates it from competitors' products through the use of a name, term, design, symbol, or any other feature. A brand name is that part of a brand that can be spoken—letters, words, or numbers. The element of a brand that cannot be spoken (a symbol, a design) is called a brand mark. A trademark is a legal designation indicating that the owner has exclusive use of a brand or part of a brand and that others are prohibited by law from using it. A trade name is the legal name of an organization, not of a specific product. Buyers benefit from branding because it identifies a manufacturer or company whose products buyers may or may not like. Brands thus help facilitate the purchase process. Sellers benefit from branding because it facilitates repeat purchases. In addition, branding facilitates promotional efforts because each branded product indirectly promotes all the firm's products that are branded similarly. Manufacturer brands are initiated by producers and identify producers with their products at the point of purchase. Private distributor brands, or private brands, are initiated and owned by resellers. A generic brand indicates only the product category and does not include the company name or other identifying terms.

    Marketers should choose a brand name that is easy to say, spell, and recall. If possible, the brand name should allude to the product's uses, benefits, or special characteristics in a positive way. To protect the firm's exclusive rights to a brand, the company should be certain that a selected brand name does not infringe on brands already registered with the U.S. Patent Office. Also, a firm must guard against a brand name becoming a generic term—a term used to refer to a general product category—because generic terms cannot be protected as exclusive brand names.

In establishing branding policies, the first decision is whether the firm should brand its products at all. When an organization's product is homogeneous and similar to competitors' products, it may be difficult to brand. Assuming that a firm chooses to brand its products, marketers may opt for one or more of the following policies: individual branding, overall family branding, line family branding, or brand-extension branding. In individual branding, every product is named differently. In overall family branding, all of a firm's products are branded with the same name or at least part of the same name. In line family branding, the same brand is used only for products within the same line. In brand-extension branding, a firm uses one of its existing brand names as part of a brand for an improved or a new product that is usually in the same product category as the existing brand. Marketers are not limited to a single branding policy. An organization's branding policies are influenced by the number of products and product lines, target markets, the number and type of competing products, and available resources.

A growing number of companies are participating in brand licensing; that is, they let approved manufacturers use their trademark on other products for a licensing fee. Advantages include extra revenue, free publicity, and trademark protection. Disadvantages are lack of manufacturing control and an excess of unrelated products bearing the same name.

Packaging involves the development of a container and a graphic design for a product. Buyers' impression of a product at the point of purchase or during use can be influenced greatly by packaging characteristics. A package performs the function of product protection, convenience, and promotion. Marketers must consider many factors when developing packages. One major consideration is cost. Marketers should try to determine how much customers are willing to pay for packages that are more protective, convenient, safe, or attractive. Another consideration is whether to package a product in single or multiple units. When developing packaging (existing organization) marketers should consider whether continuity among package designs is desirable. Packaging is also a promotional device, attracting buyers' attention and providing product information. Verbal and nonverbal symbols describe the product's content, features, uses, advantages, and hazards. A firm can create desirable images and associations by using certain sizes, shapes, textures, colors, and graphics. Other considerations include how to make the package tamper-resistant, whether to use multiple packaging and family packaging, how to design the package as an effective promotional tool, how best to accommodate middlemen, and whether to develop environmentally responsible packaging.

Packaging can be a major component of a marketing strategy. An effective package can give a firm a competitive edge. For established brands, marketers should keep package designs up-to-date. Packaging policies should also take into account middlemen's transporting, storing, and handling needs.

Labeling is an important product feature, not only for promotional and informational purposes but for legal ones as well. Federal agencies and laws now require that certain products be labeled with warnings, instructions, certifications, manufacturer identifications, and content information. Labels can be used to encourage proper use, which can increase consumers' satisfaction with a product, or to promote a manufacturer's other products.

MATCHING EXERCISES

Use the following set of terms to identify the sentences and phrases below. On the blank line next to each sentence or phrase, place the letter of the term that the sentence or phrase describes. Do not use a term more than once.

a. Labeling
b. Family packaging
c. Brand-extension branding
d. Brand name
e. Overall family branding
f. Trademark
g. Manufacturer brand
h. Universal product code

i. Trade name
j. Line family branding
k. Individual branding
l. Brand
m. Brand mark
n. Generic brand
o. Private distributor brand

_____ 1. The element of a brand, such as a symbol or design, that cannot be spoken. *Brand Mark*

_____ 2. The legal name of an organization. *Trade Name*

_____ 3. A policy in which all of a firm's products are branded with the same name or at least a part of the same name. *Overall Family*

_____ 4. A branding policy in which an organization uses family branding only for products within a line, not for all its products. *Line Family Brandi*

_____ 5. A branding policy in which each product is named differently. *Individual Branding*

_____ 6. A legal designation indicating that the owner has exclusive use of a brand or part of a brand and that others are prohibited by law from using it. *Trademark*

_____ 7. The part of a brand that can be spoken, including letters, words, and numbers. *Brand Name*

_____ 8. A type of branding in which a firm uses one of its existing brand names as part of a brand for an improved or a new product that is usually in the same product category as the existing brand. *Brand-extension*

_____ 9. A brand initiated by a producer; it makes it possible for a producer to be identified with its product at the point of purchase. *Mfgr Brand*

_____ 10. A name, term, symbol, design, or combination of these that identifies a seller's products and differentiates them from competitors' products. *Brand*

_____ 11. A brand that indicates the product category only and does not include the company name. *Generic*

_____ 12. A brand that is initiated and owned by a reseller. *Private (distributor)*

_____ 13. An organizational policy of making all packaging similar or including one major element in the design. *Family Pkgg.*

_____ 14.ᵃ An element closely related to packaging that facilitates the identification of a product by presenting the brand and a unique graphic design. *Labeling*

_____ 15.ⁿ Part of a product label; it consists of a series of thick and thin lines that identify a product and provide inventory and pricing information.

Universal Product Code

TRUE OR FALSE STATEMENTS

T   F   1. A brand is a name, term, symbol, design, or combination of these that identifies a seller's products and differentiates them from competitors' products.

T   F   2. Manufacturer brands give retailers higher gross profit margins than do private brands.

T   F   3. Branding primarily benefits the sellers of a product.

T   F   4. Private distributor brands identify the product's manufacturer.

T   F   5. A marketer should work to have a brand name become a generic term.

T   F   6. In overall family branding, each product is branded differently.

T   F   7. The primary function of packaging is to promote a product.

T   F   8. Product packaging—a unique closure, more durable container, size—can give a firm a competitive advantage in the market.

T   F   9. When labeling a product, a manufacturer must consider promotional, informational, and legal implications.

T   F   10. Branding plays a significant role in differentiating a product.

T   F   11. Green Giant, Levi's Jeans, and Apple Computer are private distributor brands.

T   F   12. Private brand labels are bought mostly by low-income shoppers.

T   F   13. A package can influence customers' attitudes toward a product and so affect their purchase decisions.

T   F   14. A brand helps to reduce a buyer's perceived risk of purchase.

T   F   15. Branding has a detrimental effect on buyers.

T   F   16. Retailers and wholesalers use manufacturer brands to develop more efficient promotion and to improve store images.

T   F   17. Private distributor brands now account for slightly over 82 percent of all retail grocery sales.

T   F   18. Cigarette smokers are highly brand loyal.

T   F   19.   Margarine containers, jelly jars, and L'eggs eggs are examples of secondary-use packages.

T   F   20.   Brand extensions have lower product introduction costs and better chances for success than new product introductions.

T   F   21.   Of the 22 best-selling brands from 1925 or before, three still lead their product categories.

MULTIPLE-CHOICE QUESTIONS

_____   1.   A brand name is
   a.   that part of a brand which can be spoken.
   b.   the element of a brand that consists of a symbol or design.
   c.   a legal designation indicating that the owner has exclusive use of a brand.
   d.   the full and legal name of an organization, rather than the name of a specific product.
   e.   required by federal law for all products.

_____   2.   Brands help buyers in all the following ways *except*
   a.   identifying specific products a buyer likes or does not like.
   b.   assisting buyers in evaluating the quality of products.
   c.   providing buyers with psychological rewards.
   d.   making product selection a random process.
   e.   helping buyers to avoid products that they do not like.

_____   3.   Which is an example of a suggestive brand type?
   a.   Dr. Pepper
   b.   Minute Rice
   c.   Aluminum Foil
   d.   Exxon
   e.   Spray 'N Wash

_____   4.   Borden Vitamin D Milk would be classified as a _____ brand, while Kroger Vitamin D Milk would be classified as a _____ brand.
   a.   manufacturer; generic
   b.   private; dealer
   c.   private distributor; store
   d.   dealer; store
   e.   manufacturer; private distributor

_____   5.   Which of the following statements about manufacturer and private distributor brands is true?
   a.   Manufacturer brands are becoming more popular.
   b.   There is no competition between manufacturer and private brands.
   c.   Manufacturers are developing multiple brands and distribution systems.

d. Consumers are buying fewer private distributor brands.

e. The market shares for manufacturer and private brands are about equal.

6. Howard Archer is responsible for choosing the name for a new trucking company that is about be launched. The company initially will serve customers on the West Coast, primarily in California. Which of the following should Howard choose, based on the criteria for naming service organizations?
a. Western Transport
b. California Transport
c. Reliance Company
d. Western Trucking
e. Reliance Trucking

7. Lever Brothers gives each product in its line of soaps a different name, such as Lever 2000, Dove, Shield, Lux, Lifebuoy, and Camay. This strategy is known as _____ branding.
a. line family
b. segment
c. overall family
d. brand-extension
e. individual

8. Healthy Choice packages all its foods in an attractive dark green color. This is an example of _____ packaging.
a. multiple
b. family
c. brand-extension
d. line
e. coordinated

9. Gillette produces a line of men's shaving products, including razors, shaving cream, and after-shave, all of which carry the Gillette brand. This is an example of a(n) _____ branding strategy.
a. segment
b. brand-extension
c. overall family
d. line family
e. individual

10. This branding policy occurs when a firm uses one of its existing brand names as part of a brand for an improved or a new product that is usually in the same product category as the existing brand.
a. Individual branding
b. Brand-extension branding
c. Line family branding
d. Overall family branding
e. Continuous branding

_____ 11. Which of the following is *least* likely to be the goal in a retailer's decision to use a private distributor brand?
   a. To purchase products of a specified quality at the lowest cost
   b. To promote a manufacturer
   c. To develop an efficient promotion scheme
   d. To generate higher gross profit margins
   e. To improve a store's image

_____ 12. The choice of a branding policy is influenced by all the following *except*
   a. the number of products and product lines produced by the firm.
   b. target market characteristics.
   c. package size.
   d. the extent of the firm's resources.
   e. the number and types of competing products available.

_____ 13. Coca-Cola's biggest reason for licensing its trademark for use on glassware, radios, trucks, and clothing was to
   a. diversify.
   b. increase revenues.
   c. protect its trademark.
   d. enter the consumer goods market.
   e. gain manufacturing control.

_____ 14. Which of these is *not* an advantage a brand extension has over a new product introduction?
   a. Consumers, reassured by a proven brand, are more likely to try a related newcomer.
   b. Product innovation is more likely.
   c. Cost of advertising and promotion is about one-third less.
   d. Success is more likely.
   e. Cost of test marketing is reduced.

_____ 15. Packaging design directly involves all the following *except*
   a. labeling.
   b. the inclusion of one or more units in a package.
   c. cost considerations.
   d. production.
   e. decisions about colors.

_____ 16. Which of the following statements about labeling is false?
   a. Labels can be used to promote the manufacturer's other products.
   b. Labels can encourage proper use of products.
   c. Labels are primarily promotional devices and provide little useful information.
   d. Content labeling can be required by federal law.
   e. Labels are attention-getting devices.

_____ 17. A package does *not* have the ability to
   a. make a product more versatile.
   b. make a product safer.
   c. make a product easier to use.

d. influence customers' attitudes toward a product.

e. improve product quality.

_____ 18. To promote an overall company image, a firm may decide that all packages are to be similar or that one major element of the design will be included in all packages. This approach is called

a. family promotion.

b. line family branding.

c. overall family packaging.

d. family packaging.

e. overall branding.

_____ 19. When the Sunshine Ice Cream company became concerned that its cartons did not stand out in the freezer case next to those of competitors, they hired a consultant. The consultant recommended redesigning the package with _____ to make Sunshine's product appear larger than those of its competitors.

a. vertical lines

b. darker colors

c. horizontal lines

d. pastel colors

e. diagonal lines

_____ 20. Packaging should be viewed as a major strategic tool, especially for

a. consumer convenience products.

b. durable goods.

c. industrial products.

d. big-ticket items.

e. power tools.

_____ 21. Cool Whip has made its product more desirable by using

a. a "tamper proof" package.

b. secondary-use packaging.

c. an environmentally responsible package.

d. a squeeze bottle for convenience.

e. a brightly colored package to catch the consumer's eye.

_____ 22. Greg Hoskins works in the marketing department of a firm that produces disposable tableware, including Styrofoam plates and cups and plastic eating utensils. He recently presented his supervisor with a proposal to sell "picnic-paks"—assortments of plates, cups, and utensils packaged in shrink wrap and sold as a unit. Greg's boss showed strong support for picnic paks but insisted on an alternative to shrink wrap. As she put it, "While shrink wrap is cost-effective, our company doesn't need any more criticism about a lack of concern for

a. functionality.

b. safety.

c. economical packaging.

d. the environment.

e. convenience.

_____   23. Procter & Gamble markets Downy fabric softener in concentrated form. In doing this, Procter & Gamble was motivated by
a. reduced costs.
b. convenience to the customer.
c. environmental concerns.
d. increased availability.
e. increased consumer awareness.

_____   24. If Heinz Ketchup were to switch from its plastic squeeze bottle back to the traditional glass bottle, the switch would be motivated by _____ concerns.
a. safety
b. environmental
c. design
d. convenience
e. distribution

_____   25. Mrs. Norton has been saving plastic milk cartons for five months so that the first-graders in her class can use them to make bird feeders. For Mrs. Norton, the cartons would be termed _____ packaging.
a. secondary-use
b. category-consistent
c. multiple
d. innovative
e. handling-improved

_____   26. Using traditional package shapes and color combinations to ensure that customers will recognize a new product as being in a specific product category is an example of
a. category-consistent packaging.
b. generic branding.
c. family branding.
d. secondary-use packaging.
e. global packaging.

_____   27. Chuck's Condiments has decided to introduce mayonnaise into its product mix. Bernie Maxwell, a newcomer to the company's marketing department, wants to package the product in a squeezable flip-top bottle to distinguish Chuck's Mayonnaise from competitors. The marketing director rejects Bernie's suggestion, noting that experience has shown a(n) _____ package sells mayonnaise most effectively.
a. innovative
b. multiple
c. secondary-use
d. category-consistent
e. handling-improved

_____ 28. If Quaker Oats were to change its traditionally cylindrical package to a square shape for the sake of shelf display and shipping efficiency, the company would be following a(n) packaging strategy.
   a. category-consistent
   b. innovative
   c. handling-improved
   d. multiple
   e. secondary-use

MINICASE: ELEGANT FRAGRANCES

Elegant Fragrances (EF) was founded in 1950 by Samuel Garrison, a postwar immigrant from southern France. Mr. Garrison brought his twenty-two years of experience in the fragrance industry to the United States with the dream of owning his own business. Now, over forty years later, EF is known worldwide as a high-quality producer of only the finest colognes and perfumes. Traditionally, EF positions its products in the upscale market and to the well-to-do consumer. Its products, found in top-of-the-line specialty shops and in such fine department stores as Saks Fifth Avenue and Bloomingdales, are very expensive, averaging $100 per ounce, a markup of up to 1000 percent.

The flagship brand, Elegance, was EF's first product in 1950 and has been highly successful from the start. EF's sales were $300,000 in the first year, with net income of $27,000. Elegance made up 80 percent of sales and 82 percent of net income. For the current year, EF's sales are projected to be above $30 million, and Elegance should make up approximately 20 percent of those sales. Today, EF produces twenty-three products, including Elegant Lady, Debonair Man, and Desire. Many of these products, sixteen of which are for women, have the word *elegant* in the title.

EF is considering a new line of perfume, targeted at the average woman who wants a special fragrance for a special occasion. This would be a gift to herself, not to be worn every day. The firm is attempting to increase sales through a new market segment without damaging its "only the best" image. Two brand names being considered are Elegant Evening and Elegance II.

Questions

_____ 1. If Elegant Fragrances were to introduce this special-occasion fragrance under the brand name "Elegance II," it would be using _____ branding.
   a. brand-extension
   b. brand license
   c. individual
   d. generic
   e. repositioning

_____ 2. Elegant Fragrances is using multiple branding policies. Many of its products have the word *elegant* in the title. This is _____ branding.
   a. generic
   b. individual
   c. overall family
   d. trademark
   e. fanciful

_____ 3. If Elegant Fragrances were to produce "Desire" in a small, one-ounce bottle for the traveler in addition to the regular size, it would be using _____ branding.
   a. brand-extension
   b. overall family
   c. description
   d. line family
   e. category

_____ 4. Fred Wilmington, vice-president of marketing, has proposed that Elegant Fragrances put every product in a carriage-shaped package. This approach is called _____ packaging.
   a. multiple
   b. tamper-proof
   c. family
   d. secondary-use
   e. category-consistent

PROGRAMMED COMPLETION EXERCISES

name, term, symbol, design

1. A brand is a _____, _____, _____, or _____ or a combination of these, that identifies a seller's products.

generic brand,

2. A _____ _____ indicates only the product category and does not include the company name.

trademark, brand, prohibited

3. A _____ is a legal designation indicating that the owner has exclusive use of a _____ and that others are _____ by law from using it.

Manufacturer

4. _____ brands are initiated by the producer and enable the producer to be identified with the product at the point of purchase.

private distributor

5. Retailers and wholesalers use _____ _____ brands to achieve more efficient promotion and higher gross margins and to improve store images.

Resellers, manufacturers

6. _____ and _____ are competing to determine who will control brand names.

individual branding, overall family branding, line family branding, brand-extension branding

7. Assuming a firm chooses to brand its products, marketers may use one or more branding policies, including _____ _____, _____ _____ _____, _____ _____ _____, and _____ _____.

customer loyalty

8. When a firm develops some degree of _____ _____ to a brand, it can charge a premium price for the product.

promotion, quality control, guarantees

9. Brand loyalty is created by _____, _____ _____, and _____.

line family, brand-extension

10. With _____ _____ branding, all products carry the same name, but with _____ branding, this is not the case.

protection, convenience, promotion

11. Packaging as a marketing activity is concerned with _____, _____, and _____.

demand

12. A package performs a promotional function if its characteristics help stimulate _____.

Multiple, increase   13. _____ packaging is likely to _____ demand because it increases the amount of the product available at the point of consumption.

recycling   14. Procter & Gamble and Unilever are making products with a green spot that indicates their packaging is part of a _____ system.

label, information   15. The _____ is that part of a product that carries _____ about the product or the seller; it may be part of a package, or it may be attached to the product.

multiple   16. Six-packs are an example of _____ packaging.

promotional, informational, legal   17. Labeling is an important aspect of packaging for _____, _____, and _____ reasons.

ANSWERS TO OBJECTIVE QUESTIONS

Matching		*True or False*		*Multiple-Choice*		*Minicase*
1. m	9. g	1. T	12. F	1. a	15. d	1. a
2. i	10. l	2. F	13. T	2. d	16. c	2. c
3. e	11. n	3. F	14. T	3. e	17. e	3. d
4. j	12. o	4. F	15. F	4. e	18. d	4. c
5. k	13. b	5. F	16. F	5. c	19. a	
6. f	14. a	6. F	17. F	6. c	20. a	
7. d	15. h	7. F	18. T	7. e	21. b	
8. c		8. T	19. T	8. b	22. d	
		9. T	20. T	9. d	23. c	
		10. T	21. F	10. b	24. b	
		11. F		11. b	25. a	
				12. c	26. a	
				13. c	27. d	
				14. b	28. c	

11 MARKETING CHANNELS

CHAPTER OUTLINE

The structures and types of marketing channels
    Channels for consumer products
    Channels for business-to-business products
    Multiple marketing channels
Justifications for intermediaries
Functions of intermediaries
    Sorting out
    Accumulation
    Allocation
    Assorting
Channel integration
    Vertical channel integration
    Horizontal channel integration
Intensity of market coverage
    Intensive distribution
    Selective distribution
    Exclusive distribution
Selection of distribution channels
    Organizational objectives and resources
    Market characteristics
    Buyer behavior
    Product attributes
    Environmental forces
Behavior of channel members
    Channel cooperation
    Channel conflict
    Channel leadership
Legal issues in channel management
    Dual distribution
    Restricted sales territories
    Tying contracts
    Exclusive dealing
    Refusal to deal

CHAPTER SUMMARY

Distribution, a major component of the marketing mix, is the process of making products available to consumers. A channel of distribution, or marketing channel, is a group of interrelated intermediaries who perform the activities necessary to direct products to customers. There are two major types of marketing intermediaries: Merchants take title to products and resell them; functional middlemen do not take title. Each member of a marketing channel holds a different responsibility within the system. The effectiveness of a system thus depends on the cooperation of all its members.

Channel structure defines the arrangement and relationships of units in the distribution system. Marketing channels are classified generally as channels for consumer products or channels for business-to-business products. Producer to wholesaler to retailer to consumer is a typical channel structure for consumer products. Because business-to-business products are used in the production of other products, retailers are seldom a part of their distribution channels. Agents, however, often are used in channels for business-to-business products when those products are standardized and when selling functions and information gathering are important. Because the consumer is the ultimate concern in designing a marketing channel, different channels may be needed to reach diverse markets or unique market segments.

The press, consumers, public officials, and marketers themselves have raised questions about the costs of intermediaries. Consumers in particular believe that the fewer the intermediaries, the lower the price—that the shorter a distribution channel, the better. But critics who suggest that eliminating wholesalers would lead to lower prices do not understand that eliminating wholesalers would not do away with the services they provide. Those services would still have to be performed, and consumers would still have to pay for them.

The basic services that intermediaries perform are sorting out, accumulating, allocating, and assorting products for buyers. Through these activities, the channel resolves discrepancies in quantity and assortment. That is, the channel makes mass distribution possible while satisfying consumers' different wants and needs. The number of intermediaries in a distribution system, and their responsibilities, are determined by the necessary assortments and the efficiency of channel operations.

Many marketing channels are determined by consensus: Producers and intermediaries coordinate their efforts for the general good. Other marketing channels are organized and controlled by a channel leader: a producer, a wholesaler, or a retailer. The channel leader establishes policies and coordinates development of the marketing mix. The various units in the channel can be combined or integrated either vertically or horizontally. Vertical integration combines two or more stages of the channel under one management. Horizontal integration combines institutions at the same level of channel operation under a single management. Channel integration can stabilize supply, reduce costs, and increase coordination.

The intensity of market coverage is a critical component of channel design. To achieve the wanted intensity, distribution must correspond to buyers' behavior patterns and to the products they buy. Intensive distribution is used for convenience products; it uses all available outlets to distribute a product. Selective distribution is used for shopping products; it uses only certain outlets in an area. Exclusive distribution is used for specialty products; it limits distribution to just one outlet in a large geographic area.

Selecting distribution channels is a complex procedure. Producers must choose intermediaries with care, not only by evaluating sales and performances but by examining other influencing factors. A producer must first consider what it wants to accomplish and the amount of resources necessary to reach its goals. A producer must also examine market characteristics such as geography and market density. Next, a producer must understand how buyer behavior influences channel selection. Product attributes such as perishability and technical complexity should also be considered. Finally, a producer's choice of intermediary will be influenced by environmental forces, such as economic conditions and technology.

A marketing channel is a social system. Each member of that system has a unique role and specific responsibilities that contribute to the effectiveness of the system. Cooperation is critical: The failure of one link in the chain could destroy the channel. Roles are the means of integrating and coordinating system members and activities. Actual or perceived deviation from a role is a major source of channel conflict. The ability of one channel member to facilitate or hinder the achievement of the system's overall goals is a measure of that member's power. Power can be based on authority, coercion, rewards, referents, or expertise. Leadership is a power relationship within the system, and any of its members can assume it.

Producers' attempts to control distribution functions may have legal repercussions. Several channel management practices are often subject to legal restraint, depending on whether the practices strengthen or weaken competition and free trade. Dual distribution occurs when a producer sells the same product through two or more channel structures. Producers may attempt to restrict sales territories to tighten control over product distribution. Tying contracts exist when a supplier furnishes products to a channel member with the stipulation that the channel member also purchase other products from the producer. Exclusive dealing occurs when a producer forbids an intermediary to carry products of competing manufacturers. Finally, refusal to deal is the producers' right to choose the channel members with whom they will do business.

MATCHING EXERCISES

Use the following set of terms to identify the sentences and phrases below. On the blank line next to each sentence or phrase, place the letter of the term that the sentence or phrase describes. Do not use a term more than once.

a. Selective distribution
b. Retailers
c. Assorting
d. Accumulation
e. Marketing channel
f. Channel power
g. Vertical marketing system
h. Channel of distribution
i. Channel leadership
j. Vertical channel integration

k. Marketing intermediary
l. Channel cooperation
m. Horizontal channel integration
n. Merchant wholesalers
o. Allocation
p. Channel conflict
q. Exclusive distribution
r. Functional middlemen
s. Assortment
t. Intensive distribution

u. Sorting out
v. Sorting activities
w. Exclusive dealing

x. Tying contracts
y. Dual distribution
z. Direct channel

_s_ 1. A combination of products put together to provide benefits. *Assortment*

_b_ 2. Marketing intermediaries who purchase products for the purpose of reselling them to ultimate consumers. *Retailers*

_g_ 3. A type of market coverage in which only one outlet is used in a relatively large geographic area. *Exclusive Distribution*

_o_ 4. Breaking down large, homogeneous inventories into smaller lots. *Allocation*

_p_ 5. Friction among channel members that often results from role deviance or malfunction. *Channel Conflict*

_c_ 6. Combining products into collections or assortments that buyers want to have available at one place. *Assorting*

_a_ 7. A form of market coverage in which only some available outlets in an area are chosen to distribute a product. *Selective Distribution*

_m_ 8. Combining institutions at the same level of operation under one management. *Horizontal Channel Integration*

_j_ 9. Combining two or more stages of a marketing channel under one management. *Vertical Channel integration*

_d_ 10. The development of an inventory of homogeneous products that have similar production or demand requirements. *Accumulation*

_t_ 11. A form of market coverage in which all available outlets are used for distributing a product. *Intensive Distribution*

_k_ 12. A member of a marketing channel (primarily a merchant or functional middleman) who performs the activities necessary to direct products to buyers. *Mktg Intermediary*

_u_ 13. The first step in developing an assortment; it involves separating conglomerates of heterogeneous products into relatively uniform, homogeneous groups. *Sorting Out*

_n_ 14. A marketing intermediary who takes title to products and resells them for a profit. *Merchant Wholesaler*

_n_ 15. A group of individuals and organizations that direct products from producers to customers. *Channel of Distribution*

_f_ 16. The ability of one channel member to influence the goal achievement of another channel member. *Channel Power*

_v_ 17. The way channel members divide roles and separate tasks, including the roles of sorting out, accumulating, allocating, and assorting products. *Sorting Activities*

_e_ 18. A helping relationship among channel members that enhances the welfare and survival of all channel members. *Channel Cooperation*

r 19. Marketing intermediaries who do not take title to products. *Functional middlemen*

L 20. Guidance provided by channel members with one or more sources of power to other channel members to help achieve channel objectives. *Channel leadership*

l 21. Another term for channel of distribution. *Mktg Channel*

g 22. A marketing channel in which channel activities are coordinated by a single channel member to achieve efficient, low-cost distribution. *Vertical Mktg System*

X 23. Furnishing a product to a channel member with the stipulation that the channel member purchase additional products. *Tying contracts*

Y 24. Selling similar products through different channels under different brand names. *Dual Distribution*

W 25. An arrangement in which a manufacturer forbids an intermediary to carry products of competing manufacturers. *Exclusive dealing*

TRUE OR FALSE STATEMENTS

T F 1. As the length of a marketing channel increases, there are fewer opportunities for intermediaries.

T F 2. Intermediaries deal with the general need for distribution.

T F 3. Channel functions cannot be passed on to buyers or performed by producers.

T F 4. Intermediaries play a minor role in marketing channel systems.

T F 5. Manufacturers may use multiple marketing channels to reach different target markets.

T F 6. A marketing channel is a system of unrelated functions that expedite the distribution of goods.

T F 7. Producers may be willing to supply products and consumers may be willing to buy them, but no transactions can take place unless a relationship between sellers and buyers is facilitated.

T F 8. Agents and brokers are the chief types of merchants.

T F 9. Agents take title to merchandise and resell it.

T F 10. A distribution network helps overcome discrepancies in quantity and quality.

T F 11. Any sequence of interrelated intermediaries from producers to final users or consumers is called a marketing channel.

T F 12. Channel leadership is involved primarily with whether a product is new to the marketplace.

T F 13. Channel decisions have little to do with product availability.

T F 14. The various links of a channel can be brought together by vertical integration.

T F 15. Horizontal integration is accomplished by combining the leadership of several institutions.

T F 16. Manufacturers of consumer packaged goods rely on selective distribution.

T F 17. Combining various links in the marketing channel always increases efficiency.

T F 18. As the channel moves from intensive to exclusive distribution, it gives up exposure in return for some other advantage—including greater dealer control of the channel.

T F 19. Channel power is measured by the ability of a member in a channel to facilitate or hinder the attainment of the channel's overall goals.

T F 20. All channel efforts must be oriented toward understanding and serving buyers.

T F 21. Wholesaler channel leaders include Sears, J. C. Penney, and K mart.

T F 22. More and more retailers are functioning as channel leaders.

T F 23. Merchants expedite exchanges for a commission or fee.

T F 24. Selecting appropriate distribution channels is usually a simple process.

T F 25. Market density is one factor that influences channel selection.

T F 26. When a given channel management practice strengthens weak competitors or increases competition, the courts usually consider it illegal.

T F 27. Federal, state, and local laws regulate channel management to promote competition and free trade.

MULTIPLE-CHOICE QUESTIONS

_____ 1. Intermediaries, especially large-scale retailers, can create marketing channel conflict by demanding
a. large discounts.
b. special promotional allowances.
c. special shipping arrangements.
d. protection against price changes.
e. all of the above.

_____ 2. Of the following, the most important dimension of a marketing channel is the
a. number of retailers involved.
b. total amount of goods distributed.
c. number of activities performed at a particular stage.
d. economic environment.
e. amount of vertical integration.

_____ 3. What type of integration brings together the processes and functions of two or more stages of the channel under one management?
   a. Conventional
   b. Vertical
   c. Traditional
   d. Horizontal
   e. Concentric

_____ 4. The Bellmark Corporation recently purchased Walls Distributing, a wholesaling operation in BellMark's channel of distribution. BellMark now controls all the channel functions from production to warehousing, to distribution to final consumers. What type of change has BellMark's marketing channel undergone?
   a. Vertical channel dispersion
   b. Vertical channel integration
   c. Horizontal channel integration
   d. Horizontal channel dispersion
   e. A vertical leveraged buyout

_____ 5. Radson Distribution, Inc., a wholesaler of plants, trees, and shrubbery, just finished buying the last remaining wholesaler in its distribution channel. By combining all of its holdings, Radson now controls all plant wholesaling operations in the southwestern United States. What type of change has Radson's marketing channel undergone?
   a. Vertical channel dispersion
   b. Vertical channel integration
   c. Horizontal channel integration
   d. Horizontal channel disperson
   e. A horizontal leveraged buyout

_____ 6. Horizontal channel integration can reduce costs because
   a. the combined units operate more efficiently than independent institutions.
   b. the market is made more heterogeneous.
   c. a number of institutions are combined under a common management.
   d. the functions of an intermediary are performed at some other channel level.
   e. government regulations protect independent institutions.

_____ 7. Changes in which of the following would have the *most* profound effect on the structure of a marketing channel?
   a. Industrial technology
   b. Marketing technology
   c. Consumer purchase patterns
   d. Wholesaling
   e. Integrative technology

_____   8. Channel leadership is based on control over many factors. According to
the text, which of the following is *not* one of them?
a. Products
b. Markets
c. Technology
d. Knowledge about markets
e. Consumer behavior

_____   9. Retailers can be all the following *except*
a. merchants.
b. agents.
c. marketing channel members.
d. wholesalers.
e. channel leaders.

_____ 10. Which of the following terms describes a wholesaler who receives a commission or fee for expediting exchanges?
a. Merchant
b. Agent
c. Channel leader
d. Negotiation merchant
e. Specialty wholesaler

_____ 11. Which of the following terms can be used to describe the marketing
channel?
a. Channel of distribution
b. Communication channel
c. Promotional channel
d. Trade flow
e. Vertical marketing system

_____ 12. The sorting activity that develops an inventory of homogeneous products
is
a. allocating.
b. combining.
c. assorting.
d. accumulating.
e. sorting out.

_____ 13. The power relationship is defined as
a. the ability of one channel member to facilitate or hinder the goal
attainment of other channel members.
b. the functions and services that a channel member has to offer compared with others in the channel.
c. the structure that facilitates the movement of a product through the
channel.
d. something that does not exist between channel members.
e. usually turbulent in marketing channels.

_____ 14. When Western Manufacturing recently introduced its new line of sharkskin boots, the company provided large financial incentives to retailers to get them to carry and promote the new line. These incentives are so effective that Western now has power over its retailers. What type of power does Western hold?
   a. Reward power
   b. Legitimate power
   c. Expert power
   d. Coercive power
   e. Referent power

_____ 15. Horizontal channel integration involves
   a. bringing under one management organizations that function at the same basic level.
   b. bringing several channel stages under one common management.
   c. acquiring the operations present at different levels in the channel.
   d. assuming the functions performed at one level into the operations that take place at another level.
   e. intensive or selective distribution.

_____ 16. Decreased flexibility is one of the limitations inherent in
   a. physical distribution.
   b. horizontal channel integration.
   c. marketing channel leadership.
   d. multiple marketing channels.
   e. using agents.

_____ 17. If a supplier drops a dealer for resisting anticompetitive practices, the supplier is engaging in
   a. restricted selling.
   b. exclusive dealing.
   c. dual distribution.
   d. refusal-to-deal actions.
   e. tying contracts.

_____ 18. Whenever the May Company sells a restaurant franchise, it insists that the franchisee buy equipment and supplies as well. The May Company justifies this policy as being necessary for quality control and protection of the company's reputation. What type of arrangement is taking place in this example?
   a. Exclusive dealing
   b. A restricted sales territory
   c. Dual distribution
   d. A tying contract
   e. Refusal to deal

_____ 19. Channel leaders are responsible for
   a. physical possession.
   b. coordination of channel members and activities.
   c. market risk.

    d. market possession.

    e. channel noise.

_____ 20. Which of the following is *not* a power base involved in channel leadership?
    a. Authority
    b. Reference groups that channel members try to please
    c. Coercion
    d. The desire to influence overall channel performance
    e. Expertise about products, markets, or technology

_____ 21. Selective distribution is the form of distribution utilized with
    a. specialty products.
    b. infrequently purchased products.
    c. convenience products.
    d. products that require controlled sales and special services.
    e. products that have a high replacement rate.

_____ 22. The Spike Company is about to introduce its new line of athletic footwear —the XgT Crosstrainer. The company must now decide what type of market coverage it wants for the XgT. Product differentiation and customer service are very important to the success of the brand. In addition, the company wants to maintain a certain degree of control over the distribution process. What type of market coverage do you recommend?
    a. Intensive distribution
    b. Inclusive distribution
    c. Exclusive distribution
    d. Controlled distribution
    e. Selective distribution

_____ 23. Guitars are generally marketed through _____ distribution.
    a. concentrated
    b. intensive
    c. selective
    d. exclusive
    e. cooperative

_____ 24. Which of the following occurs when one of the members of a marketing channel fails to fulfill its expected role?
    a. Channel cooperation
    b. Channel conflict
    c. Channel leadership
    d. Channel integration
    e. Channel distribution

_____ 25. Which of the following statements is true?
    a. Selective distribution is commonly needed for convenience goods.
    b. Intensive distribution uses just a few outlets in a given area.
    c. Consumers are likely to devote more time and effort when shopping for products available through selective distribution than for those available through intensive distribution.

    d. Only products that are marketed through exclusive distribution require special services or information.

    e. Selective distribution uses most of the available resellers.

26. All the following are prerequisites for channel leadership *except*

    a. a channel member has to command a comfortable margin of power over other channel members.

    b. a channel member must conform to the expectations of both retailers and producers in providing coordination, functional services, and communication.

    c. other channel members have to tolerate the leader's use of power.

    d. the leader must want to influence the behavior of other channel members and actually exert leadership power.

    e. the leader must have the ability to influence another channel member's goal achievment.

MINICASE: MARKETING CHANNELS FOR MICROWAVE OVENS

In the 1980s, microwave oven sales rose rapidly. Microwave ovens can be found in over half of all U.S. households and clearly have become a mass market item. Marketers are trying to expand the market even further by offering lower prices and product innovations such as combination units that bake, broil, toast, and microwave.

Both domestic and foreign manufacturers have significant market shares. Among the U.S. leaders are Litton Industries and Amana. Foreign competitors include Japan's Sharp Electronics, Sanyo, Panasonic, and Toshiba, as well as Korean contenders Samsung and GoldStar.

Amana and Litton rely on independent wholesalers and have used pull strategies consisting of heavy advertising supported by product innovations to create consumer demand. Channel cooperation is maintained through demonstrations or "cooking schools" presented by manufacturers' representatives. Sears, with its Kenmore microwave ovens, maintains sales through effective price cutting, in-home free trial periods, and miscellaneous retail premiums. Sears has been the largest national chain retailer of microwave ovens, purchasing products from Litton, Sharp, and Sanyo but offering them under its Kenmore private label. Amana and Litton focus on supporting their own marketing channels of independent wholesalers and appliance retailers and some department stores.

Questions

1. The case states that Litton relies mostly on independent wholesalers, yet Sears purchases microwave ovens from Litton and offers them under its own private label. For Litton this is an example of

    a. intermediaries.

    b. multiple marketing channels.

    c. accumulation.

    d. channel integration.

    e. intensive distribution.

_____ 2. What intensity of market coverage do microwave oven manufacturers utilize?
   a. Protective
   b. Exclusive
   c. Selective
   d. Competitive
   e. Intensive

_____ 3. Sears's source of power in the distribution channel is most likely
   a. authority.
   b. coercion and authority.
   c. rewards and expertise.
   d. referents.
   e. universal.

_____ 4. Manufacturers' representatives run product demonstrations to maintain channel operations. This implies that the _____ is attempting to manage channel conflict.
   a. retailer
   b. producer
   c. wholesaler
   d. agent
   e. broker

_____ 5. Which type of intermediary might be used if a manufacturer decided to pursue the consumer discount market?
   a. Dealer-wholesaler
   b. Vertically integrated channel to the mass seller
   c. Broker
   d. Distributor
   e. Industrial distributor

PROGRAMMED COMPLETION EXERCISES

authority, coercion,
rewards, referents,
expertise

1. The power bases of channel leadership include

_____, _____, _____, _____, and _____.

merchants, agents

2. Marketing channel intermediaries can be either

_____ or _____.

channel

3. The word _____ implies a linkage of units to carry product flows to the marketplace.

assortment

4. An _____ is a collection of products that complement one another or possess some common want-satisfying attributes.

intermediaries

5. The number and type of _____ in the channel are determined by the assortments buyers want and the efficiency of channel arrangements.

channel selection

6. Buyer behavior, product attributes, and organizational objectives are among the variables influencing _____ _____.

leader

7. The channel _____ may establish distribution policies and coordinate the development of the marketing mix.

coordination, flexibility

8. The limitations of horizontal channel integration include difficulties in _____, a decrease in _____, and an increase in planning and research.

retailers, wholesalers

9. Marketing channels are an interrelated group of inter-mediaries, such as _____ and _____, who perform the activities necessary to direct products to consumers.

producer, wholesalers, retailers, consumers

10. The most traditional channel for consumer products is _____ to _____ to _____ to _____.

assortments

11. The basic functions of channels include sorting out, accumu-lating, allocating, and providing _____ for buyers.

Agents

12. _____ often are used in the business-to-business channel when products are standardized and when information gathering and selling functions are important.

utilities, product benefits

13. The channel system builds up a collection of _____ or _____ _____ by performing activities that facilitate exchanges.

Vertical, horizontal

14. _____ and _____ integration strategies can be used to stabilize supply, reduce costs, and increase channel control.

conflict

15. Role deviance or malfunction is a major source of channel _____.

integration, coordination

16. Role expectations are a means of _____ and _____ to enhance channel effectiveness and efficiency.

Producers, wholesalers, retailers

17. _____, _____, or _____ can assume leadership and guide the channel.

understood, realized, shared

18. Control of the marketing channel is tolerated only when the benefits of that control are _____, _____, and _____ by all channel members.

sales

19. A major change in the marketing channel can have a profound impact on product _____.

competition, free trade

20. Protection of _____ and _____ _____ is the general principle underlying the government regulation of channel management practices.

ANSWERS TO OBJECTIVE QUESTIONS

Matching		*True or False*		*Multiple-Choice*		*Minicase*
1. s	14. n	1. F	15. T	1. e	14. a	1. b
2. b	15. h	2. T	16. F	2. c	15. a	2. c
3. q	16. f	3. F	17. F	3. b	16. b	3. c
4. o	17. v	4. F	18. T	4. b	17. b	4. b
5. p	18. l	5. T	19. T	5. c	18. d	5. b
6. c	19. r	6. F	20. T	6. a	19. b	
7. a	20. i	7. T	21. F	7. c	20. d	
8. m	21. e	8. F	22. T	8. e	21. d	
9. j	22. g	9. F	23. F	9. d	22. e	
10. d	23. x	10. F	24. F	10. b	23. c	
11. t	24. y	11. T	25. T	11. a	24. b	
12. k	25. w	12. F	26. F	12. d	25. c	
13. u		13. F	27. T	13. a	26. b	
		14. T				

12 WHOLESALING

CHAPTER OUTLINE

The nature and importance of wholesaling
The activities of wholesalers
    Services for producers
    Services for retailers
Classifying wholesalers
    Merchant wholesalers
    Agents and brokers
    Manufacturers' sales branches and offices
Facilitating agencies
    Public warehouses
    Finance companies
    Transportation companies
    Trade shows and trade marts
Changing patterns in wholesaling
    Wholesalers consolidate power
    New types of wholesalers

CHAPTER SUMMARY

Wholesaling involves all transactions in which the purchaser intends to use the product for resale, for making other products, or for general business operations. A wholesaler is an individual or organization that facilitates and expedites exchanges that are primarily wholesale transactions.

    Wholesaling activities must be performed for the distribution of all goods, whether or not a wholesaling institution is involved. These activities include wholesale management, planning and negotiating supplies, promotion, warehousing and product handling, transportation, inventory control and data processing, security, pricing, financing and budgeting, and client management and merchandising assistance. Producers have a distinct advantage when they use wholesalers. By performing specialized accumulation and allocation functions for a number of products, wholesalers allow producers to concentrate on developing products to match consumers' wants. Wholesalers also sell products and initiate sales contacts, assist producers financially, and relay valuable information within the marketing channel. Wholesalers help retailers select inventory, negotiate purchases, and coordinate supply sources. Because they carry products for many customers, wholesalers can maintain a wide product line at relatively low cost. By buying in large quantities and delivering to customers in small lots, wholesalers perform physical distribution activities more efficiently and provide more services than producers or retailers can by establishing their own distribution systems.

Four factors influence the classification of wholesalers: (1) whether the wholesaler is producer-owned, (2) whether the wholesaler takes title to the products it handles, (3) the range of services the wholesaler provides, and (4) the breadth and depth of the wholesaler's product lines. The three general categories of wholesalers are merchant wholesalers, agents and brokers, and manufacturers' sales branches and offices. Merchant wholesalers take title and assume risk. They generally are involved in buying and reselling products to industrial or retail customers. The two broad categories of merchant wholesalers are full-service and limited service wholesalers. Full-service wholesalers provide most services that wholesalers can perform. Types of full-service wholesalers include general merchandise wholesalers, who carry a very wide product mix; limited-line wholesalers, who carry only a few product lines; and specialty-line wholesalers, who stock a narrowly defined line of products, such as shellfish. Limited service merchant wholesalers offer only certain services. Typical limited service wholesalers are cash-and-carry wholesalers, truck wholesalers, drop shippers, and mail-order wholesalers.

Agents and brokers negotiate purchases and expedite sales, but they do not take title to products. They are called functional middlemen because they perform a limited number of marketing activities in exchange for a commission. Manufacturers' agents, selling agents, and commission merchants are typical functional middlemen. Brokers bring together buyers and sellers and offer their customers specialized knowledge of a particular commodity.

Manufacturers' sales branches and offices are wholesaling operations that are owned and controlled by the manufacturer. Manufacturers may set up sales branches and offices to reach customers more effectively by performing wholesaling functions themselves or because certain specialized wholesaling services are not available through existing middlemen.

Facilitating organizations perform highly specialized wholesaling functions but do not buy, sell, or transfer title to products. Sometimes these organizations make it unnecessary for manufacturers or retailers to use a wholesaling establishment. Common facilitating organizations are public warehouses, finance and transportation companies, and trade shows and trade marts.

New marketing methods that offer more services and lower prices have triggered a move away from traditional wholesaling. This is especially evident in the food industry, where several large grocery wholesalers are now operating retail stores. Mergers also are more common today, the end product of economic conditions and advances in materials handling and communication technology. The nature of future wholesaling establishments will depend on the changing mix of marketing activities that producers and retailers perform and the innovative efforts of wholesalers to increase efficiency in the marketing channel.

MATCHING EXERCISES

Use the following set of terms to identify the sentences and phrases below. On the blank line next to each sentence or phrase, place the letter of the term that the sentence or phrase describes. Do not use a term more than once.

a. Trade show
b. Mail-order wholesaler
c. Wholesaling
d. Drop shipper
e. Agent
f. Wholesaler
g. Limited-line wholesaler
h. Public warehouses
i. Functional middlemen
j. Full-service wholesaler
k. Cash-and-carry wholesaler
l. Broker
m. Merchant wholesaler

n. General merchandise wholesaler
o. Manufacturers' agent
p. Specialty-line wholesaler
q. Selling agents
r. Limited service wholesaler
s. Truck wholesaler
t. Rack jobbers
u. Trade marts
v. Commission merchant
w. Sales office
x. Food broker
y. Facilitating agency
z. Sales branch

_p_ 1. A merchant wholesaler who carries a very limited variety of products designed to meet customers' specialized requirements. *Specialty-line Wholesaler*

_d_ 2. A limited service wholesaler that takes title to products and negotiates sales but never takes actual possession of products. *Drop Shipper*

_i_ 3. Agents or brokers who negotiate purchases and expedite sales but do not take title to products; they perform a limited number of marketing activities for a commission. *Functional Middleman*

_f_ 4. An individual or organization that facilitates exchanges that are primarily wholesale transactions and performs marketing activities—such as transportation, storage, and information gathering—that are necessary to expedite exchanges. *Wholesaler*

_t_ 5. Specialty-line wholesalers that own and maintain their own display racks in supermarkets and drugstores. *Rack Jobbers*

_l_ 6. A functional middleman whose primary function is to bring together buyers and sellers for a commission. *Broker*

_v_ 7. An agent who receives goods on consignment from local sellers and negotiates sales in large central markets; this agent has broad powers regarding prices and terms of sales. *Commission Merchant*

_b_ 8. A middleman who uses catalogs instead of a sales force to sell products to retail, industrial, and institutional customers. *Mail Order Wholesaler*

_s_ 9. A wholesaler who transports a limited line of products directly to customers for on-the-spot inspection and selection. *Truck Wholesaler*

j 10. A merchant wholesaler who provides most services that wholesalers can perform. *Full-service Wholesaler*

g 11. A full-service merchant wholesaler who carries only a few product lines but offers an extensive assortment of products within those lines. *Limited line Wholesaler*

X 12. An intermediary who sells food and general merchandise items to retailer-owned and merchant wholesalers, grocery chains, industrial buyers, and food processors. *Food broker*

M 13. A marketing intermediary who takes title to products, assumes risk, and generally is involved in buying and reselling products to industrial or retail customers. *Merchant Wholesaler*

N 14. A full-service merchant wholesaler who carries a very wide product mix with limited depth within the product lines. *General Mdse Wholesaler*

Z 15. Manufacturer-owned middlemen who sell products and provide support services for the manufacturer's sales force. *Sales Branch*

Y 16. An organization that performs activities that enhance channel functions; it does not buy, sell, or transfer title to products. *Facilitating Agency*

W 17. Provides service normally associated with agents; owned and controlled by the producer. *Sales Office*

C 18. All transactions in which the purchaser intends to use the product for resale, for making other products, or for general business operations. *Wholesaling*

a 19. Industry exhibitions that assist manufacturers and wholesalers in the selling and buying functions; commonly held annually at a specified location. *Trade Show*

K 20. A limited service wholesaler whose customers pay cash and furnish transportation or pay extra to have products delivered. *Cash & carry Wholesaler*

R 21. A merchant wholesaler who provides only some marketing services and specializes in just a few functions. *Limited Service Wholesaler*

H 22. Business organizations that provide storage facilities and related physical distribution facilities for a fee. *Public Warehouse*

q 23. Intermediaries who market all of a specified product line or a manufacturer's entire output; they perform every wholesaling activity except taking title to products and can be used in place of a marketing department. *Selling Agents*

l 24. An intermediary who receives a commission or fee for expediting exchanges; this intermediary represents either buyers or sellers on a permanent basis. *Agent*

O 25. An independent businessperson who sells the complementary products of several producers in assigned territories and is compensated through commissions. *Mfgr's Agent*

U 26. Relatively permanent facilities that firms can rent to exhibit products year-round. *Trade Marts*

TRUE OR FALSE STATEMENTS

T F   1. Wholesaling includes all transactions in which purchases are intended for resale, for making other products, or for general business operations.

T F   2. Eliminating wholesalers would eliminate the need for the functions they provide because direct channels are more efficient.

T F   3. Wholesaling involves exchange activities between organizations that deal directly with ultimate consumers.

T F   4. One major advantage of using wholesalers is that they perform accumulation and allocation roles for a number of products, saving producers money and allowing them to concentrate on producing, assembling, and developing quality products.

T F   5. About one-third of all goods are exchanged through wholesaling institutions.

T F   6. Wholesaling exists to provide services and functions that for the most part are unrelated to basic marketing functions.

T F   7. Wholesaling activities must be performed during distribution for all goods, whether or not a wholesaling institution is involved.

T F   8. Wholesalers can provide information about markets and products that helps retailers understand consumers.

T F   9. Financing, inventory control, and billing are areas of service wholesalers rarely handle.

T F 10. Wholesalers usually have closer contact with retailers than do producers.

T F 11. Wholesaling is concerned only with those marketing activities that are related to the actual handling and moving of physical goods.

T F 12. Wholesalers provide form utility, which allows manufacturers to avoid the risks associated with holding large inventories.

T F 13. Buying, selling, storing, transporting, financing, risk taking, and gathering market information are the basic activities of wholesalers.

T F 14. Wholesalers who buy must understand market conditions but do not have to be experts at negotiating final purchases.

T F 15. Any classification of wholesalers is meaningful only at a point in time because wholesalers continuously adjust their activities to changes in the marketing environment.

T F 16. Wholesalers are classified according to their position in the marketing channel.

T F 17. Merchant wholesalers do not take title to products.

T F 18. Agents and brokers take title to products and are compensated by commissions for negotiating transactions between manufacturers and retailers.

T F 19. The broad categories of merchant wholesalers are full-service wholesalers and limited service wholesalers.

T F 20. General merchandise wholesalers are full-service merchant wholesalers who carry a wide product mix.

T F 21. Drop shippers take title to products and negotiate sales but do not take actual possession of products.

T F 22. Rack jobbers provide only transportation, delivering products directly to customers for inspection and selection.

T F 23. Manufacturers' sales offices differ from manufacturers' sales branches in that sales offices carry no inventory.

T F 24. Public warehouses, finance and transportation companies, and trade shows and marts are all limited service merchant wholesalers.

MULTIPLE-CHOICE QUESTIONS

_____ 1. Wholesalers
   a. perform those marketing activities necessary to expedite exchanges.
   b. usually can be eliminated with no loss in efficiency.
   c. are engaged primarily in selling products to ultimate consumers.
   d. create higher consumer prices by performing their functions.
   e. appear in almost all channels.

_____ 2. Which of the following services does a wholesaler usually *not* offer?
   a. Management assistance and marketing research
   b. Handling credit and financing
   c. Selling activities
   d. Physical distribution activities
   e. Making sales to ultimate consumers

_____ 3. Wholesaling functions are performed
   a. when products are produced.
   b. for transactions in which purchases are intended for resale or for making other products.
   c. when ultimate consumers buy products.
   d. when ultimate consumers allocate products.
   e. mainly by producers.

_____ 4. Which of the following is *not* a major category of facilitating organizations?
   a. Finance companies
   b. Transportation companies
   c. Brokers
   d. Public warehouses
   e. Trade marts

_____ 5. Which of the following statements is true?
  a. Accumulation and allocation are roles performed by wholesalers.
  b. The distinguishing characteristic of rack jobbers is that they take title to products and negotiate sales but do not physically handle products.
  c. Products offered by a manufacturers' agent, of necessity, must be competing and noncomplementary.
  d. Rack jobbers sell only clothing.
  e. Rack jobbers are functional middlemen.

_____ 6. Limited service wholesalers
  a. provide much more service than customers want.
  b. are specialists in most of the wholesaling functions.
  c. are restricted to boundaries of competition set forth by the government.
  d. provide only some marketing services and specialize in just a few functions.
  e. are agents.

_____ 7. Tropic Distributors is a full-service merchant wholesaler that carries only fresh fruit that is flown in daily from Hawaii. What type of wholesaler is Tropic Distributors?
  a. Limited-line wholesaler
  b. Rack jobber
  c. Specialty-line wholesaler
  d. General merchandise wholesaler
  e. Air delivery wholesaler

_____ 8. OfficeMart is a limited service merchant wholesaler that sells office supplies to small retailers and industrial firms. OfficeMart does not provide delivery or credit services to its customers. What type of wholesaler is OfficeMart?
  a. Cash-and-carry wholesaler
  b. Rack jobber
  c. Specialty-line wholesaler
  d. Drop shipper
  e. Mail-order wholesaler

_____ 9. By buying in large quantities and delivering to customers in smaller lots, a wholesaler can perform all the following activities *except*
  a. transportation.
  b. materials handling.
  c. selling the retailer's product.
  d. inventory planning.
  e. warehousing.

_____ 10. The classification of wholesalers is based on
  a. the state of the economy.
  b. categories set forth by the government.
  c. the nature of the marketing environment.
  d. the activities they perform.
  e. their size and organizational structure.

_____ 11. Wholesalers
   a. increase the total number of negotiations and selling transactions among manufacturers and consumers.
   b. increase the costs associated with exchanges through intermediaries.
   c. promote both specialized mass production and the satisfaction of varied consumers' needs.
   d. increase costs to consumers.
   e. eliminate the need for retailers.

_____ 12. Wholesaling usually does *not* include the marketing activities performed by
   a. manufacturers' sales branches.
   b. agents.
   c. commission merchants.
   d. resellers.
   e. retailers.

_____ 13. Part of Steve's job as an agent in agricultural marketing involves receiving goods on consignment from local sellers and negotiating sales in large central markets. When a sale is completed, Steve deducts his fees and then turns the remaining profit over to the producer. What type of agent is Steve?
   a. Manufacturer's agent
   b. Commission agent
   c. Selling agent
   d. Food broker
   e. Agricultural agent

_____ 14. Which of the following are *not* limited service merchant wholesalers?
   a. Cash-and-carry wholesalers
   b. Mail-order wholesalers
   c. Specialty-line wholesalers
   d. Drop shippers
   e. Truck wholesalers

_____ 15. Agents and brokers
   a. take title and assume risk and generally are involved in buying and reselling products to industrial or retail customers.
   b. take title to products and negotiate sales but do not physically handle products.
   c. negotiate purchases and expedite sales but do not take title to products.
   d. are part of the producer's vertically integrated distribution channel.
   e. are highly specialized wholesalers who act as facilitating agencies for producers.

_____ 16. A distinct advantage of wholesalers is their ability to
   a. provide time and place utility.
   b. deal directly with ultimate consumers.
   c. increase the number of sales contracts.
   d. offer trade discounts to retailers.
   e. attract ultimate consumers.

_____ 17. Linda is the owner of TBL Wholesaling, a tire distributor. Linda is interested in exhibiting her products to potential buyers as well as gaining access to tire manufacturers. Which of the following would you recommend to Linda?
a. Contact a tire manufacturer's agent.
b. Call a tire broker.
c. Buy a copy of the *Census of Wholesale Trade*.
d. Attend a trade show or trade mart.
e. Hire an advertising agency to handle her needs.

_____ 18. The basic difference between channel members and facilitating agencies is that
a. channel members are independent organizations; facilitating agencies are producer-owned.
b. channel members are functional specialists; facilitating agencies direct channel decisions.
c. channel members are producer-owned; facilitating agencies are independent organizations.
d. channel members buy, sell, and transfer title to products; facilitating agencies do not.
e. facilitating agencies buy, sell, and transfer title to products; channel members only take physical possession of the products.

_____ 19. A channel member may place products in a bonded warehouse to
a. use the goods as collateral for a loan.
b. retain both possession and control of the products.
c. avoid the cost of building its own warehouse.
d. exhibit the goods to potential buyers.
e. qualify for a type of financing called "floor planning."

_____ 20. Roger Davis is considering going into the wholesaling business with his brother to form Davis and Davis Wholesaling. As Roger contemplates his decision, which of the following is a threat to the wholesaling industry that Roger should be aware of?
a. The shortage in the number of available facilitating agencies to help wholesalers
b. The trend toward larger and more powerful retailers
c. The disappearance of the trade show and trade mart
d. The trend toward larger and more powerful producers
e. The shortage of manufacturer's agents

MINICASE: WHOLESALE FOOD SUPPLY, INC.

Wholesale Food Supply, Inc., is one of the largest wholesale food operations in the United States. The firm supplies its customers (food stores) with food and nonfood products and a variety of operational, merchandising, and administrative services, including site selection, store engineering and interior design, financing, inventory control, and merchandising. The total offering of wholesale and support activities enables Wholesale Food Supply's independent customers to compete effectively with chains and other food stores in their area.

The wholesale food business is basically regional, with distance from the firm's distribution center a key cost factor. Wholesale Food Supply and other large wholesalers represent the end product of many past mergers and acquisitions of smaller regional firms. Wholesale Food Supply competes with other voluntary food wholesalers as well as cooperative food wholesalers and national chain stores such as Safeway and A&P. New customers can be awkward to serve until sufficient area volume is developed, which is why many food wholesalers prefer to expand sales volume by increasing sales to established customers rather than by developing new customers.

Wholesale Food Supply, however, is building a customer base among the large regional and national food chains currently replacing or supplementing their integrated wholesaling systems with traditional wholesalers. Some wholesalers are not interested in serving national chain stores, believing that this market would conflict with their service to independent retailer clients. Most of the other wholesalers, however, do serve or would serve food chains but have not sought this business as aggressively as Wholesale Food Supply has. To date, wholesale business to the independent retailer market appears stable despite sales to the national chain market.

As labor and overhead costs increase, Wholesale Food Supply believes more and more food chains will specialize in retailing and contract with wholesalers on a management fee basis. The increasing use of wholesalers by retail chains promises the chains greater profitability on existing assets as well as the possibility of greater instability or volatility in earnings.

Questions

_____ 1. Which of the following is *not* a service that Wholesale Food Supply would provide for retailers?
   a. Physical distribution
   b. Inventory selection
   c. Merchandising assistance
   d. Inventory control
   e. All the above are wholesaling services.

_____ 2. Based on the information supplied in this case, Wholesale Food Supply is a
   a. limited service merchant wholesaler.
   b. full-service merchant wholesaler.
   c. specialty-line wholesaler.
   d. drop shipper.
   e. buying agent.

_____ 3. Trends in wholesaling indicate that wholesalers who provide services similar to Wholesale Food Supply
   a. are increasing.
   b. are decreasing.
   c. remain constant.

d. have been eliminated.
e. None of the above.

_____ 4. If Wholesale Food Supply serves more large food chain stores and independent customers complain, this would result in
a. increased profits.
b. decreased profits.
c. channel conflict.
d. government regulation.
e. less service.

_____ 5. By selling to both corporate chains and independent retailers, Wholesale Food Supply demonstrates that
a. most wholesalers are evolving gradually into retail organizations.
b. food producers are relinquishing power within marketing channels.
c. wholesalers must look to mass merchandisers for most of their business.
d. wholesalers must adjust their activities as the marketing environment changes.
e. wholesalers are not concerned with market segmentation.

PROGRAMMED COMPLETION EXERCISES

Full-service,
limited service

1. _____ wholesalers provide most of the services that can be performed by wholesalers; _____ _____ wholesalers provide only some marketing services.

ultimate consumers

2. Wholesaling includes all exchange activities among organizations and individuals except transactions with _____ _____ .

distribution,
wholesaling

3. Wholesaling activities must be performed for all goods during _____ , whether or not a _____ institution is involved.

public, finance,
transportation, trade
shows, trade marts

4. Facilitating organizations that perform wholesaling functions include _____ warehouses, _____ and _____ companies, and _____ _____ and _____ _____ .

general merchandise,
limited-line,
specialty-line

5. The three types of full-service merchant wholesalers are
_____ _____ wholesalers, _____
wholesalers, and _____ wholesalers.

Facilitating agencies

6. _____ _____ sometimes make it
unnecessary for manufacturers or retailers to use wholesaling
establishments.

activities

7. The kinds of wholesale establishments that develop in the
future will depend on the changing mix of _____ that
retailers and producers perform.

industrial, reseller,
government,
institutional

8. Wholesale establishments are engaged primarily in selling
products directly to _____, _____,
_____, and _____ users.

Sales offices,
owned, operated

9. _____ _____ provide services normally
associated with agents; they are _____ and
_____ by the producer.

large, small,
transportation,
materials handling,
inventory planning,
communication,
warehousing

10. By buying in _____ quantities and delivering to
customers in _____ lots, a wholesaler can perform
such physical distribution activities as _____,
_____ _____, _____
_____, _____, and _____.

wholesalers,
accumulation,
allocation

11. The use of _____ is a distinct advantage to producers
because they perform _____ and _____
roles for a number of products.

Merchant, title

12. _____ wholesalers take _____ to goods and
assume risk; they generally are involved in buying and
reselling products to industrial or retail customers.

agents, several,
product line

13. Manufacturers' _____ represent _____ sellers and usually offer customers a complete _____ _____.

Cash-and-carry, truck,
drop shippers, mail-
order

14. _____ wholesalers, _____ wholesalers, _____ _____, and _____ wholesalers are typical limited service wholesalers.

functional middlemen

15. Agents and brokers are called _____ _____. Their distinguishing characteristic is that they do not take title to products.

full-service,
limited service

16. Two broad categories of merchant wholesaler are _____ wholesalers and _____ _____ wholesalers.

branches, offices,
merchant wholesalers'

17. Manufacturers' sales _____ and _____ are producer-owned middlemen who resemble _____ _____ operations.

wholesaler

18. Although the _____ is a distinct business entity, its activities can be performed by any marketing channel member.

ANSWERS TO OBJECTIVE QUESTIONS

Matching		*True or False*		*Multiple-Choice*		*Minicase*
1. p	14. n	1. T	13. T	1. a	11. c	1. e
2. d	15. z	2. F	14. F	2. e	12. e	2. b
3. i	16. y	3. F	15. T	3. b	13. b	3. a
4. f	17. w	4. T	16. F	4. c	14. c	4. c
5. t	18. c	5. F	17. F	5. a	15. c	5. d
6. l	19. a	6. F	18. F	6. d	16. a	
7. v	20. k	7. T	19. T	7. c	17. d	
8. b	21. r	8. T	20. T	8. a	18. d	
9. s	22. h	9. F	21. T	9. c	19. a	
10. j	23. q	10. T	22. F	10. d	20. b	
11. g	24. e	11. F	23. T			
12. x	25. o	12. F	24. F			
13. m	26. u					

13 RETAILING

CHAPTER OUTLINE

The nature of retailing
Major types of retail stores
    Department stores
    Mass merchandisers
    Specialty retailers
Nonstore retailing and direct marketing
    In-home retailing
    Telemarketing
    Automatic vending
    Mail-order retailing
Franchising
    Major types of retail franchises
    Advantages and disadvantages of franchising
    Trends in franchising
Strategic issues in retailing
    Location
    Product assortment
    Retail positioning
    Atmospherics
    Store image
    Scrambled merchandising
    The wheel of retailing

CHAPTER SUMMARY

Retailers operate in an extraordinarily dynamic environment and are an important link in the marketing channel because they are both buyers and sellers. Retailing involves those activities that facilitate exchanges with ultimate consumers. By providing assortments of products that meet consumers' wants, retailers create place, time, and possession utilities. In the case of service products, retailers themselves develop most of the product utilities as well. Services are unique because of their intangible nature, their perishability, the heterogeneity of their delivery, and the fact that they are inseparable from the retailer.

Retail stores may be classified into three major categories. Department stores offer a wide product mix and are distinctly service-oriented. Mass merchandisers, which include discount stores, supermarkets, superstores, home improvement centers, hyper-markets, warehouse/wholesale clubs, and warehouse and catalog showrooms, usually focus on low prices, high turnover, and large sales volume. They generally have a wider and shallower product mix than department stores. Specialty stores, which include traditional specialty retailers and off-price retailers, carry a narrow product mix with deep product lines. They often compete on the basis of service or store image.

Nonstore retailing and direct marketing take place outside the retail store. In-home selling and telephone selling are types of personal nonstore retailing; automatic vending and direct mail are nonpersonal types. Direct marketing is the use of nonpersonal media to introduce products to consumers, who then buy products by mail or telephone.

Franchising is an arrangement whereby a supplier (franchisor) grants a dealer (franchisee) the right to sell products for some type of consideration (such as a per-centage of sales). The producer may franchise a number of stores to sell a particular brand; it may franchise wholesalers to sell to retailers; or it may simply supply brand names, techniques, procedures, or other services.

Franchising offers advantages to both the franchisee and the franchisor. The franchisee is able to start a business with limited capital and receives support from the franchisor. The franchisor gains a more effective distribution system through a franchisee and benefits from the work of a highly motivated individual. Drawbacks of franchise arrangements to franchisees include the often strict control franchisors have over an establishment's decor, employees' uniforms, and numerous operating details and the extremely hard work and long hours needed to build a franchise into a successful business.

Since the mid-1960s, franchising has experienced enormous growth. This growth has paralleled the expansion of the fast-food industry, which uses franchising widely. Fran-chise arrangements for health clubs, exterminators, hair salons, tax preparers, and travel agencies are also widespread. The largest franchise sectors (ranked by sales) are auto-mobile and truck dealers, gasoline service stations, restaurants, and nonfood retailing.

To increase sales and store patronage, retailers must consider several strategic issues. Because consumers shop for a variety of reasons, retailers must make desired products available, create stimulating shopping environments, and develop effective marketing strategies.

A store's location determines the trading area from which a store must draw its customers. When choosing a location, retailers consider such issues as the location of the firm's target market within the trading area, the kinds of products being sold, the availability of public transportation, customer characteristics, competitors' locations, and the relative ease of movement to and from the new site. Retailers also evaluate the characteristics of the site itself: the types of stores in the area, the physical traits of the building or lot under consideration, and the rental or ownership arrangements. Retailers must select from among several general types of locations: freestanding structures, traditional business districts, neighborhood shopping centers, community shopping centers, regional shopping centers, or nontraditional shopping centers.

The width, depth, and quality of a retailer's product assortment should satisfy cus-tomers and is evaluated in terms of its purpose (how well an assortment satisfies con-sumers while furthering the retailer's goals), status (the relative importance of each product in an assortment), and completeness (the products necessary to satisfy a store's customers). How much to include in an assortment depends on the needs of the retailer's target market.

Retail positioning involves identifying an unserved or underserved market niche and serving the segment through a strategy that distinguishes the retailer from others. For example, a retailer may position itself as a seller of high-quality, premium-priced products or as a seller of reasonable-quality products at everyday low prices.

Atmospherics are the physical elements in the store's design that can be adjusted to appeal to consumers' emotions so that consumers will be encouraged to buy. Exterior and interior characteristics, layout, and displays all contribute to a store's atmosphere.

Store image, which different customers perceive differently, is associated with atmosphere but also includes location, products offered, customer services, prices, promotion, and the store's overall reputation. Characteristics of the target market— social class, lifestyle, income level, and past buying behavior—help form store image as well.

Scrambled merchandising adds unrelated product lines to an existing product mix to generate sales. Through scrambled merchandising, retailers hope to convert their stores into one-stop shopping centers, generate more traffic, realize higher profit margins, and increase impulse purchases. The practice of scrambled merchandising may blur a store's image and intensify competition among traditionally distinct types of stores.

The wheel of retailing hypothesis holds that new retail institutions develop as low-status, low-margin, low-price operators. As they increase services and prices, the institutions become vulnerable to newer institutions, which enter and repeat the cycle.

MATCHING EXERCISES

Use the following set of terms to identify the sentences and phrases below. On the blank line next to each sentence or phrase, place the letter of the term that the sentence or phrase describes. Do not use a term more than once.

a. Regional shopping center
b. Traditional specialty retailer
c. Discount store
d. Nonstore retailing
e. Catalog retailing
f. Wheel of retailing
g. Off-price retailer
h. Retailing
i. In-home retailing
j. Neighborhood shopping center
k. Telemarketing
l. Superstore
m. Scrambled merchandising
n. Franchising

o. Atmospherics
p. Automatic vending
q. Department store
r. Community shopping center
s. Mail-order retailing
t. Catalog showroom
u. Warehouse showroom
v. Mass merchandiser
w. Warehouse/wholesale club
x. Hypermarket
y. Direct marketing
z. Supermarket
aa. Retail positioning
bb. Home improvement centers

j   1. A shopping center that usually consists of several small convenience and specialty stores and serves consumers who live less than ten minutes' driving time away. *Neighborhood Shopping Center*

b   2. A type of store that carries a narrow product mix with a deep product line. *Traditional Specialty Retailer*

f   3. A hypothesis that holds that new types of retailers usually enter the market as low-status, low-margin, low-price operators and eventually evolve into high-cost, high-price merchants. *Wheel of Retailing*

a   4. A type of shopping center that usually has the largest department stores, the widest product mix, and the deepest product lines of all shopping centers in an area and a target market of at least 150,000 customers. *Regional Shopping Cntr*

x   5. A combination of a supermarket and a discount store; it is larger than a superstore. *HyperMkt*

u   6. A type of retail facility characterized by low overhead, warehousing technology, vertical merchandise display space, large inventory, and minimal customer services. *Warehouse Showroom*

d   7. Retailing in which consumers purchase products without visiting a store. *Nonstr Retailing*

l   8. A giant store that carries all food and nonfood products found in supermarkets as well as most products purchased on a routine basis; a high-volume, low-margin, low-price operation. *Super Str*

i   9. A type of nonstore retailing that involves personal selling in consumers' homes *On-Home Retailing*

n   10. An arrangement in which a supplier grants a dealer the right to sell products in exchange for some type of consideration. *Franchising*

z   11. A large self-service store that carries broad, complete lines of food products and usually some nonfood products. *Super Mkt*

t   12. A type of retail facility in which consumers shop from a mailed catalog and buy at a warehouse where one of each product is on display with all other products stored out of buyers' reach. Products are provided in the manufacturer's carton. *Catalog Showroom*

s   13. A type of nonpersonal, nonstore retailing that uses direct mail advertising and catalogs to reach consumers. Selling is by description; the buyer usually does not see the actual product until it is delivered. *Mail Order Retailing*

k   14. A direct selling by telephone based on a cold canvass of a telephone directory or a prescreened list of prospective clients. *Telemktg*

o   15. The conscious design of a store's space to create emotional effects that enhance the probability that consumers will buy. *Atmospherics*

R   16. A shopping center that includes one or two department stores and some convenience and specialty stores; it serves several neighborhoods and draws consumers who are not able to find products in neighborhood shopping centers. *Community Shopping Cntr*

_____ 17. A type of mail-order retailing in which catalog orders are placed by mail, by telephone, or by in-store visits, and products are delivered by mail or picked up by the customers.

_____ 18. A self-service general merchandise store that regularly offers brand-name merchandise at low prices.

_____ 19. A retail operation that tends to offer fewer customer services than department stores and focus its attention on lower prices, high turnover, and large sales volume; it includes supermarkets and discount houses.

_____ 20. A form of nonpersonal retailing that uses coin-operated, self-service machines.

_____ 21. A type of retail store that has a wide product mix; it is organized into departments to facilitate marketing efforts and internal management.

_____ 22. Includes all transactions in which the buyer intends to consume the product through personal, family, or household use.

_____ 23. A large-scale, members-only selling operation that combines features of cash-and-carry wholesaling with discount retailing.

_____ 24. The use of nonpersonal media to introduce products to consumers, who then purchase the products by mail or telephone.

_____ 25. A store that buys manufacturers' seconds, overruns, returns, and off-season production runs at below-wholesale prices for resale to consumers at deep discounts.

_____ 26. The process by which a retailer identifies an underserved market segment and serves this segment through a strategy that distinguishes the retailer from competitors in the minds of people in the market segment.

_____ 27. The fastest growing form of retailing in the United States.

TRUE OR FALSE STATEMENTS

T   F   1. The wheel of retailing hypothesis holds that new types of retailers enter the market as low-status, low-margin, low-price operators.

T   F   2. In community shopping centers there is greater emphasis on shopping and specialty products that are not available in neighborhood shopping centers.

T   F   3. Today, many specialty retailers appear to be following the wheel of retailing by offering more service, better locations, quality inventory, and therefore higher prices.

T   F   4. Atmospherics are important to the appearance of a store, but there is no evidence to support the belief that they can affect sales.

T   F   5. Understanding the nature and development of marketing methods is the guiding philosophy of retailing.

T F 6. Retailers are not middlemen because they sell to ultimate consumers.

T F 7. Retailing involves primarily the development of a satisfying assortment of products for some market segment.

T F 8. In some cases, retailers create form, place, time, and possession utilities.

T F 9. Retailers are customers for the marketing efforts of suppliers, wholesalers, and manufacturers.

T F 10. Satisfying the needs of a market segment is one objective of retailers.

T F 11. Telemarketing is done through the cold canvass of the phone directory or by using prescribed lists.

T F 12. Traditional business districts are generally undesirable locations for retailers.

T F 13. The hypermarket is a fairly new idea that started in Japan.

T F 14. Discount stores can be described as self-service/general merchandise stores that, like department stores, carry a wide assortment of products.

T F 15. Retailing is oriented toward accomplishing exchanges for the purposes of industrial and business use.

T F 16. Mail-order retailing represents a form of nonstore retailing.

T F 17. Wholesale clubs require large amounts of capital to cover their high carrying costs.

T F 18. Franchising is currently experiencing declining growth.

T F 19. A business that develops a vague image bordering between a discount store and a department store will draw from both clienteles.

T F 20. Retailers must be inflexible in controlling product mix, product line depth, store location, and level of service.

T F 21. Retail positioning involves the use of a strategy that allows a retailer to distinguish itself from competitors in the minds of consumers.

T F 22. It is impossible for a retailer to create more than one atmosphere in a store to appeal to multiple segments.

T F 23. It is correct to assume that if target customers do not think a store is going to satisfy their needs, they will not shop there and therefore will have no exposure to the products there.

T F 24. Mass merchandisers typically are organized into separate departments to facilitate such store functions as marketing efforts and internal management.

T F 25. Labeling a store according to the consumer's image of the product assortment limits the store to one type of merchandise.

T F 26. The superstore prototype is usually the same size as a discount store or supermarket.

T F 27. A major weakness of the wheel of retailing theory is that it predicts what and when new innovations will develop rather than describing new retail stores.

T F 28. The wheel of retailing hypothesis states that increasing the level of services, and thus costs, makes established retail institutions vulnerable to the entry of new low-margin, low-price retailers.

T F 29. Door-to-door selling is generally more efficient than other forms of in-home retailing that rely on lists of prospects.

T F 30. Warehouse clubs serve small retailers who may be unable to obtain wholesaling services from larger distributors.

MULTIPLE-CHOICE QUESTIONS

_____ 1. The guiding philosophy of successful retailers can best be stated as
   a. convincing target customers that they have the best store to shop in.
   b. foreseeing changes and estimating their impact on the existing retail structure as well as on their own channel.
   c. developing product assortments and distribution methods that satisfy consumers' wants.
   d. offering products at a profitable price and convincing target customers that they have the best selection of merchandise.
   e. always use the golden rule of retailing.

_____ 2. The middlemen most visible to ultimate consumers are
   a. agents.
   b. brokers.
   c. distributors.
   d. retailers.
   e. rack jobbers.

_____ 3. The main difference between superstores and hypermarkets is
   a. store size and prices.
   b. credit availability.
   c. store size and size of product offering.
   d. size of product mix and store size.
   e. location.

_____ 4. Of the following services, which distinguishes the role of retailers in the marketing channel?
   a. Providing assortments of products that match consumers' wants
   b. Developing and designing products to match consumers' wants
   c. Offering service to wholesalers
   d. Performing marketing functions that wholesalers refuse to perform
   e. Providing services at the lowest prices

_____   5. The Hall Company is engaged in operations associated primarily with nonstore retailing. With which of the following types of retailing is the Hall Company most likely to be involved?
a. Catalog showroom
b. Vending machine
c. Specialty retailing
d. Off-price retailing
e. Boutique

_____   6. What term is used to describe the conscious design of store space to create emotional effects that enhance the probability that customers will buy?
a. Merchandising
b. Trading up
c. Internal environment
d. Atmospherics
e. Store layout

_____   7. Whitney's is a popular department store chain in the southeastern United States. Like all department stores, Whitney's offers a wide variety of consumer services. Which of the following services is Whitney's least likely to offer to its customers?
a. Delivery
b. Personal assistance
c. Pleasant atmosphere
d. Credit
e. Centralized checkout counters

_____   8. Which of the following statements best describes a customer's view of a specialty store?
a. The customer wants to compare both products and store product mixes.
b. The customer will buy any brand at the most accessible store.
c. The customer prefers both a particular product and a particular store.
d. The customer likes the wide product mix found there.
e. The customer has no concept of a specialty store.

_____   9. The least flexible of the strategic retailing issues is
a. store image.
b. atmospherics.
c. location.
d. product assortment.
e. customer services.

_____   10. Which of the following statements is false?
a. When a retailer allows expenses and prices to increase, vulnerability to competition from new institutions also increases.
b. Today there is a sharp delineation between discount stores and department stores.
c. The wheel of retailing hypothesis works reasonably well in industrialized expanding economies.

d. Retailers are customers of wholesalers and producers.
e. There are more than 1.5 million retail stores operating in the United States, according to the text.

11. Which of the following statements best characterizes superstores?
a. They have three times the sales and four times as many products as department stores.
b. They are a combination specialty store and supermarket.
c. They carry few nonfood products.
d. They are low-cost, high-volume, limited service operations.
e. They are the original mass merchandisers.

12. Off-price retailing can be a source of tension between department stores and manufacturers when off-price stores
a. locate in factory outlet malls.
b. obtain in-season, top-quality merchandise.
c. refuse to extend credit.
d. remove labels from products.
e. provide delivery services.

13. Specialty stores differ from department stores in that specialty stores usually have a very narrow product
a. line.
b. mix.
c. type.
d. perspective.
e. angle.

14. Superstores have been designed to sell products efficiently by means of their
a. size and operating methods.
b. legal advantages.
c. direct approach to consumers.
d. services for consumers.
e. services provided to producers.

15. Status in the product assortment identifies the relative importance of each product by
a. purpose.
b. purchase.
c. rank.
d. selection.
e. price.

16. A welcome change for consumers dissatisfied with the impersonal nature of large retailers can be found in the close personal contact at
a. superstores.
b. department stores.
c. supermarkets.
d. specialty stores.
e. fast-food franchises.

_____ 17. The warehouse club is a type of mass merchandiser that
   a. sells primarily to ultimate consumers and occasionally to small retailers.
   b. combines features of discount retailing with a high level of customer service.
   c. gave rise to the modern discount store and has now largely disappeared from the retail scene.
   d. combines features of cash-and-carry wholesaling with discount retailing.
   e. sells only to institutions, such as schools, hospitals, banks, credit unions, and government agencies.

_____ 18. Over the past few years, Loves has experienced a dramatic growth in its retail operations. In fact, Loves is just one of many companies that represent the fastest growing type of retailing in the United States. What type of retailer is Loves?
   a. A hypermarket
   b. A grocery store
   c. A warehouse club
   d. A discount merchandiser
   e. A home improvement center

_____ 19. Bob Jones recently entered into an agreement with The Blue Lagoon, a chain of upscale seafood restaurants. According to the agreement, Bob gets the right to operate a Blue Lagoon restaurant in return for 20 percent of the profits. Based on this scenario, Bob is a(n)
   a. franchisor.
   b. franchisee.
   c. independent retailer.
   d. outlet manager.
   e. operations supervisor.

_____ 20. Rachel was recently promoted to manager of the Banana Factory, a local candy store. As a new store manager, Rachel is very concerned about the functional and psychological picture that consumers have about her store. From a retail strategy perspective, Rachel seems to be concerned about the Banana Factory's
   a. image.
   b. product assortment.
   c. location.
   d. positioning.
   e. atmospherics.

MINICASE: THE ITALIAN RESTAURANT

The Italian Restaurant is operated by John Barboni and his son-in-law, Tim. Their main strategy is to provide friendly service, good food, and drinks while keeping costs and prices as low as possible. The menu includes sandwiches, pizza, complete meals, beer, and cocktails.

The restaurant's advertisements, which run in the local newspaper, focus on the variety and quality of food available at a reasonable price. Word of mouth is so strong and so successful that it is no longer necessary to promote the restaurant's atmosphere through advertising.

One of the most unusual aspects of the Italian Restaurant is its clientele, which is difficult to describe. On a typical day, the restaurant serves retired couples, teachers from a local high school, construction workers, college students, lawyers, and political figures. Barboni states that this too is one of his main objectives: to cater to all types of people.

The restaurant's somewhat archaic interior creates a certain ambience. Neither the exterior nor the interior has changed much in the last seventy-five years; the restaurant resembles an old neighborhood tavern. Although the atmosphere is friendly and relaxed, Barboni believes that the furniture should not be too comfortable or else people will stay too long. This is a special problem during the noon rush, when incoming customers often have to wait for a table.

Questions

_____ 1. The Italian Restaurant is a
   a. service retailer.
   b. nonstore retailer.
   c. franchisee.
   d. franchisor.
   e. specialty retailer.

_____ 2. The Italian Restaurant's competitive advantage appears to be its
   a. good location.
   b. good management.
   c. atmosphere.
   d. menu variety.
   e. clientele.

_____ 3. Which of the following does *not* contribute to the restaurant's atmosphere?
   a. Clientele
   b. Old neighborhood tavern look
   c. Archaic interior
   d. Friendly, relaxed feeling
   e. Price

_____ 4. Which of the following is most likely the Italian Restaurant's main retail positioning objective?
   a. Good food at good prices
   b. Fast and friendly service
   c. Old neighborhood tavern ambience
   d. Catering to all types of people
   e. Having a complete line of menu options

PROGRAMMED COMPLETION EXERCISES

in-home, tele-
marketing, automatic
vending, mail-order

1. Four types of nonstore retailing are _____,
_____, _____ _____, and
_____ retailing.

Retail positioning,
distinguishes, minds

2. _____ _____ involves identifying an underserved market segment and serving it with a strategy that
_____ the retailer from competitors in the
_____ of consumers.

franchise

3. A _____ system is an arrangement in which a
supplier grants dealers the right to sell products in exchange
for some type of consideration.

link

4. Retailers are an important _____ in the marketing
channel.

Scrambled
merchandising

5. _____ _____ consists of adding unrelated
products and product lines to an existing product mix.

wheel of retailing

6. The _____ _____ _____
hypothesis describes a cycle in the evolution of retail stores:
As the level of services increases, established retail institutions
become vulnerable to the entry of newer institutions.

central management
control

7. The expansion of the franchise system to many industries
illustrates the advantages of _____ _____
_____ and coordinated marketing efforts for
franchise members.

low-status, low-
margin,
low-price

8. The wheel of retailing hypothesis suggests that new types of retailers begin as _____, _____, _____ operators and gradually, as competition increases, acquire more expensive facilities.

department stores,
mass merchandisers,
specialty stores

9. The major types of retail stores that account for most retail shares are _____ _____, _____ _____, and _____ _____.

Retailers

10. _____ are the most visible middlemen because most of their contacts are with ultimate consumers.

place, time,
possession

11. Retailers create _____, _____, and _____ utilities by providing assortments of products that match consumers' wants.

product mix,
product line depth

12. One of the main functions of retailers is to provide a _____ and a _____ _____ _____ that gives consumers opportunities to compare, shop, and make purchasing decisions.

Purpose, status,
completeness

13. _____, _____, and _____ are three criteria for evaluating product assortments.

Atmospherics

14. _____ is the term used to describe the purposeful design of store space to create emotional conditions that enhance the probability that customers will buy.

marketing efforts,
internal management

15. Department stores have a wide product mix and are organized into different departments to facilitate _____ _____ and _____ _____.

narrow, deep

16. Specialty retailers are stores that carry a _____ product mix and _____ product lines.

department store

17. A good example of a shopping store where the customer compares the prices, quality, and services of one store with its competitors is the _____ _____.

warehouse showroom

18. The introduction of sophisticated mass merchandising to the highly fragmented furniture industry created the _____ _____.

neighborhood, community, regional

19. Types of planned shopping centers include _____, _____, and _____ shopping centers.

Mass merchandisers

20. _____ _____ appeal to large, heterogeneous target markets; images of efficiency and economy distinguish the atmosphere of these stores.

consumers, manufacturers

21. Retailers are in a strategic position to collect feedback from _____ and to channel this information back to _____ or resellers.

image

22. A retail store must project an _____ that is acceptable to its target market.

ANSWERS TO OBJECTIVE QUESTIONS

Matching		*True or False*		*Multiple-Choice*		*Minicase*
1. j	15. o	1. T	16. T	1. c	11. d	1.a
2. b	16. r	2. T	17. F	2. d	12. b	2.c
3. f	17. e	3. F	18. F	3. d	13. b	3.e
4. a	18. c	4. F	19. F	4. a	14. a	4.d
5. x	19. v	5. F	20. F	5. b	15. c	
6. u	20. p	6. F	21. T	6. d	16. d	
7. d	21. q	7. T	22. F	7. e	17. d	
8. l	22. h	8. T	23. T	8. c	18. e	
9. i	23. w	9. T	24. F	9. c	19. b	
10. n	24. y	10. T	25. F	10. b	20. a	
11. z	25. g	11. T	26. F			
12. t	26. aa	12. F	27. F			
13. s	27. bb	13. F	28. T			
14. k		14. T	29. F			
		15. F	30. T			

14 PHYSICAL DISTRIBUTION

CHAPTER OUTLINE

CHAPTER SUMMARY

Physical distribution is the set of activities involved in managing the movement of products from producers to consumers and end users. For most companies, the main objective of physical distribution efforts is to decrease distribution costs while increasing service. Because these goals are difficult to achieve in real-world situations, physical distribution managers strive for a balance among service, costs, and resources. The distribution cost objective should be to keep the lower overall cost compatible with the company's stated service objectives.

A major issue to consider in a physical distribution system is order processing—the receipt and transmission of sales order information. Order processing is composed of order entry (when customers or salespersons place purchase orders), order handling (verifying product availability), and order delivery (scheduling pickup with an appropriate carrier). Order processing can be performed either manually or electronically.

Materials handling refers to the physical movement of products. The characteristics of the product itself (e.g., liquid or gas) as well as the product's packaging are important considerations.

Another major consideration is the design and operation of facilities for storing and moving goods, or warehousing. A private warehouse is operated by a company for distribution of its own products. Public warehouses rent out storage space and related physical distribution facilities to firms and sometimes provide distribution services. A distribution center is a large, centralized warehouse that receives goods from factories and suppliers, regroups the goods into orders, and quickly ships the orders to customers.

Inventory management involves the development and maintenance of adequate assortments of products to meet customers' needs. To avoid both stockouts and high carrying costs, inventory managers must know when to order and how much. The economic order quantity (EOQ) specifies the order size that minimizes the total cost of ordering and carrying inventory. Specialized equipment and certain management techniques, such as JIT, are available to improve inventory control.

Another distribution variable is transportation, which creates time and place utilities for a firm's products. The major modes of transportation are railways, motor vehicles, inland waterways, airways, and pipelines. Criteria to consider in transportation selection include cost, transit time, reliability, capability, accessibility, security, and traceability. Marketers often coordinate and combine two or more modes of transportation to take advantage of the benefits and minimize the deficiencies of various carriers.

The strategic importance of physical distribution can be seen in each element of the marketing mix. Product design and packaging affects storage and transportation, pricing may depend on the ability to provide timely delivery, promotion must be coordinated with distribution functions, and each element of the physical distribution system must be continually evaluated and adjusted to ensure maximum effectiveness in maintaining company goals.

MATCHING EXERCISES

Use the following set of terms to identify the sentences and phrases below. On the blank line next to each sentence or phrase, place the letter of the term that the sentence or phrase describes. Do not use a term more than once.

a. Materials handling
b. Containerization
c. Physical distribution
d. Private warehouse
e. Freight forwarders
f. Public warehouses
g. Inventory management
h. Unit loading
i. Transit time
j. Field warehouse
k. Stockout

l. Bonded storage
m. Safety stock
n. Transportation modes
o. Economic order quantity (EOQ)
p. Megacarriers
q. Order processing
r. Distribution center
s. Intermodal transportation
t. Reorder point
u. Warehousing
v. Just-in-time (JIT)

d 1. A storage facility operated by a company for the purpose of distributing its own products.
Private Warehouse

l 2. A service many public warehouses provide; the goods are not released until U.S. customs duties, federal or state taxes, or other fees are paid.
Bonded Storage

k 3. The condition that exists when a firm runs out of a product.
Stockout

m 4. Inventory needed to prevent a stockout.
Saftey Stock

b 5. The practice of consolidating many items into one container, sealed at the point of origin and opened at the destination.
Containerization

e 6. Businesses that consolidate shipments from several organizations into efficient lot sizes, which increases transit time but can lower shipping costs.
Freight Forwarder

c 7. An integrated set of activities that deals with managing the movement of products within firms and through marketing channels.
Physical distribution

i 8. The total time that a carrier has possession of the goods.
Transit time

h 9. Grouping one or more boxes on a pallet or skid.
Unit loading

n 10. Railways, motor vehicles, waterways, pipelines, and airways used to move goods from one location to another.
Transportation Mode

o 11. The order size that minimizes the total cost of ordering and carrying inventory.
Economic Order Quanity

a 12. Physical handling of products.
Materials handling

f 13. Business organizations that rent out storage and related physical distribution facilities.
Public Warehouses

j 14. A temporary storage space established by a public warehouse at the owner's inventory location.
Field Warehouses

g 15. The development and maintenance of an adequate assortment of products.
Inventory Mgmt

t 16. The inventory level that signals that more inventory should be ordered.
Reorder Pt

p 17. Freight transportation companies that provide several methods of shipment.
Megacarrier

r 18. A large, centralized warehouse that receives goods from factories and suppliers, regroups the goods into orders, and quickly ships the orders to customers.
Distribution Center

v 19. An inventory management technique whereby a company maintains low inventory levels and purchases materials in small quantities as they are needed for production.
Just-in-Time

s 20. The integration of two or more modes of transportation.
Intermodal Transportation

q 21. The receipt and transmission of sales order information.
Order Processing

u 22. The design and operation of facilities for storing and moving goods.
Warehousing

TRUE OR FALSE STATEMENTS

T   F   1. When sales volumes are fairly stable, the ownership and control of a private warehouse can provide several advantages, including financial ones, such as property appreciation and tax shelters realized through depreciation of the facility.

T   F   2. Order handling refers to the physical movement of products from producer to end user.

T   F   3. Materials handling procedures and techniques can reduce the number of times a good is handled and improve service to customers as well as customer satisfaction with the product.

T   F   4. Transportation systems must take into account both cost factors and customer requirements.

T   F   5. The protective functions of packaging are an important consideration in physical distribution.

T   F   6. The development of an efficient physical handling system depends in part on packaging materials and methods.

T   F   7. Containerization has revolutionized physical distribution by broadening the capabilities of the transportation system, enabling shippers to handle a wider range of cargoes with speed, reliability, and stable costs.

T   F   8. Electronic order processing is more practical than manual processing for a large volume of orders but is less flexible in special situations.

T   F   9. Changes in customers do not usually affect the overall structure of physical distribution in the marketing strategy.

T   F   10. Speed of delivery, reliability, and economy of service are marketing considerations that help develop the total product in customers' eyes.

T   F   11. A physical distribution system must be able to adjust to changing environmental circumstances while continuing to give customers what they want.

T   F   12. Changes in transportation, order processing, warehousing, materials handling, and inventory can increase or decrease speed of delivery and other services.

T   F   13. A physical distribution system is not a part of the marketing strategy.

T   F   14. Physical distribution is an integrated set of activities that deals with the movement of products from producers to consumers and end users.

T   F   15. Physical distribution creates time and place utilities by performing the activities that store, transport, handle, and process orders for products.

T   F   16. Whatever the role of physical distribution in the marketing strategy, someone must make distribution decisions for the physical movement of goods to occur.

T F 17. Inventory management requires a systematic approach to determining efficient reorder points, which can help eliminate stockouts and too much capital being tied up in inventory.

T F 18. The problem of trade-offs between the costs of carrying larger inventories and the costs of frequent orders can be solved by finding the optimal marginal order quantity (MOQ).

T F 19. Transportation decisions should be integrated with other marketing strategy decisions.

T F 20. The selection of a transportation mode usually is based on cost, transit time, reliability, capability, accessibility, security, and traceability.

T F 21. Warehousing involves only the design and operation of facilities to store goods.

T F 22. Materials handling, or the physical handling of products, is an important element of the inventory management system.

T F 23. Just-in-time inventory management requires considerable coordination between an organization and its suppliers.

T F 24. The physical distribution system is often adjusted to meet the unique needs of a channel member.

T F 25. The "total cost approach" to physical distribution emphasizes lowering the separate costs of individual functions.

MULTIPLE-CHOICE QUESTIONS

_____ 1. Which of the following is *not* one of the main tasks of order processing?
a. Order verification
b. Order delivery
c. Order entry
d. Order handling
e. All of the above are main tasks of order processing.

_____ 2. Which of the following statements about physical distribution is true?
a. Physical distribution usually deals with the physical movement of goods and raw materials between storage and production facilities within a firm.
b. Physical distribution deals only with the holding of inventory until it is needed.
c. Physical distribution deals with the movement of products from producers to consumers and end users.
d. Physical distribution concerns the sorting, grading, sampling, and physical movement of goods within and among intermediaries.
e. Physical distribution deals only with the physical movement of goods from producer to ultimate consumer.

_____ 3. In order to increase customer service and lower costs, Rogers Distributing is interested in integrating its order processing, inventory, accounting, and transportation planning into a total information system. Which of the following systems would you recommend to Rogers Distributing so they can meet their objectives?
   a. A just-in-time (JIT) system
   b. An electronic data interchange (EDI) system
   c. A computer-based planning (CBP) system
   d. A manual order processing system
   e. A materials handling system

_____ 4. Mills Brothers Distributing has a big problem with its products being damaged or broken during handling and transportation. This indicates that Mills Brothers has a problem with the _____ of its products.
   a. order processing
   b. shipment
   c. handling
   d. internal packaging
   e. quality

_____ 5. Inventory management is essential to
   a. production planning and control.
   b. increasing inventory carrying and ordering costs.
   c. inventory pricing.
   d. a sound physical distribution system.
   e. inventory financing.

_____ 6. The total time that a carrier has possession of goods is known as
   a. transit time.
   b. holding time.
   c. lead time.
   d. carrying time.
   e. possession time.

_____ 7. To buyers, speed of delivery, service, and dependability are
   a. less important than the cost of the product.
   b. more important than the quality of the product.
   c. unimportant when compared to price.
   d. as important as the cost of the product.
   e. of no significance whatsoever.

_____ 8. Ace Tea, Rosedale Distribution, and Hilltop Stores are a group of interrelated organizations that direct the flow of various food products to customers. This group can best be described as a(n)
   a. sales channel.
   b. distribution channel.
   c. marketing force.
   d. intermediary.
   e. marketing channel.

_____ 9. Which of the following are most likely responsible for delivery delays, thereby causing a loss of sales and customers?
   a. Wide assortment of bulky goods
   b. Stockouts
   c. Late deliveries
   d. Failure to use air freight
   e. Distant business locations

_____ 10. The management decision to accept higher transportation costs in exchange for lower warehousing costs is an example of
   a. cost optimization.
   b. cost trade-off.
   c. intermodal transportation.
   d. economic order cost.
   e. inventory management.

_____ 11. The Bach Company consolidates all of its shipments with a system that allows cargo to be stacked and shipped via rail or waterway. When the cargo reaches its destination, wheel assemblies are added so that the cargo can be hauled with ground transportation. What type of system is the Bach Company using?
   a. Containerization
   b. Unit loading
   c. An EDI system
   d. A JIT system
   e. A transmodal system

_____ 12. Which of the following is *not* a criterion in selecting a transportation mode?
   a. Reliability
   b. Variety
   c. Security
   d. Accessibility
   e. Capacity

_____ 13. Assuming similar benefits and services, which of the following remains an important consideration in selecting a transportation mode?
   a. Cost
   b. Security
   c. Speed
   d. Dependability
   e. Capability

_____ 14. The ability of a carrier to move goods over a specific route or network is known as its
   a. accessibility.
   b. dependability.
   c. reliability.
   d. capability.
   e. capacity.

_____ 15. The design and operation of facilities to store and move goods is an important
   a. physical distribution activity.
   b. selling activity.
   c. facilitating function.
   d. inventory planning and control activity.
   e. transportation activity.

_____ 16. According to the text, changes in which of the following can have the most profound effects on the overall structure of physical distribution in the marketing strategy?
   a. Transportation
   b. Customers
   c. Technological advances
   d. Physical handling system
   e. Materials handling practices

_____ 17. Which of the following is *not* one of the functions performed by a warehouse?
   a. Identifying goods
   b. Sorting goods
   c. Bearing the loss of damage to goods while in storage
   d. Recalling, selecting, or picking goods from storage
   e. Dispatching shipments

_____ 18. There is often a trade-off between inventory carrying costs and
   a. stockouts.
   b. inventory holding costs.
   c. the probability of stockouts.
   d. the chance of losing sales.
   e. order lead time.

_____ 19. Economic order quantity (EOQ)
   a. reduces the inventory carried in stock.
   b. minimizes the cost per unit of inventory.
   c. guarantees a sufficient inventory level at all times.
   d. minimizes the total cost of ordering and carrying inventory.
   e. minimizes only total carrying costs.

_____ 20. Many firms establish a customer service policy of minimum order sizes to ensure that
   a. surplus inventory does not build up.
   b. orders can be shipped at full carload rates.
   c. transactions are profitable.
   d. product quality remains high.
   e. sales are not lost to competitors.

_____ 21. The 80/20 rule of inventory management holds that
   a. 20 percent of the customers account for 80 percent of the sales.
   b. 20 percent of the firm's items must be reordered 80 percent of the time.

c. 20 percent of a firm's items account for 80 percent of its sales.

d. 20 percent of the inventory moves slowly while 80 percent moves quickly.

e. 80 percent of a firm's inventory will usually be delivered on time while 20 percent will usually be delivered late.

22. The Ford Motor Company practices an inventory management technique whereby it maintains very low inventory levels and purchases materials in small quantities only as they are needed for production. What type of technique is Ford using?

a. The economic order quantity (EOQ) technique

b. The just-as-needed (JAN) technique

c. The only-as-needed (OAN) technique

d. The just-in-time (JIT) technique

e. The limited order quantity (LOQ) technique

23. Thompson Plastics, Inc., is in need of a new warehouse to add to its distribution system. Thompson's products require special handling and storage features. In addition, the company wants to maintain complete control over the design and operation of its new warehouse. What type of warehouse should Thompson use?

a. A public warehouse

b. A distribution center

c. A private warehouse

d. A combination warehouse

e. A public-limited warehouse

24. Which of the following has as one of its primary functions accepting merchandise delivered from outside transportation or an attached factory and taking responsibility for it?

a. Public warehouse

b. Wholesaler

c. Channel member

d. Warehouse

e. Field warehousing company

25. The text indicates that transit time affects a marketer's ability to

a. select a suitable marketing mix.

b. increase sales volume.

c. utilize a carrier to capacity.

d. provide service.

e. transport the largest quantity of goods to the marketplace.

26. The integration of all those activities that help to store, transport, handle, and process orders and that are necessary to provide a level of service satisfactory to customers is known as

a. production strategy.

b. sales strategy.

c. physical distribution.

d. inventory planning and control.

e. the physical movement of goods.

_____   27. Planning an effective means of physical distribution can be a significant decision point in developing a
        a. marketing strategy.
        b. product strategy.
        c. promotion strategy.
        d. sales strategy.
        e. transportation system owned by the firm.

_____   28. A systematic approach must be taken to determine efficient reorder points to
        a. ensure higher levels of inventories.
        b. decrease shortages.
        c. eliminate stockouts or avoid having too much capital tied up in inventory.
        d. ensure regular and uniform supply.
        e. minimize inventory ordering costs.

_____   29. The overall safety stock
        a. must be greater than the average inventory.
        b. depends on the general level of demand.
        c. depends on the level of supply.
        d. is determined by the inventory cost.
        e. is determined by the cost of stockouts.

_____   30. Bob and Sylvia King, owners of the King Dairy Farm, recently signed a contract to supply raw milk to a milk processing plant in the next state— over 600 miles away. Bob and Sylvia are concerned about the best way to transport their milk to the processing plant. The King Farm is located next to a regional airport, three major interstate highways, and a major rail line. Which transportation mode would you recommend to Bob and Sylvia?
        a. Air
        b. Truck
        c. Waterways
        d. Railroad
        e. Pipeline

MINICASE: THE BLACK HAWK COMPANY

The Black Hawk Company was established approximately fifty years ago. It is a linen supply company that serves twelve midwestern states with uniform rentals, toweling, and paper products. The company deals with many types of customers, from small service stations to large corporations. The market, which includes all organizations that need towels and uniforms, is highly competitive, and the profit margin is low.

Black Hawk has three general divisions: marketing centers, processing plants, and warehouses. The marketing centers are involved only with selling activities. The plants process the merchandise (dry cleaning, washing, pressing), which then is shipped to the warehouses and on to the ultimate consumers. For the most part, customer records, billing, and inventory control have been maintained both in plants and warehouses but not in the marketing centers. Recently, however, Black Hawk purchased computer services with terminal time. Management hopes that there will be less reliance on duplicate records and more reliance on centralized computer control.

Common carriers and, in some cases, buses are used to transport supplies to customers. Although buses are more expensive, the cost is balanced against faster delivery and greater customer satisfaction. On occasion, two different carriers are used on the same day for freight destined to the same location—a practice that can lead to higher per weight shipping charges. This can happen when rush orders are made or when the shipments come from two different warehouses. Presently, there is little coordination among the firm's warehouses.

Questions

_____ 1. Black Hawk occasionally uses buses because of
    a. an insufficient fleet of trucks.
    b. unreliable common carriers.
    c. the needs of the market.
    d. poor assembling procedures.
    e. lack of proper communication.

_____ 2. An integrated communications and data processing system would *not* help Black Hawk solve its problem of
    a. higher per weight shipping charges.
    b. using buses for emergency situations.
    c. multiple invoicing.
    d. poor management.
    e. freight destined to the same location from different warehouses.

_____ 3. Black Hawk's biggest problem appears to be
    a. intense competition.
    b. warehousing.
    c. materials handling.
    d. inventory planning and control.
    e. communication and data processing.

_____ 4. What is the firm's major consideration in selecting buses as a mode of transportation?
    a. Transit time
    b. Accessibility
    c. Security
    d. Cost
    e. Reliability

_____ 5. What seems to be the firm's major consideration in using common carriers as its primary mode of transportation?
    a. Transit time
    b. Needs of the market
    c. Security

      d. Capability

      e. Cost

_____ 6. Which of the following types of warehouses does Black Hawk use?

      a. Private

      b. Public

      c. Field

      d. Private and public

      e. Public and field

PROGRAMMED COMPLETION EXERCISES

products, consumers, end users

1. Physical distribution is a set of activities used in the movement of _____ from producers to _____ and _____ _____.

time, place, value

2. Physical distribution creates _____ and _____ utilities, which maximize the _____ of products by delivering them when and where they are wanted.

Planning, physical distribution, developing

3. _____ an effective means of _____ _____ can be a significant decision point in _____ an overall marketing strategy.

important variable, costs, customer satisfaction

4. Physical distribution is an _____ _____ in a marketing strategy, in that it can decrease _____ and increase _____ _____.

speed, delivery, services, dependability

5. To buyers, _____ of _____, _____, and _____ are often as important as cost.

marketing channel, interrelated, direct

6. The _____ _____ is a group of _____ organizations that _____ products to customers.

physical distribution,
adjusted, unique

7. The _____ _____ system often is
_____ to meet the _____ needs of a
channel member.

cost trade-offs,
customer service,
total cost

8. Physical distribution managers use _____
_____ to provide a specific level of _____
_____ for the lowest possible _____
_____.

satisfied customers,
repeat orders,
increased profits

9. Efficient order processing contributes to _____
_____, _____ _____, and
_____ _____.

Electronic, total
information system

10. _____ order processing allows an organization to
integrate several distribution activities into a _____
_____ _____.

Materials handling,
warehouse,
production,
consumption

11. _____ _____ is important in efficient _____
operations as well as in transportation from points of
_____ to points of _____.

usable capacity,
number, times,
product

12. Materials handling procedures should increase the
_____ _____ of a warehouse, reduce the
_____ of _____ a good is handled, and
improve service to customers as well as their satisfaction with
the _____.

Warehousing, design,
operation, activity

13. _____ refers to the _____ and
_____ of facilities to store and move goods and is
another physical distribution _____.

Warehousing, storage,
goods, services

14. _____ is not limited to providing space for the
_____ of _____ but also includes offering
_____ for the distribution of the goods.

Inventory management, development, maintenance

15. _____ _____ refers to physical distribution activities that aid in the _____ and _____ of adequate assortments of products to meet customers' needs.

costs, inventory, controlled

16. The _____ involved in obtaining and maintaining _____ must be _____ so that profit goals can be met.

planned, products sold, products, stock

17. An inventory system should be _____ so that the number of _____ _____ and the number of _____ in _____ can be determined at certain checkpoints.

systematic, reorder, shortages, capital

18. A _____ approach must be taken to determine _____ points to avoid _____ without too much _____ being tied up in inventory.

safety stock

19. The overall _____ _____ depends on the general level of demand.

reorders, larger, processing

20. Individual _____ depend on the trade-off between the cost of carrying _____ average inventory and the cost of _____ small orders.

transportation modes, marketers, risk

21. Because all _____ _____ have security problems, _____ must determine the relative _____ associated with each mode before making a selection.

consolidating, container, destination, containerization

22. The practice of _____ many items into one _____, sealed at the point of origin and opened at the _____, is called _____.

half, marketing

23. According to the text, physical distribution functions account for about _____ of all _____ costs.

target markets,
distribution systems,
products, costs

24. Consumer-oriented marketers analyze the characteristics of their _____ _____ and then design _____ _____ to provide _____ at acceptable _____.

ANSWERS TO OBJECTIVE QUESTIONS

Matching		*True or False*		*Multiple-Choice*		*Minicase*
1. d	12. a	1. T	14. T	1. a	16. b	1. c
2. l	13. f	2. F	15. T	2. c	17. c	2. d
3. k	14. j	3. T	16. T	3. b	18. c	3. e
4. m	15. g	4. T	17. T	4. d	19. d	4. a
5. b	16. t	5. T	18. F	5. d	20. c	5. e
6. e	17. p	6. T	19. T	6. a	21. c	6. a
7. c	18. r	7. T	20. T	7. d	22. d	
8. i	19. v	8. T	21. F	8. e	23. c	
9. h	20. s	9. F	22. F	9. b	24. d	
10. n	21. q	10. T	23. T	10. b	25. d	
11. o	22. u	11. T	24. T	11. a	26. c	
		12. T	25. F	12. b	27. a	
		13. F		13. a	28. c	
				14. a	29. b	
				15. a	30. b	

15 PROMOTION: AN OVERVIEW

CHAPTER OUTLINE

The role of promotion
Promotion and the communication process
Promotion and the product adoption process
The promotion mix
  Promotion mix ingredients
  Selecting promotion mix ingredients
  Push policy versus pull policy

CHAPTER SUMMARY

The role of promotion is to communicate with individuals, groups, or organizations to facilitate exchanges directly or indirectly by informing and persuading one or more of these audiences to accept an organization's products. Communication here is defined as a sharing of meaning. The process begins with a source—a person, group, or organization that has a message it wants to share with an audience. Through the coding process, the source converts the meaning into a series of signs that represent ideas or concepts. These signs must be familiar to the audience or receiver and must clearly transmit the intended meaning. Once the message is encoded, it is transmitted to the audience or receiver through a medium of transmission, a communication channel that carries the coded message. When the audience receives the message, it must decode it to obtain meaning: The receiver must convert the signs into concepts and ideas. When the decoded message is different from the encoded message, a condition called noise exists. The receiver's response to the message is feedback to the source. It is encoded, transmitted, and decoded in turn. The communication process, then, is circular. Each communication channel can handle only a limited amount of information effectively. Channel capacity is determined by the least efficient component of the communication process.

Marketers communicate to facilitate exchanges. One of their primary objectives is to influence and encourage buyers to accept or adopt goods, services, and ideas. To set realistic expectations for promotional strategies, they must understand the product adoption process, which involves five stages: awareness, interest, evaluation, trial, and adoption. In the awareness stage, individuals become aware that the product exists, but they have little information about it and are not concerned about getting more. They enter the interest stage when they are motivated to get information about the product's features, uses, advantages, disadvantages, price, and location. During the evaluation stage, buyers consider whether the product satisfies their specific needs. In the trial stage, they use or experience the product for the first time. Finally, they move into the adoption stage, the point at which they begin using the specific product whenever the need arises for that general type of product. Rejection can occur at any stage, including adoption, and can be temporary or permanent.

Most people respond to different information sources at different stages of the adoption process. For example, mass communication sources are effective for moving large numbers of people into the awareness stage; personal sources are more effective during the evaluation and trial stages. Other factors—product characteristics, price, use, and buyer characteristics—also play a part in how consumers respond to information. And all these factors must be considered in developing a promotional strategy.

The time people take to adopt a new product is another factor that affects buyers' reactions to the form of communication and the type of information transmitted. There are five major adopter categories: innovators, early adopters, early majority, late majority, and laggards.

A promotion mix is the combination of promotional methods used to communicate with consumers. Advertising, personal selling, publicity, and sales promotion are four of the elements that make up a promotion mix. Advertising is a paid form of nonpersonal communication about an organization or its products that is transmitted to a target audience through a mass medium. Advertising can be an extremely cost-efficient promotional method because it reaches a vast number of people at a low cost per person. Also, advertising allows the user to repeat a message and can enhance a firm's public image. On the other hand, advertising can entail a high absolute dollar outlay; it can be slow to provide feedback; and its effect on sales is difficult to measure.

Personal selling is the process of informing customers and persuading them to purchase a product through personal communication in an exchange situation. Whereas advertising is aimed at a relatively large target audience, personal selling is aimed at one or several individuals. The cost of reaching one person through personal selling is considerably more than through advertising, but personal selling often has greater impact on customers.

Publicity, like advertising, is a form of nonpersonal communication. With publicity, however, the organization does not pay media costs and is not identified, and the communication is presented as a news story. As much as possible, publicity must be planned and implemented so that it is compatible with, and supportive of, other elements in the promotion mix.

Sales promotion is an activity or material that acts as a direct inducement, offering added value, or incentive for the product, to resellers, salespersons, or consumers. Often marketers use sales promotion to improve the effectiveness of their advertising and personal selling efforts. (Sales promotion can be, but seldom is, the primary promotion vehicle.) Sales promotions usually are used to produce immediate short-run sales increases.

The specific promotion-mix ingredients employed and the intensity at which an organization uses them depends on a number of factors. The size of an organization's promotional resources affects the number and relative intensity of promotional methods. If a company's promotional dollars are limited, the firm is likely to concentrate on personal selling. The firm's objectives also influence the makeup of the promotion mix. For example, if a company wants to create awareness of a new convenience product, its promotion mix is likely to be heavily oriented toward advertising and sales promotion, and possibly publicity. If a company wants to educate consumers about the features of a durable good, its promotion mix generally involves a large amount of personal selling.

The size, geographic distribution, and socioeconomic characteristics of the target market also influence the promotion mix. When the size of a market is limited or customers are concentrated in a small area, personal selling is most effective. When a market is very large or customers are highly dispersed across a vast geographic area, advertising and sales promotion are most effective. Buyers' age, income, and education also are factors in the makeup of the promotion mix. For example, less-educated people respond better to personal selling than to print advertising.

Product characteristics also affect the promotion mix ingredients. Generally, promotion mixes for industrial products concentrate on personal selling, and advertising plays a major role in promoting consumer goods. High-priced products require promotion mixes with a great deal of personal selling. For low-priced convenience items, marketers use advertising because the profit margin on many of these items is too low to justify the cost of personal selling and because most consumers do not need advice from sales personnel when buying convenience products. The stage of the product life cycle is another element in the decision about the promotion mix, as is the intensity of market coverage. For products marketed through intensive distribution, the organization depends strongly on advertising. Items distributed through selective distribution require a variety of promotional methods. Items distributed through exclusive distribution often are promoted through personal selling. The ways products are used also affect the combination of promotional methods in the mix.

The costs and availability of promotional methods are major factors in developing a promotion mix. National advertising and sales promotion efforts require large expenditures. And a firm may not be able to advertise to a certain market because no available advertising medium effectively reaches it.

Policy plays a role here too. Using a push policy, the producer promotes the product only to the next institution down the marketing channel; using a pull policy, the producer promotes directly to consumers. The pull policy is designed to "pull" goods down through the marketing channel by creating demand at the consumer level.

MATCHING EXERCISES

Use the following set of terms to identify the sentences and phrases below. On the blank line next to each sentence or phrase, place the letter of the term that the sentence or phrase describes. Do not use a term more than once.

a. Pull policy
b. Promotion
c. Laggards
d. Tactile communication
e. Coding process
f. Personal selling
g. Push policy
h. Communication
i. Medium of transmission

j. Advertising
k. Innovators
l. Source
m. Receiver
n. Proxemic communication
o. Early adopters
p. Promotion mix
q. Durable good
r. Decoding processs.

s. Late majority
t. Kinesic communication
u. Publicity
v. Sales promotion

w. Product adoption process
x. Noise
y. Feedback
z. Channel capacity

_____ 1. Promotion of a product directly to consumers with the intention of developing strong consumer demand. *Pull Policy*

_____ 2. Among the first to adopt new products, this group is viewed as "the people to check with" by persons in the remaining adopter categories. *Early Adopters*

_____ 3. The element that carries the coded message from the source to the receiver or audience; examples include ink on paper or vibrations of air waves produced by vocal cords. *Medium of Transmission*

_____ 4. Moving one's head, eyes, arms, or hands as a form of communication; body language. *Kinesic Commun.*

_____ 5. The receiver's response to a decoded message. *Feedback*

_____ 6. A person, group, or organization that has a meaning it wants to share with a receiver or an audience. *Source*

_____ 7. The process by which a meaning is placed into a series of signs that represent ideas. *Coding Process "encoding"*

_____ 8. The specific combination of promotional methods an organization uses for a particular product. *Promotion Mix*

_____ 9. The volume of information that a communication channel can handle effectively. *Channel Capacity*

_____ 10. Promotion of a product only to the next institution down the marketing channel. *Push Policy*

_____ 11. The type of communication that occurs when one party moves closer to or farther away from the other party. *Proxemic Communi*

_____ 12. An activity or material that acts as a direct inducement, offering resellers, salespersons, or consumers added value, or incentive for the product. *Sales Promotion*

_____ 13. A paid form of nonpersonal communication about an organization or its products, that is transmitted to a target audience through a mass medium. *Advertising*

_____ 14. The communication with individuals, groups, or organizations to facilitate exchanges directly or indirectly by influencing audience members to accept an organization's products. *Promotion*

_____ 15. The five-stage process that buyers go through in accepting a product: awareness, interest, evaluation, trial, and adoption. *Product Adoption Process*

_____ 16. A sharing of meaning through the transmission of information. *Communication*

_____ 17. A condition in the communication process that exists when a decoded message is different from what was coded. *Noise*

_f_ 18. The process of informing customers and persuading them to purchase products through personal communication in an exchange situation.
Personal Selling

_e_ 19. The stage in the communication process in which signs are converted into concepts and ideas.
Decoding

_d_ 20. Handshaking is a form of this type of communication.
Tactile Communi.

_m_ 21. The individual, group, or organization that decodes a coded message.
Reciever

_c_ 22. The last group to adopt new products.
Laggards

_u_ 23. Nonpersonal communication in news story form, about an organization or its products, that is transmitted through a mass medium at no charge.
Publicity

TRUE OR FALSE STATEMENTS

T F 1. Meaningful communication is achieved through the transmission of any symbols.

T F 2. During the encoding process, the source must be careful to avoid signs that have multiple meanings.

T F 3. The decoding process is the source of most of the noise that arises in the communication process.

T F 4. Feedback is the stage in the communication process that makes the process circular.

T F 5. Channel capacity is the volume of information that can be handled effectively through a specific communication channel.

T F 6. The basic role of promotion is to communicate.

T F 7. A single information source, such as mass communication, is effective during all stages of the product adoption process.

T F 8. Rejection can occur at any stage in the product adoption process.

T F 9. Four possible ingredients of a promotion mix are advertising, personal selling, publicity, and sales promotion.

T F 10. Advertising is a nonpersonal paid form of communication that is transmitted by a mass medium.

T F 11. Because it is so expensive, advertising is not cost efficient.

T F 12. Usually marketers design sales promotion to produce long-run sales increases.

T F 13. A marketer's use of sales promotion is usually on an irregular, not a continuous, basis.

T F 14. Industrial products generally are promoted through a heavy concentration on advertising in the promotion mix.

T F 15. Sales promotion and promotion mean about the same thing.

T F 16. In making promotion-mix decisions, marketers must consider not only the mix ingredients but market and product characteristics.

T F 17. Publicity gives an organization a means of free communication.

T F 18. Because the intensity of distribution generally is determined after the promotion mix is created, it is not an important consideration in developing that mix.

T F 19. When a push policy is used, the producer promotes the product directly to consumers.

T F 20. When a company's customers are numerous and highly dispersed, advertising may be a more practical promotional method than personal selling.

T F 21. High-priced products require promotion mixes with a great deal of advertising, publicity, and sales promotion.

T F 22. Manufacturers of highly personal products depend heavily on personal selling.

T F 23. The stage of the product life cycle has little effect on the makeup of the promotion mix for a specific product.

T F 24. A firm may not be able to advertise to a certain market because no available advertising medium effectively reaches it.

MULTIPLE-CHOICE QUESTIONS

_____ 1. According to the text, communication is best defined as
   a. a transmission of meaning.
   b. information transmitted in form or pattern.
   c. the sending and receiving of information.
   d. the coding and decoding of information.
   e. a sharing of meaning.

_____ 2. The coding process is
   a. performed by the receiver.
   b. always ineffective because of noise.
   c. performed by the medium used for transmission.
   d. the conversion of meaning into signs that represent ideas.
   e. the process of interpreting messages.

_____ 3. Procter & Gamble's program of donating part of the purchase price of each jar of JIF peanut butter to local schools is a direct example of
   a. mass marketing.
   b. channel-driven marketing.
   c. cause-related marketing.

        d. macro marketing.

        e. the marketing concept.

_____ 4. When coding meaning into a message, a marketer must do all the following *except*

        a. know what level of language the target market can understand.

        b. avoid signs that have several meanings.

        c. select a medium of transmission that will reach the target market.

        d. include all possible product information.

        e. attempt to minimize noise.

_____ 5. An audience is best defined as

        a. two or more receivers who decode a message.

        b. the component in the communication process responsible for transmitting a message.

        c. the major source of noise.

        d. the component in the communication process responsible for encoding.

        e. the people who receive a message.

_____ 6. HEB grocery stores wants to indicate to its customers that it now offers an expanded range of services, including late hours and check cashing. In the communication process, HEB would be considered the

        a. source.

        b. audience.

        c. decoder.

        d. transmission medium.

        e. receiver.

_____ 7. When a decoded message is different from the coded message,

        a. the message was not encoded properly by the source.

        b. a condition called noise exists.

        c. the wrong receivers have been reached.

        d. an inappropriate medium of transmission was used.

        e. it is the source's fault.

_____ 8. Channel capacity is determined by the

        a. medium of transmission chosen.

        b. intended receiver's prior knowledge.

        c. complexity of the information transmitted.

        d. least efficient component of the communication process.

        e. size of the intended audience.

_____ 9. The stage in the adoption process in which buyers are motivated to find information about a product is the

        a. interest stage.

        b. awareness stage.

        c. adoption stage.

        d. evaluation stage.

        e. trial stage.

10. Individuals often seek information, opinions, and reinforcement from friends and relatives during the
    a. trial and adoption stages.
    b. awareness and interest stages.
    c. evaluation and trial stages.
    d. interest and evaluation stages.
    e. interest and trial stages.

11. Steve Roberts of Roberts Auto Sales states in his television commercial that his cars are "bad." Seeing this, Calvin Peters wonders why any of these cars are sold. This situation is an example of a communication problem stemming from the absence of
    a. encoding.
    b. noise.
    c. decoding.
    d. shared meaning.
    e. a medium of transmission.

12. Immediate feedback and knowledge of customers' needs are advantages of
    a. advertising.
    b. publicity.
    c. sales promotion.
    d. public relations.
    e. personal selling.

13. According to the text, advertising is
    a. a process of informing customers and persuading them to purchase products through personal communication.
    b. nonpersonal communication in news story form.
    c. the same thing as sales promotion.
    d. a paid form of nonpersonal communication transmitted through a mass medium.
    e. an activity that acts as a direct inducement, offering customers added value for the product.

14. Which of the following is an activity or a material that serves as a direct inducement to resellers, salespersons, or consumers?
    a. Advertising
    b. Personal selling
    c. Packaging
    d. Publicity
    e. Sales promotion

15. Which of the following is a characteristic of sales promotion?
    a. It is used on a continuous or cyclical basis.
    b. It may be aimed at either final consumers or trade people.
    c. It is used to increase long-run sales.
    d. It is a comprehensive area that includes promotion.
    e. It generally is used as the primary promotion vehicle.

____ 16. A form of communication that is transmitted through mass media at no charge is
   a. advertising.
   b. personal selling.
   c. sales promotion.
   d. publicity.
   e. packaging.

____ 17. Most firms with limited promotional resources use mainly personal selling because
   a. measuring a salesperson's contribution to sales is easy.
   b. it is the most cost-efficient method.
   c. the per-unit cost of advertising is higher than the per-unit cost of personal selling.
   d. a small firm finds it difficult to obtain publicity.
   e. it supplies the greatest diversification at the lowest price.

____ 18. As Joe is wondering what to do this weekend, an advertisement for Flemming Furniture is aired on the television station to which Joe's set is tuned. Joe never even thinks about furniture or the Flemming store during the commercial. In this instance, _____ has (have) blocked the communication process.
   a. poor encoding.
   b. inefficient medium of transmission.
   c. the absence of shared meaning
   d. promotion complexity
   e. perceptual processes

____ 19. State University has been running a student government blood drive for the past three years. This year the group ran radio spots announcing the drive on the student radio station. The number of people participating grew by 25 percent. This increase in participation represents the communications'
   a. attention level.
   b. perceptual congruence.
   c. mode of transmission.
   d. feedback.
   e. decoding accuracy.

____ 20. Tom Gregory is in the market for a new car. He has obtained information on some models he is interested in, and now he is trying to decide which car would best satisfy his specific needs. Tom is in which stage of the product adoption process?
   a. Awareness
   b. Interest
   c. Evaluation
   d. Adoption
   e. Trial

_____ 21. Custom Schooners, Inc., makes heavy use of the _____ element of the promotion mix because the number of valid prospects for ships costing over $125,000 is limited.
   a. advertising
   b. publicity
   c. sales promotion
   d. public relations
   e. personal selling

_____ 22. When a toy manufacturer advertises a product on Saturday-morning television and tells children to ask for the product at their favorite toy stores, it is implementing a _____ policy in its promotion mix.
   a. differentiated
   b. penetration
   c. push
   d. pull
   e. concentrated

_____ 23. A push policy is characterized by
   a. heavy promotional concentration at the level of ultimate consumers.
   b. heavy promotional emphasis at the retail level.
   c. concentration of promotional efforts on the next institution down the marketing channel.
   d. the manufacturer's supplementing the promotional efforts of all members of the marketing channel.
   e. required compliance with the manufacturer's marketing objectives throughout the marketing channel.

_____ 24. A pull policy is characterized by
   a. producers' domination of the marketing channel.
   b. promotion aimed directly at consumers.
   c. a short marketing channel.
   d. heavy emphasis on personal selling throughout the marketing channel.
   e. heavy promotional emphasis at the wholesale level.

_____ 25. If a company's objective is to educate consumers about the features of a home appliance, its promotion mix should emphasize
   a. advertising.
   b. sales promotion.
   c. publicity.
   d. personal selling.
   e. packaging.

_____ 26. Organizations that sell convenience products in markets containing millions of customers are most likely to use
   a. advertising and sales promotion.
   b. personal selling and publicity.
   c. advertising, publicity, and sales promotion.
   d. personal selling and sales promotion.
   e. advertising and personal selling.

_____ 27. A daily newspaper in Atlanta runs an article each week featuring a description of various new products that are available and gives the opinions of the editors who tested the products. One week the paper featured a new camera by Polaroid called the Cool Cam. This article represented which one of the following elements of the promotion mix for Polaroid?
   a. Advertising
   b. Personal selling
   c. Sales promotion
   d. Publicity
   e. Telemarketing

MINICASE: THE KITTY CHOW COMPANY*

The Kitty Chow Company, a leader in the pet food market, is trying to convert even more cat owners to the fast-growing dry cat food market with a new dry cat food, Cat's Meow. Kitty Chow anticipates its largest spending program to introduce this new offering. The new brand, a combination of three flavors—tuna, chicken, and liver—will hit the shelves very soon.

   Although Kitty Chow would not reveal its promotional budget for Cat's Meow, it is said to be the largest ever used by the company. When they introduced a new product two years ago, the company's budget for promotion was reported to be $16.5 million. It would appear that even more money has been allocated for promoting Cat's Meow.

   The promotion mix for Cat's Meow has not been finalized. However, the tentative promotion mix includes the following:

* Fourteen weeks of continuous network television, with 70 percent of it on prime time
* Color advertisements, including a detachable coupon, in nine women's magazines
* More than 160 million coupons, mostly 25 cents off, to be distributed through magazines, Sunday newspaper inserts, and door-to-door deliveries

Dry cat foods currently represent more than 30 percent of the $900 million cat food market. More than 50 percent of the market uses canned cat foods; this segment of cat owners who do not use dry food is Cat's Meow's target market. Competitive information indicates Kitty Chow is not the only company that intends to expand into the dry cat food market; two major competitors are now test marketing dry cat foods.

Questions

_____ 1. Based on the information in the case, Kitty Chow currently intends to use which of the following promotion mix ingredients?
   a. Advertising
   b. Personal selling
   c. Sales promotion
   d. Advertising and personal selling
   e. Advertising and sales promotion

*Contributed by Steven J. Skinner, University of Kentucky.

_____ 2. Which channel member is likely to handle most of the promotional efforts for Cat's Meow?
a. Producer
b. Agent
c. Wholesaler
d. Retailer
e. Advertising agency

_____ 3. In making its final decisions on the promotion mix, Kitty Chow will have to consider
a. its available promotional resources.
b. the characteristics of the target market.
c. the characteristics of the product.
d. the cost and availability of promotional methods.
e. all of the above.

_____ 4. Kitty Chow is ahead of its competition in expanding the dry cat food market. It is most important that its initial message
a. informs the audience about dry cat food.
b. educates the audience about how bad canned cat food is.
c. influences the audience to buy.
d. entertains the audience.
e. is similar to advertisements used for other Kitty Chow products.

_____ 5. A major problem Kitty Chow may encounter in marketing Cat's Meow to the canned cat food market is
a. changing consumer attitudes toward dry cat food.
b. having sufficient resources.
c. competing with other dry cat food producers.
d. understanding the pet food market.
e. finding an advertising medium that reaches the right target market.

PROGRAMMED COMPLETION EXERCISES

communicate,
individuals, groups,
organizations,
influencing

1. The primary role of promotion is to _____ with _____, _____, or _____ to facilitate exchanges directly or indirectly by _____ one or more of the audiences to accept an organization's products.

sharing of meaning,
transmission

2. For promotional purposes, a useful approach is to define communication as a _Sharing of meanin_ _____; implicit in this definition is the notion of _transmission_ of information.

source, person,
group, organization

3. Communication begins with a _Source_, which can be a _person_, a _group_, or an _Organization_

source, signs, ideas,
concepts

4. The coding process, or encoding, requires the _Source_ to convert the meaning into a series of _Sign_ that represent _Ideas_ or _Concepts_.

signs, familiar

5. To facilitate the sharing of meaning, the source should use _Sign_ that are _familiar_ to the receiver or audience.

limit, channel
capacity

6. Each communication channel has a _limit_ regarding the volume of information it can handle effectively. This is called _Channel Capacity_

influence, encourage,
accept, adopt

7. One long-run purpose of promotion is to _influence_ and _encourage_ buyers to _accept_ or _adopt_ goods, services, and ideas.

awareness, interest,
evaluation, trial,
adoption

8. One of the more common approaches to the product adoption process is to view it as consisting of five stages: _awareness_, _interest_, _evaluation_, _trial_, and _adoption_

relatives, friends,
associates

9. During the evaluation stage of product adoption, people often seek information from their _____, _____, and _____.

promotion mix

10. The specific combination of promotional methods an organization uses is its _Promo Mix_.

Advertising, trans-
mitted, mass medium

11. _____ is a paid form of nonpersonal communication about an organization or its products that is _transmitted_ to a target audience through a _mass medium_.

purchase, personal, exchange

12. <u>Personal selling</u> is a process of informing customers and persuading them to _purchase_ products through _personal_ communication in an _exchange_ situation.

inducement, resellers, salespersons, consumers, added, incentive

13. <u>Sales promotion</u> is an activity or material that acts as a direct _inducement_, offering _salesperson, consumer_, or _resellers_ _added_ value, or _incentive_ for the product.

news story, mass medium, no charge

14. Publicity is communication in the form of a _news story_, regarding an organization or its products, that is transmitted through a _mass medium_ at _no charge_.

personal selling, consumer goods

15. Generally, promotion mixes for industrial products concentrate heavily on _personal selling_ whereas <u>advertising plays</u> a major role in promoting _consumer goods_.

personal selling

16. When the size of a market is limited, _personal selling_ probably will be emphasized because it is effective for reaching small numbers of persons.

push policy

17. When a _push policy_ is used, the producer promotes the product only to the next marketing institution down the channel.

pull policy, pulling, demand

18. A _pull polic_ is directed toward _pulling_ goods down through the channel by creating _demand_ at the level of consumers.

ANSWERS TO OBJECTIVE QUESTIONS

Matching		*True or False*		*Multiple-Choice*		*Minicase*
1. a	13. j	1. F	13. T	1. e	15. b	1. e
2. o	14. b	2. T	14. F	2. d	16. d	2. a
3. i	15. w	3. F	15. F	3. c	17. a	3. e
4. t	16. h	4. T	16. T	4. d	18. e	4. a
5. y	17. x	5. T	17. F	5. a	19. d	5. a
6. l	18. f	6. T	18. F	6. a	20. c	
7. e	19. r	7. F	19. F	7. b	21. e	
8. p	20. d	8. T	20. T	8. d	22. d	
9. z	21. m	9. T	21. F	9. a	23. c	
10. g	22. c	10. T	22. F	10. c	24. b	
11. n	23. u	11. F	23. F	11. d	25. d	
12. v		12. F	24. T	12. e	26. a	
				13. d	27. d	
				14. e		

16 ADVERTISING AND PUBLICITY

CHAPTER OUTLINE

The nature of advertising

The uses of advertising

Promoting products and organizations

Stimulating primary and selective demand

Offsetting competitors' advertising

Making salespersons more effective

Increasing the uses of a product

Reminding and reinforcing customers

Reducing sales fluctuations

Developing an advertising campaign

Identifying and analyzing the advertising target

Defining the advertising objectives

Creating the advertising platform

Determining the advertising appropriation

Developing the media plan

Creating the advertising message

Executing the campaign

Evaluating the effectiveness of the advertising

Who develops the advertising campaign?

Publicity

Publicity and advertising compared

Kinds of publicity

Uses of publicity

Requirements of a publicity program

Dealing with unfavorable publicity

Limitations in using publicity

CHAPTER SUMMARY

Advertising is a paid form of nonpersonal communication that is transmitted to consumers through the mass media. Businesses are not the only users of advertising; many types of organizations—governments, churches, universities, civic groups, and charities —use advertising as a part of their promotion mix.

Organizations use advertising in many ways and for many reasons. How a firm uses advertising depends on its objectives, resources, and environment. Advertising can promote goods, services, images, issues, ideas, and people and can be classified into two categories: institutional advertising and product advertising. Institutional advertising promotes organizational images, ideas, and political issues. Product advertising promotes goods and services and often serves to stimulate demand directly. Examples of product advertising are pioneer advertising (to stimulate primary demand) and competitive advertising (to stimulate selective demand). An increasingly popular form of competitive advertising is comparative advertising, which compares two or more specific brands on the basis of one or more product attributes. When marketers advertise to offset the effects of a competitor's promotional program, they are using defensive advertising.

Businesses that allot a significant part of their promotional effort to personal selling often use advertising to increase the effectiveness of sales personnel. This kind of advertising tries to presell buyers, informing them about a product and encouraging them to contact local dealers or sales representatives. The demand for any product is limited in that the market can consume only so much of it. One way to increase sales is to expand the number of product uses through advertising. Reminder advertising lets consumers know that an established brand is still available and that it has certain uses, characteristics, and benefits. Reinforcement advertising assures current users that they have made the right choice of product. And finally, advertising is a way to reduce the sales fluctuations of seasonal products.

There are eight major steps in creating an advertising campaign. First, the advertiser must identify and analyze the advertising target, the group of people toward whom the advertisements are aimed. Second, the advertiser should define the advertising objectives—determine what the campaign is intended to accomplish. The third step is developing an advertising platform, which consists of the basic issues or selling points that the advertiser wants to include in the campaign. The platform provides a base on which to build the message. The fourth step is to determine the advertising appropriation, the total amount of money allocated for advertising during a specific time period. To determine that appropriation, the marketer can use the objective-and-task approach, the percent-of-sales approach, the competition-matching approach, or the arbitrary approach. Fifth, the marketer must develop a media plan, which specifies which media will be used to achieve the appropriate reach and when they will be used. Sixth, the advertiser must create the message through the use of copy and artwork. Copy is the verbal portion of an advertisement—the headlines, subheadlines, body copy, and the signature. Artwork includes illustrations and the physical arrangement (layout) of the copy components. In the seventh step, the campaign is executed, a process that requires an extensive amount of planning and coordination. The eighth and final step is evaluating the effectiveness of the campaign. Although this obviously is important after a campaign, it is also a critical process both before and during a campaign.

An advertising campaign may be handled by an individual or a few persons within the organization, an advertising department within the organization, or an advertising agency. In very small firms, one or two individuals are responsible for performing advertising activities. In certain types of large businesses, especially larger retail organizations, advertising departments handle the creation and implementation of advertising campaigns. When an organization uses an advertising agency, the development of the advertising campaign is usually a joint effort of both the firm and the agency. The advantage of using an advertising agency is the service of highly skilled, objective specialists who have broad experience in the advertising field.

Publicity is communication in news story form regarding an organization or its products and transmitted through a mass medium at no charge. Within an organization, publicity is sometimes treated as part of public relations. Public relations is a broad set of communication activities used to create and maintain favorable relations between the organization and its publics: customers, employees, stockholders, government officials, and society in general. Compared with advertising, publicity is mainly informative and more subdued. Also, the organization does not pay for it, which may give publicity greater credibility among consumers. However, publicity does not give the organization control or the opportunity to repeat messages.

The most common form of publicity is the news release, usually a single page of typewritten copy with no more than three hundred words. A feature article is a longer manuscript that generally is prepared for a specific publication. Captioned photographs can be effective for illustrating a new or improved product that has highly visible features. A press conference is a meeting used to announce major news events. Letters to the editor and editorials sometimes are prepared and sent to newspapers and magazines. Finally, films and tapes occasionally are distributed to broadcast stations. The choice of a specific type of publicity depends on several factors, among them the type of information being transmitted, the characteristics of the target audience, the receptivity of media personnel, the importance of the item to the public, and the amount of information.

Publicity often is used to make people aware of a firm's products, brands, or activities; to maintain a certain level of positive public visibility; and to promote a particular image. To obtain maximum benefit from publicity, a firm should create and maintain a systematic, continuous publicity program. It is important too to establish good working relationships with media personnel and to give them material that is both newsworthy and well written. Finally, the firm must develop a way to measure the effectiveness of its publicity efforts.

Not all publicity is favorable. The impact of negative publicity can be immediate and dramatic, destroying consumer attitudes that have taken years of promotional effort to build. Although the firm may not be able to avoid unfavorable publicity completely, it can take steps to lessen its effects. The first and most important is to reduce negative incidents through safety programs, inspections, and effective quality control procedures. The second is to establish policies and procedures for dealing with those incidents when they do happen. In most cases, this means expediting new coverage rather than impeding it.

The media do not charge for transmitting publicity. Although this is a financial advantage for the firm, it brings with it a lack of control that can limit the effectiveness of a publicity program.

MATCHING EXERCISES

Use the following set of terms to identify the sentences and phrases below. On the blank line next to each sentence or phrase, place the letter of the term that the sentence or phrase describes. Do not use a term more than once.

a. Benchmark
b. Press conference
c. Advertising
d. Regional issues
e. Cost comparison indicator
f. Source
g. Captioned photograph
h. Institutional advertising
i. Copy
j. Media plan
k. Feature article
l. Product advertising
m. Closing
n. Storyboard
o. Arbitrary approach
p. News release
q. Pioneer advertising
r. Artwork
s. Headline
t. Competition-matching approach
u. Public relations

v. Competitive advertising
w. Illustrations
x. Percent-of-sales approach
y. Publicity
z. Comparative advertising
aa. Layout
bb. Objective-and-task approach
cc. Aided recall test
dd. Channel power
ee. Defensive advertising
ff. Pretest
gg. Advertising appropriation
hh. Unaided recall test
ii. Signature
jj. Reminder advertising
kk. Consumer jury
ll. Advertising platform
mm. Recognition test
nn. Reinforcement advertising
oo. Posttest
pp. Advertising target

_____ 1. Advertising used to offset or lessen the effects of a competitor's promotional program. *Defensive Advertising*

_____ 2. A form of advertising that promotes organizational images, ideas, or political issues. *Institutional Advertising*

_____ 3. Advertising that compares two or more specific brands on the basis of one or more product characteristics. *Comparative Advert*

_____ 4. A method for determining an advertising appropriation whereby a high-level executive states how much can be spent on advertising over a certain period of time. *Arbitrary Approach*

_____ 5. A paid form of nonpersonal communication about an organization or its products that is transmitted to a target audience through a mass medium. *Advertising*

_____ 6. A method of determining an advertising appropriation whereby an advertiser tries to match a major competitor's appropriation in terms of absolute dollars or percentage of sales used for advertising. *Competition-Matching Approach*

cc   7. A posttest method of evaluating the effectiveness of advertising whereby subjects are asked to identify advertisements they have seen recently and are shown a list of products, brands, company names, or trademarks to jog their memories. *Aided Recall test*

j   8. A plan that sets forth the exact media vehicles to be used and the dates and times that advertisements will appear. *Media Plan*

k\l   9. A panel used to pretest advertisements; it consists of people who are actual or potential buyers of the advertised product. *Consumer jury*

u   10. A broad set of communication activities employed to create and maintain favorable relations between the organization and customers, employees, stockholders, government officials, and society in general. *Public Relations*

i   11. The verbal portion of advertisements; it includes headlines, subheadlines, body copy, and signature. *Copy*

hh   12. A posttest method of evaluating the effectiveness of advertising whereby subjects are asked to identify advertisements that they have seen recently but are not shown any clues to stimulate their memories. *unaided Recall test*

R   13. The illustrations for and layout of an advertisement. *ART WORK*

v   14. Advertising that points out a brand's uses, features, and advantages that may not be available in competing brands. *Competitive*

nn   15. An advertisement that tries to assure current users that they have made the right choice and tells them how to get the most satisfaction from the product. *Reinforcement Advert.*

l   16. Advertising that promotes goods and services. *Product Advert*

ll   17. The basic issues or selling points that an advertiser wants to include in an advertising campaign. *Advertising Platform*

k   18. A form of publicity that is up to three thousand words long and usually is prepared for a specific publication. *Feature Article*

x   19. A method for determining an advertising appropriation whereby marketers simply multiply a firm's past sales, forecasted sales, or a combination of the two by a standard percentage based on both what the firm traditionally spends on advertising and what the industry averages. *Percent of Sales Approach*

d   20. Versions of a magazine that differ across geographic regions, in which a publisher can vary both advertisements and editorial content. *Regional Issues*

bb   21. A method for determining an advertising appropriation whereby marketers first set campaign objectives and then identify the tasks required to accomplish those objectives; the costs of the tasks are added to determine the total appropriation. *Objective & task Approach*

n   22. A blueprint that technical personnel use to produce a television commercial; it combines copy with visual material to show the sequence of major scenes in a commercial. *Storyboard*

_OO_   23. Evaluation of advertising effectiveness after a campaign.
Posttest

_E_   24. Allows an advertiser to compare the costs of several vehicles within a specific medium in terms of the number of people reached by each vehicle.
Cost Comparison Indicator

_mm_   25. A posttest method of evaluating the effectiveness of advertising whereby individual respondents are shown the actual advertisement and asked whether they recognize it. *Recognition Test*

_gg_   26. The total amount of money that a marketer allocates for advertising over a specific time period. *Advertising Appropriation*

_b_   27. A meeting used to announce major news events.
Press Conference

_P_   28. A form of publicity that is usually a single page of typewritten copy containing fewer than three hundred words. *News Release*

_y_   29. Nonpersonal communication in news story form regarding an organization or its products and transmitted through a mass medium at no charge. *Publicity*

_jj_   30. Advertising used to remind consumers that an established brand is still around and that it has certain uses, characteristics, and benefits.
Reminder Advert.

_w_   31. Photographs, drawings, graphs, charts, and tables used to encourage an audience to read or watch an advertisement. *Illustrations*

_aa_   32. The physical arrangement of illustrations, headline, subheadline, body copy, and signature within an advertisement. *layout*

_g_   33. A photograph with a brief description that explains the picture's content.
Captioned Photograph

_pp_   34. The group of people toward which an advertisement is aimed.
Advertising target

_q_   35. A type of advertising that tells people what a product is, what it does, how it can be used, and where it can be purchased. *Pioneer Advert.*

_bb_   36. Evaluation of an advertisement before it actually is used.
Pretest

TRUE OR FALSE STATEMENTS

T ~~**F**~~   1. Advertising can compensate for most weaknesses in a firm's marketing strategy.

T ~~**F**~~   2. It is illegal to mention the name of a competing brand in an advertisement.

T ~~**F**~~   3. Building primary demand means creating demand for a specific brand of product.

~~**T**~~ **F**   4. Defensive advertising is used most often by firms in extremely competitive consumer product markets.

~~**T**~~ **F**   5. Both reminder and reinforcement advertising are used to prevent a loss in sales or market share.

T F 6. Advertising can be used to reduce fluctuations in sales.

T F 7. Advertising objectives need not be clear, precise, and measurable because they are only estimates of what an advertiser wants to accomplish.

T F 8. A benchmark is used in advertising as a point of reference for defining advertising objectives.

T F 9. "Our primary advertising objective is to increase monthly sales from $300,000 to $500,000" is an example of a good advertising objective.

T F 10. Even though the long-run goal of an advertiser is to increase sales, not all campaigns are aimed at producing immediate sales.

T F 11. Although an advertising platform defines basic issues, it does not indicate the form in which those issues should be presented.

T F 12. Advertising appropriations for industrial products are usually much larger than those for consumer convenience items.

T F 13. The advertising appropriation is the total amount that a marketer allocates for advertising for a specific period of time.

T F 14. The percent-of-sales approach is based on the incorrect assumption that sales create advertising.

T F 15. The main problem with the objective-and-task approach to setting an advertising appropriation is that is often results in underspending or overspending of the firm's resources.

T F 16. Marketers usually are concerned about the type and intensity of competitors' advertising.

T F 17. The arbitrary approach to setting an advertising budget uses the opinion of a high-level executive in the firm.

T F 18. The cost and impact of a television commercial can be compared accurately with the cost and impact of a newspaper advertisement.

T F 19. A cost comparison indicator allows an advertiser to compare the costs of several vehicles within a medium in terms of the number of people reached by each vehicle.

T F 20. The signature is the written portion of an advertisement.

T F 21. Because radio listeners often do not listen attentively, radio copy should be formal and straightforward to attract their attention.

T F 22. Television copy should be written so that the visual material overpowers the audio portion of the commercial.

T F 23. The advertising platform is the foundation on which campaign messages are built.

T F 24. The artwork in an advertisement includes the illustrations and the physical arrangement of the illustrations, headline, subheadline, body copy, and signature.

T   F   25. The effectiveness of advertising can be evaluated before, during, and after it appears.

T   F   26. The major justification for using recognition and recall methods to evaluate the effectiveness of advertising is that if individuals can remember an advertisement, they are more likely to buy the product.

T   F   27. Publicity is a paid form of advertising.

T   F   28. Publicity is communication in news story form that is transmitted through a mass medium at no charge.

T   F   29. Publicity releases always identify sponsors.

T   F   30. Publicity can be used to make people aware of a firm's products, brands, or activities.

T   F   31. A news release in a manuscript of about three thousand words that usually is prepared for a specific publication.

T   F   32. A captioned photograph is a form of advertising, not a type of publicity.

T   F   33. To obtain the maximum benefit from publicity, a firm should try to establish and maintain good relationships with media personnel.

T   F   34. The effectiveness of publicity is evaluated on the basis of how many releases are published or broadcast.

T   F   35. The best way to deal with negative publicity is to ignore it.

T   F   36. One limitation of publicity is that the firm cannot control the content or timing of the communication.

MULTIPLE-CHOICE QUESTIONS

_____ 1. The kind of advertising that promotes organizational images, ideas, or political issues is
a. product advertising.
b. governmental advertising.
c. political advertising.
d. pioneer advertising.
e. institutional advertising.

_____ 2. Pioneer advertising
a. compares a product to other similar products.
b. emphasizes the brand name of a product.
c. reminds consumers that a brand is still around.
d. stimulates primary demand.
e. improves the image of a firm.

3. Ralph Johnson, president of Johnson Real Estate, rejects Mary King's proposal that the firm double its radio spots on WHOS for the next quarter. Ralph bases his reaction on higher interest rates on mortgages in recent months. This reaction relates to the _____ dimension of the value of advertising.
   a. important features
   b. economic conditions
   c. resource commitment
   d. marketing expertise
   e. competitive environment

4. Competitive advertising
   a. offsets or lessens the effects of a competitor's promotional campaign.
   b. stimulates a selective demand.
   c. reinforces a product's image.
   d. introduces a new product.
   e. stimulates primary demand.

5. The type of advertising in which an advertiser mentions the actual names of competing brands is
   a. comparative advertising.
   b. competitive advertising.
   c. selective advertising.
   d. defensive advertising.
   e. pioneer advertising.

6. In a business organization in which a sizable portion of promotion efforts are aimed at personal selling,
   a. advertising often is used to improve the effectiveness of sales personnel.
   b. advertising is seldom used.
   c. reminder advertising is used.
   d. advertisements are used to stimulate primary and selective demand.
   e. advertising emphasizes new product uses.

7. When an organization advertises to offset or lessen the effects of a competitor's promotional program, it is using
   a. defensive advertising.
   b. competitive advertising.
   c. comparative advertising.
   d. selective advertising.
   e. reinforcement advertising.

8. Travis Manufacturing Company has asked its advertising agency to develop a campaign that promotes its organizational image. What kind of advertising is Travis asking for?
   a. Competitive
   b. Institutional
   c. Product
   d. Reinforcement
   e. Comparative

_____   9. Advertising that shows consumers new ways to use a certain product is employed
a. to enlarge the geographic market and sell to more people.
b. to increase sales after the demand for a product has reached its limit.
c. sparingly because the demand for competitive brands also increases.
d. to remind consumers that the brand is still around and that it has certain uses, characteristics, and benefits.
e. to reduce seasonal fluctuations in sales.

_____   10. When advertisers try to increase sales by promoting new uses for a product, they should
a. advertise established products to remind consumers that the products are still around.
b. assure current users that they have made the right choice and indicate how to get the most from the product.
c. allocate a sizable portion of the promotional effort to personal selling.
d. adjust the advertising campaign so that it is aimed only at current users of the product.
e. attempt to increase demand for the product without increasing the demand for competing brands.

_____   11. Reinforcement advertising is focused on consumers who
a. have not used the product.
b. purchased the product and were dissatisfied.
c. use another brand of the same product.
d. already use the advertised brand.
e. would like to try the advertised brand but are unsure that it will provide satisfaction.

_____   12. A marketer uses pioneer advertising to
a. promote established brands.
b. compare brand names.
c. promote a product in the introductory stage of the life cycle.
d. introduce a competitive version of a product.
e. appeal to rural consumers.

_____   13. The advertising target is
a. the location and geographic distribution of the market.
b. the distribution of age, income, race, sex, and educational level.
c. consumers' attitudes regarding the purchase and use of a product.
d. what the advertiser wants to accomplish with the advertising campaign.
e. the group of people at which the advertisement is aimed.

_____   14. The first step in the development of an advertising campaign is to
a. set an advertising budget.
b. develop a media plan.
c. identify and analyze a target market.
d. define the advertising objectives.
e. create an advertising platform.

15. Bob of Bob's Burger Bar calls his advertising agency. He tells the account representative that the competition is indicating in its ads that his burgers are not 100 percent pure beef. The account representative indicates that the appropriate response is a(n) _____ campaign.
    a. institutional
    b. product
    c. pioneer
    d. defensive
    e. traditional

16. A statement that indicates a firm's current condition or position is commonly known as a
    a. platform.
    b. media plan.
    c. primary objective.
    d. benchmark.
    e. secondary objective.

17. Which of the following statements about advertising objectives is false?
    a. Advertising objectives that are not clearly defined are seldom successful.
    b. Advertising objectives can be stated in terms of sales or communication.
    c. An advertising objective should not be restricted in terms of the time needed to accomplish it.
    d. Precision and measurability are required to allow advertisers to evaluate their campaigns.
    e. Not all advertising objectives are designed to produce immediate sales.

18. The campaign referring to Pepto-Bismol as "old reliable" is an example of which one of the following categories of advertising?
    a. Pioneer
    b. Defensive
    c. Reminder
    d. Comparative
    e. Offensive

19. An advertising platform consists of
    a. the basic issues or selling points that an advertiser wants to include in a campaign.
    b. issues that are of little importance to consumers.
    c. selling features included in an advertisement.
    d. the objectives of the advertising campaign.
    e. a survey of consumers' feelings about the product.

20. Which of the following is an example of an advertising objective stated in terms of sales?
    a. Increase brand awareness
    b. Make consumers' attitudes more favorable

    c. Increase the firm's market share

d. Increase product awareness

e. Increase consumers' knowledge of product features

_____ 21. Using the objective-and-task approach to determine an advertising budget, a marketer would
   a. simply multiply the firm's past sales, forecasted sales, or a combination of the two by a standard percentage based on what the firm traditionally has spent on advertising.
   b. adjust the amount previously spent on advertising relative to the increase in sales.
   c. study the type and intensity of advertising performed by competitors and adjust the budget accordingly.
   d. request an executive of the firm to set the amount of the appropriation.
   e. determine the objectives that the campaign should achieve and then estimate how much must be spent to accomplish those objectives.

_____ 22. The major disadvantage of the percent-of-sales approach for determining an advertising budget is
   a. the difficulty of trying to estimate how much money is needed to achieve a certain goal.
   b. that it is based on the incorrect assumption that sales create advertising rather than that advertising creates sales.
   c. that it often results in either underspending or overspending of the firm's resources.
   d. that the firm's competitors probably use greater amounts of resources for advertising.
   e. that is does not take into consideration the sizes and types of audiences that are reached by specific media vehicles.

_____ 23. The media planner's primary goal is to
   a. formulate a media plan that allows an advertisement to reach the largest number of people in the advertising target per dollar spent.
   b. decide what type of medium is best for a product.
   c. decide which specific media vehicles to use.
   d. formulate a media plan that allows the advertisements to reach a majority of the advertising target.
   e. create a media time schedule.

_____ 24. When advertisers want to show textures as well as numerous details, they should use
   a. radio.
   b. newspapers.
   c. outdoor displays.
   d. mass transit vehicles.
   e. magazines.

_____ 25. The part of an advertisement that links the headline to the body copy is the
   a. signature.
   c. subheadline.
   d. artwork.
   e. primary copy.

_____ 26. When creating a television commercial, the copywriter and the artist combine the copy with the visual material through the use of a
   a. storyboard.
   b. layout.
   c. body copy.
   d. media plan.
   e. parallel script form.

_____ 27. A consumer jury consists of
   a. people who have never purchased the advertised product.
   b. consumer advocates who will decide the safety of the product.
   c. consumers who will report how effective an advertising campaign has been.
   d. consumers who will pretest an advertisement.
   e. consumers who will judge whether an advertisement is misleading.

_____ 28. Effectiveness during a campaign usually is measured by
   a. posttests.
   b. pretests.
   c. consumer juries.
   d. paired comparisons.
   e. inquiries.

_____ 29. In evaluating the effectiveness of advertising, subjects may be asked to identify advertisements that they have seen recently but are not shown any clues to stimulate their memories. This evaluation technique is known as
   a. the recognition method.
   b. the posttest method.
   c. a consumer survey.
   d. the aided recall method.
   e. the unaided recall method.

_____ 30. Which one of the following media would be least appropriate for Kodak's advertisements of its new color print film?
   a. Television
   b. Magazine
   c. Newspaper
   d. Outdoor
   e. Direct mail

_____ 31. Publicity
   a. is transmitted through the media for a fee.
   b. usually has a sponsor.

c. usually is designed to have an immediate impact on sales.

d. is transmitted through the mass media at no charge.

e. is usually persuasive and informative.

32. If an advertiser pays $25,000 for a one-page magazine advertisement and that magazine is read by ten million people, how much is the advertiser paying to reach a thousand people?
    a. $25
    b. $2.50
    c. $250
    d. $5
    e. $50

33. To determine the effectiveness of a recent advertising campaign for Coast soap, market researchers provided subjects with a list of soap brands and asked if the subjects remembered seeing advertisements for any of the listed products. This is an example of which one of the following types of advertising evaluation methods?
    a. Pretest
    b. Recognition test
    c. Unaided recall test
    d. Aided recall test
    e. Consumer jury test

34. Publicity is used to
    a. have an immediate impact on sales.
    b. inform and persuade consumers.
    c. make people aware of a firm's products, brands, or activities.
    d. reach a different target market from the one that advertising reaches.
    e. increase consumers' awareness of a firm as well as to persuade them to buy its products.

35. Which of the following statements concerning the differences between advertising and publicity is false?
    a. Advertising is informative and persuasive; publicity is mainly informative.
    b. Advertisements identify sponsors; publicity releases do not.
    c. Sponsors pay for publicity but not for advertising.
    d. Advertisements are separated from broadcast programs or editorial portions of print media; publicity releases are part of a program or editorial content.
    e. Publicity may have greater credibility among consumers.

36. Which of the following is *not* a type of publicity?
    a. Press conferences
    b. Films distributed to broadcast stations in the hope that they will be aired
    c. Captioned photographs
    d. Direct mail pamphlets promoting greeting cards and including an order blank
    e. Letters to a newspaper editor

_____ 37. To obtain the maximum benefit from publicity, a firm should
   a. include various types of publicity in the promotion mix.
   b. spend as much money as possible on publicity.
   c. create and maintain a systematic publicity program.
   d. publish or broadcast as many publicity releases as possible.
   e. block all negative publicity.

MINICASE: SOLARCO—WILL PUBLICITY WORK?*

Solarco, a St. Louis firm little more than one year old, designs, manufactures, and sells one type of solar heating system, an active flat-plate collector system. This type of system consists of tilted rectangular "black boxes" that are oriented southward to absorb the sun's heat energy. (Black absorbs sunlight better than any other color.) Heat can then be blown directly into the space to be heated or into an insulated storage tank for later use. Flat-plate collectors are presently used to heat homes and distill fresh, salt-free water from sea water. Such systems can be used to heat air or water and, if well designed, could probably halve a home's hot water and space heating costs.

In another type of solar heating system, which transforms solar energy into electrical power, photovoltaic cells that receive the sun's rays are wired to electrical circuits. This type of system is currently far more expensive and has a low conversion efficiency (about 10 percent). In the next decade, however, as the technology progresses and becomes more economically feasible, photovoltaic electricity is expected to receive large-scale use by electric companies for "peak shaving"—generating power during periods of peak demand—in areas with much sunlight and high utility rates.

Today the buyers of solar products are generally well-educated upper-middle-class home owners. Approximately 75 percent of all flat-plate systems are installed on new homes; the remainder are used to retrofit existing structures. In the past, the large initial outlay required to purchase a solar energy system precluded many people from buying one, but current state and federal tax credits for users of energy-saving systems, economies of scale in the manufacturing process, and the lower operating cost of a solar system as compared to other types are making solar products increasingly attractive to less affluent home owners. With an expanding customer base, solar products are beginning to flood the market.

Solarco employs five salaried business people and ten machinists and skilled workers; most of them have engineering backgrounds. Although the company has reliable technical directorship, it has limited funds for promotional efforts.

Recently, the engineers at Solarco developed a unique flat-plate device that can be sold at a price 30 percent lower than existing models. It also can be used to retrofit existing homes for considerably less money because fewer alterations are required. In addition, the new flat plate collects solar energy more efficiently than competitive plates.

*Information taken from E. H. Warren, Jr., and A. L. Walton, "The Solar Alternative," *USA Today*, September 1984, pp. 80–84; Jon R. Luoma, "A Forecast of Sun," *Audubon*, November 1983, pp. 44, 46, 47; and "Solar Energy," *The World Book Encyclopedia*, World Book Inc., Scott Fetzer Co., 1984, vol. 18, p. 472.

Questions

_____ 1. Solarco's management is interested in using publicity as much as possible. Which of the following factors is most likely to have prompted this interest?
   a. Lack of qualified personnel to manage an advertising campaign
   b. Failure of previous advertising attempts
   c. Lack of funds for extensive advertising
   d. Competition from other solar product manufacturers
   e. Expressed interest from the media

_____ 2. Which of the following forms of publicity seems *least* appropriate for Solarco to use at this time?
   a. News releases
   b. Feature articles
   c. Press conferences
   d. Captioned photographs
   e. Letters to the editor

_____ 3. To obtain maximum benefit from publicity, Solarco should
   a. include various types of publicity in the promotion mix.
   b. create and maintain a systematic publicity program.
   c. spend as much money as possible.
   d. block all negative publicity releases.
   e. hire an employee to handle all publicity.

_____ 4. Solarco's publicity efforts should focus on
   a. educating consumers about the uses of solar energy.
   b. educating consumers about the economics of solar energy.
   c. the reliability of solar energy.
   d. securing a competitive advantage for its products.
   e. educating consumers about the economies, uses, and reliability of solar energy as well as securing a competitive advantage for its products.

PROGRAMMED COMPLETION EXERCISES

paid, nonpersonal

1. Advertising is a major promotion mix ingredient. It is a _____ form of _____ communication that is transmitted to consumers through the mass media.

institutional, product

2. Depending on what is being promoted, advertising can be classified into one of two categories: _____ advertising and _____ advertising.

pioneer, primary
demand

3. When a firm is the first to introduce a revolutionary new product, it should use _____ advertising to stimulate _____ _____.

selective,
competitive

4. To develop _____ demand, a firm employs _____ advertising, which points out a brand's uses, features, and advantages.

Reinforcement

5. _____ advertising is aimed at individuals who already use the advertised brand.

objectives, resources,
environment

6. The manner in which a firm uses advertising depends on the firm's _____, _____, and _____.

targets, base

7. Advertisers analyze advertising _____ to develop an information _____ for a campaign.

Precision,
measurability

8. _____ and _____ allow advertisers to evaluate the degree to which advertising objectives have been accomplished.

how far, what
direction

9. An advertising objective should clearly indicate _____ _____ and in _____ _____ the advertiser wants to move from a benchmark.

sales,
communication

10. Advertising objectives are usually stated in terms of _____ or _____.

basic issues,
selling points

11. An advertising platform consists of the _____ _____ or _____ _____ that an advertiser wants to include in an advertising campaign.

easy to use, less
disruptive, market
share

12. The percent-of-sales approach often is used for setting an advertising budget because it is _____ _____ _____ and is _____ _____ competitively in that it stabilizes a firm's _____ _____ within an industry.

arbitrary approach

13. When using the _____ _____ to set an advertising budget, a high-level executive in the firm states how much can be spent on advertising over a certain period of time.

media plan, largest
number, per dollar

14. The media planner's primary goal is to formulate a _____ _____ that allows an advertisement to reach the _____ _____ of people in the advertising target _____ _____ spent on media.

Print, broadcast

15. _____ media are more effective than _____ media when an advertiser wants to present many issues or numerous details.

Copy, headlines,
subheadlines, body
copy, signature

16. _____ is the verbal portion of advertisements; it includes _____, _____, _____ _____, and _____.

illustrations, layout

17. Artwork consists of the _____ in and the _____ of an advertisement.

before, during, after

18. The effectiveness of advertising can be evaluated _____, _____, and _____ a campaign.

recognition, recall

19. Posttest methods based on memory are called _____ and _____ tests.

news story, mass
medium, no charge

20. Publicity is communication in _____ _____ form
about an organization or its products and transmitted through
a _____ _____ at _____ _____.

informative

21. Advertising messages tend to be informative, persuasive, or
both, whereas publicity messages are mainly _____.

sponsors

22. Publicity releases do not identify _____.

aware

23. Publicity can be used to make people _____ of a firm's
products, brands, or activities.

newsworthy, timely,
interesting, accurate

24. Media personnel must believe that publicity messages are
_____, _____, _____, and _____.

information,
characteristics,
receptivity,
importance, amount

25. The selection of a specific form of publicity depends on the
type of _____ being transmitted, the _____ of the
target audience, the _____ of media personnel, the
_____ of the news item to the public, and the
_____ of information to be presented.

rejected, news-
worthiness, poorly
written

26. A great deal of publicity material is _____ by media
personnel because it lacks _____ or is _____
_____.

safety programs,
inspections, quality
control procedures

27. The main way to avoid unfavorable publicity is for an
organization to reduce the likelihood of negative incidents
through _____ _____, _____, and effective
_____ _____ _____.

ANSWERS TO OBJECTIVE QUESTIONS

Matching		*True or False*		*Multiple-Choice*		*Minicase*
1. ee	19. x	1. F	19. T	1. e	20. c	1. c
2. h	20. d	2. F	20. F	2. d	21. e	2. c
3. z	21. bb	3. F	21. F	3. b	22. b	3. b
4. o	22. n	4. T	22. F	4. b	23. a	4. e
5. c	23. oo	5. T	23. T	5. a	24. e	
6. t	24. e	6. T	24. T	6. a	25. c	
7. cc	25. mm	7. F	25. T	7. a	26. a	
8. j	26. gg	8. T	26. T	8. b	27. d	
9. kk	27. b	9. F	27. F	9. b	28. e	
10. u	28. p	10. T	28. T	10. e	29. e	
11. i	29. y	11. T	29. F	11. d	30. c	
12. hh	30. jj	12. F	30. T	12. c	31. d	
13. r	31. w	13. T	31. F	13. e	32. b	
14. v	32. aa	14. T	32. F	14. c	33. d	
15. nn	33. g	15. F	33. T	15. d	34. c	
16. l	34. pp	16. T	34. T	16. d	35. c	
17. ll	35. q	17. T	35. F	17. c	36. d	
18. k	36. ff	18. F	36. T	18. c	37. c	
				19. a		

17 PERSONAL SELLING AND SALES PROMOTION

CHAPTER OUTLINE

The nature of personal selling
Elements of the personal selling process
Prospecting and evaluating
Preparing
Approaching the customer
Making the presentation
Overcoming objections
Closing
Following up
Types of salespersons
Order getters
Order takers
Support personnel
Management of the sales force
Establishing sales-force objectives
Determining sales-force size
Recruiting and selecting salespeople
Training sales personnel
Compensating salespeople
Motivating salespeople
Managing sales territories
Controlling and evaluating sales-force performance
The nature of sales promotion
Sales promotion opportunities and limitations
Sales promotion methods
Consumer sales promotion methods
Trade sales promotion methods

CHAPTER SUMMARY

Personal selling is the process of informing customers and persuading them to purchase products through personal communication in an exchange situation. Personal selling gives marketers the greatest freedom to adjust a message to satisfy customers' information needs. At the same time, it is the most expensive ingredient (per person reached) in the promotion mix. The specific goals of personal selling efforts vary from one firm to another. In general, though, they involve finding prospects, convincing them to buy, and keeping customers satisfied.

The exact activities involved in selling are different among salespersons and in particular selling situations. Nonetheless, most salespersons move through a similar process as they sell: prospecting and evaluating, preparing, approaching the customer, making a presentation, overcoming objections, closing, and following up. It helps salespeople if they are aware of competitors.

Most businesses use different kinds of sales personnel. The choice is determined by the product's uses, characteristics, complexity, and price; the number of customers and their characteristics; the kinds of marketing channels; and the intensity and type of advertising. Based on the functions they perform, salespersons can be classified into three groups: order getters, order takers, and support personnel. One person can, and often does, perform all three functions. The job of order getters is to increase the firm's sales by selling to new customers and by increasing sales to current customers. Both inside and field order takers seek repeat sales. Support personnel work primarily with business-to-business products. They locate prospects, educate customers, build goodwill, and provide service after a sale. Three common types of support personnel are missionary, trade, and technical salespersons.

The sales force is directly responsible for generating an organization's primary input: sales revenue. The effective management of the sales force is a critical determinant of a firm's success. That management focuses on eight general areas: (1) establishing objectives for the sales force, (2) determining its size, (3) recruiting and selecting salespeople, (4) training sales personnel, (5) compensating salespeople, (6) motivating salespeople, (7) managing sales territory, and (8) controlling and evaluating the sales force.

Sales objectives are usually established for the total sales force and for each salesperson. They should be stated in precise, measurable terms, and they should be specific regarding the time period and the geographic areas involved. These objectives tell salespersons what they are expected to accomplish during a specified period of time. Marketers can use several methods for determining the optimal size of a sales force.

Recruiting is a process by which a sales manager develops a list of applicants for sales positions. To ensure that the applicants are qualified, the sales manager must establish specific requirements. These requirements are based on job descriptions and trait analyses. Usually applicants come from several sources: departments within the firm, other firms, employment agencies, educational institutions, advertisements, and current employees' recommendations. The process of hiring a sales force varies in complexity from one firm to another. Sales management should design a selection procedure that satisfies the company's specific needs.

Salespeople, whether new or experienced, require sales training. The developers of a training program must consider what to teach, who to train, and how to train them.

A compensation plan should attract, motivate, and hold the firm's most effective salespeople. It should give sales management the necessary level of control and sales personnel an acceptable level of freedom, income, and incentive. A firm can use one or more of three basic compensation methods: straight salary, straight commission, or a combination of salary and commission.

Although financial compensation plays an important role in motivating salespeople, a motivational program must also satisfy their nonfinancial needs. Examples of motivational incentives are enjoyable working conditions, power and authority, job security, and an opportunity to excel. Some organizations also use negative motivational measures—financial penalties, demotions, even terminations.

Decisions about sales territories can determine the effectiveness of a sales force that must travel. These decisions must consider the size and shape of territories and routing and scheduling, all of which are influenced by many factors.

To control and evaluate a sales force properly, sales management must have information. That information comes from salespeople's reports, customer feedback, and invoices. The dimensions used to measure performance are determined largely by sales objectives. The process does not end with the evaluation. Where there are problems, the sales manager must take corrective action, which may involve comprehensive changes in the sales force.

Sales promotion is an activity or material that acts as a direct inducement, offering added value, or incentive for the product, to resellers, salespersons, or customers. It includes all promotional activities and materials that are not a part of advertising, publicity, or personal selling. It is often used to facilitate personal selling and advertising. Consumer sales promotion techniques encourage or stimulate consumers to patronize a specific store or to try a particular product. They include coupons, demonstrations, frequent user incentives, point-of-purchase displays, free samples, money refunds, premiums, cents-off offers, and contests and sweepstakes. Trade sales promotion techniques stimulate wholesalers and retailers to carry a producer's products and to market them aggressively. They include buy-back allowances, buying allowances, counts and recounts, free merchandise, merchandise allowances, cooperative advertising, dealer listings, premium or push money, sales contests, and dealer loaders.

MATCHING EXERCISES

Use the following set of terms to identify the sentences and phrases below. On the blank line next to each sentence or phrase, place the letter of the term that the sentence or phrase describes. Do not use a term more than once.

a. Dealer loader
b. Personal selling
c. Coupons
d. Trade sales promotion methods
e. Sales contest
f. Prospecting
g. Demonstration
h. Consumer sales promotion techniques
i. Allocation
j. Push money
k. Approach
l. Frequent user incentives
m. Sales promotion
n. Dealer listing
o. Closing

p. Point-of-purchase materials
q. Combination compensation plan
r. Cooperative advertising
s. Order getter
t. Free samples
u. Sales training
v. Straight commission compensation plan
w. Free merchandise
x. Order taker
y. Straight salary compensation plan
z. Count-and-recount promotion method
aa. Support personnel
bb. Money refund
cc. Cold canvass

dd.	Buy-back allowance	kk.	Cents-off offer
ee.	Missionary salespersons	ll.	Target market
ff.	Sales potential	mm.	Merchandise allowance
gg.	Premiums	nn.	Consumer sweepstakes
hh.	Recruiting	oo.	Technical salespersons
ii.	Buying allowance	pp.	Consumer contest
jj.	Trade salespersons		

_____ 1. Salespeople who are not strictly support personnel because they perform the order-taking function as well.
Trade Salespersons

__q__ 2. A plan by which salespeople are paid a fixed salary and a commission based on sales volume. *Combination Compensation*

__y__ 3. A plan by which salespeople are paid a specific amount per time period.

__a__ 4. A gift, often part of a display, that is given to a retailer who purchases a specified quantity of merchandise.

__mm__ 5. A sales promotion method, aimed at retailers, consisting of a manufacturer's agreement to pay resellers certain amounts of money for providing special promotional efforts. *Allowa*

__h__ 6. Sales promotion methods that encourage or stimulate customers to patronize a specific retail store or purchase a particular product.

__EE__ 7. Support personnel, usually employed by a manufacturer, who help the producer's customers sell to their own customers.

__N__ 8. An advertisement that promotes a product and identifies the names of participating retailers who sell the product.

__OO__ 9. Support personnel who provide the firm's current customers with technical assistance and offer advice on product characteristics and applications and system design and installation.

__W__ 10. A sales promotion method aimed at retailers whereby goods are given to resellers who purchase a stated quantity of a product.

__L__ 11. A sales promotion method used to reward specific customers who engage in repeat purchases.

__aa__ 12. Members of the sales staff who facilitate the selling function but usually are not involved just with making sales.

__c__ 13. A sales promotion method used to stimulate consumers to try a new or established product, to increase sales volume quickly, to attract repeat users, or to introduce new package sizes or features.

__hh__ 14. A process by which a sales manager develops a list of applicants for sales positions.

__NN__ 15. A sales promotion device for established products in which entrants submit their names for inclusion in a drawing for prizes.

g   16. A sales promotion method manufacturers use to show how a product actually works to encourage trial use and purchase of the product.

pp 17. A sales promotion device for established products that has individuals competing for prizes based on their analytical or creative skills.

s   18. A salesperson who increases the firm's sales by selling to new customers and by increasing sales to present customers.

m   19. An activity or material that acts as a direct inducement to resellers, salespersons, or consumers by offering added value, or incentive for the product.

R   20. An arrangement in which a manufacturer agrees to pay a certain amount of a retailer's media costs for advertising the manufacturer's products.

B   21. The process of informing customers and persuading them to purchase products through personal communication in an exchange situation.

BB 22. A sales promotion technique in which a consumer submits proof of purchase and is mailed a specific amount of money.

K   23. The manner in which a salesperson contacts a potential customer.

X   24. A type of salesperson who primarily seeks repeat sales.

F   25. Developing a list of potential customers for personal selling purposes.

t   26. A consumer sales promotion technique marketers use to stimulate trial of a product, to increase sales volume in early stages of the product's life cycle, or to obtain desirable distribution.

O   27. The element in the selling process in which the salesperson asks the prospect to buy the product.

II 28. A temporary price reduction to resellers for purchasing specified quantities of a product.

d   29. Sales promotion techniques that stimulate wholesalers and retailers to carry a producer's products and to market those products aggressively.

KK 30. A sales promotion device for established products in which buyers receive a certain amount off the regular price shown on the label or package.

J   31. Funds used to push a line of goods by giving salespeople additional compensation.

Z   32. A sales promotion method whereby the producer pays the reseller a specific amount of money for each product unit moved from the reseller's warehouse in a given period of time.

P   33. A sales promotion method that uses outside signs, window displays, and display racks to attract attention, to inform customers, and to encourage retailers to carry particular products.

gg 34. Items offered free or at minimum cost as a bonus for purchasing a product.

35. A sales promotion method used to motivate distributors, retailers, and sales personnel by recognizing outstanding achievements.

 36. A sales promotion method that gives a reseller a sum of money for each unit bought after an initial deal is over.

 37. A plan by which a salesperson's compensation is determined solely by the amount of his or her sales for a given period of time.

TRUE OR FALSE STATEMENTS

T   F   1. Business organizations spend more on personal selling than on any other promotion mix ingredient.

T   F   2. Personal selling is usually the least expensive ingredient in the promotion mix.

T   F   3. Personal selling gives marketers their greatest opportunity for adjusting a message to satisfy customers' information needs.

T   F   4. The sales presentation gives a salesperson the greatest opportunity for determining a prospect's specific product needs.

T   F   5. One of the best ways for a salesperson to overcome objections is to anticipate them.

T   F   6. The personal selling process begins with approaching the customer.

T   F   7. Salespersons who seek repeat sales are classified as order takers.

T   F   8. Support personnel facilitate the selling function but usually are not involved solely with making sales.

T   F   9. Trade salespeople usually are employed by manufacturers and help the producer's customers sell to their own customers.

T   F   10. An important function of the technical salesperson is to advise the customer about product characteristics and applications.

T   F   11. Sales objectives usually are established for the entire sales force, not for each salesperson.

T   F   12. Currently, there is no set of generally accepted guidelines that a sales manager can use to ensure the recruitment of good sales personnel.

T   F   13. Both experienced salespeople and new salespeople require sales training.

T   F   14. When the straight commission method is used to compensate salespeople, the commission must be based on a single percentage of sales.

T   F   15. The straight salary compensation method is useful when the firm moves into new sales territories that require developmental work.

T   F   16. When deciding territory size, a sales manager should attempt to create territories that have different sales potential.

© 1993 Houghton Mifflin Company. All rights reserved.

T   F   17. A sales manager should develop a systematic approach for motivating salespeople.

T   F   18. The dimensions used to measure a salesperson's performance are determined largely by the firm's sales objectives.

T   F   19. Sales promotion usually is used in conjunction with other promotion mix ingredients.

T   F   20. Consumer sales promotion techniques stimulate resellers to carry a product and promote it aggressively.

MULTIPLE-CHOICE QUESTIONS

_____   1. Personal selling is an important marketing function because it
   a. lets marketers zero in on the most promising sales prospects.
   b. is the most expensive promotion-mix ingredient.
   c. produces more profit than other promotional methods.
   d. is the least flexible promotion-mix ingredient.
   e. is the main thrust of the marketing field.

_____   2. Compared with other promotional tools, personal selling is
   a. the least expensive.
   b. the most precise.
   c. the least flexible.
   d. usually not used in an organization's total promotion activities.
   e. more often used in conjunction with other promotion-mix ingredients.

_____   3. The most widely used promotion-mix ingredient is
   a. publicity.
   b. sales promotion.
   c. personal advertising.
   d. personal selling.
   e. public relations.

_____   4. In the general selling process, developing a list of potential customers is called
   a. evaluating.
   b. preparing.
   c. prospecting.
   d. preselling.
   e. searching.

_____   5. When salespeople approach potential customers without their prior consent, they are using
   a. the cold canvass technique.
   b. repeat contact.
   c. the referral technique.
   d. the blind technique.
   e. hard sell.

_____ 6. This Tuesday, Sharon Spencer has a sales trainee riding with her. She states that today will be her first call on Dunbolt Electronics. She explains that in the approach phase of this call her goal, as usual, will be to
a. get an order.
b. get referrals.
c. gather information.
d. explain the product's benefits.
e. establish her company as the low-price leader.

_____ 7. As Ken Gerrard enters Steve Long's office, he explains that Steve's close friend at Apple suggested that he come by and see if his firm could improve his communication system as it had done last month for Apple. Ken is using which one of the following types of approach in this instance?
a. Cold canvass
b. Follow-up
c. Preparation
d. Referral
e. Creative

_____ 8. One of the best ways for a salesperson to overcome a prospect's objections is to
a. attract and hold the prospect's attention.
b. demonstrate the product to get the prospect more involved with it.
c. listen to the prospect's comments and responses.
d. fulfill the prospect's needs for information.
e. anticipate and answer them before the prospect has an opportunity to ask.

_____ 9. During the presentation, the salesperson may ask questions based on the assumption that the prospect will buy the product. This is known as a
a. follow-up.
b. closing.
c. cold canvass.
d. trial close.
e. referral.

_____ 10. Salespersons can be classified into three groups according to the functions they perform:
a. order getters, order takers, and support personnel.
b. order getters, current customer sales, and new customer sales.
c. past customer sales, current customer sales, and new customer sales.
d. inside order takers, outside order takers, and support salespeople.
e. missionary, trade, and technical salespeople.

_____ 11. Salespersons who facilitate the selling function but usually are involved with more than just making sales are known as
a. support personnel.
b. inside order takers.
c. outside order takers.
d. order getters.
e. agents.

_____ 12. Ben explains to Marty that if he were hired by American, his job would be to call customers who had not placed their orders by the scheduled weekly cut-off time. Marty's job would be best classified as which type of selling?
   a. Field order taker
   b. Missionary salesperson
   c. Trade salesperson
   d. Inside order taker
   e. Current-customer salesperson

_____ 13. The missionary salesperson's major function is to
   a. promote products to potential customers.
   b. perform the order-taking function.
   c. help the producer's customers sell to their own customers.
   d. advise customers about product applications.
   e. generate the bulk of the firm's total sales.

_____ 14. Salespeople who direct much of their effort toward helping customers promote products are called
   a. technical salespeople.
   b. missionary salespeople.
   c. trade salespeople.
   d. inside salespeople.
   e. outside salespeople.

_____ 15. Bill Smith tells the other sales managers at Pitney Bowes that before they can identify qualified applicants, they first must sit down and develop a
   a. training manual.
   b. recruiting plan.
   c. job description.
   d. set of sales objectives.
   e. compensation plan.

_____ 16. Chemisell Company is in the process of training new salespeople. So far they have been familiarized only with the products they will be selling. In what other major areas should they receive training?
   a. Competitors' products and strategies
   b. Selling techniques and company policies
   c. Public relations and physical distribution
   d. Sales promotion and pricing decisions
   e. Consumer behavior and management techniques

_____ 17. Items such as outside signs, window displays, counter pieces, display racks, and self-service cartons are
   a. trade sales promotion methods.
   b. point-of-purchase displays.
   c. premiums.
   d. merchandise allowances.
   e. dealer loaders.

_____ 18. Additional compensation provided to salespeople to encourage them to push a line of goods is called
   a. commission.
   b. salary.
   c. a buy-back allowance.
   d. push money.
   e. a bribe.

_____ 19. Which of the following statements about compensation programs is *most* correct?
   a. Most compensation programs place salespeople on an equal basis, with each person receiving approximately the same pay.
   b. When a straight salary method is used, compensation is determined solely on the basis of sales for a given time period.
   c. When a straight commission method is used, the salesperson is paid a fixed salary plus a commission based on sales volume.
   d. Good compensation programs usually are developed solely on the basis of the product being sold.
   e. Sales compensation programs usually reimburse salespeople for their selling expenses, provide fringe benefits, and deliver the necessary compensation level.

_____ 20. Sales compensation plans
   a. are easy to design.
   b. should be designed to maintain a productive sales force.
   c. have very little to do with customers.
   d. pertain only to the salaries of salespeople.
   e. are not described by any of the above statements.

_____ 21. In presenting the firm's new sales-force compensation plan to the executive committee, vice-president of sales Betty Roberts proclaims that the need for incentive and control leads to the development of a _____ compensation plan.
   a. combination
   b. straight salary
   c. regular
   d. continual
   e. straight commission

_____ 22. One major disadvantage of the straight commission compensation method is that it
   a. results in selling expenses that are directly related to sales revenues.
   b. gives salespeople little financial security.
   c. gives salespeople no incentive.
   d. causes fluctuating sales revenue.
   e. results in stable selling expenses during periods of declining sales.

_____ 23. In attempting to set the size of a territory, the sales manager should try to
   a. create territories that have relatively dissimilar sales potentials but require about the same amount of work.
   b. form territories that are as nearly equal in size as possible.
   c. create territories that have relatively similar sales potentials or that require about the same amount of work.
   d. establish territories mainly on the basis of sales potential.
   e. create territories that facilitate the effective distribution and servicing of the product first and benefit the salesperson second.

_____ 24. One major goal of the planner when routing and scheduling a salesperson is to
   a. construct the routes and schedules in such a way that sales potential can be measured easily.
   b. employ symmetrical patterns to maximize the effectiveness of the salesperson.
   c. allow for flexibility in the routes and schedules so that the salesperson can handle special accounts properly.
   d. minimize the salesperson's nonselling time.
   e. minimize selling costs.

_____ 25. An activity or material that acts as an inducement to resellers, salespeople, or consumers by offering added value or incentive for the product is known as
   a. publicity.
   b. advertising.
   c. personal selling.
   d. sales promotion.
   e. personal communication.

_____ 26. The dimensions used to measure a salesperson's performance are determined largely by
   a. sales objectives.
   b. projected sales volume.
   c. anticipated profit margin.
   d. the profit impact point.
   e. the total number of sales calls made.

_____ 27. Dickerson Foods Company is using sales promotion to motivate wholesalers and retailers to carry a new product and to market the product aggressively. What type of sales promotion is Dickerson using?
   a. Consumer sales promotion
   b. Product sales promotion
   c. Trade sales promotion
   d. Merchandising promotion
   e. Pull promotion

_____ 28. An example of a sales promotion technique for a new product is
   a. push money.
   b. cooperative advertising.
   c. a buy-back allowance.
   d. a sales contest.
   e. free samples.

_____ 29. Sales contests are examples of a sales promotion method aimed at
   a. selling new products.
   b. resellers.
   c. manufacturers.
   d. selling established products.
   e. consumers.

_____ 30. If, as part of its sales promotion efforts, Campbell Soup Company placed 1 million fifteen-cent coupons in ads in major national magazines, given that Campbell's redemption rate is near average, it could expect to get back how many coupons?
   a. 15,000
   b. 35,000
   c. 70,000
   d. 100,000
   e. 200,000

MINICASE: DR PEPPER'S SALES PROMOTION EFFORTS*

Dr Pepper's taste is unique—so unique that the National Soft Drink Association had to name a soft-drink category after it. But that uniqueness makes it difficult to describe what Dr Pepper tastes like for those who have never tried it.

Executives of Dr Pepper Company wanted to build consumer loyalty based on taste preference. They believed the way to go about this was through sampling. Bottlers were told to find ways for consumers to try Dr Pepper under the most favorable circumstances. Goals also were set to attain high visibility and availability of Dr Pepper brands and to develop pull pressure. The company wanted to avoid price discounting; it did not want customers to think of soft drinks as a commodity to be chosen according to whichever one is on sale.

To support these goals, four major sales promotions were planned, one for each quarter, along with separate promotions for Diet Dr Pepper. Following is a description of each promotion.

• "Endless Summer" offered a dream vacation for two as the grand prize. Bottlers' salespeople were offered a chance at a beach vacation for two for every one-hundred-case display built during the promotion. To encourage retailers to display Dr Pepper

---

*Information taken from Gary A. Hemphill, "Rejuvenated Dr Pepper Bounces Back," *Beverage Industry*, December 1984, pp. 4, 21; Gary A. Hemphill, "It's Fun To 'Be a Pepper'—Again," *Beverage Industry*, October 2, 1985, pp. 1, 36; and Gary A. Hemphill, "Dr Pepper Continues 'Out of the Ordinary' Ads," *Beverage Industry*, November 1985, p. 4.

with their high-margin, high-volume snack food items, consumers were offered a 50-cent cash refund on any purchase of Dr Pepper plus snack food.

- A sweepstakes offered $1 million to the grand prize winner. This promotional effort involved answering questions by phone—the correct answers were given on bottles and cans of Dr Pepper. Every correct answer won a coupon and a chance to win the grand prize.
- The "Western Pepper" promotion hoped to turn people into walking billboards for the brand by giving away T-shirts, mugs, and iron-ons. A sweepstakes tie-in offered a $100,000 customized western wardrobe and a trip to Dallas to pick it out. Bottlers were encouraged to set up local redemption centers.
- The fourth-quarter sweepstakes offered a trip to Times Square to be on television with Dick Clark on Dr Pepper's "New Year's Rockin' Eve" special.
- A final promotion was designed to support Diet Dr Pepper (then Sugar-free Dr Pepper). The promotion involved a new slogan, "Test these tastes," and offered a sports bag with a Dr Pepper logo for less than half price through the mail with proofs of purchase. Advertisements showed both men and women drinking Diet Dr Pepper.

Questions

_____ 1. Which sales promotion objective does Dr Pepper seem to be emphasizing?
   a. To increase the total number of users for an established brand
   b. To encourage greater usage among current customers
   c. To educate consumers regarding product improvements
   d. To stabilize a fluctuating sales pattern
   e. To obtain more and better shelf space and displays

_____ 2. Dr Pepper's sales promotion mix consists of
   a. consumer sales promotion techniques exclusively.
   b. trade sales promotion methods exclusively.
   c. mainly consumer sales promotion techniques.
   d. mainly trade sales promotion methods.
   e. roughly equal amounts of consumer and trade sales promotion.

_____ 3. Dr Pepper used a variety of sales promotion methods. Which of the following was *not* used?
   a. Premiums
   b. Coupons
   c. Consumer sweepstakes
   d. Retailer coupons
   e. Sales contests

_____ 4. The "Endless Summer" promotion is an example of a sales promotion aimed at
   a. sales of new products.
   b. salespeople.
   c. retail establishments.
   d. sales of established products.
   e. consumers.

PROGRAMMED COMPLETION EXERCISES

informing, persuading

1. Personal selling is a process of _____ and _____ customers to purchase products through personal communication in an exchange situation.

prospecting

2. Developing a list of potential customers is called _____.

Closing, prospect

3. _____ is the stage in the selling process in which the salesperson asks the _____ to buy the product or products.

order getters, order takers, support

4. Based on the functions they perform, salespeople can be classified into three groups: _____ _____, _____ _____, and _____ personnel.

missionary, trade, technical

5. Although there are many kinds of sales support personnel, the three most common types are _____, _____, and _____ salespersons.

technical, current customers

6. Technical salespersons provide _____ assistance to the organization's _____ _____.

product, customer, marketing channel, advertising

7. The type of sales force the firm chooses is influenced by the firm's _____, _____, _____ _____, and _____.

sales calls, travel times

8. A salesperson's workload is not just a function of the number of _____ _____; _____ _____ between customers and the amount of time spent with each account also affect workload.

management, success,
sales revenue

9. Effective _____ of the sales force is an important determinant of a firm's _____ because the sales force is directly responsible for generating an organization's primary input, namely _____ _____.

precise, measurable,
geographic

10. Sales objectives should be stated in _____, _____ terms and should specify the time period and _____ areas involved.

sales volume,
market share, profit

11. Objectives for the entire sales force should be stated in terms of _____ _____, _____ _____, or _____.

recruits,
qualifications

12. To ensure that the recruiting process produces a usable list of _____, the sales manager should establish a set of _____.

comprehensive,
refresher, products

13. Ordinarily, new sales personnel require _____ training, whereas experienced personnel need both _____ courses on established _____ and training about new products.

field, educational
institutions, facilities,
combination

14. Sales training can be performed in the _____, at _____ _____, in company _____, or in a _____ of these locations.

formulate, administer,
attracts, motivates,
holds

15. A business organization must _____ and _____ a compensation plan that _____, _____, and _____ the most effective salespeople.

sales management,
control, freedom,
income, incentive

16. A compensation plan should be designed to give _____ _____ the necessary level of _____ and sales personnel an acceptable level of _____, _____, and _____.

selling expenses,
fringe benefits

17. Sales compensation programs normally reimburse salespeople for their _____ _____, provide a certain number of _____ _____, and deliver the necessary compensation level.

motivating, motiva-
tional, nonfinancial

18. Although financial compensation plays an important role in _____ a salesperson, a _____ program also must satisfy the salesperson's _____ needs.

size, shape

19. In creating sales territories, sales managers make decisions that have to do with the _____ and _____ of those territories.

reports, customer
feedback, invoices

20. To control and evaluate sales-force activities properly, sales management needs information. The sales manager obtains this information through salespeople's _____, _____ _____, and _____.

dimensions, sales
objectives

21. The _____ used to measure a salesperson's performance are determined largely by _____ _____.

activity, material,
inducement, con-
sumers, added value,
incentive

22. Sales promotion is an _____ or _____ that acts as a direct _____ to resellers, salespersons, or _____ by offering _____ _____, or _____ for the product.

secondary,
advertising,
personal selling

23. Sales promotion efforts do not always play a _____ role; a company sometimes uses _____ and _____ _____ to support sales promotion activities.

ANSWERS TO OBJECTIVE QUESTIONS

Matching		*True or False*		*Multiple-Choice*		*Minicase*
1. jj	20. r	1. T	11. F	1. a	16. b	1. a
2. q	21. b	2. F	12. T	2. b	17. b	2. c
3. y	22. bb	3. T	13. T	3. d	18. d	3. d
4. a	23. k	4. T	14. F	4. c	19. e	4. b
5. mm	24. x	5. T	15. T	5. a	20. b	
6. h	25. f	6. F	16. F	6. c	21. a	
7. ee	26. t	7. T	17. T	7. d	22. b	
8. n	27. o	8. T	18. T	8. e	23. c	
9. oo	28. ii	9. F	19. T	9. d	24. d	
10. w	29. d	10. T	20. F	10. a	25. d	
11. l	30. kk			11. a	26. a	
12. aa	31. j			12. d	27. c	
13. c	32. z			13. c	28. e	
14. hh	33. p			14. c	29. b	
15. nn	34. gg			15. c	30. b	
16. g	35. e					
17. pp	36. dd					
18. s	37. v					
19. m						

18 PRICING CONCEPTS

CHAPTER OUTLINE

The nature of price
    Terms used to describe price
    The importance of price to marketers
Price and nonprice competition
    Price competition
    Nonprice competition
Pricing objectives
    Survival
    Profit
    Return on investment
    Market share
    Cash flow
    Status quo
    Product quality
Factors affecting pricing decisions
    Organizational and marketing objectives
    Types of pricing objectives
    Costs
    Other marketing mix variables
    Channel member expectations
    Buyers' perceptions
    Competition
    Legal and regulatory issues
Pricing for business-to-business markets
    Price discounting
    Geographic pricing
    Transfer pricing
    Price discrimination

CHAPTER SUMMARY

Price is the value of what is exchanged. The buyer exchanges purchasing power for satisfaction or utility. Purchasing power is determined by the buyer's income, credit, and wealth. Price is not always money; barter, the trading of products, is the oldest form of exchange.

Price is expressed in different terms for different exchanges. Premiums, fees, fares, tolls, rents, commissions, dues, deposits, tips, interest, and taxes are all prices. Whatever it is called, price is used to quantify and express the value of the items in a market exchange.

Price is the most flexible variable in the marketing mix. Often it is the only element that can be altered quickly in response to changes in demand or to the actions of competitors. It relates directly to the generation of total revenues. Total revenues equal price times the quantities sold; profits are what is left when total costs are subtracted from total revenues.

A product offering can compete on a price or nonprice basis. Price competition emphasizes the price of a product as a selling point. A seller who competes on the basis of price must be willing and able to change prices often and quickly and should consider the images his or her pricing policies will promote. Nonprice competition emphasizes distinctive product features, service, product quality, promotion, or packaging to distinguish a product from competing brands. Although less flexible than price competition, nonprice competition creates product loyalty. Nonprice competition is effective only under certain conditions: The product must have unique characteristics; buyers must be able to recognize those characteristics and want them; competitors should find it difficult, if not impossible, to imitate those characteristics; and the organization must be able to promote those characteristics to establish the superiority of the brand and to set it apart from the competition in the minds of consumers. A marketer who is competing on a nonprice basis still must be aware of competitors' prices and should probably price its brands near competing brands. Price, then, remains a crucial element in the marketing mix, even in nonprice competition.

Pricing objectives are overall goals that describe what the firm wants to achieve through its pricing efforts. Because pricing objectives influence decisions in most functional areas, they must be consistent with the organization's overall objectives. Survival is the broadest and most fundamental pricing objective. Because price is a flexible variable, it can be used to increase sales volume to a level consistent with the organization's expenses. Sometimes the management of a business claims that its pricing objective is to maximize profits for the firm's owners; the profit objective rarely works, however, because its achievement is difficult to measure. Pricing for a targeted return on investment is another kind of pricing objective. Many firms establish pricing objectives to maintain or increase market share. This strategy allows the manager to develop market share without depending on growth of the industry. A cash flow and recovery objective is used to recover development capital as quickly as possible. When an organization is in a favorable position, it may set for itself a status quo objective; that is, it may decide not to take further risk. Or a firm may have the objective of product quality leadership in the market, which usually means high prices. There is no one best objective, but any objective selected should be consistent with the organization's goals.

Pricing decisions are influenced by many factors, including organizational and marketing objectives, pricing objectives, costs, other marketing mix variables, channel member expectations, buyers' perceptions, competition, and legal and regulatory issues. Pricing must be consistent with a firm's overall organizational goals and sales objectives. The type of pricing objectives used by a marketer should have considerable bearing in the determination of prices. Most marketers view a product's cost as a minimum, or floor, below which a product cannot be priced. All the marketing mix variables are interrelated, which means that price can influence and be influenced by decisions that relate to product, distribution, and promotion. Marketing channel members (wholesalers, retailers) have certain expectations—about revenues and support activities. These expectations must be considered in establishing prices. The effects of a pricing strategy on related products in the company's line should be considered. The importance of price to buyers is not absolute; it can vary from market to market or segment to segment. How buyers respond to price, then, is an important element in determining price. Marketers also must know how competitors are pricing their products and how they might respond to price adjustments. This allows a firm to establish prices relative to the market. Finally, government regulations and legislation can strongly influence pricing decisions.

Business-to-business markets consist of individuals and organizations that purchase products to use in their own operations or to produce other products. Two common business-to-business pricing policies are price discounting and geographic pricing. Trade discounts, quantity discounts, cash discounts, seasonal discounts, and allowances are all forms of price discounting. Geographic pricing involves reductions for transportation costs or other costs associated with the physical distance between buyer and seller. One type of geographic pricing is freight absorption pricing, where the seller absorbs all or part of the actual freight costs.

Transfer pricing occurs when one unit in a company sells a product to another unit. The price is determined by actual full cost, standard full cost, cost plus investment, or market-based cost methods.

Price discrimination is a policy that results in different prices being charged to give a group of buyers a competitive advantage. Price differentials are legal when they can be justified on the basis of cost savings, when they meet competition in good faith, or when they do not damage competition.

MATCHING EXERCISES

Use the following set of terms to identify the sentences and phrases below. On the blank line next to each sentence or phrase, place the letter of the term that the sentence or phrase describes. Do not use a term more than once.

a.	Barter	m. F.O.B. factory
b.	Allowance	n. Transfer pricing
c.	Cash discount	o. Zone prices
d.	Purchasing power	p. Uniform geographic pricing
e.	Total revenues	q. Trade (functional) discount
f.	Pricing objectives	r. Geographic pricing
g.	Market share	s. Cumulative discounts
h.	Price competition	t. Nonprice competition
i.	Base-point pricing	u. Seasonal discount
j.	Quantity discounts	v. Price
k.	Price discrimination	w. Freight absorption pricing
l.	Noncumulative discounts	

_t_ 1. Using distinctive product features to compete with competitors. NON PRICE Competition

_h_ 2. Changes in the price of a product in response to the actions of other sellers. Price Competition

_F_ 3. Overall goals that describe the role of price in an organization's long-range plans. Pricing Objectives

_E_ 4. Price times the quantities sold. Total Revenue

_a_ 5. The oldest form of exchange; the trade of products. Barter

_v_ 6. The value placed on what is exchanged. Price

_d_ 7. A buyer's income, credit, and wealth. Purchasing Power

_g_ 8. A firm's sales in relation to total industry sales, expressed as a ratio. Market Share

_O_ 9. Regional prices that vary for major geographic zones as transportation costs increase. Zone Prices

_P_ 10. Sometimes called postage-stamp pricing; results in fixed average transportation costs; used to avoid the problems involved with charging a different price to each customer. Uniform geographic pricing

_N_ 11. Pricing when one unit in a company sells a product to another unit. Transfer Pricing

_K_ 12. A policy in which some buyers are charged lower prices than other buyers, giving them a competitive advantage. Price discrimination

_S_ 13. Quantity discounts that are aggregated over a stated period of time. Cumulative Discounts

_m_ 14. A price quotation that excludes transportation charges and indicates a shipping point. FOB Factory

_B_ 15. A concession in price to achieve a desired goal. Allowance

_W_ 16. Pricing for a particular customer or geographic area; the seller pays all or part of the actual freight costs. Freight Absorption Pricing

_J_ 17. Deductions from list price that reflect the economies of purchasing in large amounts. Quantity Discounts

_L_ 18. One-time price reductions based on the number of units purchased, the dollar size of the order, or the product mix purchased. NON Cumulative Discounts

_R_ 19. A form of pricing that involves reductions for transportation costs or other costs associated with the physical distance between the buyer and the seller. Geographic Pricing

_c_ 20. A price reduction to the buyer resulting from prompt payment or cash payment. Cash Discount

_i_ 21. A geographic pricing policy that includes the price at the factory plus freight charges from the base point nearest the buyer. Base Point Pricing

TRUE OR FALSE STATEMENTS

T F 1. The price of a product usually has little effect on consumers' purchasing decisions.

T F 2. It is a mistake to believe that price is always money or some other financial consideration.

T F 3. Price is a key element in the marketing mix because it relates directly to the generation of revenues.

T F 4. Buyers' concern for and interest in price is related to their expectations about the satisfaction or utility associated with a product.

T F 5. Sellers who use nonprice competition still must consider price in marketing their products.

T F 6. A firm always raises prices when it is actively engaged in price competition.

T F 7. Pricing objectives influence decisions in most functional areas and must be consistent with an organization's overall goals.

T F 8. A fundamental pricing objective is the firm's survival.

T F 9. Status quo pricing objectives can increase a firm's risk by creating a climate of severe price competition in an industry.

T F 10. Price usually is one of the most visible and flexible variables available to marketers.

T F 11. There are times when a marketer may sell a product below cost.

T F 12. Price affects the promotion but not the distribution of products.

T F 13. To consumers, price is always the most important factor in the buying decision.

T F 14. Quantity discounts may be cumulative or noncumulative.

T F 15. A reduction off the list price given to an intermediary by a producer is called a trade discount.

T F 16. A price quoted as F.O.B. factory means that the manufacturer pays for shipping the product from the factory.

T F 17. Knowing competitors' prices can help marketers increase their own sales.

T F 18. The purpose of price discrimination is to decrease revenues from buyers who may be reluctant to purchase a product even at a low price.

MULTIPLE-CHOICE QUESTIONS

1. Which of the following pricing objectives is oriented to the quick recovery of cash and is favored for products with a short life cycle?
   a. Return on investment pricing
   b. Profit pricing
   c. Cash flow pricing
   d. Market share pricing
   e. Status quo pricing

2. John trades his old lawn mower to his next-door neighbor, Peter, for Peter's electric sander. This transaction is known as
   a. pricing.
   b. selling.
   c. marketing.
   d. barter.
   e. reciprocity.

3. According to the text, price is
   a. purchasing power.
   b. the value placed on what is exchanged.
   c. the utility associated with a product.
   d. how much something costs in monetary terms.
   e. money paid or some other financial consideration.

4. Which of the following statements is false?
   a. Price can be changed quickly to respond to changes in demand.
   b. Price has a psychological impact on customers and can be used symbolically to emphasize a product's quality.
   c. Price is important in determining profits.
   d. Price is usually used as a tool to raise production costs.
   e. None of the above statements is false.

5. Pricing objectives are overall goals that describe the role of price and
   a. must be consistent with the organization's goals.
   b. have a minimal effect on other functional areas of a business.
   c. help determine the allocation of buyers' purchasing power.
   d. should not have an effect on the functional areas of a business.
   e. should take only profit into account.

6. Which of the following is the broadest and most fundamental pricing objective?
   a. Market share
   b. Survival
   c. Profit
   d. Return on investment
   e. Cash flow and recovery

7. Which of the following statements is false?
   a. Market share, or sales in relation to competition, is a meaningful benchmark of success for a company.
   b. An organization's sales can increase while its actual market share decreases.
   c. Market share is important but cannot be considered a pricing objective.
   d. Market share can increase even when sales for the total industry are decreasing.
   e. Market share is an important determinant of a company's relative strength.

8. If Carrier develops a new air conditioning compressor that lasts twice as long as existing compressors while using half the electricity, it will probably establish its pricing objective based on
   a. cash flow.
   b. product quality.
   c. survival.
   d. return on investment.
   e. market share.

9. Price fixing was made illegal by the
   a. Robinson-Patman Act.
   b. Sherman Act.
   c. Clayton Act.
   d. Federal Trade Commission Act.
   e. Consumer Goods Pricing Act.

10. Price discrimination is illegal when price differentials
    a. do not affect the level of competition.
    b. are used for customers who are not competitors.
    c. lessen or injure competition.
    d. occur to meet competitors' prices.
    e. are the result of different costs for different customers.

11. What effect do quantity discounts have on the marketing function?
    a. Large purchases reduce selling costs and may shift certain storage, finance, and risk-taking functions onto buyers.
    b. Because discounts are usually small, they provide no incentive for intermediaries to furnish transportation, storage, or other services.
    c. Discounts usually decrease the total number of marketing functions that are necessary to get a product to buyers.
    d. Discounts are considered bribes by intermediaries, which puts producers in a bad light.
    e. Quantity discounts have no effect on the marketing function.

12. The advantage of knowing competitors' prices is that
    a. it eliminates a marketer's need to develop cost objectives.
    b. it helps the firm adjust its prices in relation to competitors' prices.
    c. it ensures profits for a marketer who charges the same price.

d. it ensures an accurate estimate of sales.

e. industry profits are known to all.

13. Given that Nissan operates in the oligopolistic automotive industry, when Nissan lowers the price of its Sentra, other automobile makers are most likely to do what with their own comparable models?
   a. Raise prices
   b. Reduce fixed costs
   c. Match the price reduction
   d. Reposition their own products
   e. Focus on larger automobiles

14. A trade discount is
   a. a deduction from the list price that reflects the economies of buying in large quantities.
   b. a reduction off the list price given to an intermediary by a producer for performing certain functions.
   c. a price reduction to the buyer given for prompt payment or payment in cash.
   d. considered unethical and has been outlawed in some states.
   e. the only means to satisfy intermediaries.

15. Shari Thompson of Allfresh Wholesale Foods has been selling Weight Watchers frozen entrees to two different grocery chains at different prices. Under the Robinson-Patman Act, which one of the following circumstances would help her explain that her pricing practices are not discriminatory?
   a. The price differentials help one of the stores gain a competitive advantage.
   b. The two stores are competitors.
   c. Allfresh's fixed costs differ for the two chains.
   d. The chains do not have stores in the same block.
   e. The lower price at one of the chains was needed to meet competitors' prices.

16. A market structure that allows no flexibility in setting prices is
   a. an oligopoly.
   b. an unregulated monopoly.
   c. perfect competition.
   d. monopolistic competition.
   e. nonprice competition.

17. The Robinson-Patman Act
   a. prohibits the use of price maintenance agreements among producers and resellers.
   b. prohibits conspiracies to control prices.
   c. prohibits deceptive pricing.
   d. limits the use of price differentials.
   e. limits the conditions under which the federal government can invoke price controls.

18. According to the text, a low-priced pen is most likely to be sold through
   a. selective distribution.
   b. intensive distribution.
   c. exclusive distribution.
   d. channel distribution.
   e. competitive distribution.

19. Nonprice competition is workable for a particular brand if
   a. the firm promoting the brand has a limited promotion budget.
   b. a lower-priced brand with similar product features is available.
   c. the firm can distinguish the brand through unique product features that are difficult for competitors to imitate.
   d. buyers fail to recognize the brand's unique features.
   e. buyers do not want the brand's unique features.

20. A major disadvantage of price competition is that
   a. it does not provide the flexibility to alter prices in response to changes in the firm's costs.
   b. it cannot be used as a method of gaining market share.
   c. it is unworkable for a particular brand if competitors can easily imitate the brand's unique product features.
   d. competitors have the same flexibility to adjust prices.
   e. the Robinson-Patman Act prohibits the firm from cutting its price to a particular buyer to meet competitors' prices.

21. Which of the following is an example of a pricing decision that is compatible with the marketing objective of increasing unit sales by 10 percent by the end of next year?
   a. Setting a price equal to the average market price when buyers are price sensitive
   b. Reducing a price below the average market price when buyers are price sensitive
   c. Increasing a price above the average market price when buyers are not price sensitive
   d. Reducing a price below the average market price when buyers are not price sensitive
   e. Increasing a price above the average market price when buyers are price sensitive

22. Over the first eight months of the year, Davis Men's Shop has purchased sixteen dozen pairs of trousers from Thompson's Slacks. If Davis can order another four dozen by the end of December, it will receive a 10 percent discount on all pants ordered during the year. What type of discount is Thompson's offering in this instance?
   a. Cash
   b. Trade
   c. Cumulative
   d. Noncumulative
   e. Seasonal

_____ 23. Idaho Forestry Products offers a cash discount to its customers on the terms 2/10, n/30. This means that the customer must
  a. pay 2 percent of the bill within 10 days and the rest within 30 days.
  b. pay all of the bill in 10 days or be charged an extra 2 percent.
  c. pay within 10 days to receive a 2 percent cash discount, or pay the entire amount within 30 days with no discount.
  d. pay interest of 2 percent on the bill for any time after 10 days that the bill is not paid.
  e. pay interest of 2 percent on the bill for any time after 30 days that the bill is not paid.

_____ 24. If Nordica offered a 25 percent discount to retailers that ordered ski boots in February for delivery in May, the retailers would have the option of taking advantage of which type of discount?
  a. Trade
  b. Cumulative
  c. Cash
  d. Quantity
  e. Seasonal

_____ 25. Most marketers consider a product's cost
  a. a minimum price.
  b. a bench mark, or average, price.
  c. a maximum price.
  d. the price that will yield the greatest long-term profits.
  e. the price that is expected by marketing channel members.

_____ 26. A lower price may be required to generate sales of a particular product if
  a. the product is viewed as superior to most of the competing brands.
  b. the product has many loyal buyers.
  c. marketing channel members believe the product is more profitable than competing products.
  d. the status associated with ownership of the product is related to its high price.
  e. buyers have a slightly unfavorable view of the product.

_____ 27. To carry a producer's product, a distribution channel member expects to
  a. receive a profit that is comparable to what it could make from handling competing products.
  b. receive discounts for small orders.
  c. receive a low per unit profit if carrying the product requires considerable time and resources.
  d. pay the entire cost of sales training and other support activities.
  e. receive a profit that is greater than or equal to 40 percent of the product's purchase and carrying costs.

_____   28. When price competition is employed, the seller
         a. extensively promotes the unique product features of the brand.
         b. expects to win over customers who prefer a competing brand because
             of nonprice issues.
         c. always uses price differentials.
         d. expects to build customer loyalty.
         e. matches or beats the prices of competitors who also emphasize low
             prices.

MINICASE: PRICING AT AMERICAN COACHES

American Coaches is a five-year-old intercity bus company that competes directly with
Starway Lines. Since the federal government's deregulation of the airline and bus
industries, most bus companies have been losing money each year on their intercity
passenger services.

Most intercity bus passengers ride relatively short distances. About 40 percent travel
less than 200 miles per trip. Less than 5 percent travel over 1,000 miles per trip. Many
of the long-distance travelers (those who travel over 500 miles) have shifted to air
transportation because of lower prices in some cases. Passenger trains with frequently
traveled routes between major cities such as Boston and Washington, D.C., are a weak
third choice. Smaller communities are not well served by airlines or railways.

To stimulate sales, American Coaches has started offering the lowest coast-to-coast
fare and is promoting it through a national advertising campaign. Starway is meeting
American's prices. On well-traveled routes, American and Starway usually match each
other's discount fares.

Questions

_____   1. Given American's losses on intercity routes, what pricing objective has
             management selected?
         a. Product quality
         b. Market share
         c. Cash flow
         d. Status quo
         e. Return on investment

_____   2. Which of the following statements is false?
         a. Price competition is the best way to compete with the airlines for long-
             distance travel.
         b. Nonprice competition is probably the best way to compete with
             Starway for long-distance travel.
         c. American does compete with the airlines, but not on short distances.
         d. The airline industry is one of American's competitors.
         e. None of the above statements is false.

3. Starway is
   a. pricing its service based primarily on costs.
   b. engaged in nonprice competition with American.
   c. not responding to American's pricing strategy.
   d. competing with American on the basis of price.
   e. using a status quo pricing objective.

PROGRAMMED COMPLETION EXERCISES

survival, profits,
return on investment,
market share, cash,
status quo, product
quality

1. Pricing objectives can be based on _Survival_, maximizing _profits_, attaining a _R O I_ _____, maintaining or increasing _Mkt Share_ _____, recovering _cash_, maintaining the _status quo_, or _quality_ _____.

value, exchanged

2. To a buyer, price is the _value_ placed on what is _exchanged_

marketing mix,
demand, competitors

3. Price is one of the easiest variables in the _Mkts Mix_ to change; it can be adjusted quickly to respond to changes in _deman_ or the actions of _competitor_

financial price

4. In our society, _financial price_ quantifies value and is the basis of most marketing exchanges.

Pricing objectives,
organizational

5. _Pricing Obje_ influence decisions in most functional areas, including finance, accounting, and production; thus they must be consistent with overall _Organiz_ goals.

Price competition,
nonprice competition

6. _Price Competi_ emphasizes price while

_____ _____ emphasizes distinct product features as a way to stimulate consumer buying.

component, quantities sold

7. Price directly influences the profit equation because it is a major _Component_ of that equation; it indirectly influences the equation because it can be a major determinant of the _Quanities Sold_ .

price competition, matches, beats, low prices

8. When _Price Comp_ is employed, a marketer emphasizes price as an issue and _Match_ or _beats_ the prices of competitors who also emphasize _low prices_ .

unit sales, price

9. Nonprice competition affords an organization the opportunity to increase its brand's _unit Sale_ through means other than changing the _price_ of the brand.

consistent, goals

10. Marketers should set prices that are _Consistnt_ with the _goal_ and mission of the organization.

below, similar, customers

11. A market-share pricing objective usually causes a firm to price a product _below_ competing brands of _simular_ quality to attract competitors' _customer_ to the company's brand.

competition, cash flow, market share, survive

12. A firm may sell a product below cost to match _Compet_ , to generate _Cash flow_ , or even to increase _Mkt Share_ , but in the long run it cannot _Survive_ by selling a product below cost.

product, distribution, promotion

13. Pricing decisions can influence the decisions and activities associated with _Product_, _Distrib_, and _Promotion_ variables.

time, resources, expectations

14. The amount of _tim_ and the _Resource_ required to carry a product influence the _expectation_ of intermediaries.

varies, product categories, markets, segments

15. The importance of price to buyers _Varies_ across different _product categories_, target _mkts_, and market _Segment_.

injure, lessen, discriminatory

16. If price differentials tend to _injure_ or _lesson_ competition, they are considered _discriminatory_ and are prohibited.

trade, quantity, cumulative, non-cumulative, cash, seasonal, allowances

17. The types of price discounting policies are _trade_ discounts to intermediaries for performing certain functions; _Quanit_ discounts, which can be _Cumulative_ or _non-cumu-lative_; _Cash_ discounts for prompt payment or payment in cash; _Seasonal_ discounts to buyers who purchase out of season; and _allowances_, concessions in price to achieve a certain goal.

discriminatory

18. Price differentials become _discriminatory_ when a seller charges one reseller less than other similar resellers.

ANSWERS TO OBJECTIVE QUESTIONS

Matching		*True or False*		*Multiple-Choice*		*Minicase*
1. t	12. k	1. F	10. T	1. c	15. e	1. c
2. h	13. s	2. T	11. T	2. d	16. c	2. b
3. f	14. m	3. T	12. F	3. b	17. d	3. d
4. e	15. b	4. T	13. F	4. d	18. b	
5. a	16. w	5. T	14. T	5. a	19. c	
6. v	17. j	6. F	15. T	6. b	20. d	
7. d	18. l	7. T	16. F	7. c	21. b	
8. g	19. r	8. T	17. T	8. b	22. c	
9. o	20. c	9. F	18. F	9. b	23. c	
10. p	21. i			10. c	24. e	
11. n				11. a	25. a	
				12. b	26. e	
				13. c	27. a	
				14. b	28. e	

19 SETTING PRICES

CHAPTER OUTLINE

Selection of pricing objectives
Assessing the target market's evaluation of price and its ability to buy
Determining demand
    The demand curve
    Demand fluctuations
    Gauging price elasticity of demand
Analysis of demand, cost, and profit relationships
    Marginal analysis
    Breakeven analysis
Evaluation of competitors' prices
Selection of a pricing policy
    Pioneer pricing policies
    Psychological pricing
    Professional pricing
    Promotional pricing
    Experience curve pricing
Development of a pricing method
    Cost-oriented pricing
    Demand-oriented pricing
    Competition-oriented pricing
Determining a specific price

CHAPTER SUMMARY

The eight stages of setting prices are (1) selecting pricing objectives; (2) assessing the target market's evaluation of price and its ability to purchase; (3) determining demand; (4) analyzing the relationships among demand, cost, and profit; (5) evaluating competitors' prices; (6) selecting a pricing policy; (7) developing a pricing method; and (8) determining a specific price.

Marketers must be certain that the pricing objectives they set are consistent with the organization's overall goals as well as its marketing objectives. Poor coordination here can cause internal conflict and confusion and can prevent the organization from meeting its overall goals. Most organizations set multiple pricing objectives, some short term and some long term. A firm should have at least one pricing objective for each product, and for each segment in which the product is marketed. Many firms have several. Over time, these objectives may have to be altered.

The second stage in setting prices is assessing the target market's evaluation of price and its ability to purchase. The importance of price depends on the type of product and the type of target market. By understanding how the target market responds to price, a marketer is in a better position to know how much emphasis to place on price. Customers' ability to buy also has direct consequences for marketers. The ability to purchase involves resources, such as money, credit, wealth, and other products that can be exchanged.

In the third stage, marketing managers, with the help of marketing researchers, should attempt to determine demand for the product. For most products there is an inverse relationship between price and demand: As demand goes up, price goes down; as price goes up, demand goes down. Changes in buyers' attitudes, other components of the marketing mix, and uncontrollable environmental factors all influence demand, which in turn influences pricing. Price elasticity of demand is the relative responsiveness of demand to changes in price. When demand is elastic, it is very sensitive to price changes; that is, demand moves in the direction opposite to price. When demand is inelastic, price changes have little effect on it; that is, it moves parallel to price.

The production of any good or service has costs associated with it. Fixed costs do not vary with changes in the number of units produced or sold. Variable costs vary directly with changes in the number of units produced or sold. Total costs are the sum of fixed and variable costs times the quantity produced. Marginal cost is the extra cost a firm incurs when it produces one more unit of a product. There are two approaches to understanding demand, cost, and profit relationships: marginal analysis and breakeven analysis. Marginal analysis combines demand with a firm's costs to develop an optimum price for maximum profit. It is most effective for setting prices for established products, especially in competitive situations. To use breakeven analysis, a marketer must determine the breakeven point—the point at which the cost of producing a product equals the revenue from selling the product—for several alternative prices. This makes it possible to determine the effects on total revenues, total costs, and the breakeven point on each price under consideration. Although it is simple and straightforward, breakeven analysis assumes that demand is inelastic and that the major function of price is to recover costs.

The fifth stage is an evaluation of competitors' prices. The first step here is determining what those prices are—a relatively simple task at the retail level, a more difficult one at producer and reseller levels. How a product is priced in relation to competitors' brands affects both the sales and image of the product.

The sixth stage in setting prices is selecting a pricing policy—a guiding philosophy or course of action designed to influence and determine pricing decisions. In general, pricing policies describe how price will be used as a variable in the marketing mix. One common pricing policy is pioneer pricing, setting the base price for a new product. There are two kinds of pioneer pricing: price skimming is charging the highest possible price that buyers will pay; penetration pricing is setting a price below that of competitors in order to penetrate the market and increase unit sales. Another pricing policy is psychological pricing, which is designed to encourage emotional, rather than rational, purchases. It is used most often at the retail level and has only limited effectiveness in pricing industrial products. Types of psychological pricing include odd-even pricing, customary pricing, prestige pricing, and price lining. Professional pricing is a policy used by people who provide highly skilled services. The concept carries with it the idea that professionals have an ethical responsibility not to overcharge unknowing customers. Price often is coordinated with promotion. Promotional pricing includes price leaders, special-event pricing, and superficial discounting. Finally, using experience curve pricing, a company fixes a low price that high-cost competitors cannot match and thus expands its market share.

After selecting a pricing policy, a marketer must choose a pricing method, a mechanical procedure for setting prices on a regular basis. The nature of a product, its sales volume, or the amount of the product carried by the organization determines how prices are calculated. Cost-oriented pricing adds a dollar amount or percentage to the cost of a product. Two cost-oriented pricing methods are cost-plus pricing and markup pricing. Demand-oriented pricing methods use the level of demand for a product as the basis for price. When demand is strong, price is high; when demand is weak, price is low. Competition-oriented pricing considers cost and revenue secondary to competitors' prices.

Pricing policies and methods should direct and structure the selection of a final price. How well that price works for the organization is a function of how well the marketer has established pricing objectives, understood the market, determined demand and its relationships to cost and profit, and evaluated competitors' prices. In practice, prices are often finalized after limited planning, due to external circumstances such as time requirements.

MATCHING EXERCISES

Use the following set of terms to identify the sentences and phrases below. On the blank line next to each sentence or phrase, place the letter of the term that the sentence or phrase describes. Do not use a term more than once.

a. Prestige pricing
b. Total costs
c. Pioneer pricing
d. Marginal revenue
e. Price lining
f. Customary pricing
g. Competition-oriented pricing
h. Variable costs
i. Experience curve pricing
j. Demand curve
k. Price elasticity of demand
l. Odd-even pricing
m. F.O.B. pricing
n. Pricing method
o. Breakeven point
p. Penetration price

q. Cost-plus pricing
r. Fixed costs
s. Marginal cost
t. Professional pricing
u. Average fixed cost
v. Average variable cost
w. Total revenue
x. Price differentiation
y. Demand-oriented pricing
z. Superficial discounting
aa. Pricing policy
bb. Price leaders
cc. Psychological pricing
dd. Special-event pricing
ee. Cost-oriented pricing
ff. Markup pricing

aa 1. A guiding philosophy or course of action designed to influence and determine pricing decisions. *Pricing Policy*

cc 2. A pricing method designed to encourage purchases that are based on emotional, rather than on rational, responses. *Psychological Pricing*

t 3. Pricing used by people who have great skill or experience in a particular field or activity; instead of pricing in relation to the time and involvement in a specific case, a standard fee is charged. *Professional Pricing*

E 4. A form of psychological pricing in which an organization sets a limited number of prices for selected groups of products. *Price lining*

Q 5. A form of cost-oriented pricing in which the seller's costs are determined first, then a specified dollar amount or percentage of the cost is added to the seller's cost in order to set the price. *Cost Plus Pricing*

pf 6. A pricing method through which a product's price is derived by adding a predetermined percentage of the cost to the cost of the product. *Markup Pricing*

f 7. A type of psychological pricing in which certain goods are priced primarily on the basis of tradition. *Customary Pricing*

g 8. A pricing method in which an organization considers costs and revenues secondary to competitors' prices. *Competition Oriented Pricing*

a 9. A type of psychological pricing in which prices are set at an artificially high level to create a quality image for the product. *Prestige Pricing*

bb 10. Products sold at less than cost to increase sales of regular merchandise. *Price Leaders*

i 11. A type of pricing in which a company fixes a low price that high-cost competitors cannot match and thus expands its market share. *Experience Curve Pricing*

ee 12. A pricing policy in which a firm determines price by adding a dollar amount or percentage to the cost of a product. *Cost-Oriented Pricing*

dd 13. Advertised sales or price cutting to increase revenue or to lower costs. *Special Event Pricing*

p 14. A price below that of competing brands, designed to penetrate the market and quickly increase unit sales volume. *Penetration Pricing*

o 15. The point at which the costs of producing a product equal the revenues made from selling the product. *Breakeven Pt*

d 16. The change in total revenue that occurs after an additional unit of a product is sold. *Marginal Revenue*

u 17. The fixed cost per unit; calculated by dividing the fixed costs by the number of units produced. *Average Fixed Cost*

b 18. The sum of fixed costs and variable costs. *Total Costs*

w 19. Price times quantity. *Total Revenue*

r 20. Costs that do not vary with changes in the number of units produced or sold. *Fixed Costs*

C   21. Setting the base price for a new product. *Pioneer Pricing*

h   22. Costs that vary directly with changes in the number of units produced or sold. *Variable*

j   23. The relationship, usually inverse, between price and quantity demanded; classically, a line sloping downward to the right, showing that as price falls, demand increases. *Demand Curve*

S   24. The cost of producing one more unit of a product. *Marginal Cost*

V   25. The variable cost per unit; calculated by dividing the variable costs by the number of units produced. *Average Variable Cost*

m   26. The relative responsiveness of changes in demand to changes in price. *FOB Pricing*

N   27. A mechanical procedure for setting prices on a regular basis. *Pricing method*

TRUE OR FALSE STATEMENTS

T F   1. Professional pricing is based on the belief that professionals who provide services have an ethical responsibility not to overcharge customers.

T F   2. Marginal analysis is most effective in setting prices for new products.

T F   3. A pricing policy is a systematic procedure for calculating prices on a regular basis.

T F   4. Penetration pricing can help a marketer gain a large market share.

T F   5. Odd-even pricing, customary pricing, prestige pricing, and price lining are types of promotional pricing.

T F   6. Price leaders are products that management prices below cost in the hope of attracting new customers.

T F   7. Knowing competitors' prices can help marketers increase their own sales.

T F   8. Superficial discounting is unethical and, in some states, illegal.

T F   9. Cost-plus pricing is a pricing method in which a specified dollar amount or percentage of the seller's cost is added to the seller's cost to set the price.

T F   10. Demand-oriented pricing involves using a low price when product demand is strong and a high price when product demand is weak.

T F   11. An inverse relationship exists between the price of most products and the quantity demanded.

T F   12. Demand should be the major consideration in setting a price for a product.

T F 13. Pricing objectives influence decisions in most functional areas and must be consistent with an organization's overall goals.

T F 14. The point at which marginal costs equal marginal revenues is called the breakeven point.

T F 15. When demand is elastic, a change in price has little effect on total revenue.

MULTIPLE-CHOICE QUESTIONS

_____ 1. A pricing policy is
   a. designed to encourage purchases based on emotional reactions.
   b. a guiding philosophy that determines how price will be used as a variable in the marketing mix.
   c. a method for calculating the base price of a product.
   d. a mechanical procedure for setting prices on a regular basis.
   e. the same thing as a pricing objective.

_____ 2. A psychological price is designed to encourage purchases based on emotional, rather than rational, responses. One approach to psychological pricing is
   a. customary pricing.
   b. loss-leader pricing.
   c. competition-oriented pricing.
   d. unit pricing.
   e. cash discounting.

_____ 3. A penetration price
   a. is a price established primarily by tradition.
   b. is a price that is set artificially high to provide a certain image.
   c. is used by persons who have great skill in a particular field.
   d. can help a marketer gain a larger market share and discourage competitors from entering a market.
   e. usually requires the firm to employ a price leader.

_____ 4. The demand curve illustrates the effect of
   a. a change in price caused by an equal change in total revenue.
   b. different pricing policies.
   c. one variable, price, on the quantity demanded.
   d. dependent variables, such as the environment and buying behavior, on price.
   e. price on the amounts of products supplied by producers.

_____ 5. Which of the following helps identify the target market's evaluation of price?
   a. Understanding customers' needs, willingness, authority, and ability to buy
   b. Discovering the top prices customers will pay for a product

    c. Stretching demand for a product

    d. Evaluating competitors' prices

    e. Discovering the lowest price customers will pay for a product

6. If Perrier notices that a change in the price of a six-pack of bottled water from \$2.75 to \$4.25 increases the quantity demanded of the product by 21 percent, this item is probably a(n) _____ product.

    a. normal

    b. breakeven

    c. prestige

    d. highly competitive

    e. value-priced

7. Pricing objectives are overall goals that describe the role of price and

    a. help an organization achieve its long-range plans.

    b. have little effect on other functional areas of a business.

    c. help determine the allocation of buyers' purchasing power.

    d. should not have an effect on the functional areas of a business.

    e. help determine an organization's short-range plans.

8. Elasticity of demand describes

    a. changes in demand that result from changes in price.

    b. changes in total revenues that result from changes in demand.

    c. changes in price that result from changes in demand.

    d. an inverse change in total revenues that results from changes in price.

    e. a parallel change in total revenues that results from changes in price.

9. The breakeven point is the point at which

    a. marginal revenues equal marginal costs.

    b. a reasonable profit has been earned.

    c. all variable costs have been recovered.

    d. marginal revenues equal total revenues.

    e. the costs of producing a product equal the revenues earned from selling the product.

10. With what types of products would it be a good idea to lower prices?

    a. Prestige products

    b. Products with elastic demand

    c. Products that exhibit a direct, positive relationship between price and quantity demanded

    d. Products with inelastic demand

    e. It is never a good idea to lower prices because it makes your product look cheap.

11. Professional pricing

    a. is a pioneer pricing policy.

    b. is a form of psychological pricing.

    c. often involves standard, rather than hourly, fees.

    d. assumes that demand is elastic.

    e. is penetration pricing.

12. An advantage of knowing competitors' prices is that it
    a. eliminates a marketer's need to develop cost objectives.
    b. can enable a marketer to set prices slightly lower and thus increase sales.
    c. ensures profits for a marketer who charges the same price.
    d. ensures an accurate estimate of sales.
    e. ensures that all firms engage in price competition.

13. Which of the following policies is *most* effective at gaining maximum unit sales volume when introducing a new product?
    a. Price skimming
    b. Psychological pricing
    c. Customary pricing
    d. Penetration pricing
    e. Professional pricing

14. Which of the following statements is false?
    a. Profits are what is left after expenses are paid and are included in costs to determine the breakeven point.
    b. The breakeven point is the point at which variable costs and fixed costs equal total revenues.
    c. At the breakeven point, no losses have been incurred and no profits have been accumulated.
    d. Breakeven analysis assumes that demand is fixed.
    e. Breakeven analysis requires that both variable and fixed costs be known.

15. In using a cost-oriented pricing method, a firm determines price
    a. by using marginal analysis.
    b. based on the level of demand for a product.
    c. based on competitors' prices.
    d. by adding a dollar amount or a percentage to the cost of the product.
    e. by determining the breakeven point.

16. A commonly employed pricing method among retailers is
    a. price skimming.
    b. demand-oriented pricing.
    c. competition-oriented pricing.
    d. penetration pricing.
    e. markup pricing.

17. Benetton is a manufacturer of knitwear that operates several plants in Europe. Which one of the following would be an example of a fixed cost for Benetton?
    a. Yarn
    b. Overtime labor
    c. Shipping cartons
    d. Rent for the plant
    e. Dye

_____ 18. The manager of Warren's Bar-B-Q discovers that when the firm sells one additional sandwich, its total revenues increase by $2.75 while its total costs increase by $2.50. It should
    a. sell more sandwiches.
    b. stay at the present level of sales.
    c. cut back on sandwich sales.
    d. look for the level at which marginal revenue increases.
    e. collect more data to decide if sales should increase or decrease.

_____ 19. The breakeven point for Dynamo Health Club is 10,000 members per year. The annual fixed cost is $100,000, and the variable cost per person is $80. What does Dynamo charge per membership?
    a. $180
    b. $100
    c. $160
    d. $110
    e. $90

_____ 20. Craven's Department Stores offers wool sweaters for sale at $15.00, $16.50, $18.75, $19.95, and $37.50. Apparently the person in charge of setting these prices is unfamiliar with or is unwilling to use
    a. odd-even pricing.
    b. customary pricing.
    c. price lining.
    d. penetration pricing.
    e. pioneer pricing.

_____ 21. Remington Manufacturing decides to use a pricing method in which it sets prices to generate a desired level of profit on each item but without any knowledge of how many items it might sell at those prices. Remington is using which one of the following pricing methods?
    a. Demand-oriented pricing
    b. Psychological pricing
    c. Price lining
    d. Price differentiation
    e. Cost-oriented pricing

_____ 22. Marketers at Vogue Department Store regularly check prices in other stores and then set their own prices 6 percent lower than competitors. Vogue uses
    a. cost-oriented pricing.
    b. competition-oriented pricing.
    c. demand-oriented pricing.
    d. superficial discounting.
    e. odd-even pricing.

MINICASE: SPECIALTY JEWELRY COMPANY

The Specialty Jewelry Company primarily produces necklaces and rings. Recently, the firm's management decided to introduce a new ring that would identify the wearer's birth month. Sales of this ring are forecasted to be 800,000 units next year. A study of the firm's costs indicate the following:

Total fixed costs   = $2,000,000
Average variable costs = $10 per unit

Specialty Jewelry's pricing objective is return on investment.

Questions

_____ 1. What is the breakeven point in units for the new ring?
a. 800,000
b. 600,000
c. 400,000
d. 200,000
e. It cannot be determined from the data given in the case.

_____ 2. If 800,000 units are sold next year, what price must be established for the firm to break even?
a. $25.00
b. $12.50
c. $4.00
d. $250.00
e. It cannot be determined from the data given in the case.

_____ 3. What will the firm's total profit be, given your answer to question 2?
a. $10,000,000
b. $6,800,000
c. $6,800,000 loss
d. Zero
e. It cannot be determined from the data given in the case.

_____ 4. If Specialty Jewelry usually adds 20 percent to total costs to determine final price, how much should it charge per unit?
a. $15
b. $12
c. $8
d. $3
e. It cannot be determined from the data given in the case.

_____ 5. What are expected profits under the price established in question 4?
a. $2,000,000
b. $3,600,000
c. Zero
d. $3,600,000 loss
e. It cannot be determined from the data given in the case.

PROGRAMMED COMPLETION EXERCISES

method, policy

1. A pricing _____ is a mechanical procedure for setting prices on a regular basis; a pricing _____ is a guiding philosophy designed to influence and determine price decisions.

pioneer

2. Market skimming and penetration pricing are _____ pricing policies.

price leaders, special-event pricing, superficial discounting

3. Promotional pricing policies include _____ _____, _____ _____, and _____ _____.

marginal analysis, breakeven analysis

4. There are two ways of understanding demand, cost, and profit relationships: _____ _____ and _____ _____.

Price elasticity

5. _____ _____ of demand is the percentage change in quantity demanded divided by the percentage change in price.

cost-oriented, demand-oriented, competition-oriented

6. Three types of pricing methods are _____ pricing, _____ pricing, and _____ pricing.

cost-plus, markup

7. Two common cost-oriented pricing methods are _____ and _____ pricing.

high, strong, low, weak

8. Demand-oriented pricing results in _____ prices when product demand is _____ and _____ prices when product demand is _____.

odd-even, customary,
prestige, price lining

9. Psychological pricing includes _____ pricing, _____ pricing, _____ pricing, and _____ _____.

objectives, target
markets, demand,
competitors' prices,
policy, method

10. Before selecting a final price, marketers should select pricing _____; identify _____ _____; determine _____; analyze demand, cost, and profit relationships; evaluate _____ _____; select a pricing _____; and select a pricing _____.

demand curve,
product, prices

11. The _____ _____ is a graph of the quantity of _____ expected to be sold at various _____.

Pricing objectives,
organizational

12. _____ _____ influence decisions in most functional areas, such as finance, accounting, and production; thus, they must be consistent with overall _____ goals.

Fixed costs, variable
costs, total cost

13. _____ _____ do not vary with changes in the number of units produced or sold; _____ _____ vary directly with changes in the number of units produced or sold; _____ _____ is the sum of the average fixed costs and average variable costs times the quantity produced.

marginal cost,
marginal revenue

14. Marginal analysis shows that maximum profit is achieved at the point where _____ _____ equals _____ _____.

elastic, inelastic

15. When demand is _____, a change in price causes an opposite change in total revenues; _____ demand results in a parallel change in total revenues.

costs, revenue, breakeven point

16. The point at which the _____ of producing a product equal the _____ made from selling the product is the _____ _____ .

penetration price, market share

17. When introducing a product, a marketer sometimes uses a _____ _____ to gain _____ _____ very quickly.

demand-oriented pricing, price differentiation

18. A marketer may favor a _____ _____ called _____ _____ when the firm wants to use more than one price in the marketing of a specific product.

ANSWERS TO OBJECTIVE QUESTIONS

Matching			*True or False*			*Multiple-Choice*			*Minicase*	
1. aa	15. o		1. T	9. T		1. b	12. b		1. e	
2. cc	16. d		2. F	10. F		2. a	13. d		2. b	
3. t	17. u		3. F	11. T		3. d	14. a		3. d	
4. e	18. b		4. T	12. F		4. c	15. d		4. a	
5. q	19. w		5. F	13. T		5. a	16. e		5. a	
6. ff	20. r		6. T	14. F		6. c	17. d			
7. f	21. c		7. T	15. F		7. a	18. a			
8. g	22. h		8. T			8. a	19. e			
9. a	23. j					9. e	20. c			
10. bb	24. s					10. b	21. e			
11. i	25. v					11. c	22. b			
12. ee	26. m									
13. dd	27. n									
14. p										

20 STRATEGIC MARKET PLANNING

CHAPTER OUTLINE

CHAPTER SUMMARY

A strategic market plan, an outline of the methods and resources required to achieve an organization's goals within a specific target market, takes into account all the functional areas of a business that must be coordinated (marketing, production, finance, personnel) as well as environmental systems. The concept of the strategic business unit is used to define areas for consideration in a specific strategic market plan. The strategic business unit (SBU) is a division, a product line, or other profit center that sells a distinct set of products or services to an identifiable group of customers and is in competition with a well-defined set of competitors.

The process of strategic market planning yields a marketing strategy that is the framework for a marketing plan. A strategic market plan is not the same as a marketing plan. It deals with all aspects of an organization's strategy in the marketplace, while a marketing plan is the blueprint for implementing and controlling an organization's marketing activities. Marketing planning is a continuous process, changing as forces in the organization and the environment change. In an established organization, marketing planning begins with the current situation, analyzing the differences between objectives and current performance, then assesses future marketing opportunities and constraints. Through this process, the organization can develop marketing strategies to help meet its overall goals. A marketing program is a set of marketing strategies used simultaneously to achieve the firm's marketing objectives. Those objectives must be consistent with the organization's overall goals.

The strategic market planning process is based on an analysis of the environment. Environmental variables affect the creation of marketing strategy in several ways. First, they have an impact on the organization's overall goals, resources, opportunities, and marketing objectives, all of which are a basis of the firm's marketing strategy. More directly, they influence consumers' needs and wants as well as marketing mix decisions.

A major component of strategic market planning is establishing organizational goals. These goals direct the firm's planning efforts. An organization's goals may focus on one or several business activities and on short- or long-term objectives.

Another major component of strategic market planning is assessing organizational opportunities and resources. This involves three elements: evaluating market opportunities, monitoring the environment, and identifying the firm's capabilities and resources. A market opportunity arises when the right combination of circumstances occurs at the right time to allow an organization to take action toward reaching a target market. Market factors (size, growth rate), competition, financial and economic factors, technological factors, and social, legal, and political factors all determine the attractiveness of a market opportunity. Market requirements relate to customers' needs or desired benefits, which businesses should attempt to satisfy. Environmental scanning is the process of collecting information about the marketing environment. That information helps marketers identify opportunities and make plans. A firm's capabilities relate to distinctive competencies that is has developed to do something well and efficiently. Resource constraints are a major concern of marketers today. Shortages in energy and other scarce economic resources often limit strategic planning options.

A third component of strategic market planning is corporate strategy, which determines the means for utilizing resources in the areas of production, finance, research and development, personnel, and marketing to reach organizational goals. Corporate strategy describes the scope and role of each strategic business unit in the organization. It also determines how resources are deployed, competitive advantages, and the overall coordination of functional areas.

In recent years, marketing managers have developed several tools to aid them in strategic market planning. The first is the Boston Consulting Group (BCG) product-portfolio analysis, which is based on the philosophy that a product's market growth rate and its relative market share should help determine its marketing strategy. All the firm's products are integrated into a single matrix and evaluated to determine appropriate strategies for individual SBUs and the overall portfolio. Managers can use portfolio models to classify each product's expected contributions and requirements. There are four basic types of products: stars, cash cows, dogs, and problem children. The long-run health of the organization depends on having a workable mix—some products that generate cash and others that use cash to support growth.

The second approach is the market attractiveness–business position model, which is also a two-dimensional matrix. The vertical dimension, market attractiveness, includes all strengths and resources that relate to the market and the overall cost and feasibility of entering the market. The horizontal dimension, business position, is a composite of factors such as sales, relative market share, research and development, price competitiveness, product quality, and market knowledge as they relate to the product in building market share. The model serves as a diagnostic tool, pinpointing those products that warrant investment and those that should be harvested or divested.

The third approach is PIMS, or Product Impact on Marketing Strategy, a research program that has available to it confidential information on the successes, failures, and marginal products of over two hundred firms. The program has identified thirty major factors that affect performance; among them are strong market position, high quality products, lower costs, and investment and capital intensity.

These three approaches are just planning tools; they are not strategic solutions. Strategic marketing planning must take into account all aspects of an organization's strategy in the marketplace. It must coordinate all functional strategies to reach organizational goals. Management must blend analytic techniques with managerial judgment to deal with the reality of the existing situation.

Competitive strategies that can be implemented through marketing include intense growth, diversified growth, and integrated growth. Intense growth is possible when current products and current markets have the potential for increased sales. The three methods for achieving intense growth are market penetration, market development, and product development. Diversified growth can take place through horizontal, concentric, or conglomerate diversification, depending on the technology of new products and the nature of new markets. Integrated growth occurs within the firm's own industry and in three directions: forward, backward, and horizontally.

Marketing planning is a systematic process that involves the assessment of marketing opportunities and resources, the determination of marketing objectives, and the development of a marketing plan. The marketing planning cycle is circular, with feedback used to coordinate and synchronize all stages of the cycle. Marketing plans may be short-range (covering less than one year), medium-range (covering two to five years), or long-range (extending beyond five years). The extent to which marketing managers develop and use marketing plans also varies.

The marketing plan offers a "road map" for implementing strategies and achieving objectives; assists in management control and monitoring of implementation of strategy; informs new participants of their role and function; specifies how resources are to be allocated; stimulates thinking and makes better use of resources; assigns responsibilities, tasks, and timing; and makes participants aware of problems, opportunities, and threats. A marketing plan typically includes sections on executive summary, situation analysis, opportunity and threat analyses, environmental analysis, company resources, marketing objectives, marketing strategies, financial projections and budgets, and controls and evaluation.

MATCHING EXERCISES

Use the following set of terms to identify the sentences and phrases below. On the blank line next to each sentence or phrase, place the letter of the term that the sentence or phrase describes. Do not use a term more than once.

a. Corporate strategy
b. Diversified growth
c. Marketing planning
d. Marketing planning cycle
e. Short-range plans
f. Medium-range plans
g. Long-range plans
h. Strategic market plan
i. Strategic market planning
j. Marketing program
k. Marketing objective

l. Market opportunity
m. Intense growth
n. Market requirements
o. Marketing plan
p. Product-portfolio analysis
q. Integrated growth
r. Market attractiveness–business position model
s. PIMS (Profit Impact on Marketing Strategy)
t. Strategic business unit

___K___ 1. A statement of what is to be accomplished through marketing activities. *Mktg Ouxective*

___j___ 2. A set of marketing strategies that are implemented and used at the same time. *Mktg Program*

___S___ 3. A databank of over 3,000 SBUs of 200 companies that provides information on successes, failures, and marginal products. *PIMS*

___b___ 4. Occurs when new products are developed to be sold in new markets. *Divisified growth*

___f___ 5. Usually encompass two to five years. *Med-Range Plan*

___g___ 6. Extend for more than five years. *Long Range Plan*

___e___ 7. Cover a period of one year or less. *Short Range Plan*

___L___ 8. Arises when the right combination of circumstances occurs at the right time to allow an organization to take action toward reaching a target market. *Mkt Opportunity*

___O___ 9. The framework and entire set of activities to be performed; the blueprint for implementing and controlling an organization's marketing activities. *Mktg Plan*

___a___ 10. Determines the means for utilizing resources in the areas of production, finance, research and development, personnel, and marketing to reach the organization's goals. *Corporate Strategy*

___i___ 11. A division, product line, or other profit center that sells a distinct set of products or services to an identifiable group of customers and is in competition with a well-defined set of competitors. *Strategic Mkt Planning*

___t___ 12. Yields a marketing strategy that is the framework for a marketing plan. *Strategic Business Unit*

___c___ 13. A systematic process that involves the assessment of marketing opportunities and resources, the determination of marketing objectives, and the development of a plan for implementation and control. *Mktg Planning*

e [handwritten] 14. A two-dimensional matrix that shows opportunities for investment, growth, harvesting, or divestment. Mkt attractiveness – Business Position Model [handwritten]

f [handwritten] 15. Classifying products in order to determine their future cash contributions and requirements; product classifications are stars, cash cows, dogs, and problem children. Product Portfolio [handwritten]

N [handwritten] 16. Satisfied by the components of the marketing mix that provide benefits to buyers. Mkt Requirements [handwritten]

h [handwritten] 17. An outline of the methods and resources required to achieve an organization's goals within a specific target market. Strategic Mkt Plan [handwritten]

d [handwritten] 18. A view of marketing planning as a circular process. Mkt Planning Cycle [handwritten]

TRUE OR FALSE STATEMENTS

T F 1. A marketing plan is the written blueprint for implementing and controlling an organization's marketing activities.

T F 2. Marketing plans help the marketing manager control marketing activities because plans include performance standards against which actual performance is measured.

T F 3. A marketing plan always encompasses a period of two to five years.

T F 4. Marketing objectives must be consistent with the firm's overall objectives.

T F 5. A marketing strategy involves selecting and analyzing a target market and creating and maintaining a marketing mix.

T F 6. Each strategic business unit is a division, product line, or profit center within the parent company.

T F 7. In implementing a marketing plan, the marketing manager must coordinate marketing activities with other functions of the firm.

T F 8. Marketing managers usually assess future opportunities and constraints, then examine the organization's current situation.

T F 9. A strategic business unit is a profit center that sells a distinct set of products or services to a distinct group of customers and is in competition with a distinct group of competitors.

T F 10. A strategic business unit's revenues, operating costs, investments, and strategic plans cannot be separated from those of its parent company.

T F 11. Each marketing strategy requires a separate marketing plan.

T F 12. A strategic market plan is developed through and is the result of a marketing strategy.

T F 13. Through their impact on consumers' needs and wants, environmental forces influence the development of a marketing strategy.

T F 14. A marketing objective should be clear and quantifiable, and should indicate a time frame for accomplishment.

T F 15. Environmental scanning should identify new developments and determine the nature and rate of change.

T F 16. A balanced product-portfolio matrix is the objective of the Boston Consulting Group product-portfolio analysis.

T F 17. Managers can use portfolio models to classify products in terms of their present cash contributions and requirements.

T F 18. The Boston Consulting Group approach is more of a guide for making strategy prescriptions than an analytical method.

T F 19. Cash cows have a dominant share of the market but need a lot of cash to finance their rapid growth.

T F 20. Of the four basic product types, dogs represent the category with the greatest market growth potential.

T F 21. The market attractiveness–business position model serves as a diagnostic tool to highlight strategic business units that have an opportunity to grow or that should be divested or approached selectively.

T F 22. Information gathered from firms for the PIMS research program is useful for analyzing current marketing strategies and evaluating alternatives.

T F 23. Management must rely heavily on analysis, to the exclusion of managerial judgment, in order to deal with the reality of the existing situation.

MULTIPLE-CHOICE QUESTIONS

_____ 1. Which of the following is *not* included as a section of a marketing plan?
   a. Executive summary
   b. Financial projections and budgets
   c. Corporate strategy
   d. Environmental analysis
   e. Marketing strategies

_____ 2. Which of the following statements about marketing planning is false?
   a. A marketing plan is the written blueprint for implementing and controlling an organization's marketing activities.
   b. Marketing planning is a circular process.
   c. Some managers do not use formal marketing plans because they spend most of their time dealing with daily problems.
   d. Marketing plans usually encompass a period equal to a firm's business cycle.
   e. Marketing planning forces the marketing manager to formulate objectives and develop a strategy.

3. Marketing planning can be viewed as a process that focuses on
    a. marketing opportunities and resources, marketing objectives, and plans for implementation and control.
    b. marketing organization and purpose.
    c. company purpose and direction.
    d. marketing objectives and organizational objectives.
    e. marketing plans and strategy.

4. Marketing objectives are important to the marketing manager because they
    a. are consistent with the firm's objectives.
    b. focus on one or several dimensions, such as market share, long-run profits, and short-run profits.
    c. indicate the point in time by which they should be accomplished.
    d. provide a foundation for making marketing decisions and implementing and controlling marketing activities.
    e. are formulate in such a way that the degree of accomplishment can be measured accurately.

5. To achieve marketing objectives and to contribute to the accomplishment of the organization's overall objectives, the marketing manager should
    a. create a marketing department.
    b. develop organizational strategies.
    c. develop a marketing strategy.
    d. identify the target market toward which activities are aimed.
    e. create a marketing mix that fits the needs of the target market.

6. Which of the following statements concerning marketing objectives is false?
    a. Marketing objectives state what is to be accomplished through marketing activities.
    b. Marketing objectives should be stated in clear, simple terms.
    c. Marketing objectives cannot be established until the firm's overall objectives have been established.
    d. Marketing objectives usually focus on the implementation of plans.
    e. Marketing objectives should be formulated in such a way that the degree of accomplishment can be measured accurately.

7. A marketing plan includes
    a. a framework and the entire set of activities to be performed.
    b. the creation of a flexible marketing unit.
    c. a sales-oriented organization.
    d. the requirement that a firm have good production.
    e. the establishment of strict performance standards.

8. Which section of the marketing plan details how the results will be measured?
    a. Situation analysis
    b. Executive summary
    c. Company resources

d. Controls and evaluation
e. Marketing objectives

9. The concept of the strategic business unit is used to define
   a. resources for implementing and controlling marketing activities.
   b. areas for consideration in a specific strategic market plan.
   c. the interrelationship of functional areas of an organization.
   d. areas of consideration in the marketing program.
   e. areas for social control.

10. Marketers at a local restaurant seek information about the marketing environment to help them identify opportunities. This process is called
    a. environmental analysis.
    b. environmental scoping.
    c. environmental scanning.
    d. opportunity search.
    e. opportunity scanning.

11. Which of the following elements is developed even before a marketing strategy?
    a. Marketing mix
    b. Measurement of performance
    c. Marketing objectives
    d. Marketing program
    e. Marketing concept

12. The marketing program is
    a. concerned with the implementation of tactics.
    b. a way of thinking about all the organization's activities.
    c. a set of marketing strategies for reaching the firm's goals.
    d. concerned with evaluating the effectiveness of competition.
    e. concerned with television advertising.

13. Which of the following statements about strategic business units (SBUs) is false?
    a. An SBU is usually a profit center.
    b. An SBU sells a distinct set of products or services.
    c. SBUs should have identifiable competitors.
    d. An SBU's marketing strategy depends on the strategies of other SBUs.
    e. An SBU has a distinctive marketing strategy.

14. A strategic market plan differs from a marketing plan in that it
    a. covers all aspects of an organization's strategy, whereas a marketing plan deals primarily with implementing the marketing strategy as it relates to target markets and the marketing mix.
    b. covers short-range plans whereas the marketing plan covers the organization's long-range plans.
    c. is developed from the marketing plan.
    d. focuses on marketing, whereas the marketing plan is designed to take into account marketing and all other functional areas of the business.
    e. focuses on the marketing concept.

_____ 15. Which of the following statements about strategic business units (SBUs) is false?
   a. An SBU's revenues can be separated from those of the parent company.
   b. An SBU can be a division, a product line, or other profit center.
   c. The concept of an SBU deals with intrafirm concerns and the interaction of functional areas of the business, excluding environmental analysis.
   d. An SBU is used to define areas of consideration in a specific strategic market plan.
   e. An SBU is usually a profit center.

_____ 16. A marketing strategy is developed through and is a result of
   a. strategic market planning.
   b. marketing planning.
   c. the marketing program.
   d. environmental monitoring.
   e. government regulation

_____ 17. According to the text, strategic market planning is composed of all the following components *except*
   a. marketing objectives.
   b. overall organizational goals.
   c. organizational resources.
   d. management time and motion analysis.
   e. assessing opportunities and resources.

_____ 18. A marketing objective is
   a. a statement of what is to be accomplished through marketing activities.
   b. usually not quantifiable.
   c. not bound by a specific time frame.
   d. a detailed analysis of actions and resources for implementing and controlling marketing activities.
   e. something you would like to accomplish.

_____ 19. All of the following are considerations in assessing opportunities and resources *except*
   a. a firm's capabilities.
   b. a firm's stock prices.
   c. market opportunity.
   d. environmental forces.
   e. the expertise of marketing personnel.

_____ 20. A market opportunity
   a. describes the fit when the key requirements of a market and the particular competencies of a firm competing in that market are at an optimum.
   b. arises when market size and growth rate, market requirements, and actions of other firms are all attractive.

c. arises when the firm has control of financial, economic, technological, and social factors.

d. arises when the right combination of circumstances occurs at the right time to allow an organization to take action toward reaching a target market.

e. develops through day-to-day operations.

21. Environmental scanning

a. involves collecting information about the marketing environment.

b. relates to customers' needs or desired benefits.

c. identifies past and current developments.

d. integrates a firm's distinctive competencies with market requirements.

e. is best implemented through the space shuttle.

22. Folgers ground coffee has had a large market share for several years in a market that is experiencing little, if any, growth. Using the product-port-folio matrix, Folgers would be classified as which one of the following?

a. Question mark

b. Star

c. Problem child

d. Cash cow

e. Dog

23. Which of the following statements about the Boston Consulting Group product-portfolio analysis is false?

a. All the firm's products should be integrated into a single overall matrix.

b. Products are classified in order to determine their future cash contributions and requirements.

c. The competitive position of a product and the opportunities for improving that product's contribution to profitability and cash flow must be examined.

d. The analysis provides data to help direct strategic market planning efforts.

e. It contains a category labeled cash cows.

24. Cash cows tend to

a. generate more cash than is needed to maintain their market share.

b. have substantial reported profit but need a lot of cash to finance growth.

c. exist at a cost disadvantage and have few opportunities for growth at a reasonable cost.

d. have an enormous demand for cash.

e. buy lots of milk.

25. Which of the following statements about dogs is false?

a. The greatest number of products fall into this category.

b. These products usually exist at a cost disadvantage and have few opportunities for growth at a reasonable rate.

c. Positive action could be taken through heavy investment over the product's foreseeable lifetime.

d. These products may be abandoned or deleted from the product line.

e. They should be carefully monitored and analyzed.

26. As Reggie prepares a market attractiveness–business position model for his firm's proposed entry into the video game market, he considers the large number of competing companies to be a
   a. plus in terms of business position.
   b. minus in terms of attractiveness.
   c. certainty that the product will become a cash cow.
   d. plus in terms of market attractiveness.
   e. minus in terms of business position.

27. In a meeting on the development of a new suncare cream, Pat Schul pushes hard for introducing a high-quality product. She firmly states that such a product would definitely have a positive impact on _____ according to the PIMS data research.
   a. supplier loyalty
   b. market position
   c. lowering costs
   d. marketing mix synchronization
   e. return on investment

28. Little Caesar's strategy of offering more pizzas for less money is most consistent with which one of the following competitive strategies?
   a. Market development
   b. Product development
   c. Diversified growth
   d. Forward integration
   e. Market penetration

29. When Honda, traditionally a marketer of motorcycles and cars, entered the lawn mower market, the move was most consistent with which one of the following competitive strategies?
   a. Concentric diversification
   b. Market development
   c. Horizontal diversification
   d. Integrated growth
   e. Conglomerate diversification

30. Ken Wright informs his management team that he is impressed with the marketing plan they have developed. His concerns center mostly on funding the efforts that have been specified for achieving the established objectives. These concerns relate to which one of the following sections of the marketing plan?
   a. Company resources
   b. Opportunity and threat analysis
   c. Situation analysis
   d. Marketing mix operationalization
   e. Financial projections and budgets

MINICASE: WORLD-WISE CORPORATION

World-Wise is a diversified company concentrating in three areas: insurance and financial services (life, property-casualty, and title insurance; insurance brokerage and management services; consumer finance), travel services (air travel, car rental), and manufacturing. Each of these three areas is in competition with a well-defined set of market rivals. World-Wise's strategy is to focus on key market segments related to its three primary businesses. Two major corporate objectives are to achieve a significant market share in each business segment and to achieve industry leadership in terms of service, reputation, innovation, and efficiency.

Subsidiaries of World-Wise benefit from being part of a larger corporation. Funds may be borrowed at a low cost; capital may be allocated among subsidiaries; and a corporate staff provides centralized strategic planning, investment, real estate management, and data processing. Among World-Wise's major subsidiaries are Rational Life, World-Wise Crossings, World-Wise Airlines, and Easy Rent-A-Car.

Rational Life insurance is sold most actively in the southwestern states. Rational's specialty is low-cost insurance with termlike rates; this type of insurance represents 85 percent of its direct ordinary volume. Rational responds to changing consumer needs with new products. Among its new product offerings are two annuities for funding IRAs (Individual Retirement Accounts) and a policy combining the features of term and whole life insurance.

World-Wise Crossings operates a transport-equipment leasing business. The equipment—including cargo containers, piggyback trailers, and over-the-road trailers—is maintained and repaired by company-owned repair shops and mobile-service units. The company enjoys operating-cost advantages resulting from economies of scale.

World-Wise Airlines flies to more locations around the world than any other airline. To compete, World-Wise has refurbished many aircraft. Improved fuel conservation and noise reduction now complement superior passenger accommodations. World-Wise's low-cost approach makes it a major national airline.

Easy Rent-A-Car provides the same services as many of its competitors but at lower rates. Easy has expanded to provide service at airports and supports its dealers with a nationwide, toll-free, computerized reservation network. It has an exclusive agreement with a leading department store chain to operate concessions for Easy's automobile rentals. All the strategies for this subsidiary are geared toward maintaining market dominions.

World-Wise is aware that the marketing environment is an important consideration in adapting a product to meet market needs. World-Wise has experienced concentric growth in many of its subsidiaries. Consistent with its strategies to achieve significant market share and become an industry leader, World-Wise is diversifying to achieve low-cost marketing in all areas. World-Wise is currently evaluating how best to proceed with its marketing strategy.

Questions

_____ 1. World-Wise's growth could best be described as
   a. integrated.
   b. short-range.

    c. intense.
    d. diversified.
    e. horizontal.

_____ 2. If World-Wise's marketing plan called for an average 5 to 6 percent growth rate from all of its subsidiaries within the next year, this would be considered a
    a. short-range plan.
    b. medium-range plan.
    c. long-range plan.
    d. strategic market plan.
    e. market opportunity.

_____ 3. World-Wise's strategic business units are
    a. each of the subsidiaries mentioned in the case.
    b. car rental, air service, insurance (corporate and individual), financial services, and manufacturing.
    c. consumer products and industrial products.
    d. products and services.
    e. insurance and financial services, travel services, and manufacturing.

_____ 4. In developing its strategic market plan, the correct process for World-Wise to use is
    a. analyzing market opportunities and corporate resources, establishing marketing objectives, and creating a marketing program.
    b. determining marketing objectives, marketing strategies, and corporate strategies, in this order.
    c. determining overall organizational goals, corporate strategies, marketing objectives, and the marketing program, in this order.
    d. analyzing market opportunities and requirements, then creating a marketing program.
    e. none of the above.

_____ 5. World-Wise's marketing objective
    a. is the means and direction for reaching its organizational goals.
    b. is a statement of what is to be accomplished through marketing activities.
    c. is a systematic process that involves assessing market opportunities and resources.
    d. usually covers a period of one year or less.
    e. relates to customers' needs or desired benefits.

_____ 6. Easy Rent-A-Car would best be categorized as a
    a. dog.
    b. star.
    c. cash cow.
    d. problem child.
    e. kangaroo

PROGRAMMED COMPLETION EXERCISES

framework,
implementing,
controlling

1. A marketing plan provides a marketing manager with a basic
_____ for _____ and _____ an
organization's marketing activities.

formulate objectives

2. Marketing planning forces the marketing manager to
_____ _____ and to think systematically
about the firm's future marketing activities.

Marketing objectives

3. _____ _____ state what is to be
accomplished through marketing activities.

marketing objectives,
accomplishment,
measured

4. For purposes of control, _____ _____
should be formulated in such a way that the degree of
_____ can be _____ accurately.

marketing manager,
consistent,
organization

5. When creating marketing objectives, a _____
_____ must be sure that they are _____
with the overall objectives of the _____.

marketing
opportunities,
implementation,
control

6. Marketing planning is a systematic process that involves the
assessment of _____ _____, the
determination of marketing objectives, and the development
of a plan for _____ and _____.

medium-range,
long-range

7. Plans extending from two to five years are considered
_____ plans; plans that extend beyond five years are
_____ plans.

actions, resources

8. The marketing plan is a complete document that details
_____ and _____ for implementing and
controlling marketing activities.

division, product line,
profit center,
products, services

9. A strategic business unit is usually a _____, _____ _____, or other _____ _____ that sells a distinct set of _____ or _____.

strategic market
planning

10. The process of _____ _____ _____ yields a marketing strategy.

marketing strategy,
set

11. To reach its marketing objectives, an organization must develop a _____ _____ or a _____ of marketing strategies.

marketing program

12. A set of marketing strategies that are implemented and used at the same time is the organization's _____ _____.

target market,
marketing mix

13. To create a marketing strategy, the marketer must select and analyze a _____ _____ and create and maintain a _____ _____ to satisfy that market.

market opportunity,
environmental forces,
firm's capabilities

14. There are three major considerations in assessing the organization's opportunities and resources: evaluating _____ _____, monitoring _____ _____, and understanding the _____ _____.

market opportunity

15. A _____ _____ arises when the right combination of circumstances occurs at the right time to allow an organization to take action toward reaching a target market.

optimum, key
requirements

16. The term *strategic window* has been used to describe the often limited periods of _____ fit between the _____ _____ of a market and the particular capabilities of a firm competing in that market.

21 IMPLEMENTING STRATEGIES AND MEASURING PERFORMANCE

CHAPTER OUTLINE

Organizing marketing activities
    Centralization versus decentralization
    The place of marketing in an organization
    Major alternatives for organizing the marketing unit
Implementing marketing activities
    Internal marketing
    Motivating marketing personnel
    Communicating within the marketing unit
    Coordinating marketing activities
    Total quality management
Controlling marketing activities
    Establishing performance standards
    Evaluating actual performance
    Taking corrective action
    Requirements for an effective control process
    Problems in controlling marketing activities
Methods of evaluating performance
    Sales analysis
    Marketing cost analysis
The marketing audit

CHAPTER SUMMARY

How effectively marketing management plans and implements marketing strategies depends on how the marketing unit is organized. The organizational structure of a marketing department establishes authority relationships and designates responsibilities. The internal structure is the vehicle for directing marketing activities.

The structures and relationships of a marketing unit strongly affect marketing activities. The influence of marketing in a company is determined largely by the extent to which a firm is marketing-oriented and how centralized or decentralized the organization is.

A marketing unit can be organized according to (1) functions, (2) products, (3) regions, or (4) types of customers. Organizing by function classifies marketing activities according to what marketing personnel are involved in doing—for example, marketing research, advertising, or customer relations. This form is fairly common, especially in small businesses with centralized marketing operations. Businesses that produce diverse products sometimes organize their marketing units according to product. Here, a product manager assumes full responsibility for the marketing of a product or product group. This form of organization gives a firm the flexibility to develop special marketing mixes for different products. A large company that markets products throughout the entire nation may organize its marketing activities by geographic region. This approach is especially effective for a firm whose customers' characteristics and needs vary greatly from one region to another. Finally, in some businesses the marketing unit is organized according to type of customer. This form of internal organization works well for a firm that has several groups of customers whose needs and problems differ significantly. Although marketing units can be structured internally using any one of these approaches, most firms use some combination of them. The use of more than one type of organization creates a flexible marketing unit that can develop and implement marketing plans to match customers' needs precisely.

Proper implementation of a marketing plan depends on internal marketing, the motivation of personnel, effective communication within the marketing unit, the coordination of marketing activities, and total quality management. Internal marketing refers to managerial actions necessary to make all members of the marketing organization understand and accept their respective roles in implementing the marketing strategy. It is used to attract, motivate, and retain qualified internal customers by designing internal products that satisfy employees' needs and wants. The second part of implementation is motivating marketing personnel to perform effectively. This means learning about employees' physical, psychological, and social needs and basing motivation methods on those needs. Without good communication, marketing managers cannot motivate personnel or coordinate their efforts. There must be an information system, then, that operates not only among the units in the organization but within the marketing unit itself as well. Because of job specialization and differences related to marketing activities, marketing managers must synchronize the activities of the marketing staff within the firm and integrate those activities with the marketing efforts of external organizations (advertising agencies, resellers, researchers, shippers). Total quality management is the coordination of efforts at improving customer satisfaction, increasing employee participation and empowerment, forming and strengthening supplier partnerships, and facilitating an organizational culture of continuous quality improvement.

To achieve marketing objectives and to help the organization achieve its overall objectives, marketing managers must control marketing efforts effectively. The marketing control process consists of establishing performance standards, evaluating actual performance, and reducing the differences between actual and wanted performance by taking corrective action. There are several requirements for creating and maintaining an effective control process. First, the control process should be designed so that the flow of information is rapid enough to allow marketing managers to detect differences quickly between actual and planned levels of performance. Second, control procedures must be flexible enough to accommodate both varied activities and changes in the environment. Third, the control process must be economical: Its costs must be low relative to the costs of having no controls. Finally, the control process should be designed so that both managers and subordinates can understand it.

When marketing managers attempt to control marketing activities, they frequently experience several problems. Often the information they need is unavailable or is available but costly. Environmental changes can hamper control. Also, the time lag between the performance of marketing activities and the effects of those activities limit marketing managers' ability to control. Because marketing activities often overlap with a firm's other activities, it can be difficult to determine the precise costs of marketing activities. Finally, marketing control may be hampered because it is extremely difficult to develop precise performance standards for marketing personnel.

Sales analysis and cost analysis are two general ways of evaluating the actual performance of marketing strategies. Sales analysis uses sales figures to evaluate a firm's current performance. To provide useful analyses, current sales data must be compared with forecasted sales, with industry sales, with specific competitors' sales, or with costs incurred to achieve the sales volume. Although sales can be measured in several ways, the fundamental unit of measurement is the sales transaction. A sales transaction involves a customer order for a specified quantity of an organization's product sold under specified terms by a particular salesperson on a certain date. A company can use these bits of information to analyze sales in terms of dollar volume or market share. Dollar volume sales analysis is a frequently used form of sales analysis because the dollar is a common denominator of sales, costs, and profits. A firm's market share is the firm's sales of a product stated as a percentage of the entire industry's sales of that product. Whether evaluation is based on sales volume or market share, sales analysis can be performed on aggregate sales figures or on disaggregated data. Aggregate sales analysis provides an overview of current sales. Although helpful, it does not indicate sales variations within the aggregate. To determine those variations, total sales figures usually are broken down by geographic unit, salesperson, product, customer type, or a combination of these categories.

Sales analysis is only a part of evaluating the effectiveness of a marketing strategy; a firm also must perform a cost analysis. A marketing cost analysis breaks down and classifies costs to determine which costs are associated with specific marketing activities. The first step in determining marketing costs is to examine accounting records. In the process, some of the costs in natural accounts (rent and salaries, for example) must be reclassified into marketing function accounts (storage, order processing, advertising, marketing research); others must be reclassified across multiple functions.

There are three broad categories of marketing costs: direct costs, traceable common costs, and nontraceable common costs. Direct costs are directly attributable to the performance of marketing functions. Traceable common costs can be allocated indirectly to the functions they support. Nontraceable common costs are assignable only on an arbitrary basis. A cost analysis can include all three cost categories (the full-cost approach), or it can include just direct costs and traceable common costs (the direct-cost approach). Marketers can analyze costs in several ways. They can analyze natural accounts; they can analyze functional accounts; or, to be more precise, they can analyze functional accounts in terms of specific products, geographic areas, or customer groups.

A marketing audit is a systematic routine examination of the objectives, strategies, organization, and performance of a firm's marketing unit. It can be specific, focusing on one or a few marketing activities, or it can be comprehensive, encompassing all of a company's marketing activities. Its scope depends on cost, the target markets served, the structure of the marketing mix, and environmental conditions.

A marketing audit should perform four major functions: (1) describing current activities and results related to sales, costs, prices, and profits; (2) gathering information about customers, competition, and environmental developments that could affect marketing strategies; (3) exploring opportunities and alternatives for improving marketing strategies; and (4) providing an overall database for use in evaluating the attainment of organizational goals and marketing objectives.

There is no single set of procedures for performing a marketing audit, but there are some general guidelines. Questionnaires should be developed carefully to ensure that an audit is directed at the right issues. To ensure that an audit is systematic, the auditors should develop and follow a step-by-step plan. Auditors should strive to talk with a diverse group of people from many parts of the company. And the results of an audit should be set forth in a comprehensive written document.

Several problems can develop in an audit of marketing activities: marketing audits can be expensive in time and money; selecting qualified auditors can be difficult; and marketing audits can disrupt a company's activities and personnel, particularly when they are performed by outside auditors.

MATCHING EXERCISES

Use the following set of terms to identify the sentences and phrases below. On the blank line next to each sentence or phrase, place the letter of the term that the sentence or phrase describes. Do not use a term more than once.

a.	Performance standard	j.	Direct-cost approach
b.	Marketing function accounts	k.	Performance evaluation
c.	Full-cost approach	l.	Marketing control process
d.	Internal marketing	m.	Centralized organization
e.	Natural accounts	n.	Marketing audit
f.	Decentralized organization	o.	Direct costs
g.	Traceable common costs	p.	Marketing cost analysis
h.	Marketing-oriented organization	q.	Nontraceable common costs
i.	Sales analysis	r.	Total quality management

_____ 1. Accounts that are based on how money is actually spent, such as rents and utilities.

_____ 2. Costs that are assigned on an arbitrary basis.

_____ 3. An organization in which the top-level managers delegate very little authority to lower levels of the organization.

_____ 4. An expected level of performance against which actual performance can be compared.

_____ 5. An organization that allows the marketing manager to participate in top-level decision making.

_____   6. A systematic examination of the objectives, strategies, organization, and performance of a firm's marketing unit.

_____   7. In cost analysis, a method that includes direct costs, traceable common costs, and nontraceable common costs.

_____   8. A process that consists of establishing performance standards, comparing those standards with actual performance, and reducing the differences between desired and actual performance.

_____   9. A way of evaluating the actual performance of marketing strategies in which sales figures are used to assess current performance.

_____   10. Efforts to improve customer satisfaction, increase employee participation, strengthen supplier partnerships, and create an environment for continuing quality improvement.

_____   11. Accounts that reclassify costs and break them down into such categories as transportation and storage.

_____   12. In cost analysis, a method that includes only direct costs and traceable common costs.

_____   13. A way of evaluating the actual performance of marketing strategies in which various costs are broken down and classified to determine which costs are associated with specific marketing activities.

_____   14. Managerial actions necessary to make all members of the marketing organization understand and accept their respective roles in implementing the marketing strategy.

_____   15. Costs that can be allocated indirectly to the functions they support.

_____   16. Costs that are directly attributable to the performance of marketing functions.

TRUE OR FALSE STATEMENTS

T   F   1. In a marketing-oriented firm, the marketing manager occupies a position above that of the financial, production, and personnel managers.

T   F   2. Organization on the basis of functions is the best approach for organizing marketing activities because it works well in all businesses.

T   F   3. Organizing a marketing department by functions works best in a large firm that produces many diverse products.

T   F   4. Organizing by product groups gives a firm the flexibility to develop special marketing mixes for different products.

T   F   5. Organizing by type of customer is most effective in small businesses with centralized marketing operations.

T   F   6. A large company that markets products nationally or internationally may organize its marketing activities by geographic region.

T   F   7. It is common for a firm to use some combination of organization by function, product, region, or customer type.

T   F   8. Marketing planning and organization guarantee the success of a marketing strategy.

T   F   9. In implementing a marketing plan, the marketing manager must coordinate marketing activities with other functions of the firm.

T   F   10. A part of implementing the marketing plan is to motivate marketing personnel to perform effectively in accomplishing their objectives.

T   F   11. Although proper implementation of a marketing plan depends on communication within the marketing unit, it is not necessary for communication to occur between the marketing manager and high-level executives.

T   F   12. The marketing control process consists of establishing performance standards, evaluating actual performance by comparing it with established standards, and reducing the differences between desired and actual performance.

T   F   13. Performance standards do not apply to a marketer's achievement of budget objectives.

T   F   14. To reduce discrepancies between planned and actual performance, a marketing manager may change a performance standard.

T   F   15. Creating and maintaining an effective control process depend heavily on the quantity and quality of information and the speed at which it is received.

T   F   16. Marketing controls should focus on the activities of the firm's marketers but should be independent of the actions of personnel in external organizations that provide marketing assistance.

T   F   17. The time lag between the performance of marketing activities and the effects of those activities increases marketing management's ability to measure precisely the effectiveness of marketing actions.

T   F   18. The information required to control marketing activities is always readily available and inexpensive to obtain.

T   F   19. Knowing that a shoe store achieved a $750,000 sales volume this year is enough for a manager to determine whether a marketing strategy is effective.

T   F   20. If a firm increased its prices by 10 percent and its sales volume by 12 percent, it has experienced a real increase in unit sales.

T   F   21. The primary reason for using market share analysis is to estimate whether sales changes have resulted from the firm's marketing strategy or from uncontrollable environmental forces.

T   F   22. Aggregated sales data provide a marketer with an overview of current sales and in-depth insight into sales variations within the aggregate.

T   F   23. If a firm finds that 10 percent of its sales are coming from an area that represents 17 percent of the potential sales for the product, it can assume that its marketing strategy is successful in that geographic unit.

T   F   24. Marketing cost analysis breaks down and classifies costs to determine which costs are associated with specific marketing activities.

T   F   25. Traceable common costs are directly attributable to the performance of marketing functions.

T   F   26. A direct-cost approach includes direct costs and traceable common costs but not nontraceable common costs.

T   F   27. An analysis of natural accounts is the most precise method of analyzing costs.

T   F   28. A marketing audit is a systematic examination of the objectives, strategies, organization, and performance of a firm's marketing unit.

MULTIPLE-CHOICE QUESTIONS

_____ 1. If Procter & Gamble is eliminating brand managers and developing division managers, this will limit the amount of authority that is delegated down to the lower levels of the organization. Based on this example, P&G's organizational structure is becoming more
   a. democratic.
   b. decentralized.
   c. autonomous.
   d. centralized.
   e. marketing-oriented.

_____ 2. The design of internal products that satisfy employees' needs and wants is an element of
   a. the marketing concept.
   b. the coordination of marketing activities.
   c. internal marketing.
   d. motivation of personnel who perform marketing activities.
   e. effective communication within the marketing organization.

_____ 3. Federal Express has been widely recognized for its ability to rapidly and successfully introduce new services. Due to a strong _____ program, the field employees are excited about and prepared for these new products.
   a. control
   b. evaluation
   c. product development
   d. internal marketing
   e. product promotion

_____ 4. Which of the following does *not* commonly serve as a basis for a marketing unit's internal organization?
   a. Functions
   b. Products
   c. Geographic regions
   d. Types of customers
   e. Types of marketing strategies

_____ 5. At Galliger, Inc., there are several people with a great deal of expertise in their respective areas, but on specific projects there are a large number of problems in coordinating these areas. Based on this information, Galliger is exhibiting tendencies of a company that is organized by
   a. product.
   b. function.
   c. region.
   d. customer type.
   e. market.

_____ 6. An organization that produces a diverse set of products probably should organize its marketing departments according to
   a. product groups.
   b. functions.
   c. geographic regions.
   d. types of customers
   e. competitive standards.

_____ 7. When marketing operations are organized on the basis of products,
   a. product lines are concentrated under a single product manager, who is responsible for them all.
   b. a product manager assumes full responsibility for the marketing of a particular product or product group.
   c. marketing activities are not duplicated among units.
   d. the product manager's authority in the organizational hierarchy is equal to the financial manager's
   e. the firm loses the flexibility to develop special marketing mixes for different products.

_____ 8. A large company that markets products nationally or internationally may organize its marketing activities by
   a. product groups.
   b. functions.
   c. geographic regions.
   d. types of customers.
   e. competitive standards.

_____ 9. Which of the following organizations creates a flexible structure that allows marketers to develop and implement plans to fit customers' needs more precisely?
   a. Organization on the basis of regions
   b. Organization on the basis of types of customers
   c. Organization on several bases

d. Organization on the basis of products
e. Organization on the basis of functions

10. To implement a marketing plan properly requires
    a. the coordination of marketing activities.
    b. the creation of a flexible marketing unit.
    c. a sales-oriented organization.
    d. first that a firm produce a good product.
    e. the establishment of strict performance standards.

11. To compare actual performance with performance standards, a marketing manager should
    a. monitor just the activities of personnel in external organizations.
    b. monitor the activities of marketers within the firm and those of personnel in external organizations that provide the firm with marketing assistance.
    c. change planned performance standards.
    d. establish a marketing strategy.
    e. convert specific performance standards into broad performance standards.

12. At the same time Laughlin Metals's marketing department institutes a program to expand the firm's customer base, Laughlin's accounting department introduces tighter standards on setting up customer accounts. The firm is experiencing problems in which one of the following areas?
    a. Organization structure
    b. Motivation
    c. Communication
    d. Control
    e. Coordination

13. Given that sales have declined for the past two years, the vice-president of marketing for Brayco decides to do a detailed investigation of the firm's advertising agency, Drummond & Wallace. He concludes that the only option is to call for open proposals from various agencies as part of which phase of the marketing control process?
    a. Evaluating actual performance
    b. Taking corrective action
    c. Establishing performance standards
    d. The marketing audit
    e. Marketing coordination

14. Which of the following is *not* a requirement for creating and maintaining an effective control process?
    a. The flow of information should be rapid.
    b. A variety of control procedures is necessary to monitor different kinds of activities.
    c. Control procedures should be flexible.
    d. The costs of the control process should be high relative to sales.
    e. Both managers and subordinates should understand the control process.

_____ 15. Which of the following would *not* help a marketing manager reduce discrepancies between planned and actual performance?
 a. Meeting with personnel to discuss morale problems
 b. Examining competitors' prices
 c. Reviewing product displays in local stores
 d. Starting research on a new product line
 e. Meeting with the sales manager to discuss customers' reactions to a product

_____ 16. Which of the following is the *best* reason for making marketing control procedures flexible?
 a. Marketing personnel are not always motivated to work.
 b. The marketing environment is always changing.
 c. Managers and workers may need several explanations to understand procedures.
 d. A competitor may suddenly change the price of a product.
 e. Short-range plans sometimes must be changed to long-range plans.

_____ 17. Dollar volume sales analysis is a frequently used form of sales analysis because
 a. it gives an accurate indication of a firm's current performance.
 b. it indicates whether sales changes are the result of the firm's marketing strategy or of environmental factors.
 c. the dollar is a common denominator of sales, costs, and profits.
 d. it is reliable and inexpensive.
 e. inflationary price changes do not affect the analysis.

_____ 18. When a company's sales volume increases and its market share stays the same, the marketer can assume that
 a. the firm's marketing strategy brought about the change in sales.
 b. industry sales increased and this increase was reflected in the firm's sales.
 c. the firm's marketing strategy failed.
 d. there has been no real change in dollar volume sales.
 e. there has been unethical behavior in the organization.

_____ 19. The iceberg principle refers to
 a. finding that a large portion of aggregate sales comes from a small number of products, geographic areas, or customers.
 b. disaggregated sales data characteristics.
 c. the hidden information that can be extracted from a sales transaction.
 d. the inflationary costs hidden in dollar volume sales analysis.
 e. the Titanic sales curve.

_____ 20. When total sales figures are broken down by geographic units, salespersons, products, or customer types, the analyst is evaluating the marketing strategy using
 a. segmented markets.
 b. aggregated data.
 c. the iceberg principle.

d. disaggregated data.

e. the market segmentation approach.

_____ 21. Donna is extremely pleased that during her boutique's first year the store had net sales of $230,000. Her marketing consultant tells her that this figure may or may not be favorable depending on the results of the
   a. sales and cost analyses.
   b. marketing audit.
   c. coordination assessment.
   d. internal marketing assessment.
   e. establishment of performance standards.

_____ 22. Marketing cost analysis usually requires that some of the costs in natural accounts be reclassified into marketing function accounts because
   a. marketing function accounts are less complicated and less expensive to use.
   b. natural accounts do not explain what functions were performed through the expenditure of funds.
   c. natural accounts assign costs on an arbitrary basis.
   d. marketing function accounts classify costs into general accounts, such as rent, salaries, and utilities.
   e. of government regulations.

_____ 23. Costs that are allocated indirectly, using one or several criteria, to the functions they support are called
   a. traceable common costs.
   b. natural costs.
   c. marketing function costs.
   d. direct costs.
   e. nontraceable common costs.

_____ 24. Marketers for a hospital equipment company are performing a marketing cost analysis to determine which costs are associated with which marketing activities. The salary of the hospital administrator cannot be assigned to a cost category with any logical criteria. This cost would be categorized as a _____ cost.
   a. full
   b. direct
   c. traceable common
   d. nontraceable common
   e. standard

_____ 25. Realizing that the company has a very high overhead in terms of rent, salaries, and debt service, Patty tells Bartlet's president that the only way the proposed new product will produce solid performance in its early years is through
   a. a direct-cost approach.
   b. arbitrary cost allocation.
   c. the allocation of overhead costs.
   d. market cost analysis.
   e. common costing.

26. Which of the following statements about marketing audits is false?
    a. A marketing audit is used to evaluate the effectiveness of an organization's marketing activities.
    b. A marketing audit explores opportunities and alternatives for improving marketing strategies.
    c. Marketing audits can disrupt a company's activities because employees sometimes fear comprehensive evaluations.
    d. A marketing audit is a control process that usually is effective only during a crisis.
    e. A marketing audit allows an organization to change tactics or alter day-to-day activities as problems arise.

MINICASE: HUGHES DIESEL CONSIDERS REORGANIZATION

Four years ago, after months of preparation, Jack Hughes—along with thirteen engineers and salespeople—formed Hughes Diesel, Inc. Because of adequate preparation, operations started smoothly and a satisfactory market share was achieved quickly.

Hughes Diesel produces diesel-powered pumps for the oil-drilling industry. Recently, one of the firm's engineers developed a new type of valve that has a simple but revolutionary design. Tests show that it works very well with a dense fluid similar to oil. In fact, it is superior to any valve on the market. A careful analysis has revealed excellent sales potential for the valve, especially with large oil companies engaged in offshore drilling. As a result, Hughes has made an agreement with the inventor to patent the valve.

The decision to exploit this opportunity has led to a revision of the company's objectives. Those objectives now include (1) maintaining market share for the fuel pump, (2) increasing production capacity and building sales volume and profits for the valve, and (3) finding other markets for the valve.

The firm's present organizational chart is illustrated below. The firm's executives, however, are considering organizational changes to accommodate the addition of the valve to the product mix. They feel that the company is likely to benefit from some changes as the new division becomes a major part of Hughes Diesel.

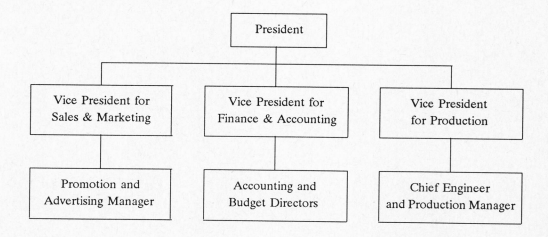

Questions

_____ 1. Hughes Diesel currently is organized by
a. functions.
b. products.
c. regions.
d. customers.
e. multiple bases.

_____ 2. Hughes has proposed a new organizational structure for the firm. He would like to see the structure remain basically as is except for the addition of a vice president of personnel and two marketing managers (each would report to the vice president of sales and marketing) for the two types of customers. His suggested structure is organized by
a. functions.
b. products.
c. regions.
d. customers.
e. multiple bases.

_____ 3. The structure proposed by Hughes assumes
a. that marketing operations should be centralized.
b. that fuel pumps and valves are significantly different products.
c. that customer characteristics vary greatly from one region to another.
d. that customer groups have distinct needs and problems.
e. nothing.

PROGRAMMED COMPLETION EXERCISES

products, product, product, product group

1. When marketing operations are organized on the basis of _____, a _____ manager assumes full responsibility for the marketing of a particular _____ or _____ _____.

characteristics, needs, region

2. The regional approach to organizing is especially effective for a firm that has customers whose _____ and _____ vary greatly from one _____ to another.

combination, forms

3. Although marketing units can be structured internally using a single base (functions, products, regions, or customer types), firms often employ a _____ of _____.

organization, develop, implement

4. By using more than one type of _____, a flexible marketing unit can _____ and _____ marketing plans to match customers' needs precisely.

Internal marketing, organization, marketing strategy

5. _____ _____ refers to the managerial actions necessary to make all members of the _____ understand and accept their respective roles in implementing the _____ _____.

purpose, direction, structure, exchanges

6. Planning and organizing provide _____, _____, and _____ for marketing activities, but implementation is necessary for _____ to occur.

coordination, motivation, communication

7. Proper implementation of a marketing plan depends on the _____ of marketing activities, the _____ of people performing those activities, and effective _____ within the marketing unit.

needs, motivation

8. To motivate marketing personnel, a marketing manager must determine their _____, then develop and use _____ methods based on those needs.

performance standards, actual performance, reducing, desired

9. The marketing control process consists of establishing _____ _____, evaluating _____ _____ by comparing it with established standards, and _____ the differences between _____ and actual performance.

marketing managers, sales managers, sales personnel

10. A marketing information system should facilitate communication among _____ _____, _____ _____, and _____ _____.

established performance standards, actual performance

11. To reduce a discrepancy between _____ _____ _____ and _____ _____, a marketing manager can take steps to improve actual performance, to reduce or totally change the performance standards, or to do both.

Total quality management, customer satisfaction, supplier, employee participation

12. _____ _____ _____ is the coordination of efforts toward improving _____ _____, strengthening _____ partnerships, increasing _____ _____, and maintaining an environment of continuous quality improvement.

operating costs, sales investments, premium pricing

13. Financial benefits derived from total quality management include lower _____ _____ higher return on _____ _____, and improved ability to use _____ _____.

sales analysis, marketing cost analysis

14. Two general ways of evaluating the actual performance of marketing strategies are _____ _____ and _____ _____ _____.

sales volume, market share, aggregate, disaggregated

15. Sales analysis can be based on _____ _____ or _____ _____ and can be performed on _____ sales figures or on _____ data.

Marketing cost analysis, marketing activities

16. _____ _____ _____ breaks down and classifies costs to determine which are associated with specific _____ _____.

full-cost approach, nontraceable common costs, arbitrary

17. Proponents of a _____ _____ claim that for an accurate profit picture all costs must be included in the cost analysis. Opponents of this approach say it does not yield actual costs because _____ _____ _____ are determined by _____ criteria.

objectives, strategies,
organization,
performance

18. The marketing audit is a systematic examination of the marketing group's _____, _____, _____, and _____.

ANSWERS TO OBJECTIVE QUESTIONS

Matching		*True or False*		*Multiple-Choice*		*Minicase*
1. e	9. i	1. F	15. T	1. d	14. d	1. a
2. q	10. r	2. F	16. F	2. c	15. d	2. e
3. m	11. b	3. F	17. F	3. d	16. b	3. d
4. a	12. j	4. T	18. F	4. e	17. c	
5. h	13. p	5. F	19. F	5. b	18. b	
6. n	14. d	6. T	20. T	6. a	19. a	
7. c	15. g	7. T	21. T	7. b	20. d	
8. l	16. o	8. F	22. F	8. c	21. a	
		9. T	23. F	9. c	22. b	
		10. T	24. T	10. a	23. a	
		11. F	25. F	11. b	24. d	
		12. T	26. T	12. e	25. a	
		13. F	27. F	13. b	26. d	
		14. T	28. T			

22 BUSINESS-TO-BUSINESS MARKETING

CHAPTER OUTLINE

The nature of business-to-business marketing
Selection and analysis of business-to-business target markets
    Determining who potential customers are and how many there are
    Locating business-to-business customers
    Estimating purchase potential
Characteristics of business-to-business marketing mixes
    Product
    Distribution
    Promotion
    Price

CHAPTER SUMMARY

Business-to-business (or industrial) marketing is a set of activities directed at facilitating and expediting exchanges involving products and customers in business-to-business markets. Business-to-business markets consist of individuals, groups, and organizations that purchase a specific kind of product for use in producing other products or for use in day-to-say operations. Business-to-business products differ from consumer products in that they are purchased to be used to produce other products or to be used in the organization's operations. The seven categories of business-to-business products are raw materials, major equipment, accessory equipment, component parts, process materials, consumable supplies, and industrial services.

Marketing research is becoming more important in business-to-business marketing. Most of the marketing research techniques described in Chapter 7 can be applied to business-to-business marketing.

The process of selecting and analyzing business-to-business target markets follows a pattern of first determining who potential customers are and how many there are, then finding out where they are, and then estimating their purchase potential. The federal government developed the Standard Industrial Classification (SIC) system to classify selected economic characteristics of business-to-business, commercial, financial, and service organizations. This system allows business-to-business marketers to divide firms into market segments that are based mainly on the types of products produced or handled. Input-output analysis, which can be used in conjunction with the SIC system, assumes that the output (sales) of one industry is the input (purchases) of other industries. To locate business-to-business customers, business-to-business marketers use state or commercial industrial directories or commercial data companies. Finally, to estimate the purchase potential of business-to-business customers, business-to-business marketers must find a relationship between the size of potential customers' purchases and a variable available in SIC data. That relationship is applied to potential customer segments to estimate their purchases. Only then can the marketer choose customers to include in the target market.

Despite their usefulness, SIC data pose several problems. There are industries that do not have SIC designations. Double counting can occur when products are shipped between two subsidiaries within the same firm. Census Bureau limitations mean that certain data are understated. And there is usually a significant lag between the time data are collected and the time they become available.

Once a target market has been identified, the business-to-business marketer is ready to create a marketing mix that will satisfy that market. The product component should emphasize services, both before and after sales. Business-to-business customers, even more than ultimate consumers, depend on on-time delivery, quality control, custom design, and nationwide parts distribution systems. Technical advice and credit services also can be important elements. The major concern in package design is protection.

Distribution channels tend to be shorter for business-to-business products than they are for many consumer products. More than half of all industrial products are sold through direct-distribution channels. Manufacturers' agents and business-to-business distributors can serve as intermediaries. The availability of a certain channel, the buying process, the cost and characteristics of the product, the size of product and parts inventories—all these enter into the choice of a business-to-business marketing channel. Other important elements are transportation, storage, and inventory control decisions. The continuity of most business-to-business seller-buyer relationships depends on the seller having the right products available when and where the customer needs them.

Business-to-business marketers rely on personal selling to a much greater extent than do most consumer product marketers. Business-to-business customers need personal contact for technical help, reinforcement, and service. The escalating costs of this form of promotion have increased the use of telemarketing. Advertising often plays a supplementary role to personal selling, making customers aware of new products and brands, informing them about product features, and identifying prospects for the sales force. Business-to-business advertisers use print media and direct mail primarily. Sales promotion can play an important role in the business-to-business promotion mix. There is widespread use of catalogs, trade shows, and trade sales promotion methods. Business-to-business marketers use publicity in much the same way as consumer product marketers use it.

Business-to-business markets are affected by many more legal and economic forces than are consumer markets. The Robinson-Patman Act influences the pricing practices of producers and wholesalers by regulating price differentials and the use of discounts. Federal price controls tend to regulate business-to-business markets more directly and to a greater extent than they do consumer markets. And the elastic demand that is characteristic of business-to-business markets often results in stable prices and nonprice competition. Prices of business-to-business products generally are determined by the use of administered pricing, bid pricing, or negotiated pricing.

MATCHING EXERCISES

Use the following set of terms to identify the sentences and phrases below. On the blank line next to each sentence or phrase, place the letter of the term that the sentence or phrase describes. Do not use a term more than once.

a. Standard Industrial Classification (SIC) system
b. Open bids
c. Business-to-business marketing
d. Administered pricing
e. Sealed bids
f. Direct-distribution channel
g. Bid pricing
h. Input-output data
i. Negotiated pricing
j. Business-to-business distributor
k. Negotiated bids

_____ 1. Information about what types of industries purchase the products of a particular industry.

_____ 2. Prices requested from several, but not all, sellers; these bids are not made public.

_____ 3. A process in which the seller sets a price for a product and the customer pays that price.

_____ 4. A process in which prices are determined through sealed or open bids.

_____ 5. A system the federal government developed for classifying selected economic characteristics of business-to-business, commercial, financial, and service organizations.

_____ 6. An independent business organization that takes title to business-to-business products and carries inventories.

_____ 7. Prices submitted to a buyer by a specified date; these bids are made public.

_____ 8. A marketing channel in which products are sold directly from producer to users.

_____ 9. A determination of price through bargaining even when there are stated list prices and discount structures.

_____ 10. A set of activities directed toward facilitating and expediting exchanges involving business-to-business markets and business-to-business products.

TRUE OR FALSE STATEMENTS

T   F   1. Business-to-business marketers have much more information than consumer product marketers with which to select and analyze their target markets.

T   F   2. Business-to-business sellers may prefer not to sell to customers who place small orders.

T F 3. Using negotiated bids, the customer negotiates the price and terms of sale with the most favorable bidders.

T F 4. The SIC system divides business-to-business firms into market segments based on plant capacity and number of employees.

T F 5. Input-output analysis assumes that the sales of one industry are the purchases of another.

T F 6. The general concepts and methods involved in developing a marketing mix for business-to-business products are similar in many ways to those involved in marketing consumer products.

T F 7. Business-to-business product marketing mixes emphasize a product's aesthetic values more than do consumer marketing mixes.

T F 8. Many business-to-business marketers depend heavily on sizable repeat purchases from customers.

T F 9. The Robinson-Patman Act significantly affects producers of consumer goods but has little impact on the marketers of business-to-business products.

T F 10. The actual price a business-to-business customer pays is usually the list price plus shipping charges.

T F 11. A manufacturers' agent is an independent businessperson who acquires title to and possession of products.

T F 12. Market information and an established set of customers are among the benefits manufacturers' agents provide.

T F 13. Business-to-business distributors are extremely efficient in selling to local markets, but the costs to the manufacturer of that selling are high.

T F 14. All the business-to-business channels discussed in the text are equally available; a producer need only select the one that best fits the firm's needs.

T F 15. Physical distribution decisions are all geared toward minimizing costs while maintaining a level of service that will keep customers satisfied.

T F 16. The relationship between business-to-business suppliers and buyers is apt to be more independent and self-sufficient than those that develop in consumer product sales.

T F 17. Advertising is usually ineffective in the business-to-business selling context.

T F 18. Trade publications and direct mail are widely used advertising media because they allow a business-to-business marketer to reach a precise market and thus avoid wasted circulation.

MULTIPLE-CHOICE QUESTIONS

_____ 1. Which of the following is the best reason for obtaining a product that meets specifications?
  a. The firm must project an image of quality by always ordering the best materials and component parts.
  b. The use of an inferior item may result in product malfunctions, causing the firm to lose customers.
  c. Specifications are government-imposed standards that must be met if a firm wants to stay in business.
  d. Higher-quality materials and component parts allow a firm to charge a higher price for its products, ensuring a higher profit.
  e. Business-to-business buyers are allocated a certain budget that they must use up or suffer a cut in budget the following year; therefore, they buy costly high-quality supplies.

_____ 2. All the following services can be important in business-to-business selling *except*
  a. production scheduling.
  b. on-time delivery.
  c. maintaining inventory.
  d. repair services.
  e. credit.

_____ 3. Which of the following considerations is probably *least* important in a business-to-business buyer's purchasing decision?
  a. Competitors' suppliers
  b. The price of a product
  c. The services offered relative to the buyer's specific needs
  d. The anticipated level of return on investment
  e. The quality of the product

_____ 4. Williamson, Inc., is considering entry into the business-to-business adhesives market. To isolate and analyze potential target markets for such a move, the firm has identified and counted potential customers and taken steps to identify their locations. It now must
  a. contact them by phone.
  b. contact them in person.
  c. estimate their purchase potential.
  d. determine the benefits they seek.
  e. determine the names of their current suppliers.

_____ 5. That the sales of one industry are the purchases of other industries is an assumption of
  a. input-output analysis.
  b. manufacturers' agents.
  c. state industrial directories.
  d. the SIC system.
  e. negotiated pricing.

_____ 6. Which one of the following is *best* suited for telling Monsanto which industries are major purchasers of a particular chemical?
   a. The Standard Industrial Classification system
   b. Input-output data
   c. *Survey of Industrial Purchasing Power*
   d. *Census of Business*
   e. Market identifiers

_____ 7. Which of the following is *not* a source of information for locating specific business-to-business customers?
   a. *Census of Business* aggregate data
   b. Commercial industrial directories
   c. *Standard & Poor's Register*
   d. State industrial directories
   e. *Middle Market Directory*

_____ 8. What is the biggest disadvantage of employing the services of commercial data companies?
   a. They are not as effective as government sources.
   b. They tend to be expensive.
   c. They are not expedient.
   d. They may be working for competitive firms and thus have a conflict of interest.
   e. They are unable to give out certain types of important information.

_____ 9. A business-to-business marketer should select the business-to-business customers to be included in the target market immediately after
   a. determining their SIC classifications.
   b. consulting government sources for customer information.
   c. determining the specific names and locations of those customers.
   d. determining which industries purchase the output of his or her industry.
   e. estimating their potential purchases.

_____ 10. During an assessment of Blackwell & Sons' customer service levels, consultant Randy Kraft learns that the company receives over five complaints on an average day. Randy is likely to tell Blackwell's marketing director that these complaints
   a. are a problem.
   b. take employee time away from making sales.
   c. serve a useful purpose.
   d. should be avoided.
   e. are normal.

_____ 11. Compared to business-to-business marketing mixes, which of the following is *least* likely to be emphasized in consumer selling?
   a. Customer satisfaction
   b. Pricing
   c. On-time delivery

  d. Product information
  e. Packaging

_____ 12. Which of the following statements about business-to-business price lists is false?
  a. Business-to-business marketers base their prices on a series of prices printed on a price sheet or in a catalog.
  b. In many cases, customers do not usually pay list prices.
  c. The book price is a base price to which charges for customer services are commonly added to figure a final price.
  d. Functional discounts are deducted from list prices.
  e. The actual price a business-to-business customer pays is called the net price.

_____ 13. Which of the following statements about sealed bids is true?
  a. The amounts of the bids are not made public.
  b. The bids are made public.
  c. They are a form of administered pricing.
  d. They usually result in the highest bidder receiving the sale.
  e. They use a list price as a beginning point for negotiation.

_____ 14. Knox Industries historically has sold industrial clamps directly to firms using these items in their production process. Knox's president believes that it may be time to start using industrial distributors because of the ability of such firms to
  a. provide Knox with market information.
  b. supply technical information to Knox.
  c. provide customers with more competitive pricing.
  d. carry a more complete line of Knox clamps.
  e. market the products to Knox specifications.

_____ 15. Which of the following channels is *not* used in business-to-business distribution?
  a. Producer, manufacturers' agent, consumer
  b. Producer, business-to-business customer
  c. Producer, business-to-business distributor, business-to-business customer
  d. Producer, manufacturers' agent, business-to-business customer
  e. Producer, manufacturers' agent, business-to-business distributor, business-to-business customer

_____ 16. Which of the following is *not* a limitation of manufacturers' agents?
  a. The method of compensation used gives the seller little control over them.
  b. They usually want to serve only larger accounts.
  c. They may be reluctant to spend time following up sales.
  d. They often lack the technical knowledge necessary to sell and service business-to-business items.
  e. They do not maintain inventories.

_____ 17. All of the following are characteristics of business-to-business distributors *except*
   a. that they are independent business organizations.
   b. taking title to products and carrying inventories.
   c. selling at relatively low costs to a manufacturer.
   d. providing credit services to customers.
   e. specializing in items that require extraordinary selling efforts or unusual handling.

_____ 18. Walton Food Products decided to use agents to reach business-to-business accounts several years ago. Logically, this decision was based on which one of the following?
   a. Walton's steady customer demand
   b. Walton's great financial strength
   c. Walton's desire to stay close to its customers
   d. Walton's desire to reduce selling costs
   e. The willingness of agents to provide market information

_____ 19. Which of the following would be *least* important to a business-to-business seller of electronic component parts when choosing a channel of distribution?
   a. Which channels are available
   b. How the products normally are purchased
   c. The availability of raw materials
   d. The parts inventory needed in local markets
   e. The amount of technical assistance customers need

_____ 20. Which of the following statements about business-to-business advertising is false?
   a. Business-to-business marketers seldom use broadcast media.
   b. Trade publications and direct mail are the most common media business-to-business marketers use.
   c. Business-to-business marketers sometimes can stimulate demand for their products by stimulating consumer demand.
   d. The content of product advertisements has little detailed information and is highly persuasive in nature.
   e. Business-to-business marketers attempt to reach a precise group of business-to-business customers.

_____ 21. Ellen Johnson, an account mnager for The Abbott Agency, explains to Bob Green, a marketing intern from City College, that an advertisement for a business-to-business product (compared to one for a consumer product) is likely to have less _____ and more _____.
   a. text/photos
   b. persuasion/copy
   c. length/persuasion
   d. print/broadcast
   e. specific details/price orientation

_____ 22. All of the following publications are sources of business-to-business market information *except*
   a. *Federal Guide to Industrial Organizations.*
   b. *Census of Business.*
   c. *Market Identifiers.*
   d. *Sales and Marketing Management's Survey of Industrial Purchasing Power.*
   e. *Census of Manufacturers.*

_____ 23. In an effort to learn if she is going to get the order at County Hospital, Kim Henderson goes to the county courthouse to see if her firm came in with the lowest price. For this purchase, which one of the following ways of determining product price was used?
   a. Administered
   b. Negotiated
   c. Bid
   d. Administered bid
   e. Bureaucratic

MINICASE: GEORGIA-PACIFIC BUILDING PRODUCTS*

Georgia-Pacific Corporation is the nation's largest forest products company. It commands about 20 percent of the U.S. plywood market and is one of the ten largest producers of roofing materials in the world. The firm has always tried to keep pace with the marketplace as well as stay at the leading edge of product development. At present, it is actively involved in the development of lower-cost plywood substitutes—such as waferboard, composite plyboard, and oriented strand board—for which builders' demands are growing. Conversely, the company is looking to upgrade its paper production to higher-profit items, such as white paper for photocopying and computer printouts, because it sees substantial growth potential in that segment of the paper market. The benefit of both paper and composite plywood products is that they allow better use of the company's wood supply, enabling Georgia-Pacific to take advantage of new market opportunities.

In the decade spanning 1972 and 1982, Georgia-Pacific spent $3.2 billion to expand and upgrade its manufacturing facilities and move its headquarters from Portland, Oregon, to Atlanta, Georgia, a site closer to its trees. Georgia-Pacific has ten roofing plants throughout the United States that are among the industry's most efficient and modern. By the early 1990s, it plans to erect ten new oriented strand board and waferboard plants. Not only is the firm increasing the capacities of existing facilities, it also is investing heavily to build and acquire new plants and mills.

* Information taken from Barry Stavro, "Trying to Get Out of the Woods," *Forbes*, May 7, 1984, pp. 172, 174; "Business Briefs: Georgia-Pacific Corp.," *Wall Street Journal*, May 7, 1986, p. 36; and Scott Scredon and Rebecca Aikman, "Georgia-Pacific Bets on Paper to Smooth Out Its Swings," *Business Week*, Apr. 15, 1985, pp. 120–121.

As part of an ambitious, aggressive marketing program, the company's goal is to place paper on an equal footing with its building products and to become the market leader in plywood substitutes. Steady growth in the sales of cardboard boxes and tissues is anticipated over the next few years. In addition, the company expects to produce coated white paper (used in magazines and newspaper inserts) in the United States. Georgia-Pacific's strong distribution division should help the firm meet its growth expectations by supporting the manufacturing division and moving products quickly into the marketplace.

In summary, Georgia-Pacific has survived the downturn that the building products market faced in the 1980s. The firm should benefit from any surge in market demand if it keeps abreast of the changing environment and if its marketing strategies cater to the fluctuating demand for products.

Questions

_____ 1. The case says that one benefit of composite plywood products is that they allow better use of the company's wood supply. Why isn't this the only basis on which to rest a decision to manufacture these products?
   a. Because the research and development involved are costly
   b. Because it does not take into consideration consumers' needs
   c. Because the cost of building plants for the manufacture of these products makes them less profitable
   d. Because plant capacity is limited
   e. Because demand for these products is unstable.

_____ 2. Because demand for building products is derived, Georgia-Pacific may choose to
   a. add manufacturers' agents to its distribution channel.
   b. limit its promotion efforts to personal selling.
   c. use advertising that promotes the products its customers sell.
   d. increase the capacity of its manufacturing facilities.
   e. use negotiated pricing as its primary pricing policy.

_____ 3. A good source for information about Georgia-Pacific is the federal government's
   a. Standard Market Classification system.
   b. input-output analysis.
   c. Standard Product Classification system.
   d. Standard Industrial Classification system.
   e. tax records.

_____ 4. The distribution channel that Georgia-Pacific uses is
   a. institutional.
   b. indirect.
   c. direct.
   d. derived.
   e. negotiated.

_____ 5. The primary objective of Georgia-Pacific's distribution division should be to
   a. manufacture high-quality products.
   b. increase sales in the 1990s.
   c. develop new composite plywood products.
   d. make products available when and where they are needed.
   e. take advantage of industry growth.

PROGRAMMED COMPLETION EXERCISES

product quality, delivery time

1. Research shows that business-to-business buyers' complaints usually focus on _____ _____ and _____ _____.

specifications

2. Business-to-business products often must conform to a set of standard technical characteristics called _____.

limited in number, technical, dollar value

3. Personal selling usually is more effective in business-to-business rather than consumer markets because customers are _____ _____ _____, products are often highly _____, and the _____ _____ of purchases is high.

Standard Industrial Classification system, industrial, commercial, financial, service

4. The federal government developed the _____ _____ _____ _____ to classify selected economic characteristics of _____, _____, _____, and _____ organizations.

Census of Manufacturers

5. The _____ _____ _____ subdivides manufacturers into five- and seven-digit coded groups.

Market Identifiers, Survey of Industrial Purchasing Power

6. Business-to-business market data also appear in nongovernment sources, among them Dun and Bradstreet's _____ _____ and *Sales and Marketing Management's* _____ _____ _____ _____ _____.

Input-output analysis

7. _____ _____ is based on the assumption that the sales of one industry are the purchases of other industries.

commercial data company

8. An expedient but expensive approach to identifying and locating potential customers is to use a _____ _____ _____.

services

9. Compared to consumer marketing mixes, the product ingredients of marketing mixes for business-to-business goods usually include a greater emphasis on _____.

repeat purchases

10. Many business-to-business marketers depend heavily on _____ _____ based on long-term relationships with their customers.

on-time delivery

11. Because business-to-business customers must have products available when they need them, an important service in the product component of many business-to-business marketing mixes is _____ _____.

product, functional, marketing research

12. Business-to-business marketers tend to concentrate on _____ research that is directed at _____ features rather than on _____ _____.

legal, economic

13. Pricing decisions business-to-business marketers make are affected greatly by _____ and _____ forces.

multiplier

14. A business-to-business seller can change prices without having to issue new catalogs or price sheets by simply changing the _____.

shorter

15. Distribution channels for business-to-business products tend to be _____ than those for many consumer products.

direct marketing channels

16. The most widely used channels in marketing business-to-business products are _____ _____ _____.

manufacturers' agent

17. A business-to-business intermediary who does not acquire title to the products and usually does not take possession is a _____ _____.

business-to-business distributor

18. An independent business organization that acts as an intermediary and takes title to products and carries an inventory is a _____ _____.

personal selling

19. The promotional ingredient that business-to-business sellers rely on most is _____ _____.

technical, trade, missionary

20. Business-to-business salespeople can be grouped into _____, _____, and _____ categories.

interdependent

21. Compared to buyer-seller relationships that develop in consumer product sales, business-to-business buyers and sellers are more likely to be highly _____.

less

22. Advertising tends to be emphasized _____ in business-to-business than in consumer product promotion mixes.

print media

23. In choosing advertising media, business-to-business marketers use primarily _____ _____.

information,
persuasive

24. Compared with consumer product advertisements, the content of messages in business-to-business advertisements is more likely to be packed with _____ and is usually less _____ in nature.

catalogs, trade
shows, trade

25. Sales promotion efforts used in business-to-business marketers' promotion mixes include _____, _____ _____, and _____ sales promotion methods.

*Survey of Industrial
Purchasing Power*

26. Unlike most government sources, the data in the _____ _____ _____ _____ _____ are more current because they are updated annually.

ANSWERS TO OBJECTIVE QUESTIONS

Matching		*True or False*		*Multiple-Choice*		*Minicase*
1. h	6. j	1. T	10. F	1. b	13. b	1. b
2. e	7. b	2. T	11. F	2. a	14. a	2. c
3. d	8. f	3. T	12. T	3. a	15. a	3. d
4. g	9. i	4. F	13. F	4. c	16. d	4. c
5. a	10. c	5. T	14. F	5. a	17. e	5. d
		6. T	15. T	6. b	18. d	
		7. F	16. F	7. a	19. c	
		8. T	17. F	8. b	20. d	
		9. F	18. T	9. e	21. b	
				10. c	22. a	
				11. c	23. c	
				12. c		

23 SERVICES MARKETING

CHAPTER OUTLINE

The nature and characteristics of services
    Growth and importance of services
    Characteristics of services
Classification of services
Developing marketing strategies for services
    Product
    Promotion
    Price
    Distribution
    Strategic considerations
Nonbusiness marketing
    Why is nonbusiness marketing different?
    Nonbusiness marketing objectives
    Developing nonbusiness marketing strategies
    Controlling nonbusiness marketing activities

CHAPTER SUMMARY

Services are the outcome of applying human or mechanical efforts to people or objects. They are intangible-dominant products that cannot be physically possessed. Today, services are a growing part of our economy, in large part a function of the country's general economic prosperity. The growth of services affects both consumer and organizational markets.

Services have four basic characteristics: intangibility, inseparability of production and consumption, perishability, and heterogeneity. To help marketers develop marketing strategies, services can be grouped according to (1) their type of market, (2) their degree of labor intensiveness, (3) their degree of customer contact, (4) the skill of the service provider, and (5) the goal of the service provider.

The marketing concept is equally applicable to goods, services, and ideas. This means all marketers must create a marketing mix that satisfies the needs of their customers.

Service offerings often are difficult for consumers to understand and evaluate. Their only visible aspects are the tangibles (facilities, employees, communications) associated with them, and these tangibles must be managed with care. Because consumers often equate the service product with the service provider, service marketers must pay close attention to the selection, training, motivation, and control of contact people.

Their intangibility makes services difficult to promote. Most advertising stresses the tangibles associated with services, to help customers understand and evaluate those services. Personal selling is a potentially powerful tool because it allows customers and salespersons to interact. Contests and certain other sales promotion methods are feasible for service firms; displays and samples, however, are difficult to implement. Service marketers appear to rely on publicity much more than goods marketers. Although all customers value word-of-mouth communications, this is especially so with consumers of services because services are experiential in nature. Service marketers, then, must work to stimulate or simulate word-of-mouth about their products.

Price plays both a psychological role and an economic role in the service sector. In its psychological role, price indicates quality; in its economic role, it determines revenues and influences profits. Price also can help smooth fluctuations in demand.

Almost by definition, service industries are limited to direct channels of distribution. Especially in high-contact services, providers and consumers cannot be separated. Certain industries have developed unique ways of distributing their services, among them the use of intermediaries and electronic means of distribution.

Services marketers, like all other marketers, have one basic objective: to provide customers with benefits that satisfy their needs. One challenge they face in meeting this objective is matching supply and demand. Before they can use marketing and nonmarketing strategies to deal with that challenge, they first must understand the patterns and determinants of demand.

Nonbusiness marketing includes marketing activities conducted by individuals and organizations to achieve some goal other than a usual business goal (profit, market share, return on investment). The marketing concepts and methods used by businesses can be applied to nonbusiness situations as well. Nonbusiness marketing can be divided into two categories: nonprofit organizations and social marketing.

Of course, there are differences. In nonbusiness marketing, the objects of exchanges may not be specified in financial terms; usually these exchanges are facilitated through negotiation and persuasion. The primary difference is in objectives, although profit and other financial objectives are variables that only indirectly change the nature of marketing activities. Whereas the chief beneficiaries of a business organization are those who own or hold stock in it, in theory the only beneficiaries of a nonbusiness organization are its clients or members, or the public at large. Although nonbusinesses can be more creative than their business counterparts, they generally are less productive and efficient—a function of less direct accountability and the difficulty of evaluating the performance of professionals.

Nonbusiness organizations can be controversial; their goals can stir up opposition. Marketing is a body of knowledge to help further an organization's goals; it does not say what those goals should be. Nonbusiness marketers, then, must place increased reliance on individual judgment when faced with controversial goals.

Nonbusiness marketing strategies involve defining and analyzing a target market and creating and maintaining a marketing mix. A nonbusiness organization may not think in terms of the needs, perceptions, and preferences of its market or public. Often this is because the organization assumes it already knows what the public needs and wants. Moreover, it can be difficult to define a specific target market or target public. In nonbusiness organizations, direct consumers of a product are called client publics;

indirect consumers are called general publics. Client publics usually are the focus of nonbusiness marketing strategies. The methods and approaches used to segment and define target markets are the same in business and nonbusiness situations.

Marketing strategies for nonbusiness organizations include decisions about product, distribution, promotion, and price. Nonbusiness organizations deal more often with ideas and services than with goods. These elements are abstract, which means marketers must make special efforts to describe their benefits to clients. Nonbusiness marketers usually analyze distribution as it relates to decisions about product and promotion. A very short distribution channel—nonbusiness organization to client—is prevalent because the production and consumption of ideas and services often are simultaneous. Nonbusiness organizations use advertising and publicity to communicate with their client and general publics. Although personal selling may be called something else, it too is an important part of promotional efforts. Price is the value placed on the items involved in an exchange. In nonbusiness exchanges, price often is not a financial value; instead, it may be an opportunity cost—the value of a benefit that is given up by selecting one alternative over another. Pricing strategies of nonbusiness organizations often stress client and public welfare over equalization of costs and revenues.

To control marketing activities in nonbusiness organizations, managers use marketing audits to determine whether goals are being achieved. Control involves a complete inventory of the activities that are being performed and a readiness to correct deviations from standards. A major problem here is the difficulty of determining whether goals are being achieved. Techniques for controlling overall marketing performance must be compatible with the nature of the organization's operations.

MATCHING EXERCISES

Use the following set of terms to identify the sentences and phrases below. On the blank line next to each sentence or phrase, place the letter of the term that the sentence or phrase describes. Do not use a term more than once.

a. Opportunity cost
b. Product concept
c. Personal selling
d. Business services
e. Experience qualities
f. Services
g. Search qualities
h. Nonbusiness marketing
i. Inseparability

j. Negotiation
k. Persuasion
l. Credence qualities
m. Target public
n. Client publics
o. General publics
p. Heterogeneity
q. Perishability
r. Marketing concept

_____   1. The indirect consumers of a nonbusiness organization.

_____   2. Qualities that can be assessed only after purchase and consumption.

_____   3. A characteristic of services that means that their production and consumption generally occur simultaneously.

Perishability   4. *g* A characteristic of services that means they cannot be inventoried.

Search quality   5. *?* The few tangible attributes of services that can be seen before a purchase.

Heterogenity   6. *p* A characteristic of services that means they are not always performed consistently.

_____   7. *f* A collective of individuals who have an interest in or concern about an organization, a product, or a social cause.

_____   8. *h* Marketing activities conducted by individuals and organizations to achieve some goal other than ordinary business goals.

_____   9. *n* Direct consumers of a nonbusiness product.

Opportunity Cost   10. *a* The value of the benefit that is given up by selecting one alternative over another.

Marketing Concept   11. *r* Maintains that an organization's planning should be guided by the clients, members, or publics being served.

Negotiation   12. *s* The mutual discussion or communication of terms and methods.

Pursuation   13. *k* The process of convincing and prevailing on by argument.

_____   14. *l* Indirect consumers of a nonbusiness product.

TRUE OR FALSE STATEMENTS

T   **F**   1. All products, whether they are goods or not, possess a certain amount of intangibility.

T   **F**   2. All products can be classified as a pure good or a pure service.

T   **F**   3. Most products contain either tangible components or intangible components.

T   **F**   4. The dominant component determines the classification of goods, services, and ideas.

T   **F**   5. An airline's product is considered a good.

T   **F**   6. Expenditures for business services have grown even faster than those for consumer services.

T   **F**   7. Service marketers and goods marketers have the same problems in marketing.

T   **F**   8. Intangibility makes service offerings more difficult to understand.

T   **F**   9. Because they are labor intensive, services tend to be heterogeneous.

T   **F**   10. Their intangibility does not make services more difficult to advertise.

T   F   11. In addition to its economic and psychological roles in the service sector, price also helps smooth fluctuations in demand.

T   F   12. Service industries in general have many channels of distribution.

T   F   13. Because of their intangibility, the marketing concept for services is different than that for products and ideas.

T   F   14. The nonbusiness organization can serve many diverse groups, even the public at large.

T   F   15. The planning of nonbusiness marketing strategies requires less refinement and coordination of goals than does the planning of business strategies.

T   F   16. The basic objective of nonbusiness organizations is to obtain a wanted response from a target market.

T   F   17. In a nonbusiness situation, negotiation and persuasion often are conducted without an awareness of the role of marketing in transactions.

T   F   18. That the identity of the owners may be unclear in a nonbusiness organization actually increases direct accountability.

T   F   19. In the nonbusiness environment, distribution channels are important in making products available.

T   F   20. Market information is more important to a manufacturer than it is to the manager of a political campaign.

T   F   21. The time a person donates to a cause is the opportunity cost to the individual.

T   F   22. Exchange transactions and organizational goals have little impact on the marketing objectives of a nonbusiness enterprise.

T   F   23. A marketing objective for a charitable organization could be the feeling of satisfaction that comes from participating in the solving of social problems or from promoting a social cause.

T   F   24. Because they lack a profit incentive, nonbusiness organizations do not need to develop a pricing strategy.

T   F   25. Developing a marketing channel to coordinate and facilitate the flow of nonbusiness products to clients is a necessary task in nonbusiness marketing.

T   F   26. The technique of personal selling is used by many nonbusiness organizations, even though it may not be called personal selling.

T   F   27. Exchanges are never consummated in the performance of nonbusiness marketing activities because of the intangible nature of most nonbusiness products.

T   F   28. The level of application for any given marketing mix variable may range from low to high, depending on the needs of the nonbusiness industry.

MULTIPLE-CHOICE QUESTIONS

1. The South Central Credit Union supplies several financial products. Where would these products fall on the tangibility continuum?
   a. Totally tangible
   b. Tangibly dominant
   c. Neutral
   d. Intangibly dominant
   e. Totally intangible

2. A service is
   a. a tangible product that can be physically possessed.
   b. one kind of good.
   c. not particularly labor intensive.
   d. an intangible-dominant product.
   e. the same thing as an idea.

3. One major catalyst to the growth of consumer services has been the
   a. general economic prosperity in the United States.
   b. growth of business services.
   c. intangible nature of most services.
   d. expanding supply of workers.
   e. increasingly complex business environment.

4. The four basic characteristics of services are
   a. intangibility, reciprocity, perishability, and homogeneity.
   b. tangibility, inseparability, perishability, and heterogeneity.
   c. intangibility, inseparability, perishability, and heterogeneity.
   d. reciprocity, separability, perishability, and homogeneity.
   e. tangibility, separability, imperishability, and homogeneity.

5. After returning from a consultation with her accountant, Janice determined that the service she received was poor because the accountant was rude and abrupt. The aspects of the product that Janice assessed are called _____ qualities.
   a. search
   b. experience
   c. credence
   d. tangible
   e. separable

6. Service qualities that cannot be assessed even after purchase and consumption are called
   a. experience qualities.
   b. credence qualities.
   c. tangible attributes.
   d. search qualities.
   e. product qualities.

7. Kevin tells his neighbor Bill that he found termintes near his front door. After the discovery, he had Dart Pest Control treat his house. Bill asks if Dart did a good job. Kevin responds that it is hard to tell unless he sees more termites. This conversation deals with the service quality known as
   a. credence.
   b. experience.
   c. value.
   d. perishability.
   e. search.

8. Services are susceptible to heterogeneity because they are
   a. perishable.
   b. diverse.
   c. labor intensive.
   d. intangible.
   e. tangible.

9. Which of the following statements about the classification of services is false?
   a. Product classification schemes have been developed to help marketers form a specific marketing strategy.
   b. Services are a very diverse group of products.
   c. An organization may provide more than one type of service.
   d. The skill of the service provider is not one of the five categories of services.
   e. Services can be classified in terms of the market or type of customer they serve.

10. In a product planning session, Rob Harris recommends that bank customers who open Pro-Line accounts be given real leather checkbooks. Rob's suggestion addresses the _____ aspect of the financial service product.
    a. tangible
    b. heterogeneous
    c. inseparability
    d. service quality
    e. variability

11. Marketers of people-based services
    a. must recognize that service providers often are equated with the service itself.
    b. are found only in organizational markets.
    c. do not have to concentrate on selecting, training, motivating, or controlling employees.
    d. are always nonbusiness marketers.
    e. can expect consistent performance from employees.

12. Typically, high-contact services
    a. involve actions directed at things.
    b. require the consumer to go to the production facility.

    c. include movie theaters and spectator sports.

    d. separate the consumer from production.

    e. emphasize the final outcome of the production process more than the process itself.

13. Advertising a service is difficult because services are
    a. perishable.
    b. costly.
    c. labor intensive.
    d. intangible.
    e. personal.

14. In its psychological role in the service sector, price
    a. determines profits.
    b. determines revenues.
    c. is a competitive tool.
    d. defines all the intangible elements of services.
    e. indicates quality.

15. Almost by definition, service industries are limited to
    a. competitive pricing.
    b. direct channels of distribution.
    c. little contact between consumers and providers.
    d. display and sample forms of sales promotion.
    e. nonbusiness organizations.

16. Dr. Knapp, a pediatrician, has tried to find reasons for the wide fluctuations in the number of children his office sees as walk-ins on any given day. Unable to produce any reasonable explanations, he is faced with the need to
    a. raise prices during peak days.
    b. offer discounts during the summer.
    c. train the nursing and reception staff in dealing with peak patient loads.
    d. insist the walk-ins schedule appointments.
    e. promote his practice more heavily in the medial during slow days.

17. Nonbusiness marketing includes all of the following *except*
    a. the accomplishment of some goal other than profit.
    b. activities aimed at facilitating and expediting exchanges.
    c. marketing activities conducted by individuals and organizations.
    d. lack of a profit incentive.
    e. direct accountability to an owner.

18. In a nonbusiness marketing situation,
    a. the individuals involved often are unaware of the role marketing plays in transactions.
    b. the consummation of exchanges does not occur.
    c. the division of labor and specialization of labor are not required.
    d. the target market is easy to define.
    e. profits can still be an objective

19. All of the following are nonbusiness marketers *except*
    a. a private university.
    b. the National Highway Safety Council.
    c. regional planning commissions.
    d. commercial banks.
    e. the Catholic church.

20. The marketing concept for nonbusiness organizations holds that planning should be guided by
    a. the thinking of the board of trustees.
    b. clients, members, or the publics being served.
    c. a professional planner's intuition.
    d. what has always worked in the past.
    e. government regulation.

21. The basic aim of the United Way is to obtain which one of the following from its target market?
    a. Favorable comments
    b. Profit
    c. Word-of-mouth support
    d. Volunteer time
    e. A desired response

22. Nonbusiness organizations serve their clients in order to achieve
    a. maximum profit.
    b. goals outlined by society.
    c. goals established by contributors.
    d. some social or environmental goal.
    e. the breakeven point of expenses.

23. The direct consumer of the product of a nonbusiness organization is called the
    a. client public.
    b. general public.
    c. target public.
    d. public at large.
    e. consumer public.

24. Which one of the following groups of people would be considered client publics for a hospital?
    a. Patients
    b. Insurance companies
    c. Doctors
    d. Nurses
    e. Pahrmaceutical sales representatives

25. Which of the following is *not* an example of a promotional effort in the nonbusiness environment?
    a. The recruitment of new members by volunteers
    b. The use of volunteers to solicit donations
    c. The use of a contest to attract donations

d. The use of a special event to raise funds

e. Shipping material to national headquarters

_____ 26. Distribution in nonbusiness marketing involves

a. showing the organization's interest in the area.

b. facilitating the product.

c. being located near trustees.

d. providing credibility.

e. making the product available to clients.

_____ 27. In nonbusiness organizations, channels of distribution are often

a. extended.

b. long.

c. vertical.

d. very short.

e. horizontal.

_____ 28. The value of a benefit that is given up by choosing one alternative over another is called

a. economic cost.

b. social cost.

c. opportunity cost.

d. marginal cost.

e. variable cost.

_____ 29. Which of the following is *not* an example of the goals of a nonbusiness organization?

a. Providing religious values and services

b. Ensuring protection and security

c. Obtaining financial contributions

d. Providing time and support

e. Promoting goods for the purpose of financial gain

_____ 30. Which of the following statements is false?

a. Nonbusiness organizations may have goals that are opposed by members of society.

b. Marketing as a field of study attempts to make value judgments about what a nonbusiness organization's goals should be.

c. One nonbusiness organization may emerge in order to oppose a social cause or a movement that another organization is trying to market to the public.

d. Nonbusiness organizations exist to serve clients.

e. Nonbusiness organizations usually have a marketing strategy.

_____ 31. Which of the following concepts is ordinarily *not* associated with nonbusiness organizations?

a. Profit

b. Negotiation

c. Persuasion

d. Marketing objectives

e. Marketing mix

_____ 32. In applying the marketing concept to nonbusiness organizations, the text essentially is stating that
    a. all organizations are really the same although their products differ.
    b. promotional activities are easier for nonbusiness organizations to develop because the public has more interest in the commodities they offer.
    c. goods and services are easier for nonbusiness organizations to market because there is no real competition for them to contend with.
    d. the development of a product should be influenced by the clients receiving or using it.
    e. a marketing concept applies mainly to profit-oriented organizations.

_____ 33. The student team assigned ot analyze the Barton House for battered women is having difficulty with the control phase of their project. Like many nonbusiness organizations, the Barton House lacks
    a. the ability to clearly determine if its goals are being achieved.
    b. clearly defined objectives.
    c. any formal planning.
    d. a clear mission statement.
    e. strategies for achieving stated objectives.

MINICASE: RIVER COUNTY NURSING HOME

River County Nursing Home is located in central Iowa, in a city of 95,000 people It is a publicly funded nursing home for the community.

The new administrator of the nursing home, Bill Setton, is concerned about the community's negative image of and attitudes toward River County. A year ago, a series of articles was published about how poorly its residents were treated. Setton believes the articles were biased.

In order to improve the nursing home's image and to increase public support, Setton hoped to use the results of a survey conducted by the state university to uncover unknown attitudes or possible negative attitudes. The findings of the survey were:

- Those who had visited the nursing home (30.5 percent) more strongly agreed that it is meeting the needs of the county than those who had not visited the nursing home.
- Over 90 percent of the sample who had not visited the home were unaware of the nursing home and the services it provided.
- The major sources of information about the facility were a friend or relative (24.2 percent), the newspaper (19.5 percent), driving by the location (19.3 percent), and word of mouth (16 percent).

Questions

_____ 1. River County's marketing activities are directed toward achieving the goal of serving the public, not normal _____ goals.
   a. pricing
   b. professional
   c. business
   d. personal
   e. nonbusiness

_____ 2. River County Nursing Home's product offering is a
   a. public product.
   b. product mix.
   c. good.
   d. service.
   e. tangible product.

_____ 3. The nursing home has been accused of failing to implement the marketing concept. That concept holds that the organization's objectives and activities should be directed at satisfying the needs of
   a. institutions.
   b. staff members.
   c. the industry.
   d. the market.
   e. contributors.

_____ 4. River County's director, Bill Setton, should concentrate on learning more about
   a. goods marketing.
   b. developing goals.
   c. services marketing.
   d. public relations.
   e. profit maximization.

_____ 5. The nursing home's marketing objectives should state the _____ for its existence.
   a. price
   b. service
   c. goals
   d. rationale
   e. goods

_____ 6. The first indication in the case that Setton is performing marketing activities is that he is making _____ decisions.
   a. objective
   b. subjective
   c. promotional
   d. pricing
   e. distribution

PROGRAMMED COMPLETION EXERCISES

Charitable organiza-
tions, social causes

1. _____ _____ and supporters of
_____ _____ are major nonbusiness
marketers in the United States.

desired response

2. The basic objective of nonbusiness organizations is to obtain a
_____ _____ from a target market.

target market,
marketing mix

3. The two steps in developing a nonbusiness marketing strategy
are (1) defining and analyzing a _____
_____, and (2) creating and maintaining a
_____ _____.

client publics,
general publics

4. In nonbusiness organizations, direct consumers of a product
are called _____ _____, and indirect
consumers are called _____ _____.

value, benefit

5. Opportunity cost is the _____ of the _____
that is given up by choosing one alternative rather than
another.

target public

6. A _____ _____ is broadly defined as a
collective of individuals who have an interest in or concern
about an organization, a product, or a social cause.

deviations, standards

7. To control nonbusiness marketing activities, managers must
make an inventory of what activities are performed and be
prepared to correct _____ from _____.

clients, members,
public at large,
owners, stockholders

8. In theory, the beneficiaries of a nonbusiness organization are
its _____, _____, or the _____
_____ _____, while the chief beneficiaries
of a business enterprise are its _____ or
_____.

Opposing organiza-
tions, combat, success

9. _____ _____ may develop to
_____ the _____ of a movement or social
cause with which individuals disagree.

goals

10. Nonbusiness organizations may have _____ that are
not accepted by some members of society.

ideas, services, goods

11. The nonbusiness product takes the form of _____
and _____ more often than the form of
_____.

product, promotion

12. Nonbusiness marketers usually examine distribution as it
relates to decisions about _____ and _____.

short

13. The typical nonbusiness marketing channel is _____;
generally, it is made up of just the organization and the client.

profit, market share

14. Nonbusiness marketing includes marketing activities
performed by individuals and organizations to accomplish
some goal other than _____, _____
_____, or return on investment.

exchange, objectives

15. The nature of the _____ and the goals of the
organization shape nonbusiness marketing _____.

personal selling

16. Churches and charities rely on _____ _____
when they send volunteers to solicit donations.

Advertising,
publicity

17. _____ and _____ are used in nonbusiness
marketing to communicate with clients and the public.

marketing strategy

18. Control identifies those activities that conform to the
organization's _____ _____ and goals.

individuals, groups,
organizations

19. An exchange situation exists when _____,
_____, or _____ possess something of value
that they are willing to give up in an exchange relationship.

negotiation,
persuasion

20. Nonbusiness exchanges usually are facilitated through
_____ or _____.

marketing audit

21. To control marketing activities in nonbusiness organizations,
managers use information obtained through the
_____ _____ to make sure that goals are
being achieved.

intangible, deed,
performance,
possessed

22. Services are _____ products that involve a
_____, a _____, or an effort that cannot be
physically _____.

goods, services

23. Tangible-dominant products typically are classified as
_____, while intangible-dominant products typically
are classified as _____.

intangibility,
inseparability,
perishability,
heterogeneity

24. The four characteristics of services are _____,
_____, _____, and _____.

Experience,
credence

25. _____ qualities are those qualities that can be
assessed only after purchase and consumption; _____
qualities are those that cannot be assessed even after purchase
and consumption.

Inseparability,
consumed

26. _____ means that services normally are produced
and _____ at the same time.

Perishability,
inventoried

27. _____ means that services cannot be _____
or stockpiled.

heterogeneity,
labor intensive

28. The _____ of services can be attributed to their

being _____ _____.

market, degree,
labor intensiveness,
consumer, skill, goal

29. Services can be classified by their type of _____,

their _____ of _____ _____, their

degree of _____ contact, and the _____ and

_____ of their provider.

low

30. Repairs, dry cleaning, and spectator sports are examples of

_____-contact services.

interpersonal

31. The appearance of production facilities and the

_____ skills of actual service providers are critical in

high-contact services.

complexity,
variability

32. Service products can be analyzed in terms of their _____

and _____.

reduce, reassurance,
promote

33. Customer contact personnel should help _____ cus-

tomer uncertainty, give _____, reduce dissonance,

and _____ the reputation of the organization.

economic,
psychological

34. Price plays both an _____ and a _____ role

in the service sector.

direct

35. Most service industries are limited to _____ channels

of distribution.

satisfy

36. The basic concept of services marketing is to _____

customers' needs.

provider

37. The service product often is equated with the service

_____.

ANSWERS TO OBJECTIVE QUESTIONS

Matching		*True or False*		*Multiple-Choice*		*Minicase*
1. o	8. h	1. T	15. F	1. d	18. a	1. c
2. e	9. n	2. F	16. T	2. d	19. d	2. d
3. i	10. a	3. F	17. T	3. a	20. b	3. d
4. q	11. r	4. T	18. F	4. c	21. e	4. c
5. g	12. j	5. F	19. T	5. b	22. d	5. d
6. p	13. k	6. T	20. F	6. b	23. a	6. c
7. m	14. l	7. F	21. T	7. a	24. a	
		8. T	22. F	8. c	25. c	
		9. T	23. T	9. d	26. e	
		10. F	24. F	10. a	27. d	
		11. T	25. T	11. a	28. c	
		12. F	26. T	12. b	29. e	
		13. F	27. F	13. c	30. b	
		14. T	28. T	14. e	31. a	
				15. b	32. d	
				16. c	33. a	
				17. e		

24 INTERNATIONAL MARKETING

CHAPTER OUTLINE

Involvement in international marketing
  Multinational involvement
  Globalization versus customization of marketing strategies
International marketing intelligence
Environmental forces in international markets
  Cultural forces
  Social forces
  Economic forces
  Political and legal forces
  Technological forces
  Regional trade alliances and markets
  The U.S.–Canada Free Trade Agreement
  Free trade between the United States and Mexico and the *maquiladora* industries
  Europe 1992
  Pacific Rim nations
  Changing relations with Eastern Europe and the former Soviet Union
Strategic adaptation of marketing mixes
  Product and promotion
  Distribution and pricing
Developing organizational structures for international marketing
  Exporting
  Licensing
  Joint ventures
  Trading companies
  Direct ownership

CHAPTER SUMMARY

The management of international marketing activities requires an understanding of marketing variables and a grasp of the environmental complexities of foreign countries. International marketing is marketing activities performed across national boundaries. The planning and control of these activities can be significantly different from marketing within national boundaries.

The level of involvement in international marketing varies widely and includes casual or accidental exporting, active exporting, full-scale international marketing involvement, and globalization of markets. Only full-scale international involvement and globalization of markets represent a full integration of international marketing into strategic market planning. In traditional full-scale international marketing, products are customized according to cultural, regional, and national differences; and marketing strategies are developed to serve specific target markets. Globalization of markets means developing marketing strategies as if the entire world were a single entity—selling standardized products using the same marketing strategies everywhere. The economic and competitive payoffs of standardized marketing strategies are great; but not all marketing mix variables are easy to standardize. And many leading marketers believe that international marketing demands that product quality and packaging, promotion, and distribution must vary to meet the needs of specific markets.

International marketing intelligence involves analyzing markets according to culture, institutions, and buying behavior. Data for that analysis should come from both secondary and primary sources. A detailed assessment of the environment is an absolute necessity before a company enters foreign markets. For a marketing strategy to be effective across national boundaries, the complexities of all environmental forces— cultural, social, economic, technological, and political and legal—must be understood. In that process, international marketers must analyze the social, economic, and political and legal institutions that serve as structures for achieving certain societal goals.

Various regional trade alliances and markets are creating both opportunities and difficulties for marketers, including the U. S.–Canada Free Trade Agreement, the *maquiladora* industries of Mexico, the unification of Europe in 1992, the Pacific Rim markets, and changing conditions in Eastern Europe and the former Soviet Union.

Once marketers understand the foreign environment and determine foreign market potentials, they must develop and adapt a marketing mix. There are five possible strategies for adapting product and promotion variables for international markets: (1) keeping the product and promotion the same worldwide, (2) adapting promotion only, (3) adapting the product only, (4) adapting both the product and promotion, and (5) inventing new products. In international marketing, distribution between countries is as critical as distribution within countries. Among the factors that influence distribution alternatives are the availability of wholesale-retail networks, ethnodomination, and the nature of the product. Pricing decisions, too, are affected by many factors. Transportation costs, supplies, taxes, and tariffs can drive up the prices of products sold in foreign markets. To accommodate the added expenses of selling in international markets, most organizations use cost-plus pricing. Price is also a function of foreign currency exchange rates.

Multinational firms can be involved in international marketing on different levels. Exporting is the lowest level and the most flexible approach. Licensing is an attractive alternative to direct investments when the political stability of a foreign country is in doubt or when resources are not available for direct investment. Joint ventures— partnerships between a domestic firm and a foreign firm or government—often are a political necessity because of nationalism or governmental restrictions on foreign ownership. Strategic alliances are partnerships formed to create competitive advantage on a worldwide basis. Trading companies are a link between buyers and sellers in different countries. These companies take title to products and perform all the activities necessary to move products from the domestic country to markets in foreign countries, in the process reducing the risk of international marketing for domestic firms. Once a company makes a long-term commitment to marketing in a foreign nation, direct ownership of a foreign subsidy or division is a possibility. Multinational enterprise refers to firms that have operations or subsidiaries located in many countries to achieve a common goal. With direct ownership come important tax, tariff, and other operating advantages, and the advantages of a cross-cultural approach. The greatest danger here —the loss of the foreign investment—comes from political uncertainty.

MATCHING EXERCISES

Use the following set of terms to identify the sentences and phrases below. On the blank line next to each sentence or phrase, place the letter of the term that the sentence or phrase describes. Do not use a term more than once.

a. Ethnodomination
b. Direct ownership
c. International marketing
d. Political forces
e. Multinational enterprises
f. Dumping
g. Joint venture
h. Strategic alliance

i. Trading company
j. Licensing
k. Globalization
l. Economic institutions
m. Culture
n. Gross national product (GNP)
o. Political and legal institutions

_____   1. A long-run commitment to marketing in a foreign nation in which a foreign subsidiary or division is owned by a domestic investor.

_____   2. Everything in our surroundings that is made by human beings; concepts, values, and tangible items that act as a blueprint for acceptable behavior in a given society.

_____   3. The sale of products in foreign markets at lower prices when all costs have not been allocated or when surplus products are sold.

_____   4. A government's policies toward public versus private enterprise, consumers, and foreign firms that influence marketing across national boundaries.

_____   5. Firms that have operations or subsidiaries in several countries, working to achieve a common goal.

_____   6. Partnerships formed to create competitive advantage on a worldwide basis.

_____   7. Marketing activities performed across national boundaries.

_____   8. An overall measure of a nation's economic standing in terms of the value of all products produced by that nation for a given period of time.

_____ 9. An arrangement in international marketing in which the owner of a foreign operation pays commissions or royalties on sales or supplies used in manufacturing to a domestic operation.

_____ 10. A partnership between a domestic firm and a foreign firm or government.

_____ 11. Marketing standardized products the same way throughout the world.

_____ 12. A link between buyers and sellers in different countries.

TRUE OR FALSE STATEMENTS

T F 1. What complicates the marketing task in foreign countries is the fact that the environment—particularly the cultural environment—often consists of elements that are unfamiliar to, and perhaps even unrecognized by, marketing executives.

T F 2. International marketing entails marketing activities that are performed in a controlled environment.

T F 3. Multinational enterprise refers to firms that have operations or subsidiaries located in many countries.

T F 4. Direct ownership of foreign subsidiaries represents the greatest commitment and the smallest risk in international marketing.

T F 5. Rapid changes in Eastern Europe and the former Soviet Union have created new marketing opportunities for U.S. firms.

T F 6. Attempts by U.S. firms to make large payments or bribes to influence the policy decisions of foreign governments are a viable alternative in conducting international marketing.

T F 7. Environmental differences that exist among and within different nations have no effects on marketing activities.

T F 8. The degree of commitment required to maintain a position in a foreign market determines the extent to which the marketing mix must be modified or redesigned.

T F 9. When products are introduced into one nation from another, acceptance is far more likely if there are similarities between the two cultures.

T F 10. Globalization permits the development of marketing strategies as if the world (or portions of it) were a single entity.

T F 11. The export of technology having strategic importance to the United States may require Defense Department approval.

T F 12. Opportunities for international marketers are limited mainly to countries with high incomes.

T F 13. GNP per capita is a measure of standard of living.

T F 14. Most multinational firms find that it is highly desirable, if possible, to have nonstandardized brand labeling and packaging.

T F 15. When a product's function in a foreign market changes, both the product and its promotion must be altered.

T F 16. Understanding the cultural environment in a foreign market can help international marketers understand the buying motives and habits of consumers in that market.

T F 17. The competitive approach is probably the most typical international pricing method.

T F 18. Casual or accidental exporting represents the lowest level of commitment to international marketing.

T F 19. Joint ventures are often born of political necessity because of nationalism and governmental restrictions on foreign ownership.

T F 20. Sometimes a firm's foreign price may be lower than its domestic price.

T F 21. International marketing intelligence involves the analysis of markets and environments.

T F 22. Trading companies are involved in the manufacture of products.

MULTIPLE-CHOICE QUESTIONS

_____ 1. The expansion of marketing to foreign markets usually is associated with
   a. a corporate strategy of long-term growth and increased profits.
   b. a desire for more power.
   c. the loosening of tariff laws.
   d. a change in the foreign political environment.
   e. a regional trade development.

_____ 2. Which of the following statements is false?
   a. The dynamics of international marketing intelligence influence the development of marketing strategies.
   b. International marketing involves marketing activities that are performed in controlled environments.
   c. Whether a firm sells in Dallas or Hong Kong, its marketing program should be built around a satisfying product that is properly priced, promoted, and distributed to a market that has been analyzed carefully.

d. Active exporting is aimed at gaining acceptance of an existing product in a foreign market.

e. Globalizations of markets is becoming more important today.

3. Full-scale international marketing involvement means that
   a. a firm conducts most of its business overseas.
   b. management recognizes the importance of developing international marketing strategies to achieve the firm's goals.
   c. a firm concentrates on selling activities to gain foreign market acceptance of existing products.
   d. a firm carries out the lowest level of commitment to international marketing.
   e. agents are used throughout the world.

4. A systematic approach to investigating foreign markets includes all the following steps *except*
   a. gathering secondary data.
   b. gathering primary data.
   c. planning a marketing strategy.
   d. reviewing entry into a foreign market.
   e. establishing a foreign distributorship.

5. Many of the marketing problems of multinational companies stem from
   a. the need for better intelligence regarding environmental forces in international markets.
   b. political enmity between the multinational firm and foreign governments.
   c. the exploitation of foreign resources by multinational firms.
   d. the companies' failure to pay bribes.
   e. government regulations of multinational industries.

6. According to the text, which of the following is *not* a form of international marketing involvement?
   a. Joint ventures
   b. Limited-line distribution
   c. Direct ownership
   d. Licensing
   e. Trading companies

7. Datacom, a U.S. manufacturer of laptop computers, was interested in some form of international marketing. The company decided to enter into a joint venture with Datamark, a French firm, to make and sell computers in France. What is the major reason behind Datacom's decision to enter a joint venture?
   a. To bypass marketing intermediaries
   b. To provide technical assistance
   c. To compete effectively in foreign markets
   d. To minimize risk and investment
   e. To find an inexpensive and highly effective means to market products

_____ 8. Marketing activities are primarily social in purpose; therefore they are influenced by all the following social structures *except*
   a. family.
   b. education.
   c. health and recreation.
   d. trade marketing channels.
   e. religion.

_____ 9. Which of the following statements is false?
   a. In foreign markets, just as in domestic markets, consumers' buying habits are a major factor in shaping distribution channels.
   b. Distribution alternatives are determined in part by the existence of retail institutions and wholesalers that can perform marketing functions between and within nations.
   c. The sale of the same product in different distribution channels at different prices is called dumping.
   d. Products that require information about servicing need controlled distribution.
   e. Distribution channels in the domestic country and the foreign country are usually different.

_____ 10. Which of the following statements about technological forces is true?
   a. Much of the technology used in industrialized areas is ill suited for developing countries.
   b. Mass marketing technology is too simple to be of much use in developing countries.
   c. Mass marketing technology is too expensive to assist developing countries.
   d. Export of strategically important technology from the United States usually does not require Defense Department approval.
   e. Technological forces can be totally controlled by the firm.

_____ 11. Intermark, a marketing research firm, was hired to collect primary data in Australia to assess consumer opinions and needs. Which of the following is *not* a problem that Intermark will have in collecting this data?
   a. Attitudes toward privacy
   b. Attitudes toward the United States
   c. Language differences
   d. People's willingness to be interviewed
   e. Low literacy rates

_____ 12. Although Atlas Manufacturing is interested in exploring international markets, the company wants to do so at the lowest level of involvement necessary. Which of the following methods would you suggest that Atlas use?
   a. Casual exporting
   b. Active exporting
   c. Licensing

d. Joint ventures
e. Direct ownership

13. The greatest threat to a joint venture in a foreign country is
    a. loss of standardization.
    b. political uncertainty.
    c. increased tariffs.
    d. product planning.
    e. dumping.

14. A primary reason for licensing agreements is to
    a. minimize insurance expenses.
    b. avoid export agents.
    c. exchange technical assistance.
    d. bypass marketing intermediaries.
    e. lower insurance costs.

15. A major shortcoming of secondary data is
    a. their high cost.
    b. their overabundance.
    c. that they offer too much detail.
    d. the difficulty of translating them.
    e. the unreliability of some of them.

16. Foreign marketing opportunities should be investigated through the use of
    a. a firm's databank.
    b. export bank marketing research.
    c. international marketing intelligence.
    d. market review and control.
    e. the U.S. Attorney General's office.

17. A society's culture, as defined by the text, does *not* pertain to
    a. attitudes toward heterosexual relationships.
    b. common eating habits.
    c. the average age of males in urban centers.
    d. the manner in which people express pleasure.
    e. marriage and family practices.

18. The U.S.-based Landmark Corporation is very committed to international marketing. The company has subsidiaries in Japan, France, Canada, and the Ukraine. What type of company is the Landmark Corporation?
    a. A joint venture
    b. A multinational enterprise
    c. A direct subsidiary
    d. A strategic alliance
    e. An export trading company

_____   19. Worldwide sales of Zenith personal computers would at the very least require an adaptation with regard to which one of the following?
a. Product
b. Promotion
c. Sales promotion
d. Distribution
e. Advertising

_____   20. Hartco Enterprises is interested in some form of international marketing but knows very little about the laws of other countries. Which of the following is the best approach for Hartco to take as it plans to comply with foreign laws?
a. Copy the plans of other foreign markets in the particular country
b. Be guided by conscience
c. Find competent nationals in the foreign country to assist with this task
d. Put the task entirely into the hands of a partner firm in the foreign country
e. Engage the firm's attorneys to find out what the laws are

MINICASE: UNITED CHEMICAL OF AFRICA, LTD.*

United Chemical of Africa, Ltd. (UCAL), is an American-owned subsidiary that manufactures dry cell batteries, flashlights, chemicals, and plastics. The company operates in the African subcontinent as a maker of dry cell batteries for flashlights, radios, and small appliances. All employees are African, except top management, who are American. For many years UCAL controlled more than 75 percent of the battery market in this region.

Most sales (70 percent) are to consumers who purchase batteries for flashlights, bicycle lights, and portable radios. Other sales are to governments (primarily the armed forces) and to industrial customers.

UCAL's battery sales, which traditionally have enjoyed a virtual monopoly in Africa, have been challenged by the recent entry into the market of a major Japanese manufacturer of electronic products. This new competitor gained entry into the African market by using an African manufacturer of electrical products as a wholesaler.

With aggressive selling and promotional support for retailers as well as lower wholesale prices (resulting in larger markups), the new Japanese battery is becoming a more attractive brand to customers. Self-service stores are rare in Africa; customers usually are waited on by salespeople, who thus play an important role in recommending brands, however informally. With the incentive of higher markups on the new Japanese brand, retailers not only are happy to stock the new battery but are eager to push it instead of UCAL's brand.

* Contributed by Professor Benoy W. Joseph, Cleveland State University.

Questions

_____ 1. UCAL probably failed to adjust to new competition because of a lack of
    a. marketing intelligence.
    b. quality control.
    c. promotion.
    d. marketing.
    e. production.

_____ 2. UCAL developed international involvement in Africa based on
    a. exporting.
    b. licensing.
    c. joint ventures.
    d. direct ownership.
    e. indirect ownership.

_____ 3. What aspects of the marketing environment must be better understood to improve UCAL's current performance?
    a. Social forces
    b. Competitive (economic) forces
    c. Consumer forces
    d. Technological forces
    e. Political forces

_____ 4. What aspects of the marketing mix should UCAL adjust immediately?
    a. Product and price
    b. Distribution and price
    c. Distribution and product
    d. Promotion and product
    e. Promotion and distribution

_____ 5. The most important marketing mix variable in the Japanese company's marketing strategy was
    a. distribution.
    b. product.
    c. price.
    d. promotion.
    e. production.

PROGRAMMED COMPLETION EXERCISES

accidental, active,
full-scale,
globalization

1. The level of involvement in international marketing varies widely from casual or _____ exporting, to _____ exporting, to _____ commitment, to _____ of markets.

markets,
environments

2. International marketing intelligence involves analyzing foreign
_____ and _____.

economic

3. Producers, wholesalers, retailers, buyers, and other organizations that produce, distribute, and purchase products are
among the _____ institutions operating in foreign
markets.

Licensing

4. _____ is an alternative to direct investment when
production, technical assistance, or marketing know-how is
required.

divisions,
subsidiaries, risk

5. Direct ownership of foreign _____ or _____
involves the greatest _____ in international
marketing.

secondary

6. The shortcomings of _____ data in international
marketing intelligence include the reliability, validity, and
comparability of available data.

social

7. Marketing activities are primarily _____ in purpose
and therefore are structured by social institutions.

distribution

8. The existence of retail institutions and wholesalers that can
perform marketing functions between and within nations
determines _____ alternatives.

pricing

9. Transportation costs, supplies, taxes, tariffs, and other
expenses affect _____ decisions in foreign markets.

Exporting, flexible

10. _____ represents the lowest level of commitment to
international marketing and is the most _____
approach.

Active

11. _____ exporting concentrates on selling activities to gain acceptance of existing products in foreign markets.

International
marketing

12. _____ _____ involves the performance of marketing activities across national boundaries.

resources, national
boundaries

13. Before international marketing could achieve its current level of importance, organizations with the necessary _____ had to develop an interest in expanding their business beyond _____ _____.

Cultural

14. _____ aspects of the environment that are important to international marketing include concepts, values, and tangible items.

political

15. The international _____ practice of payoffs and bribes is deeply entrenched in many foreign governments.

invention

16. Product _____ is necessary when existing products cannot meet the needs of a foreign market; it is often the most expensive strategy affecting international product and promotion decisions.

regional

17. Standardization of the international marketing mix is highly desirable, but most evidence indicates that it is restricted to a _____ standardization.

Multinational
enterprise

18. _____ _____ refers to the organizational aspects of firms that have operations or subsidiaries located in many countries to achieve a common goal.

technology, strategic importance

19. The export of _____ with _____ _____ to the United States may require Defense Department approval.

market potential

20. Measures of foreign _____ _____ include per capita income, aggregate GNP, credit, and income distribution.

political, legal

21. The _____ and _____ systems—including national laws, regulatory bodies, courts, and national pressure groups—have great impact on international marketing.

Promotional

22. _____ adaption is a low-cost modification compared with the engineering and production redevelopment costs of physically changing a product.

Globalization

23. _____ of markets requires total commitment to international marketing; it embodies the view that the world is a single market.

Trading companies

24. _____ _____ act as a link between buyers and sellers in different countries; they buy in one country at the lowest price consistent with quality and sell to buyers in another country.

dumping

25. The sale of surplus products in foreign markets at low prices is called _____.

Ethnodomination, majority

26. _____ is a situation in which an ethnic group occupies a _____ position within a marketing channel.

ANSWERS TO OBJECTIVE QUESTIONS

Matching		*True or False*		*Multiple-Choice*		*Minicase*
1. b	7. c	1. T	12. F	1. a	11. b	1. a
2. m	8. n	2. F	13. T	2. b	12. a	2. d
3. f	9. j	3. T	14. F	3. b	13. b	3. b
4. d	10. g	4. F	15. T	4. e	14. c	4. b
5. e	11. k	5. T	16. T	5. a	15. e	5. a
6. h	12. i	6. F	17. F	6. b	16. c	
		7. F	18. T	7. d	17. c	
		8. T	19. T	8. d	18. b	
		9. T	20. T	9. c	19. a	
		10. T	21. T	10. a	20. c	
		11. T	22. F			